Praise for th
of *Getting to Maybe*

This is the best book I have ever seen on how law students should approach exams. It is stunningly insightful and will be useful for every type of law school exam. But the book is much more than just test-taking tips; it really is a wonderful guide for students on how to approach their courses in law school. Every law student will benefit from reading this book.

Erwin Chemerinsky
Dean and Jesse H. Choper Distinguished Professor of Law
University of California, Berkeley School of Law

This book is the definitive answer to that age-old 1L refrain... "I knew the law so much better than my study partner, so why did she get an A while I got a B?" An antidote to law professors who students claim 'hide the ball,' this book throws that ball right into their lap in easy-to-follow prose, which is equal parts humor, serious advice, and relatable examples drawn from common human experience and typical 1L hypotheticals. There are hundreds of guides to success in law school, but if I could recommend only one, this one wins by a landslide!

Nina Farber
Director, Academic Success Programs
Boston College Law School

There are many guides to success in law school, but *Getting to Maybe* is in a class by itself. Patient, friendly, and superbly clear and accessible, it teaches how to master law school exam-writing by an abundance of helpful examples from standard first-year subjects. Its secret formula is that—unlike many commercial outlines—its authors have a sure and sophisticated grasp of the structures of legal reasoning and of lawyers' techniques for analyzing and arguing their way through ambiguity. Absorbing the lessons of *Getting to Maybe* will help law students not only to perform better on exams, but to understand why.

Robert W. Gordon
Professor (Emeritus)
Stanford and Yale Law Schools

It is not enough to work *hard* in law school, you must work *smart*. *Getting to Maybe* tells you how to do exactly that. This comprehensive book is packed with practical wisdom and expert advice to guide you through every step of your law school journey. I highly recommend this exceptional book!

Ashley E. Heidemann, Esq.
Founder and CEO, JD Advising, Inc.

Jeremy Paul and Michael Fischl have incorporated decades of teaching experience in *Getting to Maybe*, a sparkling roadmap through the complexities of law school test-taking. For too long, most law students, flailing among thickets of dense knowledge, dark ambiguity, and leatherbound tomes heavy as cinder blocks, were advised to treat final exams like a game of Lincoln Logs: The mission was to pick out relevant issues from a dispersed cacophony of scattergrams and then to snap each issue together with "the" right rule. Rejecting such formulaic reductionism, Paul and Fischl provide a manual to excelling through strategic thinking, lively metaphor, and comprehensive problem-solving. With rich hypothetical problems and nuanced model answers, readers are shepherded through the habits of layered critical analysis—inspired to think, in other words, and not just "like a lawyer." *Getting to Maybe* is an indispensable guide, showing readers not simply how to pass tests but how to succeed at the highest levels—in law school, in legal practice, and ultimately in those tests of civic advocacy yet to be imagined in our rapidly changing, ethically challenged, and paradox-filled world.

Patricia J. Williams
*University Distinguished Professor of
Law and Humanities, Northeastern University*

Getting to Maybe

Getting to Maybe

How to Excel on Law School Exams

SECOND EDITION

Richard Michael Fischl

Constance Baker Motley Professor of Law
University of Connecticut School of Law

Jeremy R. Paul

Professor of Law
Northeastern University School of Law

CAROLINA ACADEMIC PRESS
Durham, North Carolina

Library of Congress Cataloging-in-Publication Data

Names: Fischl, Richard Michael, 1952- author. | Paul, Jeremy R., 1956-
    author.
Title: Getting to maybe : how to excel on law school exams / Richard
    Michael Fischl, Jeremy R. Paul.
Description: Second edition. | Durham, North Carolina : Carolina Academic
    Press, LLC, [2023]
Identifiers: LCCN 2023000036 (print) | LCCN 2023000037 (ebook) | ISBN
    9781594607349 (paperback) | ISBN 9781531024369 (epub)
Subjects: LCSH: Law examinations--United States--Study guides.
Classification: LCC KF283 .F57 2023 (print) | LCC KF283 (ebook) | DDC
    340.076--dc23/eng/20230512
LC record available at https://lccn.loc.gov/2023000036
LC ebook record available at https://lccn.loc.gov/2023000037

Carolina Academic Press
700 Kent Street
Durham, NC 27701
(919) 489-7486
www.cap-press.com

Printed in the United States of America

Contents

Acknowledgments

Helping law students cope with the mysteries of the law school exam captured our imagination from the moment we began our teaching careers at the University of Miami back in the mid-1980s. Our collaboration began with an invitation from Miami's Black Law Students Association to present a talk on exam-taking to One-Ls, and that occasion provided the opportunity to "put our heads together" and give sustained and careful thought to the anatomy of the law exam and the features of successful student answers. Over all the years since, the project has been informed and greatly improved by many talented and generous colleagues, students, and friends far too numerous to name, so we can do no more than offer our heartfelt thanks. You know who you are.

We would be remiss, however, not to give individual recognition to those who worked closely with us on this, our second edition. Julie Lipkin carefully read every word, offering us the ideal combination of precise editing and good humor that would warm any author's heart. Bob Enright brought a long-time practitioner's perspective to the manuscript and offered insightful criticisms of the material on law school success appearing for the first time in this edition. Carol McGeehan provided a keen and practiced eye that kept us focused on the reader's experience; she and Linda Lacy responded to our every anxious query with wisdom and equanimity; Book Designer Kathleen Soriano-Taylor painstakingly transformed a sprawling manuscript into a gorgeous volume; and they and all of our infinitely patient friends at Carolina Academic Press cheered us on every step of the way.

Above all, we owe a special debt to Duncan Kennedy, who inspired each of us as law students—and has done so ever since—by vividly demonstrating that great teaching and great scholarship are deeply linked and can change the world by opening new ways for generations of students and scholars to understand it. We proudly dedicate this book to Duncan, without whom it could not have been written.

Finally, we are painfully aware that the legal education project we celebrate in these pages depends upon sustained commitments to social justice and the rule of law that face dire threats in contemporary life. It is the passion for those commitments that we see in our students every day that gives us what hope we have for the future. For law students everywhere eager to participate in the next chapter in the nation's legal history, we wrote this book for you.

Michael Fischl—Hartford, CT
Jeremy Paul—Boston, MA

What's New in the Second Edition?

As we drafted the original edition of *Getting to Maybe* back in 1999, we had a particular audience in mind: first-year students disappointed with their fall term grades and thus eager for advice on doing better the next time around. The book has indeed proved to be of great value to such students, as one of us has repeatedly witnessed first-hand by assigning it as the text for academic success courses offered in the spring of first year and the following fall. But it turns out that most of our readers encounter the book long before classes begin, many of them at the prompting of law schools that include the book in summer reading lists. We have accordingly added four chapters—which appear together as Part I of the new edition—that focus on how students can tackle their law school studies "from the get-go" in ways that will better prepare them for law school success. The new chapters stress the virtues of "slow learning" and include material on critical study techniques—including case-briefing and statute-outlining—but do so with a principal focus on how those techniques can improve exam performance.

The second edition also adds an exercise we developed for exam-taking workshops that we've conducted over the years for law student audiences at UConn, Northeastern, Harvard, Minnesota, Miami, and elsewhere. It begins with a classic "issue spotter" exam question, and then walks students through a series of answers that get progressively better from first to last. These answers help students see for themselves the most common "rookie" mistakes as well as the key characteristics of better answers, demonstrating to great effect the exam-taking techniques offered in the book. The second edition likewise includes a new set of sample exam questions—testing core topics in Property, Contracts, Torts, and Constitutional Law—as well as sample answers, each introduced by a brief summary of governing legal principles (so students can think through the problem even if they haven't studied the topic under examination) and followed by a critique explicitly drawing on the lessons of the book.

As was the case in the first edition, we are unsparing in our criticism of even the most well-meaning efforts to reduce legal reasoning to a rigid multi-step one-size-fits-all formula. But two additional decades of classroom teaching—and the recent experience we've each had of watching our own kids suffer through law school—have made us more sympathetic to the eternal longing for a road map. We have thus expanded the single chapter on preparing for and taking exams that appeared in the original edition to separate chapters on exam prep (including note taking and course outlining); a chapter on issue spotting *in media res*; and—most responsive to all that longing—a chapter designed to demonstrate that the key to a successful exam answer lies not in the rote application of this year's trendy checklist but instead in learning to do what a good lawyer would do with the legal problem under examination.

Finally, the second edition adds an entirely new chapter on multiple-choice exams, recognizing (if not necessarily embracing) their increasing prominence in legal education and offering clear and useful advice for fitting the square peg of the law's many "maybes" into the tiny ovals on a multiple-choice answer sheet.

We are immensely grateful to the readers who made the original edition the best-selling book on law exams and hope that this new edition will prove more useful still to the next generation of lawyers-to-be and to those who teach them.

How to Use This Book

After an introductory chapter designed to offer an overview of our approach to law exams, *Getting to Maybe* has six parts, each with a sequence of lessons for students eager to excel on law school exams. Part I focuses on "the basics" of law school study—class attendance, case reading, and other building blocks for successful legal learning. Part II will show you how the so-called "issue spotter"—the type of exam question you'll encounter most frequently—tests what you've learned in the classroom, and Part III will help you bring that learning to the task of writing successful exam answers. Part IV focuses on the two other kinds of exam questions—policy questions and multiple choice—that law professors most often employ to supplement the ubiquitous issue spotter. Part V walks you through a series of sample exams and answers that put the book's lessons to work. And an Appendix appearing at the end of the book offers a multitude of exam-taking tips and answers to questions frequently asked by beginning students.

The book can certainly be read in one fell swoop—and be warned that we've aspired to make *Getting to Maybe* so engaging that it may prove difficult to put down. But our experience with the first edition has taught us that there are particular times during the first year of legal studies that each of these parts is likely to be most useful. Accordingly, in the next few pages we'll offer a more detailed map to the contents of the book even if it's scarily reminiscent of something you'd expect to find in an automobile owner's manual. We're betting you'll be grateful for the guidance at whatever point the felt need for exam-taking advice prompts you to give *Getting to Maybe* a try.

Part I—Exam Preparation Starts Early

This Part is designed to be most helpful just before you begin law school. (Light reading, perhaps, during one final weekend of late-summer fun.) It contains entirely new material we've added for the benefit of readers looking for a head start on "the basics" before classes meet. Because the focus of this book is exam success, however, Part I doesn't expound upon the importance of the basics "for their own sake"—tempting as that might be for two devoted educators!—but instead directly links the basics to the challenges of exam-taking.

Those of you who specifically chose this book for the exam focus suggested by its title may think you've already had your fill of general law school advice, either from friends and family who've been through it or from one of the many "how to survive law school" guides available on the market. Should that be the case, you may well decide to "cut to the chase" of exam-taking and thus begin with Part II, skipping Part I at least for now. Indeed, if you don't take a close look at *Getting to Maybe* until several weeks or more into your first semester of legal studies, turning directly to Part II is what we'd suggest as well. But you may want to put Part I in your "save for later" queue—perhaps for a leisurely read over winter break—for we'd be remiss if we didn't pass along the warnings of literally hundreds of students who learned the hard way that they should have tackled their legal studies in the manner recommended in Part I all along.

Part II—Taking Issues Seriously

Part II is ideally suited for diving in roughly midway through the first semester, around mid-October for the student who begins law school in the fall. Here's why. The exam question format you will most frequently encounter is called the "issue spotter," which tests the crucial lawyering skill of identifying legal issues presented by run-of-the-mill disputes, such as a breach of contract or an auto accident. This Part is brimming with examples and illustrations, and you'll find that they make much more sense after you've got a month or more of legal learning under your belt. At the same time, this material is not a "quick read"; getting the most from it requires serious and sustained engagement. So we wouldn't leave it until semester's end either.

Part III—Prepping for and Tackling the Issue Spotter

While Part II helps you learn what an issue *is*, the point of Part III is to assist you in figuring out what to *do* with issues as you prepare for and take exams. Here we cover some exam-prep strategies that will be familiar to most readers—e.g., taking good class notes and preparing course outlines—but do so in a manner specifically designed to help you anticipate the issues your professors are likely to test and to recognize them when they show up on the exam. We finish Part III with concrete advice about writing successful exam answers, and for obvious reasons these materials are likely to be most helpful in the final weeks of the first semester, as exams are approaching.

Part IV—Beyond Issue Spotting

Part IV is likewise end-of-term material and explores two kinds of exam questions that are less common but still used frequently enough to make it worth your while to learn how to tackle them: policy questions and multiple choice. The policy chapter will prep you for straightforward policy questions—e.g., "You are a legislative aide to U.S. Senator Gomez, and she has asked you to draft a memo outlining the pros and cons of a bill...." But the chapter has a second and equally important payoff, which is to help you draft better answers on "issue spotter" questions by incorporating policy analysis into your arsenal of legal arguments. The multiple-choice chapter, for its part, will aid you in anticipating the particular kinds of issues professors are likely to examine in this way and in coping with a test format that forces black-and-white choices in a field of study that is all about shades of gray.

Part V—Sample Questions and Answers

This Part offers you a chance to see the lessons of this book "in action" via a series of genuine law exam questions accompanied by "A" answers. It also provides a guide to practicing with a professor's old exams and suggests an approach to getting the most out of that exercise via group study. Like Parts III and IV, this is "end game" material that will benefit you the most toward the end of the semester.

Appendix: Exam-Taking Tips and Frequently Asked Questions

We have prepared this Appendix as a lifeline to students who have turned to this book at the last minute, perhaps the night before their first exam. Some may have purchased it early on and—like generations of law students before them—quickly discovered that the assigned readings for their courses ate up all the time and energy they had for schoolwork. Others may have picked up a copy in response to the urging of a fellow student or law school instructor recounting a first-hand experience of the benefits gained from *Getting to Maybe.* But if you find yourself removing the shrink wrap at the last minute, there just won't be time to work through Parts I through V of the book. Not to worry. We don't think you should even try. Your limited time would be far better spent reviewing material specific to the looming exam—like class notes, case briefs, or a course outline. So what we offer instead is this Appendix, which because of its "quick and easy" style—a multitude of concrete "tips" and answers to "frequently asked questions"—can be read in a couple of hours, thus reducing distraction from all-important subject-specific study. We do think this material is well worth the time, for at the very least it may help you avoid some common exam-taking errors. The Appendix may also be of great use to eager beavers who had read the book over the summer or early in the term and are seeking a brief review as they hunker down for finals.

However and whenever you decide to use this book, we hope you'll find it as helpful as the generation of readers who, well, got to maybe before you. When we were law students—a million years ago—we found that fear and confusion about exams all too frequently displaced the joy of learning the law and engaging with the profound issues of the day. This book represents our heartfelt effort to diminish that fear and confusion for those whose hard work—and tuition dollars!—make the jobs we love possible.

An Introduction to the Law School Exam: You're Not in Kansas Anymore

Every law student craves the answers to a few big questions. Can I handle the pressure? Will I make the Law Review? What kind of job can I get when I graduate? Does law school leave room for romance?

We suspect, however, that one question burns deepest in the hearts of all but the few students at the top of every class: How come Student X did better on (say) the Torts exam than I did, even though I studied twice as hard and knew the material much better than she did?

The point of this book is to provide you with an answer to that question from a law professor's perspective—a perspective we think you'll find useful, since it is invariably a professor who decides whether to give you or Student X the higher grade! But we want to begin by considering answers our *students* often give to this "burning question," since we think those answers reveal some common misunderstandings about law exams:

(a) Student X had a copy of a Torts outline put together by the star who "booked" last year's class and who is now the professor's research assistant.

(b) Student X was in a mega-study group, a dozen confident eager beavers who divvied up the Torts course into 12 topics and each produced a magnificent 100-plus-page summary of her assigned topic.

(c) Student X ignored everything the professor said and pulled an all-nighter streaming Quimbee just before the exam.

(d) Student X shamelessly found ways to smuggle political perspectives aligned with the professor's into her exam answers.

We hear these answers—or slight variations on them—all the time from students disappointed with their law school grades. We can safely say after decades of experience that students cannot shine on exams simply by parroting a professor's perceived political views. And we'll explain in detail in Part I of the book why commercial study aids and outlines prepared by others are likely to be of little use in the quest for exam-taking success. Indeed, our disappointed test-taker may or may not have "studied twice as hard" as Student X, but his assumption that canned resources are the key to high grades suggests that he may not have been studying *smart*.

Here's a painful truth about the law school experience. Even students who do the *right* things during the semester—those who study the assigned texts with great care and impress classmates and professors alike with their seeming grasp of the materials during class discussion—even those students more than occasionally come up short at exam time. Yet observers who conclude from this phenomenon that "grades are random," or at least impervious to the amount of work you do over the course of the semester, are basing that view on the faulty assumption that the key to excelling on law school exams lies in what you "know" coming into the test.

In point of fact, you *do* need to "know the material"—the seemingly endless collection of cases, rules, policies, and theories examined in each of your courses—in order to succeed on your exams. But the rub is that knowing the material is only a starting point, for the typical law exam doesn't simply test your ability to recall (or even to understand really well) the many things you learned from the course in question. Rather, the typical exam tests your ability to *use* the material you've learned and to *apply* it to problems you've never seen before—just as practicing lawyers are called on to do every day of their professional lives, which is precisely the reason law professors persist in testing our students in this way.

To get a sense of what we mean, forget about law for a moment. Assume instead you are taking a graduate course in engineering and have spent the semester studying the properties of various building materials and a host of theories of design. You have dedicated virtually every waking moment to this course. You have read and re-read every assignment and taken copious notes; you have come to each class session meticulously well prepared; you have taken down almost every word the instructor has uttered; you have saved and annotated every handout; and—during the two weeks just before the final exam—you have organized and reorganized and outlined and committed everything to memory with such success that, in the highly unlikely event that someone were to ask you to explain the differing properties of (say) plastic vs. glass, you could quickly rattle off everything that could possibly be said on the subject.

You enter the room for the final examination, and—to your astonishment—the proctor presents you with a large box containing a seemingly random assortment of materials of the sort studied in the course. On the blackboard, the proctor writes the following instructions: "Using the materials in the box before you, design and construct a widget according to the principles we studied in the course." (Unlike law students, engineering students know exactly what widgets look like!) Confronted with this daunting task, you would no doubt find the mass of information you have mastered in preparation for the exam helpful—indeed, crucial. But you would obviously be making a serious mistake if you left the contents of the box untouched and proceeded instead to compose an essay detailing "everything you know" about the fundamentals of materials and design, submitting the essay instead of a widget for the grade. The point of the exercise is not, after all, to regurgitate what you know, but rather to use what you know on what you find inside the box.

Perhaps the most important lesson we can offer about law exams is that each question you encounter is a lot like the engineering student's box: It's what you do with what you find *inside* the question that counts the most. In all likelihood, what distinguished Student X's performance from everybody else's on that Torts exam was less what she "knew" coming into the exam—let alone which outline she had or which commercial study aid she worked with—than *what she did with the questions she encountered on the exam itself.* And the intellectual skills that enabled her to handle the questions so well can be learned and developed by virtually any student who has secured entrance to law school and is willing to put in the time.

But truth be told, we law professors generally don't do a very good job of teaching exam skills, at least not directly. Classroom discussion often focuses on the intricacies of legal reasoning and argument—and on the policies and theories that organize and complicate each area of the law—but we seldom, if at all, explore in any depth the connection between those lessons and the challenge of law exam-taking. So even the most enterprising student has little choice but to draw upon sources that turn out to be less than fully reliable, for it's almost impossible to master law school exam-taking by relying on undergraduate habits, tips from fellow students, or even impressions drawn from the Socratic dialogue in the classroom. In the section that follows, we'll explain why those sources may send the wrong messages, and then we'll offer a better approach.

Some Lessons You May Need to Unlearn

Lesson #1—Undergraduate Exams and the "Information Dump"

Consider, first, the exam-taking habits you developed as an undergraduate and perhaps even before that. College-level testing often involves a demonstration of student knowledge. Who was William the Conqueror, and what country did he invade and when? How many hydrogen atoms make up a water molecule? Such questions conform to a vision of "memorize-and-regurgitate" learning, and, to many students, law school initially appears to be the ideal spot for raising this kind of testing to new heights. How many days do I have to file that appeal? How many witnesses must there be for the will to be valid? Given the gargantuan number of laws "on the books," law professors could easily give closed-book exams filled to the brim with nothing but questions calling for esoteric knowledge of memorized legal intricacies. *But we don't.*

It's true that failing to grasp the basic points of your courses will prove fatal to your exam performance. In Constitutional Law, for example, you need to know that *Marbury v. Madison* established our tradition in which the federal courts have the power to invalidate acts of Congress in the name of the Constitution. Going beyond the basics, however, to attempt to memorize verbatim every little rule and subrule you encountered during a course is unlikely to be particularly helpful, because law school exams will not reward mere accumulated knowledge. Indeed, testing principally for such knowledge would be foolish. As an attorney, you can almost always "look it up" if you need to; in fact, on most occasions, it would be irresponsible *not* to look it up, even if you were absolutely positive you remembered "it." Besides, to invoke once again our engineering exam analogy, a client seeking a lawyer's advice doesn't need someone who can recite legal rules from memory. Rather, she needs someone who will use all that knowledge to help her solve her "box" of problems.

Exam-taking skills developed before law school, however, cause many students to persist in treating our questions *as if* they called for a memorized answer. To see what we mean, let's watch as a well-prepared student—let's call her Ketanji—works her way through a question that is typical of the sort you are likely to encounter on a first-year Property exam:

> Katie Mathews has long owned a lovely home in a suburban neighborhood in Emerald City, the capital of Oz. (*Oh no,* Ketanji thinks. *We're in an imaginary jurisdiction, so how are we supposed to know what the law is?*) When Mathews decides to place the home on the market, it sits for a few months before the Brady family comes calling. The Bradys have two elementary school-age children and are attracted to the home because of its proximity to LaPierre Public Elementary School, about which the Bradys have heard good things. As the Bradys' broker takes them through the home, they encounter Ms. Mathews in the kitchen. The Bradys tell Mathews how much they like the home and say they hope to reach an agreement on a price soon. They also mention that they plan to send their children to LaPierre. "All three of my children attended that school," Ms. Mathews truthfully tells the Bradys. (*Okay,* Ketanji thinks. *Something about the school is going to be important here, since it's a major drawing point for buyers. But we're told that seller spoke "truthfully," so we're not dealing with misrepresentations of the sort we read about in the residential real estate sales cases we studied. What other dispute might there be?*)
>
> The Bradys reach an agreement with Mathews and take title to and possession of the home in August 2019. That October, however, the Bradys' oldest daughter is attacked and stabbed by a fellow student at LaPierre. She is traumatized and left with limited use of her left arm. A thorough investigation reveals that Ms. Mathews's oldest son, Sam, was badly beaten by

xxiv An Introduction to the Law School Exam

a fellow student at LaPierre just three years ago. (*Wow*, Ketanji thinks. *Seller didn't mention that terrible incident when she told buyers that her children had attended the school. Not a lie, exactly, but not the whole story either, and seller knew firsthand that buyers planned to send their kids there. But this is confusing. Under traditional property law, it's* caveat emptor—"*the buyer beware*"—*and sellers can keep quiet about problems so long as they don't actually lie. Yet under the modern rule adopted in many states, sellers have a duty to disclose facts about the property that are "not readily observable" and that "materially affect the value of the home." But how can we say which approach the courts will take if we don't know what state we're in? And besides, is this a fact "about the property" or just a fact about the school or about the seller's family?*) No record of the earlier assault could be found at the police station, because the incident had been kept private. Similarly, no official at LaPierre was authorized to disclose information about Sam's beating or his injuries. (*Okay*, Ketanji says to herself. *I guess this means the facts weren't "readily observable," even if someone tried to look into them. But does the earlier incident "materially affect the value of the home"? Local schools matter a lot to buyers with young children but might not matter much to the childless or to empty nesters. How can we be certain about the home's value without knowing more about the local housing market or, for that matter, the size and layout of the Mathews home?*)

If the Bradys sue to rescind the deal and get their money back, what are their chances of success, and what arguments is Ms. Mathews likely to raise in response? (*Oh boy*, Ketanji thinks. *Buyers are really going for broke here. The cases we read awarded monetary damages for such things as fixing hidden termite damage or compensating for diminished value resulting from an undisclosed problem with the septic field. But it's another thing altogether for a buyer to try to back out of a fully consummated sale of real property after title has passed, the mortgage loan funds have issued, the debt has likely been sold to a third party, seller has moved on and purchased a new home, etc. Will the courts in Oz be willing to "unwind" all of those transactions?*)

As we will shortly explain, the point of an exam question like this one is to get the test-taker to identify each of the ambiguities identified by Ketanji's italicized musings, to discuss possible resolutions of those ambiguities, and to analyze the difference all that makes to the rights and obligations of the respective parties. But in the face of exam pressure, many students respond by ignoring the ambiguities—indeed, by ignoring the facts stated in the question altogether—and treating the problem as an invitation to offer a short history of the rise and fall of *caveat emptor* or to begin writing down everything they know about the rules governing the sale of residential real estate.

We refer to an answer that replaces analysis of the question with disquisitions on the origins or state of the law as an "information dump." The student interprets the question actually asked—involving multiple issues, complex facts, and competing equities—as an opportunity to do what he used to do (and no doubt did very well) in college: Write an essay designed to persuade the grader that he "really understands" the area of law tested by the question. But what he has done instead is persuaded the grader that he couldn't—or, perhaps, that he just preferred not to—grapple with the vexing difficulties presented in the exam problem. And, like the engineering student who writes an essay rather than building a widget out of the box of materials, chances are he won't be very happy with the grade he gets as a result.

Lesson #2—Sorting Through the Law School Rumor Mill

Students begin to hear that "law exams are different" from almost the moment they set foot on their law school campus. As with most "rumor mills," however, there's a good bit of misleading advice lurking within the conventional wisdom imparted by second- and third-year students.

Imagine a rookie basketball player whose teammate's advice on covering a superstar is "force him left." The rookie enters the game and invites the star to drive left. The star promptly does so, putting the ball in the basket with a beautiful left-handed shot. During the next timeout, the rookie presses his teammate, "I thought you told me to force him left!" Without batting an eyelash, the teammate responds, "You should see what happens when he goes right!"

Law students who trade the "information dump" for the "helpful hints" from their classmates and from upper-level students may have a similarly unsettling experience. "You told me to spot the issues," a student was recently overheard complaining to a colleague, shortly after first-semester grades were released. "And the professor acknowledged that I saw most of them. But I only got a C+ on the exam!" The predictable response: "You should see what you'd get if you *didn't* spot the issues!"

Like "knowing the material," the ability to "spot the issues" is crucial to a successful exam performance; but like knowing the material, issue spotting is nowhere near enough. Recall, for a moment, our hypothetical home sale. An answer that read something like the following would almost surely get a passing grade at virtually any law school:

> The first thing we need to know is whether we are in a jurisdiction that adheres to *caveat emptor* or one that has adopted the modern rule of liability for nondisclosure. If we're in a nondisclosure state, then there is a further issue about whether the incident involving seller's child is "about the property" and, if so, whether it materially affects the value of the home. If it is and if it does, we'll also need to know whether the courts will be willing to grant rescission of the deal or limit the buyer's remedy to damages.

This student has indeed "spotted the issues" and would no doubt get credit for doing so. But like the student who "dumps" information rather than *using* it, the student who merely "spots" the issues—without going on to explain why they are issues, what difference they make, and the pros and cons of resolving them one way or another—will at best end up somewhere in the undistinguished lower middle of the class. (In Part III of the book, we will explore in great length what you *should* do with issues once you spot them.)

There are two other exam-taking bromides frequently promoted by well-meaning fellow students that may be equally misleading to a beginner. First, there is the suggestion that all you need to do on the final is to show the professor that you've "grasped the fundamentals of the course." This approach does have one thing going for it: You can organize and draft your answers well in advance of the exam, and you won't have to waste any time during the exam period itself reading—let alone thinking about—the professor's pesky questions! The downside, of course, is that this is simply a variation on the "information dump" we talked about earlier, except this kind of undifferentiated "dump" is likely to get you an even lower grade. Thus, the student who responds to our hypothetical question by "writing everything she knows" about *caveat emptor* and nondisclosure in residential real estate sales might get at least some credit for signaling to the professor that she recognizes the basic legal problem raised by the question. By contrast, the student who responds by attempting to demonstrate that she's grasped the "fundamentals" of *the entire Property course* is likely to lead the grader to the conclusion that she didn't have the faintest idea what the question was about.

The other strategy you are likely to hear about from your classmates is the so-called "IRAC" method. The idea here is that exam-taking can be reduced to four simple steps: (1) spot and state the Issue; (2) identify the Rule that governs the issue; (3) Apply the rule to the facts presented; and (4) offer a Conclusion that answers the question. We will have a lot to say about the dangers of IRAC (and other paint-by-numbers approaches with trendy acronyms) later in the book, but for now we'll just say this: We've worked with hundreds of wonderfully talented lawyers over the years and studied thousands upon thousands of judicial opinions and legal analyses, and we have never encountered one—not one—that grappled with a legal problem by attempting to reduce it to four simple steps. And since the overwhelming majority of law professors test legal reasoning skills on their exams, it is no surprise that answers deploying a submediocre form of reasoning are highly likely to earn submediocre grades. Indeed, you could write a book about the many important legal reasoning and exam-taking skills that simply cannot be captured in IRAC or in any other one-size-fits-all formula. (We have, and you're reading it!)

Lesson #3—The Dark Side of the Socratic Method: The Rulebook vs. The Loose Cannon

Perhaps the cruelest aspect of the law school exam process is visited upon students who look for lessons in the place you legitimately should expect to find them—inside the law school classroom. Many students enter law school expecting to memorize a massive quantity of legal rules for regurgitation-on-command—much in the manner that the interns and residents on *Grey's Anatomy* or *House* are asked to rattle off the names of a million and one body parts, symptoms, and diseases while making rounds with their senior colleagues. We have no idea whether those popular shows accurately capture the rigors of medical training, but the law student who anticipates a memorize-and-regurgitate model of education is in for some big surprises at most U.S. law schools.

One surprise is that most of the "rules" you are expected to master are buried in the text of judicial opinions. In spite of the fact that you're paying thousands of dollars a year to have a faculty of experts teach you the law, it turns out that your professors expect *you* to figure out the rules—often referred to as "case holdings"—on your own. What's worse, you never seem to get them right. Does the holding of *District of Columbia v. Heller* guarantee a Second Amendment right to possess handguns, or does it apply more broadly to machine guns, AK-47s, and other military-grade ordnance? Does *Hawkins v. McGee* govern damages for every breach of contract; or for broken promises in the context of medical treatment gone awry; or just for "hairy hands"?

Nor can you find the solace of certainty in the statutory supplement. It may seem that at least *these* are rules you don't have to figure out on your own; after all, they are written down in black and white. But before you've even had time to breathe a sigh of relief, you discover that it is just as difficult to determine the meaning of a statute—or a provision from the Constitution or a section from the Restatement of Torts—as it is to figure out the holding of a case. When you offer an interpretation based on the "plain meaning" of the rule ("no vehicles permitted in the park" means *all* "vehicles," period), the professor is bound to respond with a series of perplexing questions. Is the "meaning" really so "plain"? Are tricycles among the "vehicles" to which the rule refers? What did the drafters *intend*? Were they even *thinking* about tricycles? What policies were the drafters trying to further? Do tricycles produce the noise, pollution, and risks to pedestrians we associate with automobile traffic?

Worse still, if you came to law school expecting simply to memorize and regurgitate rules, the biggest surprise may be that "determining the meaning of the rule" is just the starting point in legal analysis. A lot of time is also spent "applying the rule to the facts," a task that turns out to be every bit as daunting as determining the meaning of the rule itself. Was the uncle's promise to give his nephew a large sum of money if the nephew refrained from smoking an offer proposing a bargain? Or was it merely a conditional promise to make a gift? If the host invites you but not your boyfriend to a party, and your boyfriend shows up anyway—injuring himself on his way in through an unlocked back door—is he considered a licensee or a trespasser? A significant part of what law professors teach *and test* is designed to help you learn to cope with these kinds of questions. But many students find classroom discussion maddening, because it's a rare professor who will stop to highlight or explain at any length the difference between good and bad efforts at rule identification or application.

What happens next is at the root of more exam disappointment than almost anything else we can describe. Students grow increasingly frustrated by the lack of hard-and-fast "answers" emerging from the so-called Socratic classroom, and, as a result, many are drawn toward one or the other of two highly simplified approaches to legal analysis and exam-taking. We'll refer to those approaches here as *the rulebook account* and *the judge as loose cannon*.

Simply put, the rulebook account is shorthand for the belief that once you know the rule, "the rule decides the case." On this view, "legal reasoning" is one part memorization and one part logic: The job of the judge, or the lawyer who appears before her, or the student on the exam, is simply to identify the governing rule, apply it to the facts at hand and then announce the result. ("A seller of residential real estate has a duty not to lie to buyers about defects materially affecting the value of the property. But under the doctrine of *caveat emptor*, a seller has no affirmative duty to advise buyers of such defects, even if they are not readily observable. Buyer's case—which rests not upon what seller said but instead on what she didn't say—must therefore be dismissed. Next case, please!")

With the possible exception of law enforcement personnel and others who've had frequent contact with the legal system, most nonlawyers—and thus most beginning law students—seem to think that the law works in this way, at least when it's working properly. As a consequence, the experience of the first semester of law school can come as quite a shock, since it typically consists of the study of case after case in which the rules, the facts, and the connection between the two can be argued in more than one way. (Recall, for example, all of the ambiguities and complexities in our home sale hypothetical—ambiguities and complexities that the simple syllogism at the end of the previous paragraph completely glossed over.)

Students respond to this "gestalt shift" in different ways. One approach is to cling to the rulebook account. We suspect this is an instinctive reaction because "the rules" offer a lifeboat of seeming certainty in the raging sea of ambiguity explored in the law school classroom. (You know you're not swimming, but at least you won't drown.) Some students may even begin to think of the professor as a heretic and the Socratic inquiry as a form of religious persecution. Paradoxically, this stance sometimes provokes a firmer resolve and a strengthened belief in the importance of the rules. "Okay," they think. "Maybe some smarty-pants overeducated preppy law professor can score picky debating points on helpless neophyte law students. But rules just *have to* decide cases, since the only other alternative is that judges are free to do whatever they want and to run utterly amok."

Yet another group of students comes to agree with this last point—i.e., that the only alternative to "rules deciding cases" is "judges doing whatever they want"—but from that premise they are drawn toward a more cynical conclusion. Having studied case after case in which "the rules" could easily lead to more than one result, these students embrace the approach we refer to as the judge as loose cannon—the notion that judges decide cases on the basis of values, or politics, or policy, or "what they had for breakfast," or some combination of such factors having nothing whatsoever to do with legal rules.

In point of fact, as our students line up on each side of this divide, they are in their own way reenacting a long-standing debate in American law—a debate the roots of which go back at least as far as the beginning of the last century. Fortunately for you (and for us as well), we don't have to rehearse or resolve the debate between formalism and legal realism here. Instead, what we want to do is to show you how the extremely oversimplified versions of these positions that beginners frequently espouse—that is, "naive" formalism (the rulebook account) and "vulgar" realism (the judge as loose cannon)—can undermine your capacity to make persuasive legal arguments and, with it, your ability to excel on law school exams.

In a nutshell, the students who embrace the rulebook account tend to write exams that substitute rule regurgitation for reasoning and analysis. On the upside, they frequently come to the exam having mastered, or even memorized, every little rule, subrule, and exception that was covered in the course—and, "just in case," some that the professor never even mentioned! But the trouble begins when they read the first question and encounter the sort of ambiguity that is typically present on a law exam. Perhaps it is a case in which more than one rule might govern (e.g., our residential real estate case, which might come out one way under *caveat emptor* and another under the modern rule of liability for nondisclosure). Or perhaps it is a case in which a single rule clearly governs, but the rule might be interpreted in one of two ways (e.g., one judge thinks the controlling rule requiring disclosure of hidden facts "about the property" demands that sellers reveal hidden physical characteristics of the land while a different judge expects spilling the beans on anything that might alter the economic value of the property). Or perhaps it is a case in which the rule and its meaning seem fairly clear, but the facts might be interpreted in more than one way (e.g., a transaction—like the uncle's promise to give his nephew $5,000 if the latter gives up smoking— that might fairly be characterized either as an offer proposing a bargain or as a conditional promise to make a gift).

Confronted with ambiguities like these, our rulebook devotee is stymied because there is no "rule" telling him how to resolve them. There is no small irony here: Since law professors almost invariably try to test what they teach, chances are that the student's instructor spent substantial class time working through these very problems—or problems quite like them—attempting to demonstrate through lecture and/or Socratic discussion that there was more than one way of looking at each of them. Yet our student may well have stopped taking notes at the time because he was waiting patiently through all the argument and counterargument for a punch line—waiting, that is, for a rule to come to the rescue with some definitive resolution.

As a result, when he encounters such a problem on the final, he may well experience a sense that he is the victim of a malicious bait and switch: After spending the semester teaching the class rule after rule after rule, how could the professor have decided to test the very questions for which the rules don't produce clear winners and losers? Unsure of how to deal with problems that the law doesn't seem to solve, the rulebook devotee may retreat to his natural habitat and draft answers designed to demonstrate his mastery of the rules, all the while avoiding the ambiguities that would arise in attempting to apply them to the facts presented in the question. Yet the point of the typical law exam is precisely to see whether students can identify, analyze, and argue thoughtfully about such ambiguities, and so an answer that has simply wished them all away is unlikely to distinguish itself.

By contrast, a student who embraces the judge-as-loose-cannon approach tends to write exam answers that discuss everything *but* the rules. Once she picks up on what she sees as the principal lesson of the Socratic method—that rules don't decide cases because there is always another way of looking at things—she stops taking notes every time a legal rule is discussed. "What's the point in focusing on *that*," she thinks, "since the decision is always based on something else?" That "something else" may vary from professor to professor, and even from case to case: Sometimes it seems to be "policy" (e.g., the security of transactions in Contracts or loss-spreading in Torts); sometimes it's the "equities" presented by the facts (e.g., the vulnerability of the impoverished tenant at the hands of the wealthy absentee landlord); sometimes it is the judge's "values" (when the professor agrees with her) or her "politics" (when he doesn't). Since in the view of such a student these extralegal considerations are what *really* drive judicial decisions, she sees no need to spend precious study time mastering the intricacies of the seemingly pointless array of rules.

Come the final exam, she may well be in for a complete disaster. For one thing, since most exam questions test the student's ability to use legal rules to make arguments, it is now our unsuspecting student who has become the "loose cannon," ironically entering the battle virtually unarmed. A central task of lawyering is to translate the facts, policies, equities, and values that support her client's case into the language of the law (e.g., "the landlord breached the warranty of habitability and therefore the tenant should be able to withhold her rent"), and you simply can't do this unless and until you develop a facility with the rules that form the basic rhetoric of legal argument. For another thing, when it comes to a task that separates the best answers from the merely mediocre—i.e., dealing with the ambiguities that complicate the legal analysis of the question—the loose-cannon student may not even be able to identify those ambiguities, since she has not taken the rules seriously enough to see how they might lead in several directions. (She is unlikely, for example, to figure out that the uncle's promise could be interpreted as proposing either a bargain or a conditional gift unless she understands the legal requirement of consideration.)

Of course, many students find themselves drawn simultaneously in both directions. Some offer randomly alternating approaches—consciously or unconsciously—in the hope that *something* they say will please the grader. Others try to embrace both approaches at the same time. Like the atheist who hedges his bets by sending the children to church, the rulebook proponent may conclude an extended regurgitation of rules with an abrupt loose-cannon appeal: "Of course, it depends on your politics," he writes. "I champion the weak against the strong—just like the professor!—so I think the court should rule in favor of the family farmer and against the coal company. But a more conservative judge might come out the other way."

Ironically, in the end the two approaches leave the student in much the same sorry fix. The rulebook devotee may see the ambiguities on the exam, but he ignores them because he thinks the law requires an answer and he doesn't have one; the loose-cannon student cannot even spot the ambiguities, for she has ignored the rules because they lead only to (wait for it) *ambiguities*. But like Dorothy in *The Wizard of Oz*, they've each had the ruby slippers all along, for if they had learned to embrace the ambiguities they have been so busy ignoring and denying, they'd be on their way to Law Review.

We said at the beginning of this introduction that the most important lesson we could teach you about law exams is that it's what you do with what you find inside the question that counts the most. The second most important lesson should be apparent from the foregoing discussion: What you will find inside the typical law exam question is *ambiguity*, and we think that learning to live with it—indeed, learning to search it out, embrace it, and exploit it—is the key to doing well on law school exams.

In Part I of the book we offer our best advice on how to approach law study generally. But in Part II the law exam will resume center stage as we attempt to translate the basic lessons of this chapter into a blueprint for concrete action as you pursue your legal studies and prepare for and take exams. Our aim is to *clarify*—not simplify—the examination process, and, accordingly, this book will require sustained effort on your part. We are confident, however, that there will be a big payoff in terms of improved academic performance. As for the burning question of whether law school leaves room for romance, you're on your own!

PART I

Exam Preparation Starts Early

In this part of the book, we focus on "the basics" of law school study—case reading; statutory analysis; and more—all with an eye to improving your performance on law school exams.

Chapter One

DIY—Law School Done Right

> "You had to find it out for yourself."
> —The Good Witch Glinda to Dorothy
> in *The Wizard of Oz*

A. The More Things Change...

Law school has changed a lot since the two of us struggled through it oh-so-many years ago. Those branded beverage containers now visible in every hallway and classroom? They were nowhere to be found; neither were food courts nor fitness centers. (We were undercaffeinated, hungry, *and* out of shape—and we didn't have a pandemic as an excuse for our slothful ways.) The law school bookstore was locally grown; national chains such as Barnes & Noble had yet to make their way to campus. And if you've ever been exposed to *The Paper Chase* or *One L*—the once-popular fictionalized accounts of law school in our era—you'll be relieved to learn that professorial bullies like the imperious Kingsfield and the desperately insecure Perini have been relegated to the dustbin of failed educational experiments, along with the rod and the dunce cap. Today, most law professors we know *just want to be loved*.

Yet for better or worse, some features of the law school experience remain remarkably unchanged. At least to someone on a typical student budget, law books were then, as now, the source of serious sticker shock. All those high school throwbacks—assigned classroom seating; endless

3

rows of lockers; the relentless gossip and the classmate crush—were likewise part of the landscape. And of course there were "gunners" in every
class, thrusting their hands to the ceiling and ceaselessly foisting their
self-assured brilliance upon eye-rolling classmates and professors
scarcely suppressing a cringe.

Above all, two features of law school life are so central to the experience that we began hearing of them—*repeatedly*—even before we arrived on campus, and we bet you did too. The first is that legal studies are
different, and not in a good way, from academic work you've done in the
past. Once again, you aren't in Kansas anymore—or in college or grad
school or anyplace else you might recognize. There's a lot of talk about
how you're supposed to be learning to "think like a lawyer," but pressing
professors or upper-level students to explain just what that means is likely to yield entirely unhelpful answers like "you'll know it when you see
it" and "it's confusing for everyone at first." Students accustomed to doing well in academic settings may find themselves struggling for the first
time ever, wondering more than occasionally whether they had somehow received the news of law school admission by mistake.

Which brings us to a second seemingly immutable feature of law
school life: At least for One-Ls, there's an overwhelming amount of work.
To be sure, initial appearances can be deceiving, and a cursory glance at
the opening-day assignments may lull you into thinking that reports of
impending inundation are exaggerated. The opening assignment for one
of our own classes, for example, was a single court opinion running no
more than half a page. ("I got this," we exclaimed—or would have, if we
said that in those days.) Yet there was the unsettling fact that there were
opening-day assignments *in the first place*, material we were supposed to
study and master even before we met the teacher or found our way to the
classroom; so much for the safe space of getting-to-know-you opening
lectures to which we'd grown accustomed as undergraduates. But the full
brunt of what lay in store didn't begin to hit home until we hunkered
down to read that seemingly brief opinion, and here is what we encountered in the opening paragraph:

> The appellant sued appellee for $10,000 damages for wrong-
> fully causing the death of his intestate. The court sustained
> appellee's demurrer to the complaint, and this ruling is as-
> signed as error.

Who *talks* like that? The deceptively short passage was full to the brim with words we couldn't pronounce let alone understand (like "intestate" and "demurrer"); more familiar terms that seemingly bore specialized meanings in this brave new context (like "complaint" and "assigned"); and expressions that on careful examination raised more questions than they answered (is there such a thing as *rightfully* causing a death?). The prospect of having to consult a law dictionary repeatedly to get through a two-sentence paragraph was truly daunting, all the more so when that resource was available only in hard copy and approximated the weight and dimensions of a Buick.

Moreover, the standard text for each class then, as now, was a "casebook," which almost invariably eschews the guidance one expects from an undergraduate text and instead veers back and forth between providing edited judicial opinions and offering "hypothetical" questions about what the results would be if the facts of the case had been different—which isn't much help to students still struggling to understand the results of the case on its actual facts. And finally there were the features of the court's opinion we were supposed to identify all on our own—the "holding"; the *ratio decidendi*; the *obiter dictum*—the search for which was like "stirring cement with your eyelashes," as a now-famous classmate wryly put it. Multiply that experience by multiple classes, and multiply it again as the semester got rolling and professors began to assign multiple cases for each class—virtually all of them far longer than half a page—and the monumental task before us came fully into view.

B. The Quest for Instant Enlightenment

So what happens when the irresistible force of eager-beaver students accustomed to academic success meets the immovable object of an enormous workload in a seemingly impenetrable new subject? The clash gives rise to a third abiding feature of law school, though it's one you may not hear about until classes begin. Recall the scene in *The Matrix* when Tank, holding the fort at the Mother Ship, downloads an instructional program directly into Trinity's brain, instantly enabling her to pilot the high-tech military helicopter needed for a daring rescue—no simulations, practice flights, or pesky training manuals necessary! Faced with the challenges of the first year, generations of law students have surely longed for a similar fix. ("Tank," the fantasy goes, "I need a pilot program for first-year Con Law. Hurry!" A couple of switches and rapid key-strokes later and *voila!* you're channeling famed constitutional scholar Melissa Murray.) Many students thus embark on a Quest for Instant Enlightenment, seeking salvation in the same and decidedly less exalted resources we turned to in our day: commercial study aids to clarify what the casebook obscured, and student-made outlines to unravel the mysteries of professorial thinking.

Commercial study aids come in all shapes, sizes, and formats—hornbooks, case briefs, flashcards, student guides, nutshells, and other materials promising rapid access to the secrets of each and every law school course, offering easily digestible revelations that would seemingly take eons to unearth on your own. At first, the lure of these materials may strike you as just a ruse to relieve you of more of your money. "Wait," you think upon hearing from a classmate that you simply *must* get Glannon's *Examples and Explanations* if you want to pass Civil Procedure. "Didn't I just spend a fortune on the books actually *required* for that course? And now it turns out that the one I really need is *extra*?"

Yet the experience of a class session or two spent puzzling over the meaning of "*in personam* jurisdiction" or "minimum contacts" may drive even the most budget-conscious student right to the nearest bookstore. One of us will sheepishly admit to having purchased a new study aid nearly every time he didn't understand what was going on in Property, which is not to say he ever had time to *read* any of them. The principal difference between our experience and yours is that these days many of the commercial materials are available digitally as well as in hard copy, instantly accessible via one-click ordering so you can start reading—or at least start purchasing—the moment you find yourself plagued by self-doubt and confusion.

Student-made outlines are likewise typically part of the Quest, and here the selling point is provenance, mythical or otherwise. "Psssst," whispers a well-meaning classmate who's become your first law school friend, "I've got a copy of the Civil Procedure outline put together by the Minow study group last year. One of them apparently wrote the best exam in the class, and the prof actually hired a second as her research assistant last summer." "I can top that," pipes up Student #2. "I just got my hands on the official Law Review outline for the spring elective in Tax. About a dozen superstars took the course a couple years back, and they divided up the work and each wrote the heck out of a section of the syllabus. I hear that if you study that outline, it's all you'll need to get an A."

If you're like most of us were—or like the typical One-L today—you'll be skeptical of the claim that any resource, commercial or homemade, can guarantee transport to the seemingly distant land of A's. But if you're like most of us were—or like the typical One-L today—in the throes of your befuddlement you may be seriously worried that no matter how long and hard you study you still won't "get it," and you may thus find yourself vulnerable to the lure of these promised lifelines.

The point of this chapter is to try to persuade you to resist this common reaction to the first year of legal studies—to resist the temptation to embark on the Quest for Instant Enlightenment via commercial study aids, the Outline of the Stars, or even a downloadable pilot program courtesy of your own personal Tank. Which is not to say it's an irrational impulse, and we'd be hypocrites if we didn't readily admit to succumbing to the Quest more than occasionally ourselves—or in equally counterproductive fashion, feeling pangs of apprehension when our classmates claimed to gain an advantage from a study aid we had not obtained.

But here's the thing: The Quest for Instant Enlightenment is not the solution to the challenges of the first year of legal studies; it's the *problem*. The risks of being led astray are high, the payoffs are scary-thin, and the resulting waste of time is considerable, diverting you from the work that will actually help you succeed in law school. The ruby slippers did a lot more for Dorothy than commercial study aids and student outlines could ever do for a law student, but even she had to experience Oz first-hand before she was ready to use them. And just in case you're not inclined to take our word on this—and as lawyers-to-be you *should* be skeptical of "because we said so" claims, even if the source is the bestselling book on law school exams—we elaborate our critiques in the paragraphs that follow, focusing first on commercial study aids and then on outlines produced by other students.

1. Commercial study aids

We'll start with an important caveat that we'll repeat throughout the book: When our advice conflicts with what you hear from the person who will actually be grading your law exams, *ignore us and do what your professor says*. If your professor requires or encourages you to use a commercial study aid (CSA, for ease of reference), don't leave the shrink-wrap intact on *our* account. Moreover, and as we've already noted, virtually every student finds the first few weeks of law school so overwhelming—with tons of reading and much of it in a strange and sometimes literally foreign language—that we wouldn't expect any remotely normal human being to resist turning to pretty much any resource on offer to get a little help, with or without a go-ahead from the instructor.

That said, no law professor we've ever met or heard about would recommend *replacing* the study of legal texts—judicial opinions, statutes, and the like, which will make up the vast majority of your law school readings—with commercial materials. So we strongly recommend using CSAs only sparingly, reading the assigned text first, and, if stumped, consulting the study aid afterward. If you're lucky, it may help clarify confusing points about the original text, especially early in your studies when legal language and reasoning are all so new. But armed with those clarifications, we'd head right back to the original text for a very slow and careful additional read to ensure that you can see the point on your own. And in that connection, one Texas-sized caveat: Always trust your own judgment, and—if at any point you think you disagree, even a little bit, with what the CSA says about the assigned text—go with your judgment, not the CSA. Even if you're wrong, and sometimes you will be, you can rest assured that your judgment is going to improve with time and effort. The CSA won't.

But with those exceptional situations out of the way, we'll put it as bluntly as we can: By some distance the most important skill you will need to develop as a One-L is the ability to read and understand legal texts. And it shouldn't surprise you to hear that the only way to develop that skill is by reading legal texts and learning how to make sense of them on your own. By contrast, reading *about* legal texts by consulting a CSA is a lot like training for a marathon by reading back issues of *Runner's World* or preparing for an "identify the painting" exam in art history by reviewing someone else's descriptions of the art without ever looking at the art itself. We cannot stress enough how important careful reading and thorough comprehension will be in law practice, when reliance on a CSA would get you laughed out of the office. And the ability to digest legal texts on your own is equally critical to law school success, in the classroom as well as on your exams.

In a typical class, the professor will direct much of the discussion by posing questions about the assigned readings and asking students to defend their answers by identifying and drawing from particular passages in the text, and you won't be in a position to undertake that task unless you've focused your study on the text itself. Indeed, you'll find that much of class discussion will be a deep dive into this court's reasoning; or into the precise language of that statute; or into the factual details of some particular dispute. You are unlikely to understand that discussion—let alone be able to take good class notes on it—if your familiarity with the text under discussion is limited to a secondhand account you found in a CSA.

Reliance on CSAs is likewise apt to hamper your preparation for exams. The vast majority of exam questions test your understanding of the legal texts you've studied all semester. If during the course of your studies you've distilled the assigned materials on your own based on firsthand work, a review of your notes as you prepare for finals is likely to stimulate your recall of the original texts and the lessons you drew from them. But that "recall" function won't operate unless you were the one who did the distillation work in the first place.

When it comes to exam-taking, law exams frequently present a text the class has never seen before—a court opinion, say, or a particular legal argument—and ask students to analyze, explain, critique, or respond to it. If you've been relying on CSAs rather than your own reading and detective work all semester long, it's highly unlikely that the required skill is suddenly going to spring fully formed from your brain in the high-pressure setting of an exam. To the contrary, the more in-depth analysis of legal materials you've been doing along the way, the better your chances when you are asked to deploy that skill on the final.

It's fair to ask at this point why you can't do both—why not read the assigned material as well as a CSA? And once again, that's exactly what you should do if your professor says so. But absent such a directive, there are at least four reasons to leave the CSAs behind as soon as you can and to focus like a laser beam on the assigned texts.

Reason #1: They oversimplify

CSAs face a heavy burden in persuading buyers to shell out additional funds for explanations of material presented in casebooks and covered in class. There's no doubt that the maddening nature of the typical case-book—with its endless parade of seemingly random court opinions, each of them followed by relentlessly complicating notes and problems—make the simpler and more accessible presentations of law offered by many CSAs look mighty good in comparison. But when it comes to exam preparation, CSAs have but a single virtue: They offer to spare you the tedious task of sorting through the many twists and turns that the as-signed readings and class discussion produced in favor of a straightfor-ward nutshell description of just what you need to know. How can the CSA accomplish this magical feat? Just as you would expect, through the miracle of "simplification," which in our experience invariably turns out to be "*over*simplification." Of course, there are many times in life when cutting out seemingly unnecessary details actually facilitates under-standing. But law school is not one of them.

Take a moment and imagine a recipe for a vegetable stir-fry that de-scribes in some detail the prepping of the individual ingredients (cut-ting, trimming, parboiling etc.); the sequence and timing for adding each ingredient to the wok; the varying heat settings required for each step of the process; and the colors and textures to watch for as the cook-ing is complete. Now imagine a cookbook that translated all of that into a simple directive: "Stir-fry the vegetables in a wok." To be sure, the latter is infinitely quicker to read and far simpler to follow, but the dinner pre-pared in this manner is likely to end up a soggy mess. Prep for finals by using the typical CSA, and you are likely to serve up something equally unappetizing to the professor grading your exam.

Reason #2: They get important things wrong

There are greater risks to the use of CSAs than oversimplification. Judging from our many decades of reading and grading exams—and from many discussions with other professors about their own grading experiences—CSAs are, with maddening frequency, simply mistaken in the information they provide about the cases and other materials you are expected to master. It is an all-too-common professorial experience to read a dozen or more student exam answers that all get exactly the same fact or rule or concept or argument wrong in exactly the same way, and the most common culprit these days is an errant CSA. (The second-most-common culprit is a student-made outline that has circulated in the class. More on that in a moment.)

Reason #3: They know nothing about the person grading your exam

Even when CSAs aren't in any objective sense "wrong," chances are slim that they will focus on the assigned readings from the same angle or through the same lens as your professor. A feature of American law that comes as a surprise to most beginning students is that there is seldom only "one way" to read a case or to interpret a statute—seldom, as the title of this book suggests, only "one side" to a legal argument—and different professors frequently use the same legal text to teach very different lessons and to select very different points of emphasis. Needless to say, a final exam drafted by your professor is infinitely more likely to require a thoroughgoing familiarity with *her* approach than it is to test you on whether you know what Quimbee has to say about the matter.

Reason #4: They waste precious time

Perhaps the biggest drawback of all to CSAs is that they are just not a good use of your time, and—as you will soon discover—in law school, study time is an extremely limited resource. If you are struggling to make sense out of a particular judicial opinion, say, you'd do far better to re-read it, slowly and carefully; or to consult your class notes or those of a classmate; or to read an article or an essay the professor has recommended in connection with the topic or one highlighted in the notes in your casebook; or to explore the confusion with your study group, ideally a coterie of classmates whose judgment, humanity, and sense of perspective you have come to trust. The punch line is that time spent on these resources and activities will have a far greater payoff—in terms of your legal learning and in terms of your exam performance—than any time spent on CSAs.

2. Outlines produced by other students

As you begin to prepare in earnest for finals, no resource is more valuable than a course outline; indeed, we think outlining is so productive that we devote the better part of a chapter to the topic later in the book. But we'll preview the most important takeaway from that material right now: The real point of an outline is not to have one but to *make* one. In our experience, the very process of outlining—of working your way back through the mass of course material and organizing it in a way that helps you make sense of it all—may be the most valuable part of your legal studies. In fact, we boldly predict that the more time you spend drafting and re-drafting an outline, the less time you'll spend actually referring to the document itself during your exam or wishing you could if it's closed book. You are likely to find that the outline has already done its job by helping you learn the material in the process of organizing it, thus freeing up precious exam time for reading and re-reading the questions and writing and refining your answers.

We understand that your study time is limited and that singlehandedly producing your own outline for every course may not be possible. Indeed, it would be incongruous for a book titled *Getting to Maybe* to suggest that there is one ideal study technique for all students. Students have different learning styles; some face struggles balancing school with work or family obligations; or—if only rarely in our experience—just don't need the mental discipline that outlines provide. You know your strengths and limits and, as is the case for everything we say about study techniques, we intend to offer *guidance* and not to insist on all-or-nothing strategies for success. We are pretty confident, however, that the work of outlining will pay off for our readers during exams.

By contrast, the value of outlines produced by *other* students is marginal at best. For one thing, from year to year most law professors update, re-organize, and even re-think the material they teach, which makes it a risky proposition to rely on an outline from earlier renditions—even very recent ones—of the course. An exam answer that draws on material the professor taught last year—but that she has taken the trouble to modify or transform for your class—is likely to irritate her a lot, and that's something you never want to do to someone faced with the formidable task of grading a large stack of law exams.

Outlines of the current course are obviously better, but their utility depends almost entirely on your personal role in their preparation. Thus, if your study group develops an outline through a genuine collective effort—discussing and analyzing each section of the course as a group, but perhaps divvying up topics for outlining among the individual participants—both the outline and the process of making it can be of significant educational value. Even here, however, you are going to find that your mastery of the material you outline yourself greatly exceeds your grasp of those parts of the course outlined by others, unless and until you retrace their thinking and make the material your own. Once again, it is the process of outlining, and far less the product produced, that makes a difference to exam performance. Prepping for the final by using an outline or a part of an outline that you did not write yourself—even if it is authored by someone you consider to be the class "star"—is like attempting to make the NBA by reading about LeBron James's practice regimen. To paraphrase a famous athletic shoe commercial, when it comes to the law school outline, it's not enough to have it, or to read it, or even to study it. The point is to *do it*. And to *do it yourself.*

Chapter Two

Slow Learning (a.k.a. Law School's 3Rs—Read and Re-Read)

So if we've convinced you that it's a bad idea to rely on "shortcuts" like CSAs or outlines produced by other students, what advice do we have for confronting a mountain of difficult work and a limited amount of time? Consider for a moment those occasions in life when the best advice is strikingly counterintuitive. What should you do if your car starts to slide as you're driving down an icy road? Faced with that circumstance, your brain will surely scream, "Slam on the brakes and turn the steering wheel sharply to stay on course!" But the most effective protocol is quite nearly the opposite: Keep your foot *off* the brake and carefully turn the wheel *in the direction of the slide*. And what should you do if you encounter a bear in the wild? Your brain will no doubt scream, "Turn around and run for it!" But once again, the wise counsel is to the contrary: Continue facing the bear and back away *slowly*.

Well, the advice we're about to give to law students faced with the considerable challenges of the first year will seem every bit as counterintuitive as these familiar survival techniques, and yet in our experience the steps we recommend are the best way to avoid ending up with the law school equivalent of a car stuck in a snowbank or a rear end full of ursine teeth: Unplug. And slow down.

Only disconnect...

As we noted in the previous chapter, there've been enormous changes in legal education since we were students. Many of them are positive: The coffee is better; the professors are nicer and considerably more diverse; and—far more important to the quality of American justice—the typical student body now looks a lot less like a country club circa 1950.

But the many changes wrought by the digital revolution are a decidedly mixed bag. On the upside, legal research is significantly faster and easier than it used to be, and the availability of instant global connectivity has facilitated less parochial approaches to law. Moreover, legal writing—for students and professors alike—has been simplified by digital word processing in ways we simply could not have imagined back in the days of longhand drafting on legal pads and typewritten manuscripts.

Yet digital magic has had some decidedly negative effects as well. Students accustomed to reading virtually everything on a backlit display screen develop the skill of skimming swiftly through endless quantities of text, getting "the big picture" or "the gist" or identifying key points and particular words or phrases. That skill is no doubt of considerable value in a variety of contexts, but it is downright dysfunctional in learning the law, where—as we've said—careful reading and the close analysis of text are the critical skills.

The world of law practice is changing rapidly, and in many professional settings you will be called upon to exercise business judgment, emotional intelligence, social skills, knowledge of other disciplines, the ability to hustle, and a growing list of other skills that may have figured less prominently in earlier eras. Some things don't change, though, and lawyers in every variety of practice and at every stage of a legal career are routinely required to offer close readings of cases, statutes, regulations, contracts, and other legal texts in order to determine their meaning and relevance to the situation at hand. And we do mean "close," for in most legal settings literally *every word counts*, and screen-skimming just will not suffice. Indeed, close reading is frequently facilitated by physically interacting with the text, highlighting critical passages, and drafting marginal notes to summarize key points or to pose lingering questions. Needless to say, at this stage the existing technologies for marking up a text "on screen" are kludgier and more difficult to deploy than using an old-fashioned highlighter and pen on hard copy.

There is a second feature of digital devices that is equally counterproductive for legal work: the nigh-irresistible temptation of instant access to social media, breaking news, texting, email, banking, shopping, games, music apps, and so many other diversions the devices likewise enable. ("There," thinks the student who has just finished reading the opening paragraph of an assigned case, "now I've got a good start. I'll just reward myself with a quick peek at Instagram. Oh and check to see if that payment came through on Venmo." An hour later...) At least when you are new to it—and for most of us, frankly, pretty much forever—working one's way through legal texts requires deep and sustained concentration and active intellectual engagement with the material. As you'll soon see, you are reading not just for "sense" or even for "information." You are reading the way a *lawyer* would, questioning the cogency of every argument; interrogating the likely effects—intended and otherwise—of every rule; and ferreting out and assessing the validity of all sorts of unarticulated assumptions.

A major goal of this book is to explain exactly how going beyond the straightforward reading of rules to search for alternative meanings and unintended consequences is crucial to exam performance and professional success. For now, take our word for it that, especially at first, this is a slow and heavy lift. Attempting to do serious legal work while multitasking—or even while actively resisting the temptation to do so—is a lot like trying to follow a complex noir-y mystery on Netflix while a precocious and persistent preschooler peppers you with random questions.

Yet screen-skimming and multitasking have become deeply ingrained habits by the time most students reach law school, and, like most habits, they are difficult to break. Not to put too fine a point on it, if your first effort at unplugging "cold turkey" occurs while you are struggling your way through a final exam, you are bound to get a grade that won't be much to your liking. So our advice is to practice, practice, practice close reading and focused concentration from the get-go, and thus (*here it comes*) to put away your laptop, desktop, tablet, smartphone, or whatever your favorite screen-skimming vehicle may be. Instead, read and study the assigned material in hard copy, even if it means printing out PDFs or—to the extent permitted by the publishing overlords—digital textbooks.

... even in the classroom

Unless you are a student with a disability that makes handwritten note-taking unduly burdensome, you will be well advised to leave the digital devices behind when you attend class as well; indeed, these days a great many law professors prohibit their classroom use, especially in first-year courses, and so drafting class notes via laptop may not be an option. Either way, you'll need to learn—or perhaps to re-learn—how to take good notes by hand. The vast majority of law professors make every effort to "test what they teach." There is thus no better guide to what will appear on your final exam than your class notes, and they will be of infinitely higher quality if they are handwritten rather than digitally processed. Here's why.

For one thing, there is once again the nigh-irresistible temptation of multitasking: checking for that much-anticipated text or email, taking a quick look at the latest headlines, or starting up a seemingly mindless game during a particularly dry spell in a midafternoon class. Yet what's going on in the typical law school classroom is a *conversation*—a dialogue between teacher and students that can take many twists and turns and is seldom reducible to a series of quick bullet points or sound bites. It is therefore a serious mistake to tune out and risk losing the train of thought or the conversation thread, even for a relatively short time.

But the problem with taking notes via laptops and the like runs much deeper than the likelihood of distractions that might take you "off task." The principal problem is that such devices serve you poorly even when you are very much *on* task, focused intently on class discussion and making a sustained effort to capture as much of it as possible in your notes. Why do we say that?

Partly it's the voice of experience, for we and most other law profs of a certain age warmly welcomed the laptop to the classroom when it got small and light and inexpensive enough for student use back in the early 1990s. Within a decade or so, the vast majority of our students were taking class notes that way, and we began to notice something most of us did not expect. We had assumed that laptops would make our students faster and more efficient note-takers and thus free them up to be even better participants in class discussion. In fact, though, widespread laptop usage had the opposite effect, and class discussion began to bog down as we found ourselves forced to repeat question after question we posed to the class. As it turned out, *our students were too busy typing to listen.* Channeling their inner court reporter, they were attempting to transcribe the class discussion verbatim, which meant the discussion was going directly from their ears to their fingertips without much involvement by the brain.

The dampening effect on class discussion was palpable, but the effect on the quality of the notes they took was even worse. As professors began to suspect—and as countless classroom studies have since confirmed—students who take notes by hand are forced to make choices constantly about what to write down and how to phrase things, since virtually no one can produce verbatim transcriptions in longhand. And the need to make constant choices forces the student to translate the ideas under discussion into her own words; to decide what is most critical and what might safely be left on the cutting room floor; and to organize the notes into a rough outline that distinguishes main points from subpoints from counterpoints. By contrast, transcript production incentivizes getting every word down, requiring virtually no contemporaneous engagement with the ideas the words express—yet it is by assiduously pursuing such engagement that students actually learn.

Finally, handwritten notes offer substantial advantages over the digital transcript when it comes to preparing for exams. Because of all the picking, choosing, synthesizing, and organizing they require, handwritten notes are likely to prompt a student reviewing them to recall the deep engagement—and the ideas, points, and concepts that were under discussion—that it took to produce them. With a transcript, by contrast, there was little active intellectual engagement in the first place, and thus you'll discover that there's very little to recall.

So our advice again is to leave your laptop at home when you head to class and to work hard on taking good notes by hand. This will enable you to engage in class discussion more deeply—and without distraction—and provide you with a far more effective tool for study when the semester draws to a close and you are preparing for exams.

Slow down!

Working with hard copy rather than digitally won't accomplish much if the habits developed via screen-skimming and endless multitasking are simply transplanted to the older medium. You will find that legal reading requires active and energetic engagement with the text, virtually the opposite of the far more passive posture most of us lapse into when we're reading something in digital format.

So we'll hit you with the bad news first: At least during your first year of law school, you'll need to read every legal text—cases, statutes, and the rest—*at least twice* in order to "make it yours." Fortunately, that task isn't nearly as tedious as it sounds, because each time you are reading for an entirely different purpose, and at least one of the reads might actually count as fun. What we have to say in the paragraphs that follow applies with equal force to any legal text, but to simplify things we are going to focus on judicial opinions, since they make up the lion's share of the readings in a typical first-year course.

Setting the Stage

Your favorite place for study may be an isolated carrel on the quiet floor of a library; a corner table at a busy coffeehouse; or a desk in a study area at your apartment, the go-to workspace for so many of us since the pandemic arrived in March 2020. Whatever the setting, clear the work space as best you can—"outer order equals inner calm"—and put your digital devices and other potential distractions to the side. Now you are ready to read.

First Read: A Legitimate Role for Skimming

After everything we've said so far, you may be a bit surprised by our advice for your initial read of a judicial opinion: Skim it! Each opinion tells a story of some real-world human conflict that wound its way to court, and the opinion will typically resolve the dispute in favor of one party or the other, offering reasons for reaching that disposition. Our advice: Put your highlighter and writing utensils aside and read the text from beginning to end just to get the "big picture." Who are the characters in the story (employer and employee? driver and pedestrian?); who did what to whom, and what are they fighting about (breach of contract? injuries from a car accident?); who prevailed in court; and, in broad outline, what justification does the court offer for that outcome?

We urge you to "begin with a skim" for a couple of reasons. First, subsequent reads will make much more sense if you "know who the players are" and have a fair grasp of their conflict before you bog yourself down in the details. Second, the conflicts presented in legal disputes often provoke partisan feelings in the reader, and you'll have the urge to "fast-forward" through the rest of the opinion just to see whether the court has reached the result you would have wanted—a lot like the temptation to peek at the last pages of a mystery to see "whodunit" and whether your favorite detective survives and ends up with the obligatory love interest.

It's "the rest of the opinion"—i.e., all the stuff between the real-world story and the outcome—where the lawyers and judges come into play, the former making arguments for the respective parties and the latter defending the result. That's where you'll find what you came to law school to learn, and it would be a mistake to rush through it because you are dying to know the outcome. The skim allows you to satisfy your curiosity before getting down to the business of the slower and closer reads that are critical to the development of your lawyering skills.

Second Read: Channeling Your Inner Difficult Child

Whether you've come to law school to pursue social justice work, to make the world safe for capitalism, to seek prison for some particular class of wrongdoers, to avoid blood (and thus med school) or spreadsheets (and thus biz school), or just because you really dig those black robes judges wear, chances are that at some point in your past you heard—from your parents, perhaps, or your teachers, or a coach or employer—that you would make a good lawyer.

There are a great many reasons to be proud of our profession, but those who identified us as contrarian-lawyers-to-be were less likely to be paying a compliment than complaining about our tendency to question assertions of authority by citing precedent ("but you let *Blair* do that when she was my age") or exploiting the ambiguity or vagueness in some command ("but you didn't say I had to clean the kitchen *now*") or by pointing up some unintended negative consequence of a proposed rule ("but if I have to leave the party that early I'll be the only one and will have to travel all alone"). During your second read of a judicial opinion, we urge you to channel your inner "difficult child" and to read the case from beginning to end *critically*—meaning slowly and carefully as you question each passage for meaning and logical flow.

For this read, you'll need your writing utensils so you can highlight or underline critical passages; annotate the steps in each argument and characterize the arguments deployed in support of each claim; and make notes in the margin about the relationship of the passage to something else you've studied in the course or about points that are confusing or ambiguous. In our experience, this sort of deep engagement with the text will not only enhance your understanding as you work your way through it but also provide a prompt for deep recall during later reads.

Intermission

We think it's a good idea to do the two reads in a single sitting in order to bring the full benefit of the initial skim to the subsequent close and careful read. But once you've finished the second read, it may actually be a good idea to take a brief break—for a fresh cup of coffee, a quick walk, or a little yoga—to clear your head for what comes next. Of course, if you finish the second read rarin' to get back at it, go for it and don't stop on our account.

The Next Step: Briefing and Outlining

The next step is a vital one, and for this one you may (though you need not) use your laptop or other digital device. Here you'll be preparing a case brief (if it's an opinion) or an outline (if it's a statute or pretty much anything else) that "deconstructs" the text and reassembles it according to a tried-and-true template for legal study. A template, for those of you unfamiliar with the term, is just a fancy name for a standardized set of questions, steps, or strategies designed to help you succeed in some particular task. (Think how journalists are taught to ask "who, what, when, where, and why," or how scientists learn to formulate a hypothesis, devise a method to test it, conduct an experiment, and then analyze the results.) Our briefing template is designed to help students get a better handle on the cases they read, and it's such an important step that we devote the next chapter to it. For now it's enough to explain briefly why you'll want to do this despite the fact you've already read the text twice:

(1) Because you're following a template—rather than just tracking the opinion—you are likely to see the text from a different perspective and thus to learn important new things about it. The template will also ensure that you don't leave essential questions unanswered.

(2) The template form will provide you with an easily referenced "script" for use in class in the event the professor calls on you to explicate the text—e.g., asks you to "state the case" or to explain the meaning of a statutory provision.

(3) The template will be an enormously useful tool for review during exam preparation, far shorter than the actual legal text (which is why it's called a "brief") and far more likely to prompt recall of the material (since you're the one who wrote it).

(4) You'll have the perfect document on which to make additions and corrections during the next and final stage, which brings us to...

The Final Step: Once More for Accuracy and Grace Notes

In every course we took in law school—even the handful with mediocre professors—class discussion offered fresh insights about each case we studied, even if we were absolutely sure we'd "nailed it" on our own. Sometimes we learned that we'd simply misread a passage or made a mistake about some fact or procedural maneuver. But more often than not the professor used class time to offer an entirely different way to understand the case; to put the case in some larger context (e.g., its historical or ideological background); to connect it with other materials we'd read and the larger themes of the course in ways we hadn't seen on our own; or to offer juicy bits about the decision the professor had discovered during her research or through academic scuttlebutt.

Whatever the "value added" by class discussion of a particular case, we guarantee that a fresh look at the case informed by in-class insights will put the text in a different light and offer you a valuable opportunity to amend and enrich your case brief accordingly, substantially increasing its value for study in the run-up to the exam.

And now for the good news: The work really will get easier

Imagine you are stranded on a desert island and, given the remote location, there is virtually no chance you'll be rescued for many months. Fortunately, there's plenty of food; an easily accessed freshwater stream; and a cave on high ground where you can take refuge from tropical storms. You've also got several items you managed to salvage from your dinghy as it sank, including flint, a hatchet, and your college roommate, a former summer camp counselor who is completely at home in the woods, capable of starting a fire and improvising all sorts of handy survival tools. And miracle of miracles, you're pretty sure you've got the complete set of Harry Potter books and finally enough time to read them.

But then you discover that in the mayhem of the shipwreck, you somehow managed to lose the first two volumes, *Harry Potter and the Philosopher's Stone* (naturally you have the British release) and *Harry Potter and the Chamber of Secrets*. Disappointed but undaunted, you settle in under a palm tree and begin to read *Harry Potter and the Prisoner of Azkaban*. But much to your surprise and eventual dismay, you realize that you have No. Idea. Whatsoever. What's. Going. On. Virtually every sentence introduces without explanation some person, place, or thing you've never heard of—Muggles, the Leaky Cauldron, Parseltongue, Lord Voldemort, Gryffindor. Your eight-year-old sister read every one of these books, for heaven's sake; why is this so difficult for you?

Fortunately, your college roommate is a serious Potter fan, and she's willing to answer your questions about the book as long as you save them for the end of each day so she can focus on her own reading—the *Lord of the Rings* trilogy—undisturbed. With her assistance, you resume your effort in earnest, but progress is fitful. Each day you spend several hours late into the evening peppering her with questions, so it takes you nearly a month to get through it.

At that point, you are exhausted and tempted to give up on the series. But your roommate assures you that *Harry Potter and the Goblet of Fire* is great fun, and points out that you know a lot more of the backstory than you did when you began *The Prisoner of Azkaban*. And sure enough, your read of the fourth volume is faster and easier. It's by no means a breeze—you still regularly encounter people, places, and things you haven't heard about before—but they are fewer and further between, and in any event you are finding it easier to figure out such mysteries on your own, without waiting till the end of the day for a roommate consult.

You know the rest. By Books Five through Seven, you are reading like, well, a wizard and virtually never have to query your roommate, though the two of you spend many tropical sunsets debating the finer points of plot, character development, romantic possibilities, and the mounting body count. But by the time you finish the series, there is still no sign of rescue, so you tackle *The Prisoner of Azkaban* again and you end up reading it cover to cover in a single day. And to your astonishment, you pick up on a multitude of developments and nuances you'd missed the first time through, many of which shed new light on the events portrayed in the later books and actually cause you to rethink a number of the disagreements you'd had about the series with your roommate.

We don't mean to suggest that reading American law will ever match the thrills of the Potter series, but the experience of starting law school is a lot like starting Harry Potter in the middle of the story—except that you're beginning with Volume Three Million instead of Volume Three of the American law story. The reading is thus going to be awfully slow going at the beginning, requiring—as we've said—multiple takes and a great deal of thought and effort. It certainly won't hurt if you manage to recruit the next Amy Coney Barrett or Ketanji Brown Jackson as your roommate, but failing that, it will get easier as you go along for the same reason reading Harry Potter does: Each new case will fit somewhere in the story of law so far, and the more you know about that story, the easier it will be to understand the new twists and turns.

Chapter Three

Briefing a Case—It All Begins with Three Little Questions

Learning the Law: What You Will Study and Why

In our experience it's a pair of "surprises" that pose the biggest hurdle for most One-Ls as they navigate law school's early days. The first surprise is that the "law" that students encounter in their first-year classes bears little resemblance to the "law" they come to law school expecting to study. Most entering students—like most nonlawyers generally—picture law as a large body of "rules." Yet from the very first day, law study focuses less on rules than it does on *judicial opinions*—i.e., decisions written by judges explaining and justifying the results reached in particular legal disputes.

1. Why judicial opinions?

Lawyers and clients alike worry a lot less about what the law "is" in the abstract than about how it will be applied in real-world disputes. Judicial opinions offer a unique window into this law-application process, and, when you peer through that window, what you'll see is lawyers and judges making *arguments* about rules. They might be arguing, for example, about how a particular rule should be interpreted. (Does a local ordinance barring "vehicles" from the park apply to motorized wheelchairs?) The judicial opinions you read for class are likely to resolve interpretive disputes, and an important reason to study them is to learn the reasoning techniques judges use to accomplish that task.

But equally important to an understanding of American law is the fact that the court's opinion itself becomes a "precedent" for future cases—that is, part of the law that lawyers will argue about and judges will interpret the next time a similar dispute arises. (If a court concludes that motorized wheelchairs are permitted in the park, will that precedent require the same result for electric scooters?) Thus, the "law" that students learn in law school isn't just the rules they expect but also the arguments that lawyers make—and that judges accept and reject—in thousands upon thousands of individual judicial opinions *applying* those rules.

2. "Knowing" the rules is never enough

A second surprise that students confront is closely related to the first. If the law were simply "rules," then "knowing the law" would mean "knowing the rules." And since the kind of studying to which most of us grew accustomed during earlier stages of our education consisted largely of memorizing mass quantities of material and regurgitating it all on quizzes and exams, many students arrive at law school expecting to have to memorize "the law" in just this way. To be sure, those of you craving mass quantities of "rules" will get your fill over the course of the next three years; we guarantee it. (Pop quiz: Is that a contract?) But the second surprise is that there is far less of a premium on memorizing or "knowing" rules by heart than on the skills you will develop in *using* rules the way lawyers and judges do—i.e., to make arguments about how to apply them to concrete disputes in real-world settings. And, once again, the judicial opinion is "ground zero" for seeing these techniques in action. Unsurprisingly, then, the law school exam is the proving ground for you to demonstrate that you, too, have mastered them. And the point of this book is to show you how to do so.

Briefing a Case

In the typical first-year course, in-class analysis of a particular opinion will frequently begin with the professor asking a student to "state the case"—that is, to give an oral rendition of the notes the student has taken while studying the case. The most reliable way to prepare notes for this purpose is by drafting a *case brief*. In this section, we set forth a briefing format that had its genesis in an approach we first learned from the late great Soia Mentschikoff, famously "the first woman everything" in American law. Dean Mentschikoff was the first woman to teach at Harvard Law School; one of the first to do so at the University of Chicago; and also the first to serve as president of the Association of American Law Schools. She was also a transformational dean at the University of Miami, whose iconoclastic faculty recruits in turn gave us our first jobs as junior professors. Most relevant to our efforts here, Dean Mentschikoff co-authored, with our Miami colleague Irwin Stotzky, the famous casebook that set forth the original version of the case brief. (See Mentschikoff and Stotzky, *The Theory and Craft of American Law* (1981).)

So about that briefing format. In a nutshell, you explain the *procedural posture* of the case; identify its *narrative facts*; and then analyze the *holding* as well as the *reasoning* that supports the holding. As usual, if one or more of your professors instructs you to use a different case-briefing format, follow his or her instructions "to a T." But we would nevertheless urge you to work your way through our updated and revised version of the Mentschikoff/Stotzky brief—and to try your hand at the sample briefing exercise that follows—because it will help you see just why so many legal educators stress the importance of case-*briefing* to developing the skill of effective case-*reading*. Moreover, later in the book we'll show you how the format can help in tackling questions on a law exam. And now, without further ado:

A. Procedural posture

1. <u>Court and date</u>? State the name of the court that decided the case (for example, "the New York Court of Appeals") and the year of the decision. This is like a free space on your bingo card, because the opinions appearing in your law school texts will typically be accompanied by a "citation" that displays this information prominently. (We offer an example in the opinion and case-brief exercise that follows.)

2. <u>Who's suing whom</u>? You should answer this in the context of the *relationship* between the parties—that is, the real-life commercial, professional, social, familial, or other interaction that has given rise to their dispute—e.g., "employee is suing employer" or "landlord is suing tenant" or "pedestrian is suing driver."

(Stating that "plaintiff is suing defendant" hardly advances the analysis; plaintiff is *always* suing defendant, for that's what plaintiffs *do*.)

3. <u>For what</u>? What does the party bringing the lawsuit want? Take, for example, a breach of contract suit by a would-be student against a law school (not *your* law school!) that has promised her admission but now reneges. Does the student want the court to force the law school to make good on its promise (i.e., admit her)? Would she settle for recovery of the expenses she incurred on the faith of the promise (e.g., moving costs and a lease)? Or does she just want her application fee and deposit money back? (You will learn the names of each of these "for whats" and a great deal more about them in your first-year courses.)

4. <u>On what basis</u>? What is the suing party's *theory of entitlement*? Identify the legal basis for her claim that the party she is suing owes her something—e.g., "breach of contract" or "medical malpractice." To put it another way, here we are determining the justification for summoning judicial power—and eventually the sheriff, if it comes to that—to force the adverse party to do something he is refusing to do (like paying you a lot of money or signing some legal document). Not every actual or perceived injury creates grounds for a lawsuit, as those of us who get hot under the collar when an aggressive motorist steals our parking space can attest. Identifying what legal theory might be available to a party seeking legal redress is thus a critical skill for any practicing lawyer.

A brief intermission before we proceed to the next point. Taken together, these last three questions—who's suing whom? for what? and on what theory?—comprise the single most effective on-ramp to case analysis we've ever seen, whether you're a student called on to "state the case" in a law school classroom; a lawyer explaining a recent decision to a professional colleague; an advocate arguing about a particular precedent in court; or—and most important for our purposes here—a student trying to figure out how the heck to get started on an exam problem. We'll return to this last point in Part III, but for ease of reference we invite you to join us in thinking of "who's suing whom? for what? and on what theory?" as "The

Three Little Questions." Once you get the hang of them, you are likely to use them in your legal work nearly every day.

5. <u>Proceedings below</u>? An important step in briefing a case is to note how the case got to the court that issued the opinion you are reading. If it's a trial court, the answer is likely to be very straightforward: A sued B, and here we are. But for a host of reasons, the vast majority of judicial opinions you'll study in law school are authored by appellate courts, and when that's the case, the dispute has been on a longer journey. To fill out the picture, then, you'll need briefly to describe what happened in the lower court or courts. Was there a trial—with or without a jury—or was the case decided at some pretrial stage? Who won, and who's dissatisfied and thus appealing the case to the higher court?

6. <u>Issue presented</u>?

    For purposes of "stating a case" in a first-year class, perhaps the best way to capture the "issue presented" is this: What are the lawyers arguing about in the court whose handiwork you are reading? To be sure, that seemingly simple question may have more than one answer, for lawyers frequently argue about more than one issue in a given case. In an auto accident case, for example, the parties may be arguing about the driver's fault as well as the extent of the pedestrian's injuries. Indeed, many cases fit this pattern, with the parties arguing over *liability* (is the alleged culprit legally responsible at all?) as well as the *remedy* (if so, what does he owe the aggrieved party?). Judicial opinions may raise a host of other issues as well, such as disputes about the admissibility of evidence or whether the case was properly within the jurisdiction of the trial court.

    Fortunately, many of the appellate court opinions you'll read early in law school will boil down to a single point in dispute. Alas, however, even in those cases there may be more than one way to *characterize* the disagreement. In a breach of contract case, for example, one side may say there's a breach while the other claims there isn't, so it won't be inaccurate to say that the issue is "whether there is a breach of contract." Yet that doesn't tell us very much, for the key question is *why* one party thinks there's a breach and the other doesn't, since that's the dispute the court must resolve in order to decide the case.

Consider again our law school admissions hypo. Do the parties agree that there's a contract but disagree over whether the law school breached it by denying the student permission to enroll? (Perhaps the issue is "whether the student satisfied the law school's admissions requirement of 'earning an undergraduate degree before enrollment,'" with the law school arguing that the student failed to obtain her degree before fall classes began and the student emphasizing that she completed her graduation requirements over the summer.) Do the parties agree that the law school made an offer of admission but disagree over whether the student accepted the offer? (Perhaps the issue is "whether the offer of admission had expired," with the law school arguing that the student missed the deposit deadline and the student arguing that her timely mailed check was delayed by the post office.) Do the parties disagree over whether the law school made a contractual "offer" at all? (Perhaps the issue is "whether the letter of admission constituted an 'offer' under American contract law.")

Years of experience convince us that your brief will be most useful as a guide to understanding a judicial opinion if you "drill down" into the text and identify the point of disagreement with the level of detail appearing in the foregoing parentheticals and frame the "issue" between the parties accordingly.

7.   <u>Outcome</u>? Did the court deciding the case affirm the lower court, reverse, or do something else? Who won, and what did she win?

B. Narrative facts

The "procedural posture" of the case—which we just described—can be thought of as the *lawyers'* story. It's the account of what happened after parties to some real-world dispute consulted legal professionals and decided (as the saying goes) "to make a federal case out of it"—or, more often in your first-year courses, to make a *state* case out of it. After completing the lawyers' story, it's time to turn to "who did what to whom" back in the real world. We call these "the narrative facts"—that is, the story of the conflict that prompted the parties to turn to the law for help in the first place—and offer three suggestions here.

First, as we all know from listening to a long-winded raconteur, not every part of a narrative moves the story along. As you are recounting the narrative of the case under review, you should focus on the *material facts*—i.e., those that seem to matter to the outcome of the case. Ask yourself, as you consider each fact, "Would it make any difference if this fact were otherwise?" If not, you may omit it from your brief. And whether a particular fact "makes a difference" depends entirely on what the parties are arguing about. To return to our law school admissions hypo, the fact that the admissions letter stated—in bold print at the bottom of the page—that "This letter is not intended as a legal offer" might matter a lot if the parties are arguing over whether the letter was indeed an offer. But it might be safely omitted if the law school has conceded that the parties had a binding contract and is contesting only the damages owed to the student on account of the breach. To be sure, telling the difference between material and immaterial facts is often easier said than done, and one of the skills you are in law school to develop is the ability to distinguish facts that matter legally from facts that don't.

Second, take special note of any material facts about which the parties disagree. Set forth the version offered by each and the supporting evidence, and be ready to explain exactly what difference it makes if one or the other of the parties is found to be "correct."

Finally, we find that the easiest way to analyze the narrative facts in the typical case is to arrange them in chronological order, even if this requires some rearrangement from the order of appearance in the court's opinion. This will provide you with a straightforward "timeline" that should aid your understanding of the story as well as your ability to recall it in class or on an exam.

C. Analysis

1. <u>Holding</u>. Simply put, the "holding" is the court's resolution of the "issue presented." Often that will be pretty obvious—as, for example, when the court says something like "we hold that the law school's letter of admission was indeed an 'offer.'" Sometimes, though, finding the holding will require a little detective

work, and here's a warning about "issues" and "holdings." The approach we've suggested here—that is, focusing on what the parties are fighting about and how the court resolved it—ought to work just fine when you are "stating a case" in a first-year class. But when the opinion you are reading (call it Case A) is deployed by lawyers and judges in a later dispute (call it Case B), don't be surprised if there is a great deal of disagreement over the issue as well as the holding of Case A. You'll learn a lot more about different ways to frame "issues" and "holdings" in virtually all of your law school classes, and in a later chapter we'll show you how to use such framing to your advantage on law school exams.

2. <u>Reasoning</u>.

   a. *"Must" reasons:* Courts frequently insist that they are "just following orders" in reaching a decision, doing what they "must" do because of some pre-existing legal authority. What authority does the court cite in this manner? A precedent? A long-standing common law rule? A statutory provision? The Constitution? Sometimes the court may acknowledge that the precedent or statute is ambiguous but still present its outcome as compelled after first explaining why a particular construction of the existing rule is the better one. And be warned that judges often portray their handiwork as "rule following" even when some observers— including their dissenting colleagues—think the case might fairly be decided another way.

   b. *"Should" reasons:* But rule following goes only so far. Courts also often rely on other considerations in reaching a decision—"shoulds," rather than "musts," drawn principally from notions of justice, fairness, and/or policy. Sometimes "should" reasons are coupled with a "must" reason—as in, "Our conclusion here is required by settled contract law, but we are also moved by the fact that a different result would be unfair to law school applicants who make costly life decisions based on letters of admission that bear no hint of possible revocation." Yet sometimes there *isn't* a precedent or any other pre-existing source of law that points to a particular result, and so the court is writing on a clean slate. In those cases, then, there is no "must," and the court must fall back on what the judge or judges believe "should" be the outcome, forthrightly relying on considerations of justice, fairness, and/or policy to reach a decision.

3. Critique. Briefly state points you might offer to challenge the court's reasoning, both on its own terms and with respect to considerations not addressed in the opinion. This may be difficult at first, since most people tend to accept much of what they read at face value, and perhaps this is particularly so when what they are reading has the imprimatur of those in black robes. But one of the most important skills you will develop in law school is the ability to read judicial opinions and other authoritative texts *critically*. It might help if there is a dissent—that is, an opinion by one or more of the judges disagreeing with the majority's opinion. But failing that, try to put yourself in the shoes of the losing party and her lawyer. What would *they* have to say about the court's opinion?

A DIY Case-Briefing Exercise

Instructions: Using the approach to case-reading we recommend in Chapter Two, read this opinion at least twice before attempting to brief it using the template that appears on the page following the opinion. (And no peeking at the sample brief until you've tried your hand at this!)

A little bit of background to the Johnston *case, which we have edited somewhat for ease of exposition:* Beginning in the late nineteenth century, the courts in every state embraced the "employment-at-will" rule. Under that rule, absent a contractual provision guaranteeing a specific period of employment (e.g., a month), an employer was free to fire an employee— and an employee was free to leave—at any time "for good reason, bad reason, or no reason at all." Over the course of the twentieth century, Congress and state legislatures carved out some statutory exceptions to the rule, identifying "reasons" for which one could not lawfully be terminated, such as race, gender, religion, and union organizing. But apart from those statutory exceptions, the at-will rule remained intact until the 1970s and 1980s, when courts in a majority of states began imposing a variety of judicially developed limits on its application.

Sample Case

Johnston v. Del Mar Distributing Co.

776 S.W.2d 768 (Tex. App. 1989)

BENAVIDES, Justice.

Nancy Johnston, appellant, brought suit against her employer, Del Mar Distributing Co., Inc., alleging that her employment had been wrongfully terminated. Del Mar filed a motion for summary judgment in the trial court alleging that appellant's pleadings failed to state a cause of action. After a hearing on the motion, the trial court agreed with Del Mar and granted its motion for summary judgment. On appeal, appellant... contends that her pleadings did in fact state a cause of action. We agree. Accordingly, we reverse and remand....

In her petition, appellant alleged that she was employed by Del Mar during the summer of 1987. As a part of her duties, she was required to prepare shipping documents for goods being sent from Del Mar's warehouse located in Corpus Christi, Texas to other cities in Texas. One day, Del Mar instructed appellant to package a semi-automatic weapon (for delivery to a grocery store in Brownsville, Texas) and to label the contents of the package as "fishing gear." Ultimately, the package was to be given to United Parcel Service for shipping. Appellant was required to sign her name to the shipping documents; therefore, she was concerned that her actions might be in violation of some firearm regulation or a regulation of the United [States] Postal Service. Accordingly, she sought the advice of the United States Treasury Department Bureau of Alcohol, Tobacco & Firearms (hereinafter referred to as "the Bureau"). A few days after she contacted the Bureau, appellant was fired. Appellant brought suit for wrongful termination alleging that her employment was terminated solely in retaliation for contacting the Bureau.

In its motion for summary judgment, Del Mar stated that the facts alleged in appellant's petition would be taken as true. Specifically, it acknowledged that it required appellant to package and ship firearms with labels that did not reflect the package's true contents. It further acknowledged that appellant's employment was terminated when she became concerned about such practices and sought the "advice" of personnel employed by the Bureau.

Del Mar asserted in its motion that, notwithstanding the above described facts, appellant's cause of action was barred by the employment-at-will doctrine. Specifically, Del Mar asserted that since appellant's employment was for an indefinite amount of time, she was an employee-at-will and it had the absolute right to terminate her employment for any reason or no reason at all.

It is well-settled that Texas adheres to the traditional employment-at-will doctrine. [Multiple citations omitted.] In 1888, the Texas Supreme Court first enunciated the employment-at-will doctrine in the case of *Eastline & R.R.R. Co. v. Scott* [72 Tex. 70, 10 S.W. 99, 102 (1888)]. The Texas Supreme Court held that absent a specific contractual provision to the contrary, either the employer or the employee may terminate their relationship at any time, for any reason. *Eastline & R.R.R. Co.*, 10 S.W. at 102.

Today, the absolute employment-at-will doctrine is increasingly seen as a "relic of early industrial times" and a "harsh anachronism." *Sabine Pilot Service, Inc. v. Hauck*, 687 S.W.2d 733, 735 (Tex. 1985) (Kilgarlin, J., concurring); *Little v. Bryce*, 733 S.W.2d 937, 940 (Tex. App. 1987) (Levy, J., concurring). Accordingly, our Legislature has enacted some exceptions to this doctrine, i.e., an employer may not fire an employee for (1) membership or non-membership in a labor union, (2) serving on a jury, (3) filing a workmen's compensation claim, (4) being on active military duty, (5) being of a particular race, color, handicap, religion, national origin, age, or sex. *Sabine Pilot*, 687 S.W.2d at 735; *Little*, 733 S.W.2d at 940. See also Tex. Rev. Civ. Stat. Ann. art. 6252-16a, § 2 (Vernon Supp. 1989) (a governmental body may not suspend or terminate the employment of a public employee who reports a violation of law to an appropriate law enforcement authority).

Recently, the Texas Supreme Court, recognizing the need to amend the employment-at-will doctrine, invoked its judicial authority to create a very narrow common law exception to the doctrine. *Sabine Pilot*, 687 S.W.2d at 735. In *Sabine Pilot*, the Texas Supreme Court was faced with a narrow issue for consideration, i.e., whether an allegation by an employee that he or she was discharged for refusing to perform an illegal act stated a cause of action. *Id.* The Court held that

> public policy, as expressed *in the laws* of this state and the United States which *carry criminal penalties*, requires a very *narrow* exception to the employment-at-will doctrine.... [T]hat *narrow* exception covers *only* the discharge of an em-

ployee for the *sole* reason that the employee refused to perform an *illegal act. Id.* (Emphasis ours.)

Justice Kilgarlin noted in his concurring opinion to *Sabine Pilot* that
it is against public policy to allow an employer "to require an employee
to break a law or face termination...." *Id.* He elaborated that to hold
otherwise "would promote a thorough disrespect for the laws and legal
institutions of our society." *Id.* Since the Court was faced only with this
narrow issue, it did not carve out any other "public policy" exceptions to
the doctrine. However, as Justice Kilgarlin noted in his concurring opinion, the decision does not preclude the Court from expanding the exception when warranted in a proper case. *Id.*

Del Mar... argue[s] that the narrow exception created in *Sabine Pilot*
d[oes] not apply to the instant case because mislabeling the contents of
a package is not a criminal offense under state or federal laws....
[A]ppellant alleges that her petition did state a cause of action pursuant
to the public policy exception announced in *Sabine Pilot*. In her brief,
appellant contends that since Texas law currently provides that an employee has a cause of action when she is fired for refusing to perform an
illegal act, it necessarily follows that an employee states a cause of action
where she alleges that she is fired for simply inquiring into whether or
not she is committing illegal acts. To hold otherwise, she argues, would
have a chilling effect on the public policy exception announced in *Sabine
Pilot*. We agree.

It is implicit that in order to refuse to do an illegal act, an employee
must either know or suspect that the requested act is illegal. In some
cases it will be patently obvious that the act is illegal (murder, robbery,
theft, etc.); however, in other cases it may not be so apparent. Since ignorance of the law is no defense to a criminal prosecution, it is reasonable
to expect that if an employee has a good faith belief that a required act
might be illegal, she will try to find out whether the act is in fact illegal
prior to deciding what course of action to take. If an employer is allowed
to terminate the employee at this point, the public policy exception announced in *Sabine Pilot* would have little or no effect. To hold otherwise
would force an employee, who suspects that a requested act might be
illegal, to: (1) subject herself to possible discharge if she attempts to find
out if the act is in fact illegal; or (2) remain ignorant, perform the act and,
if it turns out to be illegal, face possible criminal sanctions.

We hold that since the law recognizes that it is against public policy to allow an employer to coerce its employee to commit a criminal act in furtherance of its own interest, then it is necessarily inferred that the same public policy prohibits the discharge of an employee who in good faith attempts to find out if the act is illegal. It is important to note that we are not creating a new exception to the employment-at-will doctrine.... Rather, we are merely enforcing the narrow public policy exception which was created in *Sabine Pilot*....

Furthermore, it is the opinion of this Court that the question of whether or not the requested act was in fact illegal is irrelevant to the determination of this case. We hold that where a plaintiff's employment is terminated for attempting to find out from a regulatory agency if a requested act is illegal, it is not necessary to prove that the requested act was in fact illegal. A plaintiff must, however, establish that she had a good faith belief that the requested act might be illegal, and that such belief was reasonable....

The judgment of the trial court is reversed and remanded for trial.

Case Brief Template *(Give it a try!)*

    A. *Procedural posture*
        1. <u>Court and date</u>?

        2. <u>Who's suing whom</u>?

        3. <u>For what</u>?

        4. <u>On what basis</u>?

        5. <u>Proceedings below</u>?

        6. <u>Issue presented</u>?

        7. <u>Outcome</u>?

    B. *Narrative facts*

    C. *Analysis*
        1. <u>Holding</u>.

        2. <u>Reasoning</u>.

            a. *"Must" reasons:*

            b. *"Should" reasons:*

        3. <u>Critique</u>.

Sample case brief

A.*Procedural posture*

1. <u>Court and date</u>? Texas Court of Appeals 1989. (How did we get "Texas Court of Appeals" out of "Tex. App."? We recommend the most current edition of *The Bluebook: A Uniform System of Citation*—a key reference work for every law student and lawyer—which has tables that, among many other things, enable you to translate citation abbreviations into specific courts, and vice versa.)

2. <u>Who's suing whom</u>? An employee is suing her former employer.

3. <u>For what</u>? It's not clear from the opinion whether she is seeking money damages, or reinstatement to her former position, or both, or something else entirely.

4. <u>On what basis</u>? Wrongful termination.

5. <u>Proceedings below</u>?

   - The employee brought a lawsuit against the employer, and the employer filed a motion alleging that the employee's pleadings—i.e., the legal documents she filed to commence the lawsuit—"failed to state a cause of action." (As you'll learn in Civil Procedure and your other courses, the employer was in essence arguing that the employee had no valid legal claim even if the facts she alleged regarding the reason for her dismissal were entirely true.)

   - The trial court granted the employer's motion and dismissed the employee's case.

   - The employee appealed, contending that her pleadings did indeed state a valid legal claim.

6. <u>Issue presented</u>? In *Sabine Pilot*, the Texas Supreme Court created a public policy exception to the employment-at-will rule, prohibiting the discharge of an employee fired for refusing to commit an illegal act. In the case at hand, the issue presented is whether the *Sabine Pilot* exception is available to an employee who is fired for making a reasonable, good-faith inquiry to a government agency about the lawfulness of an act requested of her by the employer, irrespective of whether the requested act would in fact be unlawful.

7. <u>Outcome</u>? The appellate court reversed the lower court's decision and remanded the case (i.e., sent it back to the lower court) for a trial on the merits.

B. *Narrative facts*

- As a part of her duties for the employer, the employee was required to prepare shipping documents for goods sent to third parties from the employer's facility.
- During the summer of 1987, the employer instructed the employee to package a semiautomatic weapon for shipment to a customer and to label the contents of the package as "fishing gear."
- The employee was required to sign her name to the shipping documents and was therefore concerned that her actions might be in violation of some firearm regulation.
- She sought the advice of personnel at the United States Treasury Department Bureau of Alcohol, Tobacco & Firearms regarding the legality of the directive, and the employer fired her for doing so.

C. *Analysis*

1. <u>Holding</u>. It is unlawful for an employer to discharge an employee for making an inquiry to a regulatory agency into the legality of an act requested by the employer when the employee reasonably and in good faith believes the act may be illegal.

2. <u>Reasoning</u>.

   a. *"Must" reasons:* In *Sabine Pilot*, the Texas Supreme Court forthrightly declared that it was carving out a narrow exception to the employment-at-will rule based on "public policy," a classic "should" reason, when it held that an employer may not discharge an employee because of the latter's refusal to commit a criminal act. By contrast, the Court of Appeals in *Johnston* went out of its way to insist that it had "must" reasons for its decision—that it was "not creating a new exception to the employment-at-will doctrine" but was instead "merely" enforcing the narrow exception carved out in the binding precedent of *Sabine Pilot*. The court reasoned that in many cases an employee won't know for sure whether a particular act requested by the employer is unlawful and thus that a right to "find out if the act is illegal" is "implicit" in the holding of *Sabine Pilot*. The court expressed the related concern that permitting an employer to fire an employee for making an inquiry into the lawfulness of an employer directive would have a "chilling effect," prompting employees unsure about the legality of a directive to err on the side of obedience to the employer rather than fidelity to the law and thus undermining the holding of *Sabine Pilot* that fidelity to the law should come first.

b. *"Should" reasons:* The court also expressed the concern that the absence of a "right to inquire" would create an unfair double-bind for an employee who suspects but isn't certain that a requested act might be illegal, forcing the employee to: "(1) subject herself to possible discharge if she attempts to find out if the act is in fact illegal; or (2) remain ignorant, perform the act and, if it turns out to be illegal, face possible criminal sanctions[,]" since ignorance of the law would be no excuse.

3. <u>Critique</u>. Given the many laws that regulate employer activities and the fact that the overwhelming majority of employees aren't lawyers, it's difficult to quarrel with the court's logic that the right under *Sabine Pilot* to refuse to commit a criminal act would be compromised in many cases if employees didn't also have the right to "find out" whether a particular directive is unlawful in the first place. But creating a "right to inquire" opens up at least three cans of worms.

First, the court understandably limits its interpretation of *Sabine* to those cases in which the employee's good-faith inquiry into the potential illegality of employer-requested conduct is "reasonable." In our social media age, however, employees can acquire all sorts of "information" from well-meaning but mistaken sources as well as from outlets that regularly traffic in "fake news." How will courts determine when it's reasonable for employees to find such "information" credible enough to warrant inquiries about the legality of a particular employer directive?

Second, for the same reason that an employee may not be in a position to know whether a particular directive is unlawful, she may not be in a position to know which regulatory agency to contact to pose an appropriate inquiry, and accordingly she may (a) unwittingly call the wrong agency; (b) call a lawyer instead; or (c) call some other knowledgeable person, such as a business law reporter from the local press. Are any or all of those inquiries protected? If so, *Sabine Pilot* would be extended further still; if not, the right to inquire may turn out to be hollow in many circumstances.

Finally, the decision likewise potentially expands *Sabine Pilot* by protecting employees who take their concerns to a regulatory agency, for even an inquiry undertaken discreetly and entirely in good faith may alert the agency to potential illegality by the employer and thus operate as the functional equivalent of "whistleblowing." Will an employee who "lets the cat out of the bag" in this manner still enjoy protection from discharge? And if the answer is yes, has the court implicitly extended *Sabine* from a rule protecting a right to refuse to perform an illegal act to a right to "blow the whistle" on employer illegality? Would such an extension be a good or bad thing?

Chapter Four

Outlining a Statute — Six Steps Along the Yellow Brick Road

Although judicial opinions are the bread and butter of the law school experience, law school courses are increasingly focused as well on statutes, the handiwork of legislatures. Statutes play an especially important role in Criminal Law (where virtually all of the rules are statutory) and Contracts (where you'll study parts of a massive statute, the Uniform Commercial Code). You'll encounter more than a few statutes in the rest of the first-year curriculum as well. Moreover, many of the courses you'll take in the upper level will treat a particular statute as the central object of study, such as the Internal Revenue Code in Federal Income Tax and Title VII of the 1964 Civil Rights Act in Employment Discrimination. And in virtually every law school class you will encounter proposed statutes, legislation not yet on the books but designed to reform the existing law of one or more jurisdictions. Learning to read and work with statutory material is thus another critical skill for law school success.

But here's the rub. As if judicial opinions didn't present enough of a challenge for the uninitiated, statutes can be more daunting still. In terms of accessibility to the beginning student, the typical judicial opinion has the advantage of leading with a story about the particulars of some real-world dispute. Statutes, by contrast, tend to address a broad multitude of possible disputes all in one fell swoop, typically in dense prose larded with abstract and obscure terms. Consider, for example, the following language from § 1-303(e) of the Uniform Commercial Code:

> Except as otherwise provided in subsection (f), the express terms of an agreement and any applicable course of performance, course of dealing, or usage of trade must be construed whenever reasonable as consistent with each other. If such a construction is unreasonable: (1) express terms prevail over course of performance, course of dealing, and usage of trade; (2) course of performance prevails over course of dealing and usage of trade; and (3) course of dealing prevails over usage of trade.

Upon encountering such a passage, many students are tempted to give up after reading the first line or two or just to skip it altogether, hoping someone—the casebook author? the professor? a commercial study aid?—will explain in plain terms what all that fine print means. But your goal is learning to do this work on your own. And in much the same way that a case brief can aid you in organizing, understanding, and recalling the finer points of a judicial opinion, a good outline can help you make sense of a statute. The technique we recommend here will be useful in dealing with other kinds of legal rules as well, from common law rules developed by courts to regulations issued by administrative agencies to the ubiquitous "statutory wannabe" products of the American Law Institute, a prestigious private organization of lawyers, judges, and legal scholars responsible for drafting the Model Penal Code (which you'll study in Criminal Law) and the Restatements of Law (which you'll study in Contracts, Property, and Torts).

So here's some good news. At least in your first year, you will almost never be assigned a mega-statute—bursting at the seams with dozens upon dozens or even hundreds of provisions—and asked to read it from beginning to end, digesting it all on your own in a single sitting. When you encounter a statute of that magnitude, your professors will instead almost invariably explore it "one provision at a time." Indeed, professors often take this approach even to statutes of more modest length; an old joke about Labor Law is that it takes fourteen weeks of class to study fourteen provisions of the National Labor Relations Act, and at least one Labor Law professor of close acquaintance thinks fourteen weeks isn't nearly enough. The outlining technique we recommend here is designed to facilitate this granular focus and also to aid you in decoding statutes of varying sizes you'll encounter in virtually all of your law school classes.

The Long-Form Outline: A Close Look at a Fictional Statute

Gotham City (NY) Ordinances

An Act Regulating Vehicle Usage in City Center Park

§ 1 *Definitions.*

  (a) "Vehicles" means all motorized vehicles except emergency vehicles.

  (b) "Emergency vehicles" means any of the following vehicles while responding to an emergency call but not while returning from such a call: any ambulance or other vehicle operated by a member of an emergency medical service organization; any vehicle used by a fire department or by any officer of a fire department; or any state or local police vehicle operated by a police officer.

  (c) "Park" means City Center Park, including the lands, waters, pools, and playgrounds within the Park as well as the roads, paths, and trails through and within the Park boundaries.

§ 2 *Prohibition.* No vehicles are allowed in the Park.

§ 3 *Penalties.* Any person violating the provisions of this Act shall be deemed guilty of a civil infraction. During a one-year period, each violation of this Act shall constitute a separate offense. Violations of this Act shall be enforced as follows:

  (a) For the first violation, by a civil penalty of $100.00.

  (b) For the second violation, by a civil penalty of $500.00.

  (c) For the third violation and any additional violation thereafter, by a civil penalty of $1,000.00.

Most of the statutes you'll encounter in law school and in legal practice will resemble this fictional one in style, organization, and format—though candidly this one is a bit on the short side so we don't overtax the reader's patience in this "how-to" book. What should you do when you are asked to study such material? As we suggested in connection with judicial opinions, you should start by reading the text through twice: the first a quick skim to get the general idea, the second a careful read to begin absorbing the details. (And don't forget that additional run-through after your professor covers the material in class; her analysis is likely to enrich and even alter your initial understanding of a statute, much as it will with judicial opinions.)

After the two reads, you're ready to outline, and in a moment we're going to suggest a series of steps to help you organize statutory material for careful analysis and effective study. But a couple of preliminary matters before we begin. First, we're going to surprise you by recommending a reliable technique in connection with statutory outlines that in virtually any other context would get you in serious trouble: *plagiarism*. As you'll figure out soon enough, drafting a statute is one of the most demanding tasks that lawyers are called on to undertake; every word counts, and fortunes have been won and lost over the placement of a comma and the difference between an "and" and an "or." As a consequence, attempts to paraphrase key provisions of a statute or to "put it in your own words"—usually a terrific way to master reading material—will often unwittingly go awry. So as you draft your outline, don't be afraid to quote directly from the statutory text rather than trying to re-write it.

The second preliminary matter is that—like our fictional statute—virtually every statute identifies its constituent sections and subsections with numbers and/or letters (§ 1(a), § 1(b), etc.). When you refer to a particular statutory provision during class discussion, on an exam, or eventually as a lawyer in a brief or argument, the best practice is to identify it by reference to these designations, so that the listener/reader/grader can locate and verify the original statutory text. It is therefore a good idea to follow this practice in your outline, coupling each entry with the corresponding numerical and/or alphabetical reference.

So let's get down to the business of outlining. We recommend a six-step approach.

Step One: Where does the statute govern? We'll start with what will typically be a free space on your outline's bingo card: the geographical reach of the statute. Early in law school, you'll begin learning about the hierarchy of legal authority in the United States: the relationships between federal and state law, common law and statutes, international and domestic law, the laws of different states, and the laws governing political subdivisions of individual states. For our purposes, the one thing you need to know now is that statutes typically operate only *within* a particular geographic jurisdiction: federal statutes typically govern the entirety of the U.S.; the statutes of a given state govern within that state; and the statutes of counties, cities, and so on govern respectively only within the enacting jurisdiction. To be sure, the statutes of one jurisdiction can *influence* other jurisdictions; it is common, for example, for states and cities to "learn" from one another and even to copy the legislative handiwork of a sister jurisdiction. Sometimes legal provisions in one state indirectly bind citizens in another state, for example, via state tax laws that let the citizens of one state reduce their taxes based on the taxes they pay to another state. But any particular statute has legal effect only in the jurisdiction of enactment, and this is obviously an important data point for a lawyer advising a client on which laws she must follow and which she need not yet worry about. The first step in the outline, then, is to identify the jurisdiction (federal, state, county, etc.) that enacted the statute, thus defining the geographical reach of that legislation. Here's an example drawn from our fictional statute:

Step One: Where does the statute govern?
- Gotham City, NY

Step Two: Whom does the statute govern? Some statutes are "laws of general application" and thus apply to pretty much everyone. Such laws can have exceptions, of course—the laws of criminal trespass, for example, won't apply to the sheriff enforcing a home foreclosure order—but the point is that anyone and everyone outside of those specific exceptions is governed by the statute in question. By contrast, other statutes are limited to a narrower target—to a particular class of persons (e.g., merchants); to a particular kind of legal relationship (e.g., landlord and tenant); to a particular type of transaction (e.g., real estate sales); or to a type of organization (e.g., nonprofit corporations). Identifying the class of persons, relationships, transactions, or institutions governed by a statute is obviously a crucial inquiry, for you can't begin to give advice about what a statute *does* without first knowing what or whom the statute does it *to*. Accordingly, this is the second step in our recommended outline.

Yet even though this step will *appear* early in your outline, you might find yourself drafting it after you work your way through Steps Three through Six. Why's that? Though many statutes announce their intended coverage in the title (e.g., "The Florida Residential Landlord-Tenant Act"), others will make you do some detective work, and it may require a close look at the definitions section (see Step Three) and/or the command section (see Step Four) of the statute to sort that out. Our fictional statute is a case in point, for its coverage is not necessarily apparent from the title ("An Act Regulating Vehicle Usage in City Center Park"). But

§§ 1 and 2 of the statute make it clear that—with a single exception for emergency vehicles—it reaches anyone who wants to bring a motorized vehicle into City Center Park and is thus a law of general application.

So whenever you actually draft it, here's what this second step would look like in an outline of our fictional statute:

Step Two: <u>Whom</u> does the statute govern?
- It's a law of general application.
- With the exception of those driving emergency vehicles, it applies to anyone and everyone who might want to bring a motorized vehicle into City Center Park.

Step Three: Definitions. Virtually every statute has a "definitions" section that operates as a glossary of key terms used by the drafters, and many statutes begin with such a section, as our fictional statute does. Definitions frequently offer surprising details about the meaning of the words as they are used in the statute. Under the Uniform Commercial Code, for example, an "assignment" is not something a professor has asked you to prepare, but instead a transfer of your rights under a contract to a third party.

On the good news side, the number of defined terms is typically small in comparison with the total number of words used in a statute; our fictional statute, for example, has nearly 300 words and only three definitions. At least as a starting point, you may rely on conventional meanings for the rest, and you needn't include in your outline any definitions that appear to have been drafted by Captain Obvious. Instead—and here's our first and most important tip about definitions—*your outline should focus on defined terms with counterintuitive or nonobvious meanings and highlight those aspects of the defined terms.* (Would you have known, for example, that "vehicles" meant only "motorized vehicles" if the definitions section of our ordinance hadn't said so?)

Our second tip: Definitions frequently contain lists, as in "As used in this statute, 'X' includes A, B, C, and D." But it turns out there are different kinds of lists, and your outline ought to reflect that. On the one hand, consider the following definition from a typical employment law statute: "'Employer' means any private individual, firm, partnership, institution, corporation, or association that employs ten or more persons." On the other hand, consider the following definition from the Uniform Commercial Code: "'Writing' includes printing, typewriting, or any other intentional reduction to tangible form." Do you see the difference? The list offered in the first example is seemingly *exhaustive*, for we are given a complete list of what the word "employer" *means*. Either a would-be employer is on the list or it isn't, and that typically ends the matter. By contrast, in the second example the word "includes" may signal that the list of "writings" is merely *illustrative*, since the defined term may "include" additional items as well. It thus invites lawyers and judges to add "other" analogous items to the list (e.g., word processing).

This is, by the way, an excellent example of how much difference a single word can make to the meaning of statutory language. Accordingly, you'll need to watch the definitions you encounter closely for "means" and similar terms (e.g., "comprises") as well as for "includes" and similar language (e.g., "such as"). When you encounter a list in a definition, then, your outline should identify the kind of list at issue—exhaustive vs. illustrative—and either way it's a good idea to replicate the list in "bullet points" separately identifying each of the different items contained therein.

So here's an illustration of Step Three, drawing once again on our fictional statute:

Step Three: Definitions.
- § 1(a) Vehicles
  - = all *motorized* vehicles
  - excludes "emergency vehicles"
- § 1(b) Emergency vehicles
  - = the following *exhaustive* list:
    - any vehicle operated by a member of an emergency medical service organization;
    - any vehicle used by a fire department or by any officer of a fire department;
    - any state or local police vehicle operated by a police officer
  - Limitation: The listed vehicles are "emergency vehicles"
    - "when responding to an emergency call"
    - "but not while returning from such a call"
- § 1(c) Park
  - = City Center Park
  - including

- the waters and adjoining lands, pools, and playgrounds within the Park
- the roads, paths, and trails through and within the Park boundaries

Step Four: The command & the elements of proof. At the heart of most statutes is a command of some sort: You can't do X; you must do Y; in order to Z, you have to do A. (E.g., "thou shall not kill"; "you must register for the draft"; "in order to drive, you have to get a license.") Channeling Tina Fey, we think of this as "the bossy part," and we trust the reasons for careful reading here are clear: Clients are going to need to know exactly what they must or must not do in order to ensure compliance with the law.

We think the best approach to drafting the command section is to adopt the point of view of a lawyer litigating a dispute arising under the statute. If the statute *prohibits* behavior, you should play the role of a prosecutor attempting to establish a violation by the other party. If the statute *requires* behavior—on pain of punishment or in order to secure some benefit—then you should play the role of a lawyer representing the party whose compliance is required. In either case, we recommend that you adopt the point of view of the lawyer with "the burden of proof"—a prosecutor attempting to establish that a defendant did something wrong or a lawyer attempting to establish that her client did something right. "Burdens of proof" can get seriously complicated, and you'll learn a lot more about them in the course of your legal studies. But the basic idea should be clear enough, and we urge you to shoulder that burden for outlining purposes so you can focus like the proverbial laser beam on the most critical question litigating lawyers confront: *What do you need to prove?*

To aid you in this lawyering exercise, we recommend using bullet points, numbers, and/or letters to break down the statutory command into discrete elements, identifying each of the individual facts or circumstances you'll have to establish in order to prevail. In this effort, the command section (Step Four) is likely to draw heavily on the definitions section (Step Three). Thus, the command will frequently incorporate terms that the statute defines in some nonobvious way—with a list, for example, or via some unexpected twist—and you should "copy and paste" the material you've assembled in Step Three and include it here.

That way, the command section will contain a complete and comprehensive list of "what you need to prove" under the terms of the statute.

We'll offer an extended example in a moment, but first we want to emphasize that this focus on facts and proofs will help you learn to do what you'll be repeatedly called on to do in class and on law school exams: apply the statute to new and different factual situations invented by your professor. And professors do this not to torment you but to help you prepare for practice, where you'll encounter new and different statutes—and new and different factual situations in which to apply them—all the time.

So here's what Step Four of the outline looks like in the context of our fictional statute.

Step Four: The command & the elements of proof.
(A) The command: "No vehicles allowed in the Park" (§ 2)
(B) The elements of proof
    (1) Is it a "vehicle"? (§ 1(a))
        (a) Is it a "vehicle" at all?
        (b) Is it a "motorized" vehicle?"
        (c) Does it fall within the exception for "emergency vehicles"? (§ 1(b))
            (i) Is it operated by emergency medical personnel, firefighters, or police?
            (ii) Is it "responding to"—but not "returning from"—an "emergency call"?
    (2) Is it "in the Park"? (§ 1(c))
        (a) Is it in City Center Park?
        (b) Is it in
            (i) "the waters and adjoining lands, pools, and playgrounds within the park"?
            (ii) "the roads, paths, and trails through and within the park boundaries"?

Note, by the way, that we've used all three definitions from Step Three—"vehicles"; "emergency vehicles"; and "Park"—in spelling out the elements of proof under our fictional statute. And notice too that the definition of "in the Park" uses the phrase "including," thus leaving open the possibility that there might be other places in the Park where vehicles are also barred. But we can't think of any, which is why we treat the list of places as exhaustive.

Step Five: The consequences of noncompliance. So what happens if a party governed by the statute has failed to comply with it? The consequences vary from statute to statute, but there are some important patterns to watch out for.

- Statutes that require compliance in order to secure a particular benefit—e.g., a driver's license, or adherence to the provisions of a will deemed by the courts to be valid—typically "punish" simply by denying the benefit in question. Sometimes the statute will itself make the consequences of such noncompliance clear (e.g., "no driver's license for *you!*"); sometimes the consequences will be dictated by other laws (e.g., if you fail to conform to the requirements for making a valid will under Statute A, the court will proceed according to the terms of Statute B, which governs the distribution of assets of individuals who die without leaving a will). Figuring this out won't be rocket science. If the statute in question appears in your assigned readings, the accompanying material will almost invariably discuss the consequences of noncompliance and the source of those consequences; and your professor is likely to do the same thing if she brings the statute to your attention during class.
- Statutes that prohibit particular forms of conduct frequently give a special name or classification to infractions of their provisions. The failure by an employer or a union to comply with the commands of the National Labor Relations Act, for example, is denominated an "unfair labor practice"; state and federal fair trade laws typically refer to a statutory violation as an "unfair trade practice" or a "deceptive trade practice." Sometimes classifying terms signify varying degrees of culpability. Criminal statutes, for example, typically identify whether a particular infraction is a felony or a misdemeanor, and additional consequences may attach depending on the classification (e.g., in some states, convicted felons lose the right to vote).
- Statutes that prohibit particular forms of conduct typically punish noncompliance through fines and/or a requirement that the offender pay for damages caused by the wrongdoing. If it's a crim-

inal statute, imprisonment may be imposed instead of or in addition to a fine.

- Whether civil or criminal, statutes that punish in this way frequently enhance the penalty—via a scale of increasing fines or longer prison sentences—for repeat offenders or for those who violate the statute in aggravating circumstances (e.g., using a firearm in the commission of a robbery).

Although it's easy to get bogged down in the details, keep in mind that the precise consequences of statutory noncompliance are likely to be a great deal more important to a client than the embarrassment of flunking a driver's test or signing an invalid will—more important even than questions of whether a criminal conviction signals that a client has done something morally blameworthy. In this fifth step of your statutory outline, then, you should identify with particularity the consequences of noncompliance. Here's what that would look like for our fictional statute.

Step Five: The consequences of noncompliance.
- Penalties (§ 3)
  - A violation = "a civil infraction"
  - Punishment =
    - During a one-year period, each violation is "a separate offense" and is subject to a scale of increasing "civil penalties"
    - The scale:
      - (A) First violation = $100.00
      - (B) Second violation = $500.00
      - (C) Third violation and any additional violation thereafter = $1,000.00

Step Six: What does it change? Here's something you need to know about the role of statutes—those on the books as well as those merely proposed—in the courses you'll be taking in law school, especially during your first year. Far more often than not, statutes are "change agents," the product of dissatisfaction with an older body of law that prompts a legislature to toss out the old in favor of something new. In your common law courses—Contracts, Property, and Torts—this is a fairly frequent occurrence, since much of the law governing those topics was originally developed by judges in the nineteenth century or even earlier, and legislatures in the twentieth and twenty-first centuries have not always been happy with prior judicial handiwork. You'll see this phenomenon in your upper-level classes as well; for example, most of what we think of today as Employment Law is the result of statutes that have displaced much of the nineteenth-century common law of master-servant.

Casebooks often introduce "change agent" statutes toward the end of a section of materials that begins with a judicial opinion embracing the "old way" and/or an opinion discussing and rejecting an older approach in favor of some "new way." The statute will often appear in the notes and comments that follow the judicial opinion(s), offered to illustrate a legislative alternative to the common law rule. You'll discover during your legal studies that such provenance is an important data point. For one thing, statutory origins shed light on the problem that the legislature was attempting to solve with the legislation and may therefore aid in interpreting and applying the statute to particular cases. (Later in the book, we devote the better part of a chapter to the role of "statutory purpose" in tackling law school exams.) For another thing, statutes frequently enact "half measures," changing some aspects of the older rule but leaving others intact. You'll obviously need to know just what's changed and what's stayed the same as you advise a client on the consequences of the statute—or as you take on the role of giving lawyerly advice while answering a law school exam question.

Direct evidence of the statute's role as a "change agent" is frequently available in materials the professor will assign to accompany the statutory provision. The legislative history of a statute, for example, will often forthrightly proclaim the legislature's displeasure with an older rule and its intention to displace it with a new one. The "Reporter's Notes" perform a similar function for the Restatements of Law, more than occasionally revealing an intention on the part of the drafters to replace rather than merely "restate" pre-existing doctrine. Likewise, the "Official Comment" that accompanies each provision of the Uniform Commercial Code will often make explicit an intention to eliminate some common law rule or principle.

We therefore recommend that you end your statutory outline with a section briefly explaining—so far as you can tell from your assigned readings—what it was that the statute was designed to change and how far it went in doing so. Illustrating once again with our fictional statute, here's what Step Six might look like:

Step Six: What does it change?
- Prior to enactment of the ordinance, drivers could evidently bring motorized vehicles of any description into City Center Park without restriction
- The ordinance prohibits Park access for all but emergency vehicles on their way to emergencies

Summing up. Now that we've worked our way through all six steps, let's stop and take in the view from 30,000 feet. Here's what a complete outline of our fictional statute would look like, and—to get the full benefit of the view—we recommend re-reading the ordinance set forth above and then carefully reviewing the outline to see how the former is taken apart and reassembled in the latter.

Step One: <u>Where</u> does the statute govern?
- Gotham City NY

Step Two: <u>Whom</u> does the statute govern?
- It's a law of general application
- With the exception of those driving emergency vehicles, it applies to anyone and everyone who might want to bring a motorized vehicle into City Center Park

Step Three: Definitions.
- § 1(a) Vehicles
  - = all *motorized* vehicles
  - excludes "emergency vehicles"
- § 1(b) Emergency vehicles
  - = the following exhaustive list:
    - any vehicle operated by a member of an emergency medical service organization;
    - any vehicle used by a fire department or by any officer of a fire department;
    - any state or local police vehicle operated by a police officer
  - Limitation: The listed vehicles are "emergency vehicles"
    - "when responding to an emergency call"
    - "but not while returning from such a call"
- § 1(c) Park
  - = City Center Park

- including
  - the waters and adjoining lands, pools, and playgrounds within the Park
  - the roads, paths, and trails through and within the Park boundaries

Step Four: The command & the elements of proof.

(A) The command: "No vehicles allowed in the Park" (§ 2)

(B) The elements of proof

 (1) Is it a "vehicle"? (§ 1(a))

  (a) Is it a "vehicle" at all?

  (b) Is it a "motorized" vehicle?"

  (c) Does it fall within the exception for "emergency vehicles"? (§ 1(b))

   (i) Is it operated by emergency medical personnel, firefighters, or police?

   (ii) Is it "responding to"—but not "returning from"—an "emergency call"?

 (2) Is it "in the Park"? (§ 1(c))

  (a) Is it in City Center Park?

  (b) Is it in

   (i) "the waters and adjoining lands, pools, and playgrounds within the park"?

   (ii) "the roads, paths, and trails through and within the park boundaries"?

Step Five: The consequences of noncompliance.

- Penalties (§ 3)
  - A violation = "a civil infraction"
  - Punishment =
    - During a one-year period, each violation is "a separate offense" and is subject to a scale of increasing "civil penalties"
    - The scale:
      - (A) First violation = $100.00
      - (B) Second violation = $500.00
      - (C) Third violation and any additional violation thereafter = $1,000.00

Step Six: What does it change?
- Prior to enactment of the ordinance, drivers could evidently bring motorized vehicles of any description into City Center Park without restriction
- The ordinance prohibits Park access for all but emergency vehicles on their way to emergencies

The Short Form Outline:
Working with Individual Statutory Provisions

The six-step outline we recommend should work well when you encounter a short or modest-length statute in the course of your studies. Such encounters will be common in law school, but—and here's some seriously good news—you will far more frequently confront statutory material in much smaller bites. As we noted earlier, many of your professors will focus your study on individual provisions from statutes of varying size, and, as often as not, they will assign and explore those provisions one at a time. In those circumstances, there's typically no need for the "long-form" six-step outline, and you can typically shorten your effort to a two- or three-step "short-form" abbreviation. Moreover, the vast majority of free-standing statutory provisions you'll encounter will perform one of the three functions we've explored in connection with the long-form outline—it will define a term, issue a command, or impose a penalty for noncompliance—and you have already seen the outlining templates for provisions that perform those functions.

For the short-form outline, then, you might start by collapsing long-form Steps One and Two, briefly addressing the "where" and the "whom" that the statutory provision governs in a single passage. To avoid confusion with the long form, we'll use letters rather than numbers and call this Step A. Step B is to outline the provision itself, and, as we've suggested, you can use the corresponding long-form template for this purpose—i.e., Step Three (if it's a definition); Step Four (if it's a command); or Step Five (if it's about the consequences of noncompliance). Step C replicates the final step from the long form, addressing that always important question for law school study: "What does it change?" Often the content of Step B will itself answer this question, particularly when the provision amends an earlier version of the statute. When that's the case, you can collapse Step B and Step C, condensing the short-form outline into two steps.

So here is a quick example of a short-form outline, drawing one final time from our fictive "no-vehicles-in-the-park" ordinance.

> Assume that the original version of the ordinance had no exception for emergency vehicles and that—after a widely publicized incident in which the police pulled over a speeding ambulance as it cut through the park—an amendment was enacted to add the exception by changing the definition of "vehicle."

Step A: Where and whom does the statute govern?
- It's a law of general application in Gotham City, NY

Step B: A new definition & what it changes
- The original text provides "No vehicles allowed in the Park" (§ 2) and defines "vehicle" as "all motorized vehicles" (§ 1(a))
- The amendment makes three changes to the original text
  1. It changes the definition of "vehicles" in § 1(a) to "all motorized vehicles *except emergency vehicles*" (new language in italics)
  2. It adds a new § 1(b) defining "emergency vehicles"
     - The term = the following exhaustive list:
       - any vehicle operated by a member of an emergency medical service organization;
       - any vehicle used by a fire department or by any officer of a fire department;
       - any state or local police vehicle operated by a police officer
     - Limitation: The listed vehicles are "emergency vehicles"
       - "when responding to an emergency call"
       - "but not while returning from such a call"
  3. It changes the section number for the definition of "Park" from § 1(b) to § 1(c)

In a moment, we'll give you an opportunity to try your own hand at a statutory outline. But before we do, we have another good news/bad news point, and we'll start with the bad. Law exam questions almost *never* present problems that can be answered with the rote application of a particular provision of a statute. As we explore in a later chapter, the questions you'll confront will almost invariably require an interpretation of the provision and will almost invariably raise the possibility of more than one way to read it. Imagine, for example, an exam question testing our "no-vehicles-in-the-park" ordinance with a hypothetical in which an ambulance heads out from a hospital to pick up an injured patient and—having done so—is now *returning* to the hospital. May it legally drive through the Park? As you'll see, there are patterns to the arguments lawyers are likely to raise in the context of such a dispute, and that's what your professor will ordinarily be testing on an exam. Which brings us to the good news: An outline of the statute—long form or short—will typically give you just the tools you'll need to formulate the arguments you'll need to write the answer your professor is seeking.

A DIY Statutory Outlining Exercise

Here's a chance to try your hand at outlining statutory material. What follows tracks the same basic format we used for the case-briefing exercise: We start with the text of a sample statute; then we offer the long-form outlining template for you to work with; and, finally, we present a "model" outline. (Once again, no peeking until you've attempted the exercise on your own!)

To avoid adding another layer of complexity, we've selected a statute related to the same area of law raised by the *Johnston* case, i.e., the employment-at-will rule and its proliferating exceptions. Here we'll focus on a legislative rather than a judicially created exception, a whistleblower protection statute based on legislation enacted in a number of states.

Sample Statute: Whistleblower Protection Act for the State of Oz

§ 1 **Definitions**—As used in § 2, the term:

    (1) "Appropriate governmental agency" means any agency of government charged with the enforcement of laws, rules, or regulations governing an activity, policy, or practice of an employer.

    (2) "Employee" means a person who performs services for and under the control and direction of an employer for wages or other remuneration. The term does not include an independent contractor.

    (3) "Employer" means any private individual, firm, partnership, institution, corporation, or association that employs ten or more persons.

    (4) "Law, rule, or regulation" includes any statute or ordinance or any rule or regulation adopted pursuant to any federal, state, or local statute or ordinance applicable to the employer and pertaining to the business.

    (5) "Retaliatory personnel action" means the discharge, suspension, or demotion by an employer of an employee or any other adverse employment action taken by an employer against an employee in the terms and conditions of employment.

§ 2 **Retaliatory Personnel Actions**—An employer may not take any retaliatory personnel action against an employee because the employee has:

    (a) Disclosed, or threatened to disclose, to any appropriate governmental agency an activity, policy, or practice of the employer that is in violation of a law, rule, or regulation.

    (b) Objected to, or refused to participate in, any activity, policy, or practice of the employer that is in violation of a law, rule, or regulation.

§ 3 **Employee's remedy**—An employee who has been the object of a retaliatory personnel action in violation of this act may institute a civil action in a court of competent jurisdiction for the following relief:

(a) An injunction restraining continued violation of this act;
(b) Reinstatement of the employee to the same position held before the retaliatory personnel action or to an equivalent position;
(c) Reinstatement of full fringe benefits and seniority rights; and
(d) Compensation for lost wages, benefits, and other remuneration.

Outline template *(Give it a try!)*

Step One: <u>Where</u> does the statute govern?

Step Two: <u>Whom</u> does the statute govern?

Step Three: Definitions.

Step Four: The command & the elements of proof.

Step Five: The consequences of noncompliance.

Step Six: What does it change?

Model outline

Step One: <u>Where</u> does the statute govern?
The statute governs in the State of Oz.

Step Two: <u>Whom</u> does the statute govern?
Private-sector employers with ten or more employees (§ 1(3))

Step Three: Definitions. (§ 1) (All definitions are *exhaustive* except
for (4) "law, rule, or regulation")
(1) "Appropriate governmental agency" means
  - any agency of government
  - charged with
    - the **enforcement of laws, rules, or regulations**
    - **governing an activity, policy, or practice of an employer**
(2) "Employee" means
  - a person who
    - **performs services** for an employer
    - **under the control and direction** of an employer
    - **for wages or other remuneration**
  - does **not** include an independent contractor
(3) "Employer" means
  - any individual, firm, partnership, institution, corporation, or association
  - that
    - is **private** and
    - **employs ten or more persons**
(4) "Law, rule, or regulation" **includes** (use of **includes** suggests this is illustrative—other sources of law may be allowed)
  - any
    - **statute or ordinance**
    - or **any rule or regulation** adopted pursuant to any federal, state, or local statute or ordinance
  - that is
    - **applicable to the employer**
    - and **pertains to the business**
(5) "Retaliatory personnel action" means

- the **discharge, suspension, or demotion** by an employer of an employee, or
- **any other adverse employment action**
  - ○ taken by an employer against an employee
  - ○ in the **terms and conditions of employment**

Step Four: The command & the elements of proof.

(A) The command (§ 2): An employer may not take any retaliatory personnel action against an employee because the employee has

  (1) Disclosed, or threatened to disclose, to any appropriate governmental agency an activity, policy, or practice of the employer that is in violation of a law, rule, or regulation (§ 2(a))

  (2) Objected to, or refused to participate in, any activity, policy, or practice of the employer which is in violation of a law, rule, or regulation (§ 2(b))

(B) The elements of proof:

  (1) Is the alleged offender an **employer**? (§ 1(3))

   (a) Is it an **individual, firm, partnership, institution, corporation, or association**?

   (b) Is it **private**?

   (c) Does it **employ ten or more persons**?

  (2) Is the aggrieved party an employee? (§ 1(2))

   (a) Is she an **independent contractor**?

    (i) If so, she is not an employee

    (ii) If not, does she:

     (a) **perform services** for the employer?

     (b) **work under the control and direction** of the employer?

     (c) receive **wages or other remuneration** in return?

  (3) Has the employer taken a "retaliatory personnel action" against the employee? (§ 1(5))

   (a) Has the employer **discharged, suspended, or demoted** the employee?

   (b) Has the employer

(i) taken any other adverse employment action against the employee?

(ii) in the **terms and conditions of employment?**

(4) Did the employer take the retaliatory personnel action

   (a) because the employee has (§ 2(a))

      (i) **Disclosed**

         (a) an **activity, policy, or practice of the employer**

         (b) that is in violation of a **law, rule, or regulation** (§ 1(4))?

            (i) Is the activity, etc.

               (1) a violation of any

                  (a) **statute or ordinance?**

                  (b) or **any rule or regulation** adopted pursuant to any federal, state, or local statute or ordinance?

               (2) a violation of any **other** law rule or regulation (NB: definition of "law, rule, or regulation" is illustrative, not exhaustive, so other rules (e.g., perhaps a common law rule) may be "include[d]" as well)

            (i) Is the law, rule, or regulation

               (1) **applicable to the employer?**

               (2) Does it **pertain to the business?**

         (c) Was disclosure made to any **appropriate governmental agency?** (§ 1(1))

            (i) Is the party to whom disclosure was made **an agency of government?**

            (ii) Is it charged with the **enforcement of laws, rules, or regulations?**

            (iii) Do those laws, etc., **govern an activity, policy, or practice of an employer?**

      (ii) **threatened to disclose** same

   (b) because the employee has (§ 2(b))

      (i) **Objected to**

      (a) **any activity, policy, or practice of the employer**

      (b) which is in violation of a **law, rule, or regulation** (see above)

    (ii) Or **refused to participate** in same?

Step Five: The consequences of noncompliance.

- (§ 3) An employee who has been the object of a retaliatory personnel action in violation of this act may institute a civil action in a court of competent jurisdiction for any of the following forms of relief:

    (§ 3(a)) An injunction restraining continued violation of this act;

    (§ 3(b)) Reinstatement of the employee to the same position held before the retaliatory personnel action or to an equivalent position;

    (§ 3(c)) Reinstatement of full fringe benefits and seniority rights; **and**

    (§ 3(d)) Compensation for lost wages, benefits, and other remuneration

- NB: The "and" between § 3(c) and § 3(d) makes clear that the aggrieved employee is authorized to seek multiple forms of relief in a single civil action.

Step Six: What does it change?

- Under the common law employment-at-will rule, an employer could fire (and otherwise punish) an employee for any reason— good, bad, or indifferent

- This statute provides protection against discharge or other adverse action in retaliation for four kinds of "whistleblowing" by employees:

   ○ *Disclosing* unlawful employer conduct to an appropriate government agency (§ 2(a))

   ○ *Threatening to disclose* unlawful employer conduct to an appropriate government agency (§ 2(a))

   ○ *Objecting* to unlawful employer conduct (§ 2(b))

   ○ *Refusing to participate* in unlawful employer conduct (§ 2(b))

- Finally, note that in all four cases the employer conduct must actually be unlawful for the employee to receive protection. Absent judicial interpretation to the contrary, the statute does not protect employees who act on good-faith but incorrect assumptions that their employer is breaking the law.

PART II

Taking Issues Seriously

We turn now to the heart of *Getting to Maybe*. Most of the book is designed to be a relatively quick read. In contrast, this part dives deeply into our strategy for excelling on law school exams and will require your close attention for maximum results. Part II's focus is the so-called "issue spotter," the exam format you're likely to face most frequently in law school and that differs most strikingly from the kind of exams you have likely encountered before. So set aside time to work your way through it carefully, and don't try to cram it all in at the last minute.

And if it's already the "last minute," we recommend devoting your energies to your course materials—your outline, class notes, case briefs, and the like—and then spending an hour or two on the Appendix appearing at the end of the book, which contains a multitude of exam-taking tips and answers to questions frequently asked by beginning students.

Chapter Five

Issues as "Forks in the Road"

If you are even a few weeks into law school, you have no doubt encountered the word "issue" with great frequency, and you've probably figured out by now that it means different things in different contexts. When writing opinions, judges use the word as shorthand for "a question we must answer in order to decide this case." Attorneys drafting briefs, by contrast, often use the word as a tool of advocacy. To borrow from an old joke, when the law is against her, a lawyer will try to make an "issue" out of the facts; when the facts are against her, she'll attempt to make an "issue" out of the law. (What happens when the law *and* the facts are both against her? The punch line varies from "pound the table" to "attack your opponent" to the most recent version, "send out some edgy tweets.") And law students struggling with case briefs for their first-year courses can be forgiven for suspecting that "issue" is some sort of code word for the cheat sheet that allows their professors to divine the meaning of a particular case while students remain in the dark.

So it should come as no surprise to you that the word has yet another meaning when you are taking a law school examination. The typical exam question will tell a story that presents some sort of hypothetical dispute. The story may be as brief as a sentence or two, or it may go on for two to three pages. The question then calls on you to identify (or "spot") the issues that would have to be resolved if the dispute became a lawsuit.

Here's a little secret: In this context, "issue" means nothing more than "something the parties' lawyers are likely to fight about." We have found that it is helpful—and somewhat less bellicose—for beginning law students to think of these "fights" as "forks in the road" of a legal analysis. Indeed, we developed the "forks" terminology as a way of helping students see the different ways that law generates issues. Like a "fork" you encounter in a real road, an issue presents you with a choice between two (and sometimes more) paths leading in different directions. But unlike a fork in a real road or a Robert Frost poem, exam forks are more like the divide in the yellow brick road, where the Scarecrow tells Dorothy she can go "both ways." Not only do exam forks permit you to travel in different directions at the same time, but that is precisely what you *should* do, for the more paths your analysis explores, the better your answer will be.

A. The Anatomy of a Fork

Let's begin with a variation on the famous Brooklyn Bridge hypothetical, designed to teach generations of Contracts students the problem of the so-called "unilateral" contract. If you haven't encountered the term yet, contract law distinguishes between offers to make "bilateral" contracts, which invite acceptance via a *promise* (e.g., "I will sell you my old car if you promise to pay me $5,000 for it") and offers to make "unilateral" contracts, which can be accepted only by actual *performance* (e.g., "I'll pay you $100 if you clean your room in 15 minutes"). The "problem" in the latter case is that the acceptance isn't complete—and the parties have no contract—unless and until the offeree finishes the required performance, and thus a world of trouble arises if the offeror changes his mind and attempts to revoke the offer while the offeree is still in the middle of her performance. In the famous hypo, I offer to pay you $50 to walk across the Brooklyn Bridge, and I scream "I revoke" when you are halfway across. (In the classic variation—which may work better with law students who know nothing about either unilateral contracts or the Brooklyn Bridge—the offeror promises $50 if the offeree climbs to the top of a flagpole and revokes when the offeree is halfway up.)

So here is a sample exam question presenting a variation on this predicament:

> Paul Patron offers Arlene Artiste $10,000 to paint a portrait of
> the Patron family. Artiste explains that her other commit-
> ments make it impossible for her to promise a completed

work by a particular date, and Patron responds, "I don't *want* your commitment. I just want the portrait." After Artiste spends numerous hours doing preliminary sketches—but before she has put brush to canvas and begun the actual portrait—Patron advises her that he has changed his mind and is revoking the offer. What legal rights does Artiste have against Patron?

What "forks in the road" are presented by this hypothetical?

As you'll learn in Contracts—if you haven't taken the course already—the traditional common law rule permits the offeror in the unilateral contract setting to revoke at any time before the offeree completes performance. If that rule is applied to the facts presented here, then Patron is perfectly free to back out of the deal, and Artiste has no right to stop him. But you will also learn that under the "modern" rule designed for this predicament—reflected in § 45 of the Second Restatement of Contracts—a binding option contract is created once the offeree "begins the invited performance." And if *that* rule is applied, then Patron is prohibited from revoking as soon as Artiste starts the commissioned work.

In sum, then, there is a "fork in the road" with respect to the law to apply to the facts stated in the hypothetical. If you take the "road" of the traditional rule, your analysis will lead to the conclusion that Patron is free to revoke his offer at any time before Artiste actually finishes the painting. But if you take the "road" of the rule under § 45, your analysis will lead to the conclusion that Patron's offer is irrevocable as soon as Artiste begins her performance. To put the matter in more conventional terms, we would say that there is an "issue" raised by the question because there are two different legal rules that might apply to the facts presented, and each of those rules will lead to a different result. We call this a "rule vs. counter-rule" issue—but if that's too fancy, just think of it as a "fork in the law." We'll have lots more to say about issues of this sort in the next chapter.

But our map of the "forks in the road" in the Artiste/Patron example is not yet complete. To continue with our analysis, it is pretty clear where the "road" of the traditional rule will lead: Since Artiste has yet to complete the portrait, Patron is perfectly free to revoke his offer. But the "road" of Restatement § 45 leads to terrain that is more uncertain than our discussion has thus far acknowledged. True enough, under that provision Patron loses the right to revoke once Artiste "begins the invited performance." But is it clear on the facts presented that Artiste has met that requirement? On the one hand, Artiste might be said to have begun the performance when she did the preliminary sketchwork. To an artist, such sketches are as much a part of portraiture as the brushstrokes on the final canvas, and from that standpoint Artiste "began the invited performance" at the moment she started work on her first sketch. But on the other hand, Patron asked for a family portrait—not a series of sketches—in exchange for his promise of $10,000. Accordingly, you could argue that from *his* perspective "the invited performance" would be limited to the actual painting of the commissioned portrait, and that the preliminary sketches were "mere preparations" for that performance.

In sum, then, we have encountered a second "fork in the road" in the problem, and this one relates to the way we interpret the facts. If you take the "road" that interprets the performance sought from the standpoint of a portrait artist, your analysis may lead to the conclusion that the preliminary sketchwork was indeed the "beginning of performance," thus preventing Patron from revoking his offer. But if you take the "road" that interprets the performance from the perspective of Patron's focus on the end-product he sought to purchase, your analysis may lead to the conclusion that Artiste had not yet begun the invited performance and that Patron is accordingly free to revoke. To put the matter once again in more conventional terms, we would say that there is a second issue in this hypothetical—quite apart from the rule vs. counter-rule issue we discussed earlier—because there are at least two plausible ways to interpret the facts presented, and each of those interpretations may lead to a different outcome. Not surprisingly, we call this issue a "fork in the facts."

For the benefit of readers who are visual learners—and for others who still wonder why we insist on referring to issues as "forks"—below we've provided a diagram of the "fork in the law" and the "fork in the facts" in the Artiste/Patron problem. As you can see, the diagram is particularly helpful in clarifying the relationship *between* the forks, for it shows how the "fork in the facts" (beginning of performance vs. mere preparations) flows directly from the Restatement prong of the "fork in the law." We refer to such a fork-to-fork relationship as an "issue cascade," and in Chapter Ten we illustrate several different kinds of issue cascades with additional diagrams.

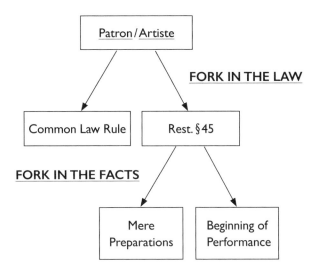

B. What Forks Can Do for You

We have good news and bad news—and then some more good news. The first bit of good news is that 99% of the issues you will encounter on law school exams will fall into one or the other of the two categories we've just identified: They will involve either a "fork in the law" or a "fork in the facts." (Indeed, as we will explain in a later chapter, a pretty fair number will involve both kinds of forks at the same time.) Thus, to coin a phrase, if you've seen two issues, you've pretty much seen 'em all.

But now for the bad news. This insight will get you absolutely nowhere on a law exam unless you already know precisely which forks in the law and precisely which forks in the facts to look for. Thus, you couldn't spot the "forks in the road" of the Artiste/Patron example unless you already knew (a) that the common law permitted the offeror in the unilateral contract setting to revoke at any time before the offeree completed performance; (b) that the Second Restatement, by contrast, protects the offeree once she begins performance; and (c) that, even under the Restatement approach, the protection the offeree enjoys during performance may not extend to activities that are "mere preparations." And you wouldn't have had a clue about (a), (b), or (c) unless you had taken—and studied pretty carefully during—a Contracts course. In sum, you can't even *begin* a search for "forks in the road" on a law exam until you've grasped the material taught in the course itself. If you were hoping for a shortcut—a way to avoid all the work it takes to engage that material seriously and make it your own—you'll have to pursue that quest elsewhere.

But now for a little more good news. Each of the two kinds of issues we've identified—forks in the law and forks in the facts—appears on law exams in recurring *patterns*. And learning to recognize those patterns can help you to (1) organize a course in preparation for an exam; (2) identify the issues that you encounter on the final; and (3) develop strategies for analyzing the issues you identify. We address each of these points at some length in Part III, but we devote the remaining chapters in this part to exploring the recurring patterns and helping you learn to recognize them on your own.

C. Taking Our Forks with a Grain of Salt

Before we turn to that task, however, we offer several important caveats about our "forks in the road" approach. First, we don't pretend for a moment that what we offer in this book is an exhaustive list of the issues that you will encounter on your law exams. Every area of law we've ever encountered has issues unique to it, and sophisticated lawyers who practice in even the most familiar areas—personal injury law, for example—come up with new ones all the time. What we've done here is to identify the issues you are most likely to encounter in the subjects most students study in law school. But for a life in the law, this is only a starting point.

Second, for exam-taking purposes, the most important issues of all are the ones that the professor stresses in your class. Most professors try to test what they teach, and so we cannot emphasize enough that the lessons you learn from this book—or for that matter from any commercial study guide—are no substitute for a mastery of the course material presented by your professor.

Third, resist the temptation—however understandable it may be—to treat the patterns of issues we identify as "answers" you can memorize and regurgitate on law exams. The point is not to memorize them; it is rather to learn how to *use* them in particular contexts. We'll have a lot more to say about this later, but for now just keep the following advice in mind: "*Utilize, don't memorize!*"

Finally, keep your eyes on the prize. The point is *not* the proper classification of the issues you encounter on your exams. In the end it really doesn't matter whether it's a "fork in the law" or a "fork in the facts." The "forks" terminology is just our way of encouraging students to focus on points of conflict, and we've been puzzled over the years when colleagues have playfully sent us problems in which it's hard to discern which type of fork is at play. So long as you are able to identify the points at which there are two plausible paths available leading to differing resolutions of a dispute, you are well on your way to success and don't need to figure out which type of fork you are facing. Indeed, though *Getting to Maybe* has been widely read, most professors won't recognize the "forks" terminology if they encounter it while grading an exam answer, so we wouldn't advise using it anyway, lest the professor wonder if you have gotten lost in Frost's yellow wood. We are confident that the "forks" approach is an extremely effective way to learn to recognize the patterns in which issues appear and thus to help you identify issues on your exams. And we are heartened by the countless students over the years who have told us that they find our approach helpful. But what matters most to us is that our readers learn to "spot" legal issues on their own, and the "right" way to do that is whatever way works best for them.

Chapter Six

Forks in the Law—Rule vs. Counter-Rule Issues

Although your professors aren't likely to label them as such, they've been teaching you about "forks in the law" since your first day of law school. Indeed, two kinds of "forks in the law" are so common in legal argument that you can expect to encounter them on virtually every law exam you ever take.

One kind of fork presents a choice between rule and counter-rule. This is neatly illustrated by our Artiste/Patron hypothetical, where the dispute in question would be resolved one way by the common law rule (which would permit Patron to revoke his offer at any time before Artiste actually completes the portrait) and another way by § 45 of the Second Restatement (which protects Artiste against revocation once she begins her performance).

A second kind of "fork in the law" presents a choice between competing interpretations of a single rule. For the classic illustration of this type of fork, consider once again the treatment of tricycles under a rule that prohibits "vehicles" in the park. There, the question might be resolved one way by an interpretation that focused on the language of the rule ("tricycles are 'vehicles' and therefore forbidden") and another way under an interpretation that focused on the rule's apparent purpose ("tricycles just don't pose the kinds of dangers in public parks that automobiles do").

This chapter zeroes in on issues that present the first kind of fork: We call them "rule vs. counter-rule" issues. We'll start by offering a "map" of the patterns in which issues of this sort appear, and then we'll explore some of the reasons that students don't recognize them as "issues" when they encounter them on an exam.

A. Patterns to Watch For

For many lawyers, the dream client would be the one who walks into your office and presents you with a problem that can be resolved in her favor simply by citing a legal rule. "The court must rule for my client," you imagine yourself solemnly declaring, "because Rule X says so"—after which you close the case file and collect your fee on the way out the courthouse door for a golf date.

If you've been in law school even long enough to have unwrapped your casebooks, chances are you've already figured out that things don't work that way very often. One reason for this—and a reason that often comes as a surprise to students who find the prospect of learning just *one* rule for every situation challenging enough—is that all too often the lawyer for the other side can respond to the rule you cite with a different rule, and under that rule her client rather than yours will prevail.

It's bad enough that your dreams of an easy win are shattered; what's far worse, at least from the perspective of most law students, is that this means that there are twice as many rules to learn! Yet the bad news comes with a silver lining, for the way most law professors test this multiplicity of rules is pretty straightforward: They will give you a hypothetical that would be resolved in one way by Rule X and in another way by Rule Y, and chances are that the difference between the rule and the counter-rule will have been analyzed in some depth in the course of class discussion. As it turns out, such rule vs. counter-rule issues appear in patterns, and an understanding of those patterns can help you recognize them when you encounter them on your exams.

1. Traditional rule vs. modern rule

In most of your law school courses, a major theme will be that law changes over time. As a result, you'll find yourself studying topic after topic in which you'll learn first about the "traditional" rule and then about the "modern" rule governing this or that particular problem. An excellent illustration is our Artiste/Patron hypothetical, where the traditional rule (a product of the common law) would permit Patron to revoke his offer at any time before Artiste completes the portrait, and the modern rule (established by the Second Restatement) would prohibit revocation once Artiste begins the requested work.

Additional examples of such traditional vs. modern rule relationships abound. Consider the following hypothetical, which raises a rule vs. counter-rule issue familiar to Torts students everywhere:

> The moment the light changes, Penny Pedestrian steps into the crosswalk without looking both ways and with the music in her headphones at full blast. Meanwhile, Danny Driver hears the ping of an incoming text and picks up his cell to read it just as he enters the intersection from behind Pedestrian and turns directly into the latter's path, striking her and causing serious bodily injury. What rights does Pedestrian have against Driver?

Do you see the issue? Everything turns on whether we apply the doctrine of contributory negligence (the traditional rule) or the doctrine of comparative negligence (the modern rule).

Thus, Driver's conduct (looking at his cellphone as he is driving) is clearly negligent, but Pedestrian's failure to look both ways before stepping into the intersection—together with her failure to turn down the volume so she can hear approaching traffic—is surely negligence on her part as well. Under the doctrine of contributory negligence, Pedestrian's own lack of due care is a complete bar to her cause of action against Driver. By contrast, under the doctrine of comparative negligence, Pedestrian would be permitted to recover that portion of her damages attributable to Driver's negligence rather than her own. Thus, if on these facts we consider Driver (say) 70% at fault and Pedestrian 30% at fault, Pedestrian can recover 70% of the damages from injuries resulting from the accident. Thus, once again we encounter an issue that arises because rule and counter-rule lead to contrasting results.

2. Different strokes for different folks

A second pattern to watch for occurs when different jurisdictions adopt different rules because of political, cultural, or regional differences among the jurisdictions in question. If enough states have adopted a particular approach, your casebook and/or your professor is likely to describe it as the "majority rule" and to refer to the less popular approach as either the "minority rule" or even the "X rule," where X = the name of a state that takes the nonconforming approach. (When we were in law school, for example, there seemed to be a special "Massachusetts rule" for just about every topic, which made us wonder whether *every* state thought its own rules were "special" or whether there was just something weird about Massachusetts.) In other contexts, however, you will learn that no rule has commanded a "majority." But regardless of the particulars, the point is that when the law on a topic is split in this way, you should watch out for a rule vs. counter-rule issue on your exam.

Consider the following problem, which is drawn from the riparian rights section of the typical Property course:

> For over a decade, Yamila has diverted water from the stream running through her land to run a generator providing electricity for her family farm. Beau purchases the land just upstream of Yamila and diverts a small portion of the stream to water his flock of sheep. Because of the diminution in flow, the stream no longer has the force to power Yamila's generator. What rights does Yamila have against Beau?

As in the other cases we've looked at so far, the issue presented here again involves rule and counter-rule. But this time, the conflict is not between traditional and modern rules, but rather between contemporary rules embraced by different jurisdictions.

Thus, under the riparian rights doctrine favored by many Western states—the rule of prior appropriation—Yamila may well have a claim against Beau for the diminution in flow, since Yamila's rights to her usage of the stream predated Beau's by many years. But under the rule of reasonable use, which is applied in many Eastern jurisdictions, Beau is entitled to his fair share of the stream no matter how much longer Yamila has owned the adjacent lot. As long as Beau's use is a reasonable one—as watering sheep from a stream running through farm country would seem to be—the fact that it deprives Yamila of the flow to which she'd grown accustomed won't get her very far if she brings a lawsuit against him.

Want to see another illustration of a "different strokes" issue? Consider a variation on the Driver/Pedestrian hypothetical we examined above. Assume that Pedestrian's husband Harry looked on helplessly and in utter horror as Pedestrian was struck by Driver's car, but that Harry managed to avoid contact with the errant vehicle himself. Driver's conduct no doubt caused Harry to experience severe "emotional distress." Yet Harry's rights against Driver may turn on another "different strokes" issue: A handful of states—we think of them as the "tough love" jurisdictions—require a direct physical impact upon the would-be plaintiff to establish a claim for emotional distress (in which case Harry would lose for want of such impact). But a large majority—the "permissive parents," of course—allow plaintiffs to pursue a claim without such impact (in which case Harry may be able to succeed in his claim).

3. Common law vs. statute

Let's end this section with one more variation on rule vs. counter-rule issues. In each of the hypotheticals discussed thus far, the issue arises in the context of a conflict between two rules, each of which has its basis in the common law. But—in your coursework as well as on your exams—you will also encounter issues that arise because of a difference between a common law rule and a statutory rule. Indeed, as state legislatures enact more and more statutes regulating matters historically governed by the common law, you are likely to confront this kind of issue on your exams with increasing frequency. Consider, then, the following illustration:

> Billy Buyer mails Sally Seller a purchase order for 1,000 of Seller's widgets, offering to pay her advertised price of $2 per widget on delivery and requesting immediate shipment. Seller replies by sending Buyer an acknowledgment of order, promising to ship 1,000 widgets immediately and agreeing to the price and payment terms. Seller's acknowledgment also states, "Seller expressly disclaims any warranties with respect to any items shipped pursuant to this acknowledgment." After Buyer receives Seller's acknowledgment—but before Seller ships the goods—Buyer telephones Seller and states that he is backing out of the deal. What rights, if any, does Seller have against Buyer?

If you've had Contracts, chances are you spotted the issue presented here straight away. Thus, under the common law "mirror-image rule," the terms of a would-be acceptance must mirror the terms of the offer in every respect. Although Seller's acknowledgment accurately recapitulates the description of goods, quantity, price, delivery, and payment terms stated in Buyer's purchase order, it "breaks the mirror" by adding a term—i.e., the disclaimer of warranties. As a result, the acknowledgment is not an acceptance of the offer, and thus there is no contract that would preclude Buyer from backing out. But under the pertinent statutory provision governing most contemporary sales of goods—U.C.C. § 2-207—an otherwise valid acceptance forms a binding contract in spite of the fact that it purports to add terms not found in the offer. And if the statutory rule were applied in this case, the Seller's acknowledgment would operate as an acceptance of Buyer's offer, thus binding Buyer to the contract and preventing him from backing out.

B. How Professors Test Rule vs. Counter-Rule Issues (and Why Students Frequently Miss Them)

As the foregoing examples suggest, rule vs. counter-rule issues are pretty straightforward: As long as you're familiar with the particular rule vs. counter-rule relationship in question, you are ready to spot it with ease when it appears on an exam. Yet law professors find that students— even students who have studied hard and prepared well—miss these issues with surprising frequency. Our view is that the principal reason for student error is not that students fail to see the rule vs. counter-rule situation, but that they don't understand that what they've seen is an "issue." Indeed, because expectations from earlier educational settings put significant psychological pressure on students to "know" the applicable rule, the idea that two different rules might apply seems inconsistent with the testing of "knowledge" they've come to expect on an exam.

Accordingly, many students ignore the rule vs. counter-rule alternatives that come to mind as they survey the exam because they figure that, at the end of the day, only one rule will govern the case at hand and their job is (a) to figure out which rule it is and (b) to apply that rule to the facts presented. Their thinking goes something like this: "Hey, I know this one: There's some old rule that lets the offeror revoke even if you're halfway up the flagpole, and there's a Restatement section that fixes all that. So who cares about the old way? The professor asked us to discuss the rights of the parties, and that must mean under the law that would apply today. Now, where's my copy of the Restatement?"

Truth be told, these students may be on the right track. Sometimes the professor has in fact constructed the question in such a way that the student will be "right" if he applies (say) the Restatement and "wrong" if he applies the common law rule. But here's an important test-taking tip: If the professor went to the trouble of teaching you about the difference between the Restatement and common law rules governing the revocation of offers—and if she also went to the trouble of designing a problem that would come out one way under one rule and another way under the other—chances are pretty good that she expects you to recognize this difference and is ready to award issue-spotting points to the students who do. And while it's true that no self-respecting lawyer would pay much attention to the "old" rule in a setting in which the Restatement alternative obviously governed, it's equally true that no self-respecting law student should pass up the chance to earn additional exam points so easily by explaining both rules!

Indeed, if you begin to tackle a question in which the choice between rule and counter-rule seems entirely straightforward, you have reason to suspect that you may be missing something in your analysis of the problem. Since only lawyer fantasies contain dream clients whose cases can be resolved by the straightforward application of a single legal rule, law professors rarely give exam questions that are this simple either. Indeed, at least nine times out of ten, the professor will aim for hypotheticals in which the choice between rule and counter-rule is not nearly so clear-cut. Fortunately, such hypotheticals tend to appear in patterns too, and we're going to help you learn to spot them.

Watch for the unidentified or imaginary jurisdiction. One common way that professors test rule vs. counter-rule issues is to set the facts of an exam question in an unidentified or even imaginary jurisdiction (e.g., "Wakanda" or "Remulak" or "the State of Oz"). When you encounter a rule vs. counter-rule issue in this setting, you can be sure that the professor is expecting you to analyze the facts at hand under both the rule and the counter-rule, since the choice between the competing rules is obviously up for grabs.

Watch for the jurisdiction whose law wasn't explored in the course. Sometimes you'll encounter an exam question set in a jurisdiction whose law you *do* know; when that happens, your job is to apply that law and then move on to other issues. If, for example, your Torts course examined Florida's approach to comparative negligence in painstaking detail, and on the final you encounter a question involving an accident that (a) occurred in Florida between Florida residents and (b) is the result of plaintiff's negligence as well as defendant's, you'd be making a serious mistake if you saw this question as an opportunity to provide a lengthy rule vs. counter-rule analysis of the difference between comparative and contributory negligence. The professor has explained Florida's embrace of comparative negligence and has designed a question specifically asking you to apply that law. It is therefore virtually certain that she wants you to focus your attention on that task. And while you might earn some issue-spotting points for offering a sentence or two contrasting the Florida law analysis with the analysis under competing approaches the professor has introduced (e.g., contributory negligence), an extended discussion of an approach that obviously doesn't apply to the facts at hand will almost surely be penalized; indeed, if your discussion suggests that you are hedging your bets because you don't know which rule applies in Florida, your answer may be in more trouble still.

But many law school courses—and especially the classic common law courses such as Contracts, Torts, and Property—examine "majority" vs. "minority" approaches and "traditional" vs. "modern" rules and rarely focus on the current law of a particular jurisdiction. If you encounter a rule vs. counter-rule issue on an exam in a course taught like this, it's a safe bet that the professor isn't testing to see whether you can guess which rule will apply, even if she has set the facts of the problem in some specifically identified jurisdiction (e.g., Idaho). She is far more likely to be testing you on what she taught you and trying to see whether you recognize that more than one rule might apply to the facts at hand.

Watch for traditional vs. modern rule issues where the modern rule has not been judicially adopted. When students learn about traditional rules and modern common law rules in a particular area of the law, many conclude that they need to know the modern rule and that the rest is "history." ("I didn't come to law school to learn how to practice in nineteenth-century England," cracked one of our students in this connection.) But this attitude can lead to serious mistakes, for the so-called "modern" rule is frequently only a trend that many jurisdictions have not yet adopted and, for all we know, might never embrace. Indeed, sometimes the modern rule isn't even a bona fide trend but is merely the approach taken by a handful of cases that have captured the fancy of the members of the American Law Institute and inspired a black-letter formulation in the latest Restatement of Law. And as we frequently remind our students, the Restatement is a beautiful thing, but (a) it isn't a statute and (b) it isn't "law" unless and until a court (or some other authoritative body) says it is.

In the end, then, our advice here is the same as in the previous point: If an exam question places you in Jurisdiction X and your professor has stressed that Jurisdiction X has adopted the modern rule on the relevant topic, then that's clearly the rule you should emphasize in your answer. But if you encounter a traditional vs. modern rule issue in virtually any other setting, you would be unwise to ignore the traditional rule and simply assume that the modern rule has been adopted.

Chapter Seven

Forks in the Law—Competing Interpretations of Statutes

The previous chapter explains how a professor may test a rule vs. counter-rule issue on a law exam by inventing a factual scenario in which the choice between two competing rules represents a "fork in the law." Each rule takes your analysis of the problem down a different path. Law professors examine a second kind of "fork in the law"—we call them "competing interpretations" issues—in much the same manner. Once again, professors design hypotheticals that can be analyzed in more than one way, but here the choice confronting the student will involve different readings of the *same* rule. The rule in question may come from any one of a number of sources, but we're going to focus here on the two you are most likely to encounter on your law exams: statutes and cases. We'll cover statutes and briefly touch on the related challenge of interpreting constitutions in this chapter. Case law comes in Chapter Eight.

We've already described the classic example of a competing interpretations issue: Does a rule that reads "No vehicles permitted in the park" apply to tricycles? The answer to that question depends on the meaning of the rule, and the meaning of the rule is not nearly so clear as it might seem to someone who's never been a target of the Socratic method. One way to read the rule is to give the word "vehicle" its common or "dictionary" definition. If we do that, the only question is whether tricycles fall within that definition and, since they probably do, we are ready to conclude that they are barred from the park. But another way to read the rule is to focus on the reasons for the prohibition. And if we read the rule that way—and conclude that the point of the rule is to reduce pollution, noise, and the risks of serious injury to pedestrians in the park—we may well decide that it wasn't designed for and therefore does not apply to tricycles.

The first time you encounter a problem like this in law school, it is tempting to conclude that the problem is just sloppy drafting. "What's the big deal?" someone might pipe up in class. "Why didn't the drafters just say '*motorized* vehicles,' since that is obviously what they meant? Wouldn't that fix the problem and spare the rest of us all this tedious discussion?" "Fair enough," responds the professor. And then she poses a question that creates a ripple of nervous laughter through the classroom: "But would your rule apply to motorized *wheelchairs*?"

As the first month or two of law school is bound to convince you, the problem of statutory ambiguity seems to lie right there in the words; and adding more words, or different words, won't make it go away. This is more than a little scary. After all, it's hard to imagine a rule that's shorter and simpler than "No vehicles allowed in the park." When we turn to the far more complex provisions of the U.C.C., the Model Penal Code, and other statutes you study in law school, the possibilities boggle the mind!

Indeed, many law schools dedicate entire courses to the problem of interpreting statutory materials, and many fine books and articles have been written on the subject. So we can't reduce the subject to five or even 50 easy lessons. But what we *can* do is help you learn to recognize a statutory ambiguity—what we call a competing interpretations issue—when you encounter it on a law exam. As in the previous section, we'll do that by describing the most common patterns of ambiguity and illustrating the kinds of problems law professors design to test them.

A. Patterns of Ambiguity

1. Plain meaning vs. purposes issues

By far the most common pattern of competing interpretations is illustrated by our "No vehicles permitted in the park" hypothetical. One way of reading that rule is to focus on the *language* (tricycle = a "vehicle"); another way is to focus on the rule's *purposes* (tricycles just don't pose the same threats as cars do). Disputes that turn on this conflict—an interpretation of a rule that is based on the so-called "plain meaning" of the words used vs. an interpretation based on the "purposes" that the rule was designed to accomplish—arise endlessly in legal practice. It should therefore come as no surprise that professors test them with great frequency on law exams.

Consider a second example:

> Horace Wholesaler receives an order from Reba Retailer for 50 high-end audio components at a total price of $20,000. Wholesaler sends Retailer an acknowledgment of order by text message, promising immediate shipment of the ordered goods. Prior to shipment, Wholesaler reneges on the deal. Retailer sues, but Wholesaler asserts that the U.C.C.'s Statute of Frauds bars the claim. What result?

Do you see the plain meaning vs. purposes issue? On the one hand, a text message that appears only as an electronically generated image on a smartphone screen may not constitute a "writing"—let alone a "signed" writing—under the plain meaning of the terms of the U.C.C. Statute of Frauds, which requires "a writing signed by the party against whom enforcement [of a contract] is sought" and defines "writing" as "printing, typewriting, or any other intentional reduction to tangible form." On the other hand, if the Statute of Frauds was enacted to minimize "he said/she said" testimonial disputes by requiring a verifiable record of certain kinds of transactions, that purpose would seem to be equally well served by a screen shot of the text readily retrievable from a smartphone's photos feature as it is by hard copy gathering dust in a file drawer.

2. Where do purposes come from?

For most students, it's easy to form at least a strong first impression of a rule's plain meaning: You know what words like "vehicle" and "writing" mean and, when you hit a rough one, you can always look it up. But purposes are a different matter, and unfortunately you won't find *those* defined in any dictionary or encyclopedia. So where do purposes come from? The two most common sources in the law-exam setting are legislative intent and policy analysis.

a. Legislative intent

The most obvious place to start in a search for a statute's purpose is the horse's mouth: What clues do we have about what the "authors" of a particular rule—Congress, the state legislature, the city council—were attempting to accomplish? We can find those clues in a number of places:

- *Legislative history.* The mass of material that lawyers refer to as "legislative history"—official reports of legislative drafting committees, statements made by legislators during floor debates, and even testimony given to the legislative body by outsiders—may shed light on what it was the drafters were attempting to achieve by enacting the statute in question. For example, recall once again our "No vehicles permitted in park" hypothetical. If the discussion in the various committee reports focused exclusively on automobile and truck traffic—citing studies of pollution and noise levels, accident statistics, damage due to weight loads, and the like—you'd have a sound basis for arguing that the purpose of the rule had nothing to do with tricycles. (A special note about legislative history: During most of the twentieth century, lawyers and judges routinely relied on legislative history to fashion arguments about how to read statutory material. But in recent years, that practice has come under sustained challenge by legal thinkers who insist that judges and lawyers should focus on the end product of the legislative process and ignore the content of the process itself. If your professor stresses this point of view—whether skeptically, enthusiastically, or simply as an important recent trend—you should obviously couple any legislative history arguments you offer in class or on your exams with an acknowledgment of the critique.)
- *Other provisions of the statute.* Another place to look for purposes is other provisions of the statute in question. To continue our "vehicle" hypo, the presence of a provision that makes revocation of the operator's license the key sanction for violations of the rule would suggest that the drafters were worried about adults in cars, trucks, and motorcycles—not children on tricycles—when they enacted the rule.
- *Official comments.* Uniform statutes such as the U.C.C. are frequently accompanied by an "official comment" specifically designed to explain the purpose of the various provisions. (Although the Restatement is not a statute, the "reporter's note" serves a similar purpose in interpreting its provisions.) To recall

once again our text message under the Statute of Frauds hypo, the official comment to the provision in question reveals that the purpose of the "signed writing" requirement is "to afford a basis for believing that the offered oral evidence rests on a real transaction"—a purpose that may be satisfied as well by a saved text message as a hardcopy document.

- *Real-world catalysts.* What was the legislature reacting to when it enacted the statute in question? Frequently there is a dramatic event that prompted the legislature to act, and this too may shed light on the purpose of a statute. If, for example, the "No vehicles permitted in the park" rule had been enacted in the wake of a tragic accident in which a sport utility vehicle had struck and fatally injured a group of joggers running together in the park, this would offer further evidence that the risks the rule was designed to eliminate were of the sort associated with automotive—rather than tricycle—traffic.

————————

We can easily imagine your reaction to all of this: "Are you guys *sure* there isn't just some dictionary I can use to find a statute's purpose? Am I really supposed to know the details of the legislative history and all that other stuff for every statute and every provision we read in class?"

As usual, we've got good news and bad news. The good news is that 99% of the time, if a law professor is going to test you on the purpose of a statute, then she will teach you about it—and do so quite explicitly—during the course. The bad news is that unless you know what to expect on exams, it will be tempting to dismiss the discussion of such material as "beside the point," since, after all, aren't you in law school to "learn the rules?" Thus, when class discussion turns to a close reading of a Senate report—or a careful analysis of the umpteenth official comment—you may see a signal to put your pen or pencil down and wait for what appears to be the only thing that matters: "So . . . what's the rule?"

This is a terrible strategy for preparing for law practice and an even worse one for exam preparation. In practice, recognizing the difference between the purpose of a rule and its plain meaning is something you'll need to do all the time, but you won't do it very well if you don't learn to pay close attention to the ways that lawyers decode statutory purpose. You'll be even worse off on an exam, for you're likely to miss altogether the issue the professor is trying to test: If you don't know the purpose of the rule, how will you be able to tell when that purpose differs from the rule's plain meaning?

b. Policy analysis

Lawyers can't always count on having direct evidence of legislative intent; for many statutes, the legislative history will be too sketchy to be useful, and the other sources we've suggested may be unavailable or inconclusive. So what do we do then?

The short answer is that we engage in "policy analysis," and perhaps the best way to do that is to imagine that you are a legislator who is trying to decide whether to support or oppose a bill containing the rule in question. What policy or policies is the rule designed to further? Why do you suppose your colleagues want to see it enacted into law? What problem or problems (social, commercial, legal, etc.) are they worried about and why do they think this rule will provide a remedy? Whether you decide to support it or not, what is it that the rule is supposed to accomplish?

Your professors have pressed you to engage in this kind of thinking from the first day of law school, and while it is befuddling at first ("How would *I* know what the rule was designed to accomplish?" more than one student has no doubt silently mused. "*I* didn't write it!"), it is a skill that gets easier with practice. Indeed, by the end of the first semester, most students have begun to ask policy questions on their own.

Of course, if you attend class regularly and take good notes, you won't have to make guesses about the policies behind the rules you encounter on an exam. As we said in connection with our discussion of legislative intent, chances are that the professor will have thoroughly explored the policies behind any statute she thinks worthy of testing on the final. At the same time, most professors would be delighted to encounter a policy analysis that goes beyond a mere parroting of points made in class. And from time to time, most of us also test you on rules and statutes you've never seen before. So developing a facility with policy analysis—in addition to good note-taking—is an important test-taking skill. A major theme of this book is that issues and arguments appear in patterns in the law—and that studying those patterns is the best way to learn to deal with those issues and arguments—so it shouldn't surprise you that there are patterns to what we're calling policy analysis as well. Indeed, we've devoted an entire chapter to this topic—Chapter Fourteen ("Policy

Czars")—and we encourage you to work your way through that material very carefully as you try to develop this skill. But we bet you're already better at policy analysis than you think you are; read on, and see if you don't agree.

3. Purposes as a source of statutory ambiguity

a. Competing purposes

Imagine a statute that protects whistleblowers—employees who "disclose to law enforcement personnel any violation of the law by the employer"—against discharge or other discipline in retaliation for their whistleblowing. Imagine further that our whistleblower statute also states a prerequisite for such protection: The employee is required to "notify the employer before disclosing the violation to law enforcement personnel." Now let's try your hand at policy analysis. Which of the following policies is the pre-disclosure notification requirement designed to further?

(a) To ensure that employees fulfill their obligation of loyalty to the employer before taking matters "outside the family";

(b) To ensure that an employer is aware of a violation of the law and has an opportunity to correct it before facing an investigation by law enforcement personnel;

(c) To encourage and facilitate voluntary employer compliance with the law in order to avoid the costs—to the taxpayers as well as to the employer—associated with government agency enforcement proceedings;

(d) All of the above.

If you picked (a), (b), or (c), congratulations! All three are policies that might indeed be furthered by the requirement of pre-disclosure notification, so you can relax a little bit about your ability to do policy analysis. (We told you that you were up to it!)

If you picked (d), you have also figured out the next point we want to make: Most rules have more than one purpose. What this means is that there is yet another source of ambiguity in statutory interpretation. In addition to the plain meaning vs. purposes issues, there are also issues that pit one statutory purpose against another. Consider, for example, how our whistleblower statute would apply to the following situation:

Emma Employee is killed in an on-the-job accident at Silver
Spoon Pharmaceuticals, Inc., and the state occupational safety
and health agency has begun an investigation of the incident.
Without a word to her employer, Wanda Whistleblower contacts agency officials and volunteers information about a safety violation—subsequently remedied by the employer—that
directly contributed to Employee's death. Silver Spoon retali-
ates by discharging Whistleblower, who sues for relief under
the statute. What result?

The analysis under a plain-meaning interpretation of the statute is
pretty clear: Whistleblower didn't "notify the employer before disclosing
the wrongdoing to law enforcement personnel." So she's out of luck.

But what about an interpretation that focuses instead on the statute's
purposes? The short answer is that it depends on *which* purposes we're
talking about. If we start with (a)—requiring employees to fulfill a duty
of loyalty by notifying the employer before "taking it outside the
family"—the result may well be the same as it would be under a plain-
meaning interpretation of the rule: Whistleblower loses because she
didn't notify the employer first.

But if we focus instead on (b), we might conclude that pre-disclosure
notification was not necessary in this case. After all, the employer was
already aware of the violation and has already corrected it, so those reasons for pre-disclosure notification are moot. Similarly, at the time of the
disclosure, the employer was already facing an investigation by law enforcement personnel, so policy (c)—avoiding unnecessary government
proceedings—is beside the point as well.

Note, by the way, that we've identified two "forks in the road" in this
problem. We started with a plain meaning vs. purposes fork, but our
analysis of purposes led us to a second fork, when we discovered there
were competing purposes. We call this a "cascading fork," and we'll have
more to say about cascading forks in Chapter Ten.

―――――――――

Policy analysis is not your only window into competing purposes. An
examination of legislative intent—through legislative history and the
like—will also frequently reveal competing purposes. One obvious reason for this is that there may be as many different purposes as there are

legislators; another is that any given legislator may be moved by multiple purposes. These differing and multiple purposes will frequently surface during the course of legislative deliberations.

Consider once again the problem of applying our "No vehicles permitted in the park" rule to tricycles. It may be clear from the committee reports and the floor debates that the legislators were concerned about many things, and most of them—pollution, noise levels, wear and tear on the park roads—may have nothing to do with tricycle traffic. That part of the record suggests that permitting tricycles in the park is perfectly consistent with the statute's purposes.

But assume that the legislative history is also rife with concerns about the park's role in enhancing the quality of life for elderly people who live in the surrounding apartments. Perhaps a representative of an advocacy group promoting the interests of the elderly was a key witness before the committee that drafted the bill; perhaps one of the catalysts for the statute's enactment was an incident in which a teenager on a bicycle struck an elderly couple. You get the picture. To the extent that "protecting the elderly users of the park" is viewed as one of the statutory purposes, the case for applying the prohibition to tricycles will be much stronger.

In the end, our point is that you should avoid the trap that befalls many law students. Having discovered that the purpose of a rule may provide a way of interpreting it that differs from a mere application of plain meaning—and having decided that this is a pretty neat trick—they stop thinking and rely on the first purpose they find in the legislative history or discern through policy analysis. Our advice: Never take any one purpose for granted, for there is frequently more than one!

b. The pattern of conflict: Broad vs. narrow purposes

Once you begin hunting for disputes that hinge on which of two or more purposes attributable to a statute is controlling, you will begin to discover familiar patterns in the way such competing purposes are pitted against one another. Perhaps the most common such pattern arises when the lawyer on one side trumpets the "broad" purposes behind the statute while the opposing attorney describes the statute's purposes as relatively "narrow." Indeed, even when those terms are not explicitly invoked, you'll often find that the conflict between broad and narrow purposes is what the lawyers on opposite sides of a case—or judges in the majority and those in dissent—are really arguing about. Broad vs. narrow purposes issues come in at least two versions.

Spin vs. counter-spin. One way to think about broad vs. narrow purposes is to put yourself in the position of the most enthusiastic supporters of a statute (on the one hand) and then of its most outspoken critics (on the other). Imagine the "spin control" that each group might attempt at a press conference on the day the statute is enacted. Typically, the supporters will declare victory in the most sweeping terms, whereas the critics will put the best possible face on defeat by acknowledging only a minor setback.

If, for example, the statute in question is a federal environmental protection act, the supporters might portray its enactment as a great victory that "marks a dramatic shift in our nation's environmental priorities" that will "forever change the way America does business." By contrast, opponents may begrudgingly acknowledge defeat by countering that the statute is "obviously not intended to affect the sound practices of the vast majority of American businesses" and insisting that "it is aimed only at the excesses of a small number of recalcitrant polluters."

When a case comes along challenging the EPA's reliance upon the statute as a basis for imposing strict emissions standards for industry, the lawyers on each side are likely to cast the broad vs. narrow purposes of the statute in similar spin vs. counter-spin terms. One strategy for the lawyers defending the strict standards will be to describe the statute's purpose as "marking a dramatic shift" in environmental policy that was obviously intended to force many firms to "change the way they do business." But lawyers challenging the standards will find them to have "gone beyond the salutary goal of targeting recalcitrant polluters" and to have intruded on the "sound environmental practices of countless law-abiding firms whom Congress never intended to reach."

Floodlight vs. laser beam. In a second version of the broad vs. narrow purposes debate, a broad purpose is invoked to defuse or weaken the effect of a statute, whereas a narrow purpose is invoked to sharpen its focus and effect. To return again to "No vehicles permitted in the park," if the purpose of the prohibition is stated in the most broad and general terms—"to protect the park and the public"—the threat posed by tricycles may seem *de minimis* when compared with the pollution, noise, and physical dangers associated with other kinds of traffic. But if the purpose is stated narrowly—"to protect the elderly, the infirm, infants and their stroller-pushing nannies, and other frequent users of the park"—the threat from tots-on-trikes may well loom larger.

———————

Competing purposes issues frequently fall into this pattern, with one side offering a broad and the other a narrow account of the purposes of the statute in question. Learn to recognize the pattern, and you'll "know it when you see it" on an exam.

4. Language as a source of statutory ambiguity: Competing meanings

A moment ago, we urged you not to stop your search for issues with the first purpose or policy that comes to mind. The same advice applies when you are focusing on the plain meaning of a rule, for—quite apart from the rule's purposes—the "meaning" of the language used frequently isn't very "plain" at all. This is a particularly important lesson to keep in mind, because "plain meaning" arguments—which were taken with a grain of salt by lawyers and judges throughout much of the twentieth century—have for a variety of reasons enjoyed a recent renaissance and are frequently deployed with a muscular confidence that can intimidate the opposition. "Just what part of 'vehicle,'" presses the plain-meaning proponent in a patronizing tone as he pointedly demonstrates the mobility of a tricycle by taking it for a test drive, "don't you understand?"

Don't be cowed. To be sure, we've assumed all along that a tricycle fits the dictionary definition of "vehicle." As it happens, however, the *Oxford English Dictionary* offers *six* definitions of the term, and only one of them could plausibly be read to cover tricycles.* Indeed, lawyers arguing about the meaning of terms used in a statute are frequently working not only with multiple definitions but also with multiple "dictionaries," looking to such sources as history and commercial context as well as to common

———————

* "A means of conveyance, usu. with wheels, for transporting people, goods, etc.; a car, cart, truck, carriage, sledge etc.…; [a]ny means of carriage or transport…." The other definitions refer to things that may end up in the park from time to time—e.g., "[a] song, play, film, etc. that is intended or serves to display the leading actor or performer to the best advantage"—but were almost surely not what our imaginary city council had in mind when it adopted the rule.

usage to determine the legal meaning of even the most seemingly self-explanatory statutory terms. To train you for this kind of work, law professors frequently draft exam questions that involve competing interpretations of the words used in rules and statutes. What follows are some of the "dictionaries"—besides Black's and the old-fashioned one—that you'll need to learn to consult.

The dictionary of statutory context. We frequently can look elsewhere in the statute to shed light on the meaning of disputed terms. In the easiest case, the legislature has provided its *own* dictionary and included a section in which various terms used in the statute are defined, a point we covered at length back in Chapter Four's discussion of how to "outline" a statute. (Indeed, recall that one of the statutes we outlined included a definition of "vehicle" that would have provided an easy-peasy resolution to the tricycle case!) In other cases, a bit of detective work may be necessary. Consider once again our vehicle hypothetical. Perhaps there is a section of the statute that prescribes different penalties for different vehicles violating the rule, and perhaps the specific vehicles listed are "motorcycles," "cars," "light trucks and vans," and then larger "trucks" with increasing numbers of wheels. This list provides evidence that when the word "vehicle" is used elsewhere in the statute, the broad plain meaning of the term should be discarded in favor of a narrower meaning limited to vehicles on the list or those closely resembling them.

The dictionary of history. It's 2035 and "hard copy" has been completely eliminated from most forms of human communication—partly because of the proliferation of electronic communications media and partly because we can't spare the trees. Four decades of efforts to amend the U.C.C. to adjust to commerce in a digital age have failed, and, as a consequence, the U.C.C.'s Statute of Frauds reads exactly as it did in 1975, quaintly requiring "a writing signed by the party against whom enforcement is sought."

In that setting, the meaning of "writing" that seems "plain" may well have changed with the social and business practices to which it once referred—and as you've no doubt already figured out, those developments will alter our analysis of the text message hypothetical. Thus, a lawyer arguing that a text message is a "writing" may well simply be stating what seems obvious, and the party responding that the Statute of Frauds is not satisfied by a text will have to cite "the dictionary of history": At the time of its enactment, "writing" meant "printing, type-writing, or any other intentional reduction to tangible form." Indeed, that's how the Code defined the term at the time, and the prospect of paperless communication could scarcely have been contemplated by most folks.

Precisely because today's "plain" meaning frequently becomes tomorrow's "historical" meaning, issues pitting historical meanings against other interpretations—based on current meanings or on statutory purpose—are extremely common in law practice and on law exams.

The dictionary of commercial context. Imagine a municipal ordinance requiring restaurants to install and maintain two flush toilets "for every 40 seats." Does that rule apply to sofas and chairs in a restaurant's lobby or waiting area? Stools at the bar? A bench at the takeout counter? Rocking chairs out front?

These are all "seats" under a plain-meaning interpretation of the rule, but to someone doing business in the restaurant industry, "40 seats" (as in a "40-seat facility") may have a more specialized meaning and refer to "seats available for meal service." For a large restaurant, the difference between the two interpretations could be worth thousands of dollars in plumbing. (The difference could also be worth a lot to a patron whose child has waited until the last moment to announce the need for a bathroom!)

Disputes that raise this issue—i.e., a conflict between a plain-meaning interpretation and an interpretation that draws meaning from the "commercial context"—arise with great frequency in the context of statutes designed to regulate a particular trade, industry, or profession. When dealing with such a statute on a law exam, then, watch for terms that may have a specialized meaning in the commercial context in question.

The dictionary of the common law. We've saved the hardest for last, so fasten your seat belts. Statutes frequently use terms (like "tenant" or "independent contractor") that had a well-developed meaning at common law. With equal frequency, statutes are enacted for the purpose of *changing* the common law. What happens when the same statute does both of these things at once: i.e., modifies the common law, but uses common law terms in the process? A concrete example may help you see how rival interpretations of the common law term can produce different meanings of the statute:

An upscale tobacco merchant sends a signed letter to a group
of selected customers announcing bargain prices on a list of
rare cigars and expressly guaranteeing those prices for a two-
week period. Three days later, one of the selected customers
attempts to purchase two cigars from the list, but the merchant
refuses to honor the price guarantee. What legal rights does
the customer have against the merchant?

At common law, the merchant's promise would have been unenforceable for want of consideration, under the famous rule of *Dickinson
v. Dodds*. But the "firm offer" provision of the U.C.C.—§ 2-205—was
specifically designed to reverse that rule. In pertinent part, that section
provides:

An offer by a merchant to buy or sell goods in a signed writing
which by its terms gives assurance that it will be held open is not
revocable, for lack of consideration, during the time stated....

Is our merchant's letter a "firm offer" under this rule? It's clear that we
have a "signed writing" from a "merchant" that "gives assurance"—indeed, in the language of our letter, *guarantees*—"that it will be held open"
for two weeks, and our customer turned up at the shop well within that
period. But what's not clear is whether the letter is also an "offer," and the
answer depends on what is meant by that term.

On the one hand, if "offer" keeps its common law meaning, the merchant's letter may fail under the common law rule that treats price lists,
advertisements, catalogs, and the like as mere invitations to deal and not
offers. But on the other hand, the purpose of § 2-205 is to hold merchants
to commitments they make and deprive them of technical objections that
are the common law's equivalent of "but-Simon-didn't-*say*-I'd-sell-cigars-
at-those-prices!" On that view, we should dispense with the common law
technicality and interpret the word "offer" more broadly, to protect the
customer's reasonable commercial expectations—based on the merchant's own signed and written assurances—that the merchant would sell
the listed cigars at the "guaranteed" prices during the stipulated period.

As the foregoing suggests, issues that present a conflict of this
sort—between the common law meaning of a term and a meaning based
on statutory purpose—can be subtle and surprisingly complex. But in a

world where statutes are ever more frequently enacted to "displace" the common law, you should expect to encounter issues of this sort often, in legal practice as well as on your exams.

5. The special case of constitutional interpretation

The "issues" we've just described—plain meaning vs. purpose, historical vs. contemporary meanings, etc.—arise with great frequency when judges interpret constitutional provisions as well as statutes, but they intersect in complex ways with the "schools of thought" that are a central point of emphasis in most contemporary Constitutional Law courses—e.g., originalism and its proliferating spawn (contemporaneous public meaning, originalism plus, and originalism lite); living constitutionalism; etc. Accordingly, when you encounter an interpretation issue in a Con Law class or exam, your professor will expect you to deploy those "schools of thought"—rather than the statutory interpretation concepts we've detailed here. To be sure, you'll see considerable overlap between the two. Con Law's rival "schools of thought" are larded with variants on "plain meaning" and "purposive" arguments—and disagreements about "competing meanings" and "competing purposes"—so the work you've done in this chapter can help a lot in understanding the debates at issue. But it is vitally important that you "render unto your Con Law professor" the analytical tools she's taught you, and accordingly we strongly advise you to use *her* lessons and not ours when drafting answers for your Con Law exam.

B. Fact Situations to Watch For

Most law professors try to test what they teach, so the best way to prepare yourself to recognize competing interpretations issues is to pay careful attention to the statutory ambiguities your professor emphasizes. If she stressed one or more of the issues we've discussed—the tension between the plain meaning of some statutory provision and its purpose, say, or between the different policies underlying a particular statute—chances are that those issues will show up somewhere on the final. Beyond that, our experience suggests that there are several factual situations that law professors routinely use to test competing interpretations of statutes. Watch out for these greatest hits on exam playlists.

- *Variation on a hypothetical examined closely in class.* One familiar fact pattern is the scenario that presents a slight variation on a hypothetical that was closely analyzed in class. If the professor devoted substantial time and attention to analyzing the "No vehicles permitted in the park" rule and its application to tricycles, watch for skateboards, wheelchairs (motorized and otherwise), and golf carts on the final!

- *New application of an old statute.* Watch for the scenario in which a statute that's been around for a while is invoked in a factual setting that was unimaginable at the time of enactment—like the Statute of Frauds applied to a transaction memorialized via text or voicemail. Precisely because they present situations that the drafters of the statute couldn't envision, new situation/old statute hypos are a great vehicle for testing the tension between plain-meaning or historical-meaning interpretations (on the one hand) and statutory-purpose meanings (on the other).

- *New or imaginary statute.* Professors who want to test their students' ability to engage in statutory interpretation (rather than just the capacity to riff off arguments rehearsed during class discussion) may design a question asking you to apply a statute you've never seen before—a recently enacted statute, perhaps, or even one that the professor has invented out of whole cloth. When you encounter a problem like this, *don't freak out.* Indeed, you should count your blessings, for this is one setting in which the professor won't expect you to know anything about legislative history! What the professor will want is for you to use policy analysis to come up with statutory purposes on your own—so keep an eye out for issues that involve policies pitted against one another and/or against the plain language of the statute.

- *A statute making a cameo appearance in a common law claim.* Finally, watch for the setting in which a statute is invoked in the context of a common law claim or defense—for example, a tenant who withholds rent on the basis of the landlord's violation of the housing code, or a defendant in a negligence suit who offers compliance with a regulatory statute as proof of reasonable care. Professors frequently invent statutes for use in settings like these, and in our experience students miss competing interpretations issues because they are drawn so powerfully to the common law issue that they pay too little attention to the statute. For example, consider a hypothetical in which an owner takes her cat on a commercial flight, and the cat escapes from its cage and bites another passenger; the bitten passenger sues for negligence, and the pet owner defends on the ground that the cage complied with pertinent FAA regulations. The "B" exam will identify and analyze the tort law issue—does statutory compliance establish reasonable care?—but the "A" exam will take analysis to the next level by focusing on competing purposes of the statute as well: Are the FAA regulations designed to protect passengers from the prospect of feline attack? If so, compliance with those regulations may help demonstrate the owner's reasonable care. But if the regulations are merely intended to protect cats from unnecessary discomfort during turbulence and to ensure that cages fit unobtrusively in the space beneath a seat, then their relevance to the duty of care with respect to fellow passengers is substantially diminished.

The steady proliferation of competing purposes such as those in our cat hypothetical would be enough to make anyone fear law school exams if the point of these exams were to choose the precise approach that we knew a court would adopt in every case. Instead, you know now that you will score points for showing your professor the many paths the analysis might take, how those paths would produce different outcomes, and why a judge might be drawn to alternative approaches. What at first seemed scary is now a chance for you to demonstrate your understanding without worrying that your doubts about the outcome will prove fatal to your cause. Indeed, the right answer to an exam question hinging on interpretation of an ambiguous statute is a careful explanation of how alternative interpretations are attractive and why that is so. In short, the right answer is that there could be *several* right answers. As we will see in the next chapter, the same spirit applies equally to exams based on case law, where the best "maybes" are yet to come.

Chapter Eight

Forks in the Law—Competing Interpretations of Case Law

"Of course, people *do* go both ways."
—The Scarecrow to Dorothy, who has happened upon a fork in the yellow brick road, in *The Wizard of Oz*

Recall the wry observation that reading your first judicial opinion is a lot like "stirring cement with your eyelashes." That was certainly our experience, and frankly things didn't improve much when we got to class, where the professor could ask virtually *anything* about a case and there seemed to be a dozen different and equally plausible answers to each question.

Believe it or not, the law exam may be just the compass needed to help negotiate this challenging terrain. For when it comes to testing your understanding of the cases you've studied, an exam problem typically asks only one question and expects only one answer. The question is "should you 'follow' the case?" and the answer (you guessed it) is "maybe." (Actually, that's two answers, but more on that in a moment.)

Perhaps the most common type of exam question you'll encounter in law school involves a scenario that is a variation on the facts of a case you've studied in the course. (The parties in the exam question may be arguing over the "capture" of underground oil deposits, while the case you studied—*Pierson v. Post*, a first-year Property classic—concerns the capture of wild animals.) The scenario thus presents you with another instance of what we've been calling a "fork in the law." If you "follow" the earlier decision (the "precedent"), you'll reach one result. But if you don't follow the precedent—if instead you "distinguish" it—your analysis may come out the other way. (The oil deposits case, for example, may lead to one result if we "follow" the rule of *Pierson v. Post* and to another if we "distinguish" that case.)

Just as the "forks in the law" we studied in the previous chapter depend on how you interpret a statute, the choice between following and distinguishing a precedent depends on how you interpret the earlier decision. And in the same way that statutory ambiguities appear in patterns you can study and learn to recognize, there are recurring patterns of ambiguity in case law as well. After an introduction to the idea of "following" and "distinguishing" precedent, we'll devote the rest of this chapter to exploring those patterns.

A. Finding Ambiguity in Case Law

1. *Stare decisis* and the quest for "like" cases

In the first weeks of law school, you'll hear it endlessly said that courts "follow precedent," a practice so basic to our idea of justice that it even sports a catchy Latin name: *stare decisis*, meaning "let the decision stand." That directive in turn reflects the principle that "like cases should be treated alike," something that dawned on most of us the first time our parents appeared to treat us with less favor than a sibling. ("No fair," you protested. "How come I have to go to bed so early and Blair gets to stay up much later?") Applying that principle to law, if courts reach a result in one case—say they find an assault and battery on a particular set of facts—then we generally expect them to reach the same result in later cases that present similar facts and are therefore "like" the first one.

But a lot depends on just what we mean by "like." The notion that your parents shouldn't treat your sibling better than you springs from the deeply felt intuition that siblings are "like" cases, deserving of equal treatment by their parents. Yet sometimes your parents might disagree and point out that your sibling's situation differs in some important respect from your own. ("Honey," they might patiently respond, "you are five years old, and Blair is 18. And when you're 18, you can stay up late too.") You'll encounter much the same move in the legal setting when lawyers point to some difference between a precedent and a later dispute—in Case #1, A tackles B as B is walking to school; in Case #2, A tackles B as B is running for a touchdown—to argue that courts should "distinguish" Case #1 and reach a different result in Case #2 ("No assault and battery here!").

It's surprising how often legal disputes turn on whether to follow or distinguish an earlier case, and thus lawyers and judges devote a great deal of effort and ingenuity to arguments over whether a precedent and a later dispute are, or are not, "like" cases. To assist you in developing this critical lawyering skill, your professors will craft exam questions offering a scenario that is *similar* to one of the cases you've studied but that also includes something *different*. And whatever might be said about the wisdom and fairness of using a graded end-of-term exam to teach this skill—rather than just spending a lot more time on it in the classroom—professors know that the exam problems they write this year are likely to be a principal focus of study for next year's students as they prepare for their own exam. So we devote considerable effort to inventing novel situations that resemble but don't mirror the cases you have mastered. The difference may shift just a fact or two from those in the original case—e.g., a reworking of *Garratt v. Dailey* in which a naughty child causes an elderly visitor to stumble to the ground as she tries to sit, not by moving the chair but instead by placing an amazingly lifelike rubber tarantula on the seat at the last moment. Or it may add something more dramatic—e.g., a free speech case in which a protester burns not a draft card but a Bible. In a moment, we'll talk about what to *do* with the similarities and differences, but first we want to offer an extended example of this sort of problem drawn from a real exam question.

2. The search for similarities and differences

In first-year Property, most students will study one or more cases on the "duty to disclose" in the context of residential real estate sales. *Johnson v. Davis*—a decision by the Florida Supreme Court—is a leading case on the topic, and let's assume you've studied it carefully in preparation for the final. In *Johnson*, an aggrieved homebuyer sued a seller seeking rescission of the sales contract and a return of money paid based on the seller's failure to disclose serious defects with the roof. (The respective parties in the case were married couples, but for ease of expression we'll refer to each side in the singular.) Under the common law doctrine of *caveat emptor* ("buyer beware"), a seller of residential real estate had no obligation to disclose such defects to a buyer; it was up to a buyer worried about defects to ferret them out. Under Florida law at the time of *Johnson*, there was an exception to *caveat emptor* for fraudulent misrepresentation, but a buyer couldn't prevail on that theory unless seller made an affirmative misrepresentation of fact—stating, for example, that "the roof was inspected this summer and passed with flying colors" when no such inspection had taken place or when such an inspection had in fact revealed serious defects in the roof. By contrast, a seller's mere *silence* about a known defect—however significant and costly that defect might be—would not support a claim of misrepresentation.

In *Johnson*, the court took the law in a new direction and reasoned as follows:

> One should not be able to stand behind the impervious shield of caveat emptor and take advantage of another's ignorance.... The law appears to be working toward the ultimate conclusion that full disclosure of all material facts must be made whenever elementary fair conduct demands it.

Turning to the case before it, the court ruled for buyer and concluded thus: "We hold that where the seller of a home knows of facts materially affecting the value of the property which are not readily observable and are not known to the buyer, the seller is under a duty to disclose them to the buyer."

Now imagine you get to the final and encounter the following problem, taken from a Property exam given a few years back:

> A visiting scholar is renting a modest home and hoping to renew the lease for the following academic year. The owner, however, puts the house on the market in December and tells the scholar he can renew only if the house isn't sold by May. The scholar's time in the house has alerted him to certain problems: basement flooding after heavy rains; loud parties every Thursday night in the rental unit across the street that is full to the brim with rowdy undergrads; frequent flickering of the outside lights. But the scholar decides to tell neither his landlord nor prospective buyers about these difficulties in the hope that a last-minute discovery will spoil a deal and give

him the chance to renew. As it happens, the owner sells the house quickly, and the defects aren't discovered until the new owner moves in. Attempts at settlement have failed, and the new owner brings suit for damages not only against the seller—who knew nothing of the defects—but also against the scholar, who was present but silent while the home inspections took place. What are the prospects for success on the claim against the visiting scholar?

What should you do if you've studied *Johnson* and you encounter the Case of the Visiting Scholar on your exam? Are these "like" cases, providing a basis for "following" *Johnson* in the exam problem and holding the scholar liable for his strategic silence? Sure enough, there are a number of similarities between the two disputes: Each involves the sale of residential real estate; in each, there were costly defects in the property; in each, the defects were known to the defendant; and in each, the defects were not disclosed to the buyer prior to entering the contract of sale. At the same time, at least one difference between the cases stands out: *Johnson* dealt with a silent *seller* and the Case of the Visiting Scholar involves a silent *tenant*, providing a basis for "distinguishing" *Johnson* and thus rejecting any claim of liability against the silent party.

As this example suggests, then, the critical first step in dealing with an exam question like this one is to identify similarities *as well as* differences between a case you've studied and a hypothetical dispute posed on an exam. (Going forward, we'll refer to the former as "the precedent" and the latter as "the exam problem.")

3. Why students identify similarities but not differences (and vice versa)

When professors draft an exam problem like the Case of the Visiting Scholar, the resemblance to a precedent covered in the course is likely to be pretty obvious to most students—the legal equivalent of a déjà vu, and, at least if you studied, you really will have "been there before." To be sure, there are steps you can take to minimize the chance of missing this moment of recognition, and we share some of those in our chapter on exam preparation and outlining. But missing the moment of recognition is not where students tend to go wrong.

Instead, the most common mistake is a failure to address the similarities *as well as* the differences between a precedent and an exam problem. And in our experience, that mistake springs not from a failure to *see* both sides but from the exam-taking reflex developed during prior schooling that finds the key to good performance in figuring out which side is "right" and which side is "wrong." We certainly don't blame our students for thinking this way, since the lion's share of the exams most of us took at earlier stages of our education asked questions that called for a single correct answer. (Math teachers of the world, this may be all your fault.)

Operating from a "one right answer" mindset, the student who spots similarities between the precedent and the exam problem may feel an enormous sense of relief. ("*Wow, we've seen* this *scenario before—the failure to disclose serious defects in the sale of a private home. It's just like* Johnson; *so follow that case, full speed ahead!*") But at this point one of two things may go wrong. Some students, thrilled at discovering what looks like *the* answer ("*It's just like* Johnson!"), may be tempted to stop thinking and even to stop reading, wanting to see no more. Better to stick with the answer you've got (goes this line of thought) than to risk learning you're wrong, so there's just no point looking for, let alone writing about, differences. Other students press on, spot a nontrivial difference, and are traumatized, perhaps to the point of forgoing discussion of *Johnson* altogether. ("*Oh no,* Johnson *was about a <u>seller's</u> failure to 'fess up to defects, and in this problem it's a <u>tenant</u> who stays mum!*") What's the point (think these students) of even *mentioning* the precedent since it's so different from the problem after all? ("*Oh well, nothing to see here. Back to the drawing board!*")

But here's the thing: No self-respecting law professor would design an exam problem presenting a 100% match with a precedent you've studied. You will *always* find differences if you look hard enough—*so look for them!* At the same time, no matter how significant a difference seems at first blush between a precedent and a problem, don't let go of that initial sense of déjà vu. Instead, dig in and search out both the similarities *and* differences as if your grade depends on it. Trust us, it does. In terms of successful exam-taking strategies, identifying similarities as well as differences means you're well on the way to earning twice the credit as the student who sees—or mistakenly decides to address—only one or the other.

4. Identifying similarities and differences that matter: Competing interpretations of precedent

The ability to identify similarities as well as differences is thus a critical exam-taking skill, but what will really set your performance apart is explaining why the similarities and differences you've identified *matter*—why the similarities justify "following" the precedent and why the differences justify "distinguishing" it. To recall a point one of our own professors was a little too fond of making while tormenting students during class discussion, "Well, the name of the plaintiff in one case is Smith, and in the other it's Jones. Is *that* a basis for distinguishing the cases?" As the Socratic needling was meant to suggest, some facts matter and some don't, and the key to telling the difference comes in understanding what the facts are supposed to matter *to*.

In a nutshell, in much the same way lawyers contend for competing interpretations of statutes (plain meaning vs. purpose, competing purposes, etc.), lawyers offer competing interpretations of precedent as well, and it is those interpretations—for the moment, it might be helpful to think of them as "points of emphasis"—that will tell you which facts matter and which facts don't. To see how this works, we'll begin with a classic example of competing interpretations, with one party stressing the *holding* of the precedent and the other stressing the court's *reasoning*. (Recall the definitions of those terms in the discussion of case-briefing back in Chapter Three: The holding is the court's resolution of the legal issue presented by the parties' dispute, and the reasoning is the analysis of authority, policy, and/or principle offered by the court to justify that resolution.) Returning to the Case of the Visiting Scholar, recall that *Johnson*—the precedent at issue—isn't shy about its holding: "[W]e hold that where the seller of a home knows of facts materially affecting the value of the property which are not readily observable and are not known to the buyer, the seller is under a duty to disclose them to the buyer." Here the holding speaks of liability for "sellers"—not for "tenants" or for any other party—so that's a factual difference between the precedent and the exam problem that clearly matters. "Simon said 'sellers,'" the argument would go. "Simon *didn't* say 'tenants.' And just what part of 'sellers' don't you understand?"

On the other hand, recall the reasoning of the *Johnson* court:

> One should not be able to stand behind the impervious shield
> of caveat emptor and take advantage of another's ignorance....
> The law appears to be working toward the ultimate conclusion
> that full disclosure of all material facts must be made whenev-
> er elementary fair conduct demands it.

While the holding mentions only "sellers," the court's reasoning broadly condemns "tak[ing] advantage of another's ignorance" and suggests
that a duty of "full disclosure" should apply "*whenever* elementary fair
conduct demands it" (emphasis ours), with no mention of—let alone
any limitation to—sellers. According to the reasoning, then, "tak[ing]
advantage of another's ignorance" is a "fact that matters" a *lot*. That's
what the seller in *Johnson* did by keeping the buyer in the dark about
the problems with the roof. And that's exactly what the Visiting Scholar
was up to as well, remaining silent about multiple defects in the rental
property in the hope that a last-minute reveal would crash the deal
between his landlord and the would-be buyer. The strategic silence is
thus a fact that matters in both cases, violating the norms of "elementary fair conduct."

In sum, then, under the *reasoning* of *Johnson*, the facts that matter are
strategic silence and unfair conduct, highlighting a factual *similarity* between the precedent and the problem. By contrast, under the *holding* of
Johnson, the fact that matters is whether the silent party was a seller,
highlighting a factual *difference* between the two cases.

B. Patterns of Competing Interpretations

1. Broadening and narrowing a precedent: Packing with a purpose

So here's a question we ask only partly in jest: As the parties in the
Case of the Visiting Scholar argue over their dispute—or, more to the
point, as you present those arguments in the course of an exam answer—which party is going to urge the court to focus on the holding in
Johnson and which party is going to emphasize the reasoning? The question answers itself, but it reflects an important feature of legal advocacy
with critical implications for successful exam-taking: *Lawyers argue for
interpretations of precedent that will serve their clients.* As a consequence,

they "go to court with the facts they have," arguing for an interpretation of precedent that makes the similarities between the cases matter (if they want the court to follow the earlier decision) or that makes the differences matter (if they want the court to distinguish it). This is a skill that takes some practice, and we have an analogy that may help you visualize these argument mobilization strategies.

Consider the lowly Rollaboard, a wheeled travel bag that is large enough to hold a weekend's wardrobe yet small enough for carry-on use, thus eliminating the risks of loss, damage, and delay (not to mention the add-on charges) associated with checked baggage. A key feature of the now ubiquitous travel companion is that—through the use of its sturdy oversized zipper—it can shrink or expand depending on the packing task at hand. When you need the bag as a carry-on, you zip it into its compact state, a perfect fit in the overhead compartment. But when you need it for other purposes—e.g., when packing for a cross-country car trip or an extended Caribbean cruise—you can unzip the zipper and expand the bag, substantially increasing its packing capacity. Over the years, we've noticed a somewhat edgier use for the expandability function. An air traveler with a bit too much in the way of clothing, gifts, or reading material can smuggle extras onto the aircraft by stuffing them into pockets, purse, or laptop case—or by wearing multiple layers of clothing—and complete the boarding process with the travel bag in its compact state, thus avoiding the eagle eye of airline personnel ready to redirect any oversized bag to the dreaded abyss of checked baggage. But once safely at the assigned seat, the traveler can surreptitiously unzip and expand the bag, squeeze in the smuggled extras, and cram the bulging Rollaboard into the overhead bin.

So what's all this got to do with competing interpretations of precedent? Pretty much everything. Simply put, a lawyer arguing that we should *follow* a precedent is going to work hard to "expand the case" so the facts of a current problem fit right in. She will therefore be looking for an interpretation of the precedent under which the facts that matter in the precedent are similar to the facts presented in the problem—that is, an interpretation that would justify placing the current facts "inside" the precedent, to continue the travel bag analogy. In the Case of the Visiting Scholar, counsel for the buyer will therefore want to focus on the reasoning of *Johnson* because it condemns all parties—not just sellers—who "take advantage of another's ignorance" and fail to meet the standards of "elementary fair conduct." Buyer suffered from precisely such misconduct at the hands of the scholar-tenant, and the current case is thus an easy "fit" when the precedent is "expanded" in accord with this interpretation.

By contrast, a lawyer who is arguing that we should *distinguish* a precedent is going to work hard to "shrink the case" so the facts of the current dispute won't fit. She will therefore be looking for an interpretation that will justify treating the facts that matter in the precedent differently from the facts of the current dispute—that is, an interpretation that would justify placing the current facts "outside" the precedent, to continue the travel bag analogy. To illustrate with the Case of the Visiting Scholar, counsel for the scholar-tenant is going to focus on the holding of *Johnson* because it imposes nondisclosure liability only upon sellers of residential real estate and bears no hint of liability for tenants; tenants just won't "fit" inside the earlier case when it's "shrunken" in accord with this interpretation.

When lawyers make these moves in a real legal dispute—*and they make them all the time*—they refer to them as "broader" and "narrower" interpretations of precedent, and these are by some distance the most common moves lawyers make when arguing about whether to follow or distinguish an earlier case. But the underlying idea is much the same as filling our travel bag, since the "broad" and "narrow" metaphors refer to the fact you can "pack" a lot more factual scenarios into a "broad" interpretation than you can into a "narrow" one. To see this in action, consider once again the competing interpretations of *Johnson* in the Case of the Visiting Scholar, where one side invoked the holding and the other the reasoning, for we can likewise describe the respective readings in "broad" and "narrow" terms. Thus, the lawyer representing the scholar-tenant offered a narrow interpretation of *Johnson* ("the case applies *only* to 'sellers,' and what part of 'seller' don't you understand?") and the lawyer representing the buyer offered a broad interpretation ("the case applies to *anyone*—not just sellers—who 'take[s] advantage of another's ignorance' and who fails to meet the standards of 'elementary fair conduct'").

We'll refer to this exchange as "Broad vs. narrow interpretations of *Johnson* #1," for it doesn't exhaust the possibilities when it comes to broader and narrower readings of the case. Let's consider some additional examples in which the parties deploy a wide range of broader and narrower interpretations to expand and shrink the precedent.

Broad vs. narrow interpretations of *Johnson* #2:

- *The buyer offers a medium broad interpretation of* Johnson: If buyer's counsel is worried that the court won't adopt an interpretation of *Johnson* that would extend the disclosure obligation to *any* party—and not merely to sellers—she might well propose a somewhat less broad interpretation of the earlier case: We impose disclosure liability on sellers not because they are "sellers" but because they have a financial interest in the transaction, and it's not fair to permit persons with such an interest to "take advantage of another's ignorance" by keeping important information about the value of the property to themselves. In the Case of the Visiting Scholar, the exam-writing professor has shared the tenant's "mum's the word" strategy in some detail, a "tell" that obviously invites the reader to consider whether that strategic silence is similar to or different from the seller's silence in *Johnson*. So what's at stake for the scholar-tenant? Well, should the sale go through, he'll have to give up a home he likes and go to the time, trouble, and costs of locating a new residence, negotiating a new lease, moving his belongings, getting accustomed to a new neighborhood and new shopping venues, etc. No wonder he's hoping that the sale of the property will fall through.

- *The scholar-tenant offers a medium narrow interpretation of* Johnson: The rejoinder by counsel for the scholar-tenant might propose a somewhat narrower interpretation of *Johnson*, arguing that the earlier case should not be read to impose nondisclosure obligations on parties whose interest in the transaction is primarily "personal," for otherwise the case would give rise to a potentially limitless expansion of liability (e.g., to neighbors who might care a great deal about who's moving in next door). Applying that standard here, the scholar-tenant's interest is less "financial" (he doesn't stand to share the profits or losses resulting from the sale of the home) than it is "personal" (comfort, convenience, avoiding the hassle of moving, etc.), and therefore *Johnson's* disclosure obligation should not apply to him.

Broad vs. narrow interpretations of *Johnson* #3:

- *The scholar-tenant offers a* really *narrow interpretation of* Johnson: If counsel for the scholar-tenant is worried that the court won't agree to limit *Johnson* to sellers, she might try yet another narrowing strategy. The opinion in *Johnson* reveals that the roof problems in that case were acute: During the period between contract and closing, buyer visited the property after a heavy rainstorm only to find water "gushing" in from the family room ceiling; from around light fixtures, glass doors, and a window frame; and from over the kitchen stove. Counsel for the scholar-tenant might focus on those facts to argue that nondisclosure liability under *Johnson* should be narrowed to cases involving defects of similar magnitude (e.g., a major termite infestation or a crumbling foundation), lest the flaws that invariably develop in a home as a result of ordinary wear and tear give rise to countless frivolous lawsuits. Judged by that standard, the problems at issue in the Case of the Visiting Scholar are small-bore: basement flooding is a common occurrence in many parts of the country; the cost of replacing a few outside fixtures is negligible in comparison with the extensive repair or replacement of a roof; and next year's student neighbors may well be a quieter and more studious lot.

- *Buyer offers a broader interpretation of* Johnson: The rejoinder by buyer's counsel might point to the language of the *Johnson* opinion, which imposed a disclosure obligation with respect to facts "materially affecting the value of the property." The multiple defects the scholar-tenant kept to himself easily meet that broader test, the argument would continue, especially the basement flooding (which would imperil some of the most common basement uses—e.g., laundry and storage—and possibly indicate significant problems with the foundation) as well as the flickering lights (which could signal a larger problem with the wiring and will at the very least require the costly services of a licensed electrician).

So now we've seen *three* pairs of broad vs. narrow interpretations of *Johnson*, with the individual readings ranging from the very broad to the very narrow. But if the Case of the Visiting Scholar were an exam question, rest assured that a student wouldn't need to come up with all of these in order to craft a successful answer; indeed, she'd be well on her way to an "A" using any one of them—or indeed other interpretations she came up with on her own. Our aim in working our way through these multiple pairings is to demonstrate that mastery of the "broadening vs. narrowing" technique can aid a student in identifying a wide range of possibilities in interpreting precedent, for the typical exam problem will give you plenty to work with once you see this larger pattern.

2. Competing meanings: Words are many-splendored things

> "Words are, in my not-so-humble opinion, our most inexhaustible source of magic. Capable of both inflicting injury, and remedying it."
>
> —Albus Dumbledore in J.K. Rowling's
> *Harry Potter and the Deathly Hallows* (2007)

The broadening and narrowing of precedent isn't the only source of competing interpretations of case law. In much the same manner that lawyers argue over the meaning of the particular words used in statutes—like the "vehicles" banished from the park—they can also argue over the meaning of words appearing in a judicial decision. Consider once again the holding in *Johnson*, which imposes a duty of disclosure whenever seller "knows of facts materially affecting the value of the property which are not readily observable and are not known to the buyer." And then consider the following scenario:

> Sam Seller is aware that three of the drains in his home—one in the master bath and shower, one in the sink in the half-bath, and one in the utility sink in the laundry room—have become increasingly sluggish during the past six months. Since it didn't happen all at once—and didn't seem to affect other drains in the house—Seller assumed the problems were attributable to the normal accumulation of detritus in the individual drains and accordingly didn't think to mention it to Betty Buyer when she purchased the home. Upon moving in, Buyer learns for the first time of the slow drains and discovers they're the result of a plumbing problem throughout the house that

will cost several thousand dollars to fix. What rights, if any, does she have against Seller?

On these facts, the parties are likely to embrace competing meanings of the word "know" in *Johnson's* holding. Thus, Seller may point to the facts he actually "knew" (i.e., the existence of three slow drains) and argue that those facts did not in themselves "materially affect the value of the property"; indeed, he had assumed that a large bottle of Drano would solve the problem entirely and just hadn't gotten around to the fix. Buyer is likely to respond that the proper test for "knowing" a fact doesn't require a seller to have the training and experience to provide a professional diagnosis of the condition in question; otherwise, *Johnson* would apply only to sellers who are licensed plumbers, electricians, roofers, etc. Rather, a seller "knows" of a problem requiring disclosure when he is aware of circumstances sufficient to prompt a reasonably prudent homeowner to take a further look into the underlying cause, and three slow drains in six months' time easily meet that test. In sum, the respective parties are once again offering competing interpretations of *Johnson* but are this time focused on a particular term. The seller urges a meaning of "know" that includes only those observable facts seller believes will have an impact on the home's value. Sellers may know many facts (e.g., house is cooler when the wind comes from one direction rather than another) that they may never mention. In contrast, the buyer will put forth an interpretation that would define "knowing" so as to take into account the way a responsible homeowner would process discrete indications of what may well be a larger problem.

Let's take a quick look at another example of "competing meanings," this one a battle over how "the value of the property" should be determined under *Johnson*.

> Oleander owns a home in a rural university town and is aware of a significant deterioration in the foundation that will eventually require its replacement, a process that can cost upwards of $100,000. Out of the blue, Oleander and the owners of the five other homes on the block are approached by Off Campus Living, Inc. (OCL), a private developer specializing in the construction of off-campus student housing in college and university towns. OCL wants to purchase the entire block, tear

down the existing structures, and replace them with a mixed townhouse and apartment complex for graduate students at the nearby university. Seeking a quick deal, OCL offered each of the owners—none of whom had been actively contemplating a sale at the time—a price well above market value for area homes, contingent on quick agreement from all parties. Each of the owners readily agreed to the proposed sale, but at no time during the course of the transaction did Oleander disclose to OCL the foundation problem with the home. OCL representatives discovered it on their own as they were surveying the area for the planned construction, and—shortly before closing—they threatened to rescind the deal unless Oleander agreed to a significant price cut. What are the rights of the respective parties in these circumstances?

OCL will argue that "the value of the property" in *Johnson* means *market value*, and there's little doubt of the impact serious foundation problems would have on the market value of a home, since virtually any potential buyer apprised thereof would at the very least require a substantial price allowance before agreeing to purchase. Oleander is likely to respond that "the value of the property" means *value to the buyer*, and—given OCL's plans to tear down the home for its student housing project—the condition of the foundation is irrelevant. Oleander will claim the suit for rescission is a bluff to scare Oleander into taking less, since presumably OCL's plans are unchanged by a flaw in a foundation that OCL will destroy. Indeed, OCL paid little heed to the market value of the homes on the chopping block, offering prices calculated to persuade owners who hadn't even been contemplating a sale to sell and to sell quickly.

The larger lesson here is the same as it was in connection with the interpretation of statutes: Legal terms frequently have more than one plausible meaning, and your legal studies will help you learn to recognize the occasions on which a claim of linguistic ambiguity is likely to get traction worthy of mention on an exam. There are times, of course, when only one meaning will be plausible—e.g., where the term has a well-settled meaning in the commercial or professional milieu giving rise to the dispute and the parties are longtime players operating within that milieu. But in most settings, we suggest you suppress your instinct to conclude "only one possible meaning" will do—e.g., "of course 'value' means 'market value,' how else could we measure it?" Explore instead the possibility of alternative meanings in the facts of a case ("the 'market value' didn't matter much to the buyer here"); in the equities ("this was a case of a buyer in a hurry, not a seller with something to hide"); or in the life experience of one or both of the parties—real estate developers, for example, may know full well that when you are buying a house to knock it down, the significant market value is not that of the house but of the land. Bakers, after all, think "a dozen" means 13. As you know, words derive their meaning from context, and context is complicated. If your exam grader has stressed dictionary definitions, then by all means shamelessly pander to the idea that terms have fixed meanings. But this will seldom be a winning strategy on any other exam or if you are preparing to practice law after graduation.

3. Competing reasons: The kaleidoscope of justification

There is a final pattern of competing interpretations of case law, and once again there is a parallel to the material on statutory interpretation. In the same way that statutory provisions are frequently enacted to serve a multiplicity of purposes, judicial opinions frequently offer multiple reasons for reaching a particular result. But once again those reasons may point in different directions or even conflict with one another in the context of a later case presenting differing facts. Assume, for example, the *Johnson* court offered the following reasoning in support of its holding:

> In particular, two considerations move us to reject the invocation of *caveat emptor*—the long-standing rule designed to incentivize vigilance on the part of buyers—in the context presented here. First, in the typical residential real estate transaction, a seller is far better positioned than a would-be buyer to unearth information about less-than-obvious defects and to do so without a needless expenditure of money and time. In the case before us, the flooding in multiple rooms in the house following a heavy rainstorm—itself a common occurrence in Florida—could scarcely have been missed by seller; buyer, by contrast, learned of the problem only through the happenstance of dropping by shortly after a downpour. Sec-

ond, it is critical to the efficient operation of this or any market that courts promote trust between contracting parties rather than sowing the seeds of cynicism. We can think of few results more likely to undermine such trust—and with it, the confidence in our courts—than a belated discovery that your trading partner deliberately withheld vital information about a costly defect in your new home and that the law will do nothing about it.

In the context of the facts presented in *Johnson*, each of these considerations points to the same result: Seller should have spoken up about that roof. But watch what happens when the considerations come into play in the Case of the Visiting Scholar. On the one hand, the buyer is likely to emphasize the importance of imposing liability on the party in the best position to acquire information about defects in the property, for in this case the scholar-tenant is the party in possession and is thus the party "in the know" about the defects. Requiring the scholar-tenant to disclose information that would be much harder for buyer to come by is thus a logical extension of the *Johnson* rule. On the other hand, we can expect counsel for the scholar-tenant to focus instead on the goal of promoting trust between contracting parties, for the contracting parties in this case are the buyer and the seller, and—whatever his obligations to the landlord—the scholar-tenant is a complete stranger to the sales agreement.

For a second example of "competing reasons" in action, let's switch gears and consider the famous example of *Griswold v. Connecticut*, a Supreme Court decision from the 1960s establishing a constitutional right to use contraceptives and striking down a state law prohibiting same. The Court's reasoning made much of the fact that a married couple brought the challenge, emphasizing that the statute at issue "operates directly on an intimate relation of husband and wife" and elsewhere decrying as "repulsive" the specter of police invading "the sacred precincts of marital bedrooms for telltale signs of the use of contraceptives." At the same time, the opinion stressed a "right of privacy" implicit in multiple constitutional provisions that apply to *all* persons, married or otherwise (e.g., the Third Amendment right not to quarter soldiers in your home and the Fourth Amendment "right of people to be secure in their persons, houses, papers, and effects"). When later cases inevitably presented the issue of whether the *Griswold* right was available to the unmarried, lawyers urging a "no" answer pointed to the marriage rationale and lawyers urging a "yes" answer emphasized the court's reliance on a broader conception of "privacy." Judges forced to choose between such "competing interpretations" later ruled in favor of extending the right to the unmarried, but had this been an issue on an exam in the years immediately following *Griswold*, students would be entirely on the right track in highlighting how language within *Griswold* points in both directions.

C. Sources of Competing Interpretations

"Where does he get all those wonderful toys?"
—The Joker, referring to the zipline device with
which the Caped Crusader rescued Vicki Vale from
the villain's clutches in Tim Burton's *Batman* (1989)

As we've seen, competing interpretations of precedent play a critical role in arguments over whether to follow or distinguish an earlier case in the context of an exam. A common and perfectly reasonable reaction to the examples offered in the previous section goes something like this: "When I see these arguments in action—broad vs. narrow interpretations, competing meanings, competing purposes—it all makes perfect sense. But how am I supposed to come up with arguments like these on my own, particularly in the middle of a law exam?"

Our response is the usual mix of good and bad news. The bad news is that identifying and deploying plausible interpretations of case law is one of the most difficult legal skills to learn, and there is really no substitute for practice. In a later chapter, we'll urge you (among other things) to get such practice via our sample questions as well as your professor's old exams. But there's good news too: Once you grasp the basic architecture of competing interpretations, coming up with case-specific arguments is easier than you might expect if you focus your efforts on three sources: the text of the precedent; class discussion and assigned readings about the case; and some "do it yourself" policy analysis. (For what it's worth, practicing lawyers draw on the same sources, though the further they get from law school, the more likely they are to consult current professional and scholarly publications rather than dimming recollections of lessons learned in their law school courses.) Let's look at each of these sources in turn.

1. Mining the text of a precedent

You may have noticed that most of the interpretations of *Johnson* we've discussed thus far are based on language quoted directly from the court's opinion—e.g., the specific references in the holding to "sellers" (which were offered as a basis for treating tenants differently from sellers) and the condemnation in the reasoning of "taking advantage of another's ignorance" and of behavior violating "elementary fair conduct" (which were offered as a basis for treating sneaky tenants the same as sneaky sellers). Simply put, there is no better way to ground a claim about what a precedent *means* than by pointing to what the precedent actually *says*. It turns out that judicial opinions say a lot of things, and a lawyer typically has a lot to work with as she searches for passages that will support her position in a current dispute—as well as passages she might expect opposing counsel to deploy against her. Here are some of the best places to begin that search.

a. Holding and reasoning

As we suggested back in Chapter Three, when you study cases and draft case briefs in preparation for class, you'll find it enormously useful to distinguish between the holding of a case (i.e., the resolution of the legal issue that brought the parties to court) and the reasoning (i.e., the analysis of authority, policy, and/or principle offered by the court to justify that resolution). Luckily for all of us, courts frequently signal a holding quite forthrightly, as the court did in *Johnson* with the words "we hold that" preceding the recitation of its seller disclosure rule. Some holdings won't be quite so obvious, but a rule of thumb we've always found helpful—and which we offered back in Chapter Three—is that the "holding" is the court's answer to the "issue" presented in the case. Courts almost invariably tell the reader what the "issue" is and do so early in an opinion. The court in *Johnson*, for example, characterized the issue as "whether a seller of a home has a duty to disclose latent material defects to a buyer," and its holding answers that question with a resounding yes. As for the "reasoning," once again that's the analysis offered by the court to explain and justify the resolution of the issue before it. In *Johnson*, and in most judicial opinions, you'll find that analysis in the material—it may be as short as a paragraph or two, or it may go on for pages—leading up to or immediately following the holding.

As you may have gathered from the examples of competing interpretations presented in the previous section, the "holding" and the "reasoning" of a precedent are rich resources for argument mobilization in the law exam setting. Accordingly your case briefs—if you've carefully identified those features in the cases you've studied—will be an invaluable asset as you prepare for and take your exams. Thus, a holding typically zeroes in on the precise point of disagreement between the parties and will therefore often read a lot like a statutory provision in its specificity. The holding in *Johnson* is a case in point: "[W]e hold that where the seller of a home knows of facts materially affecting the value of the property which are not readily observable and are not known to the buyer, the seller is under a duty to disclose them to the buyer." It's not difficult to imagine that language—minus the "we hold that"—appearing verbatim in the Restatement of Property or in a state statute governing real estate transactions. Because of this rule-like quality, it's often the case that every word counts, and the holding is therefore a great place to look for "competing meanings" issues, as we witnessed in the debates over the meaning of "know" and the meaning of "value" in *Johnson* in the previous section.

A court's reasoning, by contrast, typically draws on an assortment of authorities, policies, and/or principles and will therefore differ from the holding in at least two significant respects. First, as we've already noted, courts frequently offer more than one reason for reaching a particular result, and in later cases the differing reasons may well point in different directions. In that connection, recall the reasons offered by the Court in *Griswold*—the sanctity of the marital bedroom as well as a generalized right to privacy—and their differing implications for whether to extend a right to contraceptive use to the unmarried. A court's reasoning is thus the obvious place to look for the material that might give rise to "competing reasons" issues. A second difference is that reasoning tends to "go big" where holdings "go small." In that connection, recall that the holding in *Johnson* focused on sellers of residential real estate while the reasoning embraced a principle—thou shalt not take advantage of another's ignorance!—that might be thought to apply not just to sellers but to *any* party, and to govern not only residential real estate sales but also a long list of other transactions, including commercial real estate sales, leases, sales of goods, service contracts, employment relationships, etc. Thus, the relationship between holding and reasoning will often be fertile ground for broad vs. narrow interpretations, since the reasoning will frequently be potentially applicable to a variety of scenarios, while the holding will typically be less well-suited to disputes presenting facts that differ significantly from those in the earlier case.

———————————

The idea that reasoning will support broad interpretations and that holdings will support narrow interpretations is a useful guidepost. But be warned that both the real world and the world of law exams will occasionally serve up problems flipping that alignment—that is, problems in which the reasoning offers a basis for a narrow interpretation and the holding offers a basis for a broader one. Consider the following scenario:

> Keiko, a retired schoolteacher, is selling her long-neglected home because severe and chronic physical challenges have forced her to move into assisted living. Her daughter Chika handles the logistics of the sale and attempts to get the infirm though sharp-as-a-tack Keiko to provide a detailed list of the many problems with the home, so they can either be remedied before sale or disclosed to potential buyers. But the inquiry comes to an abrupt halt when the conversation stirs up decades of memories about the home she is leaving behind, causing the ailing Keiko to suffer a cardiac episode requiring medical intervention.
> In the meantime, responding to an online listing, Malik expresses an interest in purchasing the home. Chika advises him of Keiko's situation and explains that Keiko is willing to pay for a thoroughgoing inspection by a licensed firm of Malik's choosing, a cost that purchasers of residential real estate ordinarily shoulder on their own. After moving in, Malik discovers sporadic outages in the electrical system that the inspection failed to turn up and that will require a complete rewiring of the house. If Malik pursues legal action, what result if Keiko was aware of the outages before the sale?

Watch as the parties flip the broad vs. narrow interpretation techniques we've previously seen in action. The buyer's lawyer will obviously urge a broad interpretation of *Johnson*, and this time that's accomplished by relying on *Johnson's* holding, which imposes a disclosure duty where "the seller of a home knows of facts materially affecting the value of the property which are not readily observable and are not known to the buyer." By its very terms (the argument would go), the holding applies to *all* sellers as well as *all* failures to share knowledge of costly problems that are not readily observable, and—whatever the reason for that failure—Keiko checks both boxes. *Johnson's* holding, then, provides a basis for an interpretation of the precedent that would apply with equal force to *Malik v. Keiko*.

Counsel for Keiko will offer a narrower interpretation of *Johnson* to get her client off the hook, but this time it's the reasoning that does the work. Thus, counsel will argue that *Johnson* condemned parties who "take advantage of another's ignorance" and who violate the standards of "elementary fair conduct," and Keiko is simply not one of those parties. Far from trying to take advantage of Malik, the sellers here encouraged Malik to search out possible problems via a thorough inspection of the premises in advance of the sale. Indeed, Keiko went above and beyond the standards of "elementary fair conduct" by agreeing to cover Malik's inspection costs while preserving his right to select the firm doing the work. *Johnson's* reasoning, then, provides a basis for an interpretation of that case that would distinguish its facts from those presented in *Malik v. Keiko*.

As we noted a moment ago, problems—like *Malik v. Keiko*—in which the holding of a precedent provides a basis for a broader interpretation and the reasoning provides a basis for a narrower one are not as common as the reverse. But *Malik v. Keiko* is not a one-off. A holding is designed to resolve a particular dispute before the court and typically offers no occasion for the court to address other scenarios, let alone disputes that might call for exceptional treatment. Thus, the holding in *Johnson* seemed to speak without limitation to *all* sellers and to *all* failures to share knowledge of costly problems. By contrast, a court's reasoning may be more flexible and forgiving, for it will typically draw on authorities, policies, and/or principles that might apply to a wide range of disputes and call for a wide range of outcomes. Thus, *Johnson's* invocation of the importance of "elementary fair conduct" and the obligation not to "take advantage of another's ignorance" may justify one result in the Case of the Visiting Scholar, another in *Malik v. Keiko*, and yet another altogether when a large oil company harasses an elderly farmer until she reluctantly agrees to sell the family farm, all the while keeping mum about the infestation of poisonous snakes slithering in wait next door.

b. Two caveats: Of characterization and candor

We have been speaking thus far as if there is a clear-cut distinction between the "holding" of a case and the "reasoning," but the difference between the two can get fuzzy in the hands of real-world lawyers and judges. There is an old joke about a little boy who gets a toy hammer as a gift and suddenly thinks that everything around him, including his younger sister, is a nail. The same might be said of a lawyer urging a court to "follow precedent" or of a judge insisting that she's doing so: Suddenly everything in the earlier opinion looks like a "holding," and it's just *got* to be followed. And as for lawyers and judges attempting to distinguish a case, suddenly everything in the earlier opinion begins to look a lot less like a holding and a lot more like, well, noise. Interesting noise, perhaps, but in the end just noise and decidedly not necessary to justify the result reached in the earlier decision. As is so often the case, there is a catchy Latin phrase for statements dismissed in this manner: *dicta*. Referring to a proposition from an earlier decision as *dicta* is thus the legal equivalent of the moment in *The Wizard of Oz* when the Wizard exhorts Dorothy and her crew to "pay no attention to that man behind the curtain." Pay no attention to that statement from the earlier decision, says a lawyer or judge calling *dicta*, for the court would have reached the same result even if that particular passage had ended up on the cutting room floor.

The point is that "holding" and "*dicta*" are not only terms we use to describe different aspects of what a court has said in a particular case; they are also tools of advocacy that lawyers and judges deploy in later cases to urge or defend a desired result. To oversimplify only slightly, lawyers and judges describe reasoning that helps them as a "holding" and reasoning that hurts as "mere *dicta*." Thus, turning once again to the Case of the Visiting Scholar, when counsel for the buyer invokes the "thou shalt not take advantage of another's ignorance" language from *Johnson*, she isn't likely to pitch her argument to the court as a "broad interpretation of the precedent based on the court's reasoning in that case." She's going to call it the "holding" of *Johnson* in an effort to convince a later court that it's binding—leaving the court with no choice but to adhere to it now—in a way that "reasoning" and "interpretations" might not be. And of course counsel for the scholar-tenant is going to dismiss the very same language as "mere *dicta*."

What's all this got to do with students preparing for law exams? Just this: When a lawyer or a judge describing an earlier case labels passages from the opinion as "holding" or "*dicta*," you should take that description with a grain of salt and focus instead on the argument the lawyer or the judge is making: Is this a broad or narrow interpretation of the earlier decision? Is the author relying on a term or a phrase with a contestable meaning? Is she emphasizing a cherry-picked purpose when a different purpose—with different implications for the current case—is likewise available? Once you identify the kind of argument the lawyer or judge has made, you'll know where to look for the missing counterargument that will enable you to "get to maybe" in addressing the issue on an exam answer.

And what should *you* call it? That depends, as always, on what the question has asked you to do. If you are asked to "discuss the issues" presented by an exam problem, then you can worry less about calling things holdings or *dicta* and focus instead on the availability of competing interpretations giving rise to contestable issues. If instead you are directed to present an argument for a particular result on behalf of one of the parties to the problem—or to make like a judge and actually decide the case—then characterizing a legal proposition as a "holding" (when you're following a precedent) or "*dicta*" (when you're distinguishing it) can be an important part of the arguments you present. To be sure, if your professor has offered a strong view of whether a particular reading of a precedent is holding or *dicta*, then get on the clue bus and follow suit—though in our experience most law professors, even those with strong points of view, will appreciate and even reward an acknowledgment of what the vanquished counterargument looks like. (We'll have more to say about making the most of a professor's point of view below.)

The analysis thus far has assumed that there are only two things you can do with a precedent: Follow it or distinguish it. But, alas, following a precedent can sometimes be even more complicated than this analysis suggests. One way to follow precedent is simply to "apply" the earlier case to the present facts; another way is to "extend" the earlier case to reach this one. The difference is subtle but important; indeed, it is the sort of difference that can separate a "B" answer from an "A." Assume you are dealing with the Case of the Visiting Scholar on an exam and that the question asks you to serve as the buyer's counsel and to argue the case accordingly. Thus charged, you might draw on a broad interpretation of *Johnson* and argue—as we've just suggested—that "thou shalt not take advantage of another's ignorance" is the "holding" of the earlier case. Accordingly, your argument continues, the resolution of the case is simple and straightforward: Since the scholar-tenant took advantage of the buyer's ignorance, *Johnson's* holding "applies" here and the scholar-tenant is therefore liable for nondisclosure.

But assume instead that *Johnson* contains language specifically limiting the reach of its holding to sellers. (E.g., "Seller offers a 'parade of horribles' that might follow if we impose liability for nondisclosure in this case, predicting a 'slippery slope' that will eventually lead to lawsuits against mortgage companies, tenants, and even the gardener and the young lad who cuts the lawn. But we need not decide today whether other parties with varying degrees of interest in the transaction would be liable for nondisclosure.") In those circumstances, an argument that *Johnson* "applies" to the scholar-tenant is obviously a dog that just won't hunt; he's a tenant, not a seller, and the court expressly declined to decide his case in *Johnson*. There is, in other words, a limit on the ability of lawyers, judges, and especially exam-taking students to call something a "holding," and we are up against that limit here. But an argument that the earlier case should nevertheless be "followed" is by no means foreclosed, for you are still free to contend that the reasoning that moved the *Johnson* court should persuade the court here to confront the issue that *Johnson* avoided and "extend" the principles embraced in the earlier case to reach the scholar-tenant. Indeed, you can turn the carefully cabined issue to your favor, noting that the court itself saw the logical extension of its reasoning to cases such as those involving tenants and avoided going that far out of admirable caution—but not without flagging for readers that the law might be headed in that direction.

Understanding the difference between applying and extending a precedent can thus help you to write exam answers that impress the grader in two ways. First, she'll be impressed by your careful reading of the precedent and by your recognition of the fact that you weren't free simply to "apply" the precedent to the new facts. Second, she'll be impressed that this obstacle didn't prevent you from developing an argument for following the precedent by "extending" it rather than merely "applying" it.

Enough, then, about using the text of a case to identify and construct competing interpretations for exam problems. Let's turn now to another equally important source of material from which to fashion alternative approaches to tough issues.

2. Your professor says so

We've said it before and we'll say it again: Most professors work hard to test what they teach. Accordingly, if your professor devotes class time to offering and/or critiquing a particular interpretation of one of the cases she's assigned, don't be surprised if she fashions an exam problem designed to give students the opportunity to deploy those arguments in the analysis of a concrete dispute. If she's teaching *Johnson*, for example, she might take the position that the disclosure obligation imposed on the seller should apply only to parties with a "cognizable financial interest" in the sale, such as real estate brokers and mortgage holders. Students who bring the professor's interpretation to bear in the analysis of an exam problem like the Case of the Visiting Scholar will be miles ahead of answers that proceed as if *Johnson* readily applies to anyone privy to undisclosed defects and that blithely overlook the possibility of a "cognizable financial interest" limit.

At the same time, don't be surprised if the exam problem presents facts that test the limits of the professor's theory. The interests of our scholar-tenant in the sale of the rental unit, for example, are hardly "financial" in the same sense as that of a broker or mortgage company, but the impending sale nevertheless portends significant consequences for him, and at least some of those consequences (like the cost of moving) can be measured in dollars and cents. In this setting, we urge you to take the professor's reading of the precedent "seriously but not literally," for the vast majority of law professors we know would welcome a thoughtful critique of a position they've advocated in class. Indeed, most of us would vastly prefer respectful disagreement to a robotic repetition of material taken verbatim from lecture. But whether you "follow" or attempt to "distinguish" the professor's views of a case, you'll get points for recognizing their implications for your exam problems. Taking those views seriously enough to identify and defend a different way of reading the precedent may get you more points still.

Another important source for arguments about the interpretation of precedent can be found in the readings for the course—in particular, the notes following an opinion reproduced in the casebook or a scholarly essay assigned in connection with a particular case or line of cases. Casebook notes frequently recount the reception of the lead case in later decisions and/or other jurisdictions and frequently identify differing approaches courts take to interpreting the original case. Your professor will be well aware of those differing approaches and—especially if she flagged them during lecture or Socratic dialogue—they may well be tested by an exam problem that would come out different ways in different jurisdictions. Scholarly essays (or extended excerpts from same) frequently amplify a "take" on a case offered by the professor in class or a viewpoint she sees as important and with which she may or may not agree. If she's taken the trouble of assigning the essay—and, again, especially if she has talked about it in class—chances are that she considers the viewpoint important enough to test on the final.

In Chapter Eleven, we'll have more to say about how to make the best use of class and reading notes in a course outline, but we want to take the time here to offer an "exam prep tip" in specific reference to the cases assigned for a class: Resist the temptation to attempt a mashup of materials—the text of the decision, the professor's in-class comments, the notes following the decision in the casebook, etc.—into a single rule or idea that attempts to smooth over the different interpretations and approaches suggested by the various sources. A law exam typically tests for such differences, and not for some lowest common denominator or tweet length version of a so-called bottom line. A study plan that ignores the continuing contestation over what the law is and where it's going will not get you to the top of the class.

3. Fact-driven policy analysis ("Just add reasons")

Recall the "*really* narrow interpretation" of *Johnson* offered earlier—i.e., the argument that the case applies only to defects of the same magnitude as the roofing disaster in that case and not to minor problems that plague almost every home. Where did that interpretation come from? The *Johnson* court didn't stress the poor condition of the roof in its holding or reasoning—indeed, in the pertinent portion of the opinion, it didn't discuss the roof at all—and we weren't working from class notes or supplementary readings from our own legal education, since we both graduated well before the decision in *Johnson*. Instead, we made a move that lawyers make all the time: We took a deep dive into the facts of *Johnson*, comparing it with the Case of the Visiting Scholar and searching not just for facts that loom large in the court's analysis but also for other facts giving rise to significant similarities to or differences from the exam problem.

Once again, some facts matter and some don't, and once again the difference is determined by how we interpret the precedent. Accordingly, when you identify potentially significant factual similarities ("Hey, both cases involve water coming inside a house after a heavy rain") or differences ("Hey, the defect in *Johnson* is a major deal and the defects in the exam problem are seemingly far less so")—but those facts didn't feature prominently in the court's analysis—you'll need to come up with an interpretation of the precedent *on your own* to support the claim that these facts matter. If that sounds like too daunting a task, there is a simpler way to put it: Just add reasons! We've devoted an entire chapter to the "reasons" lawyers come up with in situations like this—see Chapter Fourteen ("Policy Czars"). Moreover, coming up with them on your own will get easier as you make your way through law school, and we'll offer a quick illustration here.

Consider the factual similarity mentioned parenthetically above between *Johnson* and the Case of the Visiting Scholar: Both cases involve water coming inside a house after a heavy rain. Try as we might, we can't come up with a plausible reason for treating "water" as a fact that mattered to the outcome of *Johnson*. Surely the case would have been decided the same way if the "invading force" in question were smoke, insects, mold, heat in the summer, cold in the winter, or anything else that does not belong inside a house and may well ruin things that do. But now consider the factual difference between the two cases likewise mentioned parenthetically above: The defect in *Johnson* is a major deal, and the defects in the Visiting Scholar problem are comparatively small-bore. That difference might provide a lawyer with a reason justifying different results in the two cases that would go something like this: Problems of the magnitude of roof leaks plaguing multiple rooms are typically known to sellers and, in any event, presumably rare among houses on the market. Affording a buyer a cause of action for nondisclosure of such defects can ensure justice in the relatively rare case without calling into question thousands of other real estate transactions. But affording a cause of action for smaller problems like those known to the scholar-tenant might well cause a flood not of water but of litigation, opening for controversy countless "done deals," destabilizing the housing market, crowding court dockets, and eventually bringing Civilization As We Know It to a bitter end. The last prediction is a bit over the top, obviously, but we include it to make the point that finding plausible "reasons" that facts might matter can actually be a bit of fun once you get the hang of it.

When we first started reading cases in law school, we (like most first-year students) tended to focus on the "law" portions of an opinion at the expense of everything else—"Hey, this isn't the University of Connecticut School of Facts!" a favorite student of ours once cracked—and it took practice and discipline to learn to pay as much attention to the factual details as to the holding and other grand pronouncements of the deciding courts. But experienced lawyers will tell you that "the facts" are where they live, and you give those short shrift—either in practice or on law school exams—at your peril.

D. Dealing with Multiple Cases

In the discussion thus far, we've been proceeding as if there's only one precedent that might govern an exam problem, but often this will not be the case. As we wrap up the chapter, we'll address two common situations in which lawyers and law students alike must grapple with multiple precedents at the same time. First, we'll talk about problems governed by a "line of cases" rather than a single precedent; then we'll talk about situations in which precedents pointing in different directions appear to govern a single problem.

1. Dealing with a line of cases

Recall our earlier discussion of *Griswold v. Connecticut*, the Supreme Court decision from the 1960s striking down a state law prohibiting contraceptive use as applied to a married heterosexual couple. Narrow interpretations of the case might have permitted states to enforce a contraceptive prohibition against unmarried persons or to regulate reproductive choices freely once pregnancy occurs. Over the course of the ensuing decades, however, the Court gave *Griswold* steadily broader readings, extending constitutional protection to the unmarried as well as to reproductive choices more generally, including the right to abortion. Broader still is the Court's more recent recognition of a robust right of intimate association, the basis for decisions condemning state laws that criminalize sodomy as well those denying same-sex couples the right to marry. Yet, as the Court's 2022 decision in *Dobbs v. Jackson Women's Health Organization* so vividly illustrated, judicial trends need not proceed in a straight line; and in that case the Court took a sharp turn in a different direction, eliminating the right to abortion and perhaps calling into question the continuing vitality of *Griswold* and the rest of its progeny.

A professor teaching this material may well decide to test it via an exam problem pitting state regulatory power against a right to engage in reproductive choices or intimate relations not yet addressed by the Court—human cloning, for example, or polyamory. Faced with such a problem, what's a student to do? We'll start with some reassuring news. A professor who teaches a particular "line" or "sequence" of cases—a "case thread," in the parlance of social media—is quite likely to explore "what's next?" scenarios via class discussion and/or assigned readings, so chances are high that the dispute presented by the exam problem won't come as a complete surprise. Moreover, it's likely that lecture and class discussion will have explored different ways to read the sequence, and a successful exam answer will obviously take "competing interpretations" emphasized in class as a starting point for analysis, if not necessarily as the final word.

Beyond that, broad generalizations about the way to approach this kind of exam problem are difficult to come by, since every line of cases has its own history, trajectory, and inflection points. But we can offer two suggestions that are likely to be useful in most case-thread settings and then one that is specific to courses in constitutional law. In terms of general advice, we start by urging you to focus your analysis on the scenario presented by the exam problem and to avoid the temptation of merely regurgitating the pertinent portion of your outline or parroting your lecture notes. The exam answers that are likely to succeed are those that use the facts presented by the problem as the lens through which to interpret the relevant case law, and, simply put, different problems are likely to bring different features of the thread into focus. (To continue with *Griswold*, an answer grappling with the regulation of human cloning is likely to emphasize the reproductive autonomy cases, whereas an answer responding to restrictions on polyamory is likely to emphasize the right of intimate association cases.)

The second general suggestion is that the same "competing interpretations" techniques we've described elsewhere in this chapter are available here as well, though in this setting you can apply them not only to individual precedents but also to the entire line of cases and/or to particular clusters of cases within the sequence. At first blush, this may sound like a recipe for way too much complexity, but we aren't suggesting that you deploy all or even most of these techniques at the same time. Rather, our point is that with this many sources of possible ambiguity, you are much more likely to find at least one that addresses the exam problem in a way that will impress the grader. To illustrate again with *Griswold*, if the problem presents a legal restriction on cloning, you might want to analyze it through a "competing meanings" analysis of the term "reproduction" in the reproductive autonomy cases, since "cloning" is literally "human reproduction," but—at least as of this writing—it's not an easy fit in the common understanding of what we mean by that term. And if instead the exam problem presents a legal restriction on polyamory, you might analyze it through competing interpretations of the intimate association case cluster, reading the cases narrowly to protect common variations on the traditional marital dyad vs. reading them more broadly to cover a multiplicity of forms of intimate human association as well.

It's not coincidental that the example we've been using thus far is a case thread from Constitutional Law, for that's the first-year course in which students are most likely to encounter and study "lines of cases." To be sure, there are famous case threads in other courses, but as it happens most of them represent topics with rules established by constitutional law (e.g., the takings cases in Property, the defamation cases in Torts, the personal jurisdiction cases in Civ Pro, and the confrontation of witnesses cases in Evidence). Despite these appearances, however, the "line of cases" is by no means unique to Con Law; indeed, when you research problems in legal practice, you will discover case threads in virtually every area of the law. But the reason students are less likely to encounter them outside of Con Law is that most law schools offer courses on the first-year common law subjects (Contracts, Torts, and Property) that "nationalize" the law, emphasizing the Restatement and so-called "majority rules," and presenting key cases from multiple jurisdictions. Accordingly, there is seldom an occasion to do a deep dive into the historical development of a particular doctrine within a particular jurisdiction.*

Here's what difference this makes for exam prep purposes. A central feature of contemporary constitutional law, and accordingly a central feature of most contemporary Con Law courses, is the view held by many American judges and legal academics that there is one "right" way to go about interpreting the U.S. Constitution, and there is a vigorous debate within the field about what that "right" way is. There are competing schools of thought on the topic, and the leading contenders are originalism and its proliferating spawn (contemporaneous public meaning, originalism "plus," and originalism lite); living constitutionalism; "common good" constitutionalism; and several varieties of functionalism. Your professor is likely to explore these approaches in some detail and may well identify others as well. She is therefore likely to devise exam questions that test these theories to see what difference they make in the resolution of a particular constitutional conflict. She might, for example, offer a problem calling for competing interpretations of *Griswold* and its progeny and expect you not only to recognize that there is more than one way to read the line of cases but also to match the interpretations with competing schools of thought. We'll have more to say about this in Chapter Thirteen, where we talk more generally about exam-taking and what to do with legal issues once you find them. But our point for now is that you should resist the temptation to dismiss schools of thought talk during class as irrelevant to your studies ("This is philosophy or maybe political science, but it's not *law*," the skeptic might think), for if your

---

* For the record, this wasn't always the case in American legal education. In the olden days, the common law subjects were taught as full-year courses at most schools, and there was much more class time to devote to each subject. As a result, professors and casebooks alike had the luxury of "going deep" and exploring case-threads on particular topics — e.g., the pre-U.C.C. indefiniteness cases in Contracts. With the advent of the single-semester common law course in the 1980s, however, professors teaching these courses began to feel pressure to go "wide" rather than "deep" with respect to the individual topics covered.

professor devotes significant time to teaching them, chances are good she'll be testing them too.

2. Competing, clashing, and interlocking precedents

In your Criminal Procedure class—or in Con Law, if your law school's version of the course features a unit on the criminal procedure provisions of the Bill of Rights—you will almost surely encounter the famous case of *Terry v. Ohio*, decided by the United States Supreme Court in 1968. In *Terry*, the Court held that a police officer does not have to comply with the Fourth Amendment's "probable cause" requirement in order to "stop and frisk" a potential suspect, so long as the officer "has reason to believe that he is dealing with an *armed and dangerous* individual" (emphasis added). Despite considerable controversy over "stop and frisk" policing—and considerable criticism of its racial impacts in particular—*Terry* has been "good law" ever since. Or at least it was until the Court decided *District of Columbia v. Heller* and, more recently, *New York State Rifle & Pistol Ass'n v. Bruen*, which taken together recognize an individual right under the Second Amendment to venture out in public while "armed and dangerous." Okay, we're kidding about the "dangerous" part, but if you put yourself in the shoes of a police officer initiating a "stop and frisk" encounter, you might well think that an individual is "dangerous" precisely *because* he is "armed." And so in the aftermath of *Heller* and *Bruen*, legal scholars and courts alike can be expected to struggle with the question of whether an officer can perform the "stop and frisk" authorized by *Terry* solely on the basis of a reasonable suspicion that the targeted individual may be bearing arms, since doing so is now constitutionally protected activity.

The apparent conflict between *Terry* and *Heller/Bruen* may well be settled by the time you read this, but our point in raising it here is that conflicts of this sort arise all the time and in virtually every area of American law. Sometimes they arise because contemporaneous understandings about the state of the law when an earlier case was decided are rejected by a later case. (When *Terry* was decided, for example, the conventional wisdom among legal thinkers was that the Second Amendment governed the maintenance of state militias and did not create an individual right to bear arms, an assumption upended by *Heller*.) Sometimes they arise not because of any inherent conflict between two decisions but because one of them spurs a line of cases that eventually winds its way into conflict with the other. (The 1991 Supreme Court decision in *Gilmer v. Interstate/Johnson Lane Corp.*, approving employment agreements mandating the arbitration of individual employment disputes, for example, triggered a sequence of cases that eventually came into conflict with older decisions involving collective bargaining and various rights under the National Labor Relations Act.) Sometimes the logic of a groundbreaking precedent calls into question all sorts of practices that were previously lawful, however problematic from a moral or ethical standpoint. (Consider, for example, *Bostock v. Clayton County*, the Supreme Court's recent decision that discrimination in employment against LGBT persons constitutes discrimination "on the basis of sex" prohibited by Title VII and the challenges likely to be mounted against precedents under a multitude of statutes with similarly worded prohibitions.) And sometimes a new practice or problem arises in the political, commercial, or social world that brings two previously unrelated cases or lines of cases into sharp and sudden contention. (Consider, for example, *U.S. Term Limits v. Thornton* (1995), where the Court had to decide whether to classify a term-limits statute as a "ballot access" measure under a line of cases granting broad leeway to such restrictions or as an additional "qualification" for public office under a line of cases sharply limiting such restrictions.)

These situations by no means exhaust the possible scenarios giving rise to "competing precedents," but they should provide you with a feel for the way cases interact with one another and a sense of the frequency with which this occurs in American law. Whatever the particular provenance of the conflict in question, though, our advice with respect to tackling it in the exam context is similar to the advice we gave with respect to exam problems that test a line of cases. First, when a conflict between precedents threatens to upend long-standing and/or important precedents in a field, chances are excellent that your professor will have highlighted the impending clash in class and carefully rehearsed and evaluated the arguments supporting different resolutions. Your class notes as well as any related readings the professor assigns will thus be your most important sources in preparing to identify and deal with the material in the context of an exam problem. Second, as usual, it's wise to present the best arguments you can muster on each side of the conflict, and if the professor has revealed a strong preference for a particular resolution, be sure to give her view a full and energetic articulation even as you canvass the arguments that point in another direction.

Finally, you can sometimes argue your way to a resolution of "competing precedents" by "interpretation and retreat" rather than annihilation. Thus, for example, as things stand as this book goes to press, it's possible that the potential conflict between *Terry* and *Heller/Bruen* might be minimized by emphasizing *Heller* and *Bruen*'s explicit recognition that firearms may be restricted in public spaces such as courthouses, government buildings, and perhaps subways and buses. If such spaces end up including parks and heavily trafficked streets, then maybe *Terry* will remain operative in most of the places where encounters between officers and members of the public take place. But a further consequence of such a reading of *Heller/Bruen* is the one that invariably flows when the Court channels King Solomon rather than declaring a winner, for it would spawn a multitude of disputes testing the boundary between "regular places" where guns must now generally be allowed and "special places" where firearms possession may be curtailed—e.g., with respect to police encounters in Times Square, at sports stadiums, outside schools, etc. We discuss strategies for identifying and handling disputes over such "competing domains" in Chapter Ten on "cascading forks."

Chapter Nine

Forks in the Facts

If we were writing an introduction to legal reasoning, or, more daunting still, a book on legal theory, we would now devote a lengthy section to explaining the difference between what we are calling "forks in the law" and what we want to discuss next, "forks in the facts." As we have explained, our legal system has so many different sources of law (statutes vs. common law, multiple jurisdictions, conflicting precedents, etc.) that it's often difficult to tell from consulting available legal materials exactly which source governs under what circumstances. Moreover, even when you have only one statute or case that seems controlling, there are typically a number of plausible interpretations available. Once again, then, it's often just not clear what the law is. Exam questions that require discussion of different rules, cases, or interpretations present what we've been referring to as "forks in the law."

If you've had more than a week or two of law school classes, however, it will come as no surprise that even when the disputing parties agree on the governing law, and even on a particular interpretation of that law, plenty remains for them to argue about. A significant number—indeed, we would guess a majority—of actual legal disputes turn not on questions of what the law is, but on questions of how the law actually *applies* to a particular case. Both parties may agree, for example, that an antidiscrimination statute prohibits gender discrimination in employment. But the employer may argue that denying a promotion to an aggrieved employee had nothing to do with discrimination, while the employee may vehemently disagree. We call such disputes about the application of law to particular situations "forks in the facts." In this chapter, we will explain why the act of applying the law to particular facts frequently gives rise to ambiguity, and we will once again map out patterns of "forks" you will encounter in law practice and, more to the point, on law school exams.

We can't emphasize enough, however, that the terminology itself doesn't matter one bit to the prospects of success on a law exam, where the point is to identify as many important issues as you can and to present the most persuasive arguments available for their resolution. Our book is designed to help you "spot" these issues by revealing the patterns in which they occur. We think the "forks" terminology can assist students in seeing and understanding those patterns. But in the context of an exam, it would be a complete waste of precious time to spend even a moment worrying about whether a particular issue is a fork in the law, a fork in the facts, or just a fork in the GPA of the law student suffering through the ordeal.

A. Where "Forks in the Facts" Come From: Categories and the Law

You can't begin to see why law school exams generate vexing problems of law application until you grasp the importance of categories to legal disputes. We'll start, then, with a simple vignette to contrast the difference between ordinary and legal conversations. Imagine you and a group of friends are gathered together thinking about where to go to lunch. One friend, Tony, says he's dying for a plate of pasta and suggests you head to an Italian restaurant. Another friend, Spanky, says he's in the mood for a diner. A third friend, Solomon, offers a concrete suggestion. "Why don't we go to Joe's Place?" he says. Joe's Place, it turns out, is just around the corner. It has booths with red vinyl benches, jukeboxes at each table, and red-and-white-checkered tablecloths. It serves hamburgers, fries, malteds and sandwiches, but the house specialties are various pasta dishes with delicious homemade sauce. The right half of the menu is printed in Italian, and pictures of Frank Sinatra, Joe DiMaggio, James Gandolfini, and Al Pacino are on the walls.

If your friends are anything like ours, the suggestion of Joe's Place will shift the focus of attention away from the type of restaurant and onto the pros and cons of the particular venue. Both Tony and Spanky are likely now to think about whether they would be happy eating at Joe's. Admittedly, Solomon's suggestion might not do the trick. Tony might say he doesn't like the pasta dishes there. Spanky might say the sandwiches aren't up to snuff. This will be a concrete dispute about the quality of particular features at Joe's Place. But it's unlikely that Tony would say something like, "I love the pasta at Joe's Place, but I really wanted to go to an Italian restaurant, and it's not really Italian." If he did, everyone else would think he was overly rigid, if not a bit nuts. The same would be true if Spanky raved about Joe's food yet resisted the selection because "it's not really a diner."

Unlike ordinary conversation, legal disputes will often pair opposing parties arguing about things like whether Joe's Place is really an "Italian restaurant" or really a "diner." Recall how the debate over whether a tricycle is a "vehicle" seemed determinative of whether the trike was allowed in the park. That's because legal rules often divide the world into categories, with one set of legal consequences applying to one category and a different set of consequences applying to a second category. Homeowners, for example, may owe a higher degree of care to invitees than they do to trespassers. Suppose, however, that I see a dangerous situation on your property and enter, uninvited, to provide assistance. Let's say I fear your child will fall into the backyard pool. If I'm hurt on the way in because I step on a sharp object among the detritus strewn throughout your yard, I might sue you to recover for my injuries. Outside the legal context, people might simply argue about whether I made the right call by dashing in to save your youngster—was he really in danger of drowning, or am I just the town busybody?

Rather than confronting such questions head-on, common law courts often respond to this situation by invoking the governing legal categories and letting them do all the work. Thus, if the court determines that I was a "trespasser," then the law says that I was just taking my chances with respect to hazards in your yard. But if the court determines that I was an "invitee," then the law says you owed me a duty of keeping the premises reasonably safe. Arguments respectively supporting the "trespasser" category (I entered the premises uninvited) and the "invitee" category (I was responding to a perceived emergency) will be the focus of the court's inquiry, and your liability for my injuries will turn entirely on the results of category placement rather than a "cut to the chase" analysis of whether I did the right thing by dashing in or whether your yard was an accident waiting to happen. This kind of problem forms the core of countless legal disputes—and of even more exam questions.

Again, if this were a book on legal reasoning, we would provide a detailed description of why the law tends to create and rely on categories. For our purposes, the simple explanation is that the notion of the rule of law has a sequential component. People want the law to be established *before* the disputed conduct occurs. Lawmakers cannot imagine every situation that might occur and devise a rule for each in advance. But the law can group activities into broad categories and establish rules covering each one. The categories give the public advance notice with respect to the law's basic content and reduce the sense that individual disputes are resolved by rules that are made up after the fact. And judges who appeal to categories already in place appear to have less room for arbitrary or biased decisions than those who are told simply to reach a fair result.

In this book, we aren't interested in whether this simple defense of law's categories is persuasive. Some of your professors may devote time to discussion about whether the law's reliance on categories really achieves larger objectives such as legitimacy, predictability, and reduced bias. But every practicing lawyer would agree that the law uses categories all the time. What we'll focus on in this chapter is where all these categories come from and how they give rise to "forks in the facts" that form the core of so many law school exam questions.

B. Oh, the Places You'll Find the Law's Categories

We start here by identifying and describing the many settings in which the law uses categories to distinguish one set of legal consequences from another. As you take your exams, you'll need to be on the lookout for these as "hiding" places for "forks in the facts." In Part C, we'll show you the ways in which professors craft exam problems that "straddle" the law's categories, creating factual ambiguities you can exploit as you draft your answers.

1. Rule vs. exception

There is perhaps no more common legal formulation than having a particular area of law governed by a basic rule but then permitting exceptions that apply to certain unusual situations. The general rule under the commerce clause is that a state cannot alter the flow of commerce in ways that favor its own citizens over those of other states. But there is an exception for those situations in which the state acts as a "market participant" and not a "market regulator." The general rule is that the prosecution can't use evidence the police have discovered during a warrantless search. But there may be an exception if the evidence was in the officer's "plain view" at the time it was seized. The general rule is that there is no duty to rescue, but there is an exception if the person refusing to give aid played a role in creating the peril. The general rule is that a landowner may exclude strangers from her property. But if the landowner invites the general public in (let's say to gamble at a casino or shop at a mall), then the law may invoke an exception that requires the owner to admit people she'd sooner keep out (let's say card counters or leafleteers).

A standard exam technique is to generate a situation in which it is unclear whether the general rule or the exception applies. If you consider the categories in our examples, it's easy to see how this can be done. It's often hard to say whether a state is regulating or participating in a market; whether evidence really was in plain view; whether the party failing to rescue helped generate the peril of the person in distress; or whether the landowner's invitation to the public was sufficiently general to trigger the exception. Such problems make good exam questions.

2. Statutory boundaries

Terms in statutes typically create categories that determine whether the statute applies. Article II of the Uniform Commercial Code, for example, governs the "sale of goods." Let's say you hire me to cater a party. You identify the dishes you want and leave the rest to me, including selecting recipes, shopping for ingredients, prepping the food (using your kitchen, utensils, pantry staples, and dishware), and serving it in the order you've requested to your guests. After all that, a dispute arises. Since the Code has many provisions favoring buyers over sellers, you may argue that I've sold you food, and, since food is a good, you'll contend the Code applies. In contrast, I'll argue that you hired me to perform "services," which are not governed by the Code. Or, to take another example, suppose I sell you a customer list. That's clearly a sale; but is it a "good" within the meaning of the Code?

Consider also the case of statutes prohibiting discrimination in "places of public accommodation." It's often unclear whether a particular establishment fits the statutory definition. Is a "members only" country club a place of public accommodation? Would it make a difference if city officials often met there for business lunches? What if local service organizations held monthly meetings in the clubhouse? Would the definition of "place of public accommodation" extend to a community reading group that meets weekly at the home of one of the participants?

There are few more common exam techniques than requiring you to read statutory language carefully to determine whether the facts at hand fall within or outside of the categories established by the statute.

3. Sequential categories

Many areas of law are organized based on a sequence of events. At some "magic moment" in the sequence, events will have proceeded far enough that the law will shift the transaction from one category into another. In contract law, for example, buyer and seller may discuss terms that might form the basis of a contract between them. As long as the language is sufficiently noncommittal, however, the law will characterize the conversation as "preliminary negotiations." Once one party commits to a particular set of terms, however, the law may characterize what he proposes as "an offer." If the other party accepts, a binding contract will be formed.

In criminal law, we see a similar structure. A deranged individual can sit in his attic all day long plotting how to kill his spouse. He can write his plans in his personal journal and draw pictures about how the crime might take place. All these activities the law might characterize as mere preparations. Once, however, the potential murderer engages in an "overt act" toward completion of the crime—let's say putting poison into a bottle of Champagne he knows his spouse plans to drink next week—then the law may characterize his activities as "attempted murder."

Drafting a problem with facts that leave you in doubt as to whether you've made the move from one legal category to another is yet one more classic exam-writing technique.

4. Crossing the line

The metaphor of proceeding step by step from one category into another is sufficiently powerful that lawyers speak of "crossing the line" even when the categories at issue are not sequential. In contract law, for example, it may be that what distinguishes a mere inquiry ("Any chance you'd consider selling your watch? I think it might be worth at least $1,000.") from an offer ("Will you sell me your watch for $1,000?") is the nature of the language used rather than some "magic moment" in a sequential chain. Sexual harassment cases force courts to distinguish between clueless banter and unwelcome sexual advances, and a supervisor might "cross the line" with an employee during their first encounter as easily as slowly building to unlawful conduct after a series of increasingly problematic interactions. The critical inquiry in such cases is whether a particular statement or act falls within the category in question (is this an offer? is this sexual harassment?) rather than whether a sequence of events has reached a tipping point. Notably, however, the language we use to describe the two situations is often the same: Did the party "go too far"? In either setting, you can expect to find exam questions that ask you whether particular conduct "crosses the line."

5. Categories as elements of legal rules: Running the gauntlet

One of our favorite Torts teachers offered students a comforting summary early in the semester to help relieve exam anxiety. Four words, he would stress, are all you need to make a good start in answering any Torts question. Those four words are *duty, breach, cause,* and *harm.* This is still sound advice, since virtually any tort suit will require the plaintiff to prove each of these elements, even if the particular content of the respective elements (e.g., the nature of the duty, species of compensable harm, etc.) can vary from tort to tort. More important for our purposes, the "four words" refrain can be generalized into a winning strategy for exam success.

Many areas of the law require a party to prove multiple elements to make out a claim or a defense. Criminal law, for example, typically requires the government to prove a specified list of the "elements" of an alleged crime. These might include "intent," "an overt act," and "causation of the forbidden result." In property law, a common definition of adverse possession requires the claimant to prove "actual possession" of the disputed acreage and that such possession was "adverse or hostile, open and notorious, continuous, exclusive, and for the time period required by statute in the jurisdiction."

Notice how the party with the burden of proof must satisfy each and every element to make out the claim. So it doesn't matter if the government can show intent and harm if there is no proof of an overt act. (If I sit alone in my house wishing my friend would die, and my friend drops dead of a heart attack, I may be a horrible person but I've committed no crime.) We call this kind of legal structure "running the gauntlet" to remind students that *each* element must be satisfied. (This contrasts with a multifactor analysis, which is more like a recipe for a vegetable stew: The absence of a particular ingredient won't spoil the dish, since it's the overall mix that's crucial. Nuisance law, where courts weigh all the surrounding circumstances, is a good example of a multifactor "stew.")

Now consider how wonderful "gauntlet running" is for exam writers. Your professor may view it as a personal challenge to see if she can write a question in which there is doubt about each of the multiple elements of a particular doctrine. And take our word for it, she can. So when you find somewhat far-fetched exam scenarios that occur on deserted islands, this may be a byproduct of your professor's taking a doctrine like adverse possession (an exam favorite) and testing her creativity. Can remote ocean locations really be possessed openly and notoriously? If boats come ashore every now and then, does this destroy exclusivity? If the marooned island dweller sticks to the beach, does she possess the inner acreage of the island? If the castaway departs the island for several weeks at a time—perhaps visiting nearby islands via homemade raft—does this undermine her claim of continuous possession? As we'll explain further in our chapter on writing exam answers, there's a tendency when you see an ambiguity in one part of the story (is possession actual?) to assume you have scoped out the whole question. But doctrines structured as a series of elements provide multiple opportunities for hard issues, so don't stop until you've "run the gauntlet."

6. Open-ended or "evaluative" categories

Classic issue-spotting exam questions get much of their mileage from legal categories that share a common border (e.g., preliminary negotiations vs. offer; residential vs. commercial lease). We would be remiss, however, if we failed to mention the many situations in which the law places an evaluative label on a party's behavior, and lawyers (and hence law students) are expected to argue whether that evaluative label applies or not. Here, it's not so much whether one of two labels (preliminary negotiations vs. offer) is applicable (a or b?), but whether a single, more open-ended label governs *at all* (yes or no?). Contract law often imposes an obligation to perform in "good faith." So an exam scenario may expect you to characterize a party's action as in good faith or not. Tort law often imposes an obligation to act as a "reasonable" person. So an exam may expect you to argue about whether particular conduct was or was not reasonable. Nuisance law requires the plaintiff to show substantial harm. So, is the harm at issue "substantial"? What you'll need to do on exam questions like this is work to identify the facts in the problem supporting a claim that the action was in "good faith"; that the behavior was "reasonable"; that the harm was "substantial." And, equally important, which facts cut the other way?

C. How Professors Construct Exam Problems That Straddle Legal Categories

We imagine many of you reading the previous section have a nagging objection to the whole endeavor. Sure, you can see that law divides things into categories and that determining which category governs is often crucial to outcomes. But what you want to know is why figuring out which category applies is such a mystery. Why aren't the law's categories sufficiently clear and determinative to enable easy application, thus permitting you to ignore all this "maybe" business and focus your energies instead on learning the rules that create the categories in the first place? In this section, we hope to demonstrate that despite the best efforts of judges and lawyers alike—or, more likely, precisely *because* of those efforts—doubts about proper categorization will be with us as long as we have law. We will detail many sources of ambiguity so you'll know exactly what to look for in the complex fact patterns that will appear on your exams.

I. Facts on both sides of a boundary

Think back to our story about the Italian restaurant and the diner. Notice how we included facts that made Joe's Place sound like a diner (booths, jukeboxes, malteds) as well as facts that made it sound Italian (wall photos, menu language, pasta dishes). This is an extraordinarily typical technique when drafting an exam question. The professor will take two well-established legal categories and write a story in which some facts point toward one and some point toward the other. And, we might add, the professors here are taking their cues from real life. There's just no reason to expect that actual human behavior will occur along the precise boundaries of legal categories, especially when those doing the behaving (or the misbehaving) aren't trained lawyers and know nothing about the legal categories at issue. Your job, then, is to see how the exam facts produce ambiguity and make the arguments for one characterization as well as the other.

In Property, you might get a landlord-tenant question involving an unrenovated loft used as a music studio, where the outcome depends on whether the lease is governed by residential or commercial rules. The teenage musicians might actually be living there with the landlord's knowledge and tacit consent. (He may have given them a key to the building for after-hours use denied to other tenants.) But the building may be otherwise commercial, and the space may have no kitchen facilities. The heat may be turned off at midnight. Yet there might be a shower in the loft space. The lease might have the words Commercial Lease written across the top in big letters. In sum, there are facts that support the "residential" lease characterization and facts that suggest a "commercial" transaction. So you need to be prepared to argue in both directions.

In Contracts, your exam might contain a lengthy letter from a seller to a buyer. The letter begins, "We would be willing to consider an agreement on the following terms." This sounds like preliminary negotiations, because the seller proposes merely to "consider" an agreement and commits to nothing. Yet the same letter may contain a great deal of detail and close with: "It is vital that you let us know immediately whether these terms are acceptable to you, so we can begin our own procurement efforts." This sounds a lot more like an offer. Since there are facts on both sides of the preliminary negotiations vs. offer line, you'll find yourself drawing on the quoted language to argue each way. Indeed, in the following sections you'll see that such linguistic ambiguities are often a source of "forks in the facts," especially when the language in question is used by a layperson rather than a lawyer.

2. Differing perspectives

It may be that the story told in an exam question looks different from the standpoint of different actors. Recall Patron's offer to pay Artiste $10,000 to paint a portrait, where the issue was whether the preliminary sketchwork was "mere preparations" or the "beginning of performance." From Patron's perspective, the deal is literally for a portrait, and thus the fact that no paint has touched the final canvas may suggest performance has not begun. Yet Artiste's understanding of what a portrait entails— born of many years of artistry—may lead her to conclude that doing the sketches is very much part of the deal, maybe even the hardest part. (Think about a paper you wrote for school where you had done all the research and even prepared an outline but hadn't actually begun drafting. You would certainly say you had started the paper. Yet a professor demanding a 25-page paper might well give you zero credit if you turned in nothing but the outline and research notes.) So, even when exam facts are undisputed, the conflicting perspectives of the parties may make it unclear whether they fall in one legal category or another.

Conflicting perspectives may also result from racial, gender, and other differences between the parties, particularly when those differences are associated with the social dynamics of subjugation and marginalization. Consider a university that insists on handing out scholarship forms personally to students so that the financial aid official can tell each applicant directly that only those with a B average are eligible to receive university funds. How likely would it be for white students to receive this message face to face and wonder whether this was specifically directed at them because the white official doubted their capacity to perform acceptably? How likely (and we might add how understandable) would it be for a Black student to have such concerns? The financial aid officer might use exactly the same words in each case, but they might be experienced very differently.

What does this have to do with sorting out facts in a legal dispute or on an exam? For one thing, language may provide a window into state of mind, and the statements of a party are often the best evidence available in antidiscrimination cases and other settings in which the invidious motive or intent of the speaker is a critical element of a claim. For another, in some areas of the law—e.g., sexual harassment—the language itself may give rise to legal consequences. In either context, differences in perspective between the speaker and the spoken-to are a common source of ambiguity. What evidently passes as harmless banter or "locker room talk" among at least some heterosexual cisgender men—or so we hear—is likely to land very differently on others subjected to such talk in the workplace. Indeed, this frequently recurring "fork in the facts" in the sexual harassment context has given rise to a parallel "fork in the law," as some courts evaluating the language at issue have replaced the law's ubiquitous "reasonable person" test with the perspective of a "reasonable woman."

Other power differentials between the parties may give rise to similar ambiguities. Suppose a supervisor is speaking with an employee who is active in union organizing and has recently gotten married. He says to her, "Congratulations, and in your position it's a really good thing you got married." If the law prohibits anti-union "threats" made by employers, is this a "threat?" The supervisor may say he was teasing and merely trying to congratulate her on her good fortune in a humorous way. Yet the employee may see this as a not-so-subtle reference to organizing activity made by someone in a position to fire her for engaging in it: It's good she got married because she's going to need someone to support her when she's out of a job.

Likewise, consider the famous case of *Anderson v. Backlund* from contract law, in which a tenant farmer in arrears on the rent was urged by the landlord to "make some money" by tripling the number of cattle on the property. When the tenant expressed concern about doing so given the risks of drought, the landlord responded, "Never mind the water, John, I will see there will be plenty of water because it never failed in Minnesota yet." From the landlord's perspective, this reassurance might be seen as merely an effort to encourage the tenant to undertake a course of action that would enable the latter to pay rent already owed. From the perspective of the tenant—who may well have been reluctant to rebuff a course of action urged by someone who could evict him at the drop of a hat—this might be understood as a promise by the landlord that there would be "plenty of water" for the thirsty herd. The punch line is that the lesson many of us learned early on from our parents—that "there are two sides to every story"—is seldom more apt than in the context of a dispute arising out of a difference in power or other perspective between the parties.

3. The snapshot vs. the film

Often the facts may be characterized in different ways depending on whether you view an event at one moment in time or as part of a longer, ongoing narrative. The most striking example of this phenomenon we've ever seen was a story presented on a television news show. The reporter opened by describing an automobile accident in which a white driver seemingly traveling at a safe speed and obeying all traffic laws ran down and killed a Black pedestrian who was crossing the street on her way to work. Black faces in local taverns were then shown denouncing the death as a product of blatant racism. White faces in different bars appeared next to accuse the first group of seeing racism everywhere, even in a simple, admittedly tragic, traffic accident. Since the story suggested no reason to think the driver had acted wrongly or possessed any ill will, it was difficult to imagine how racism could have had anything to do with the death.

The story then switched its focus, however, to show how the Black pedestrian came to be in the middle of the very busy street on which she was killed. It turned out that she had taken a city bus to her job in a large suburban shopping mall that was some distance down the street from the site of the accident. There was no bus stop at the mall entrance, and the pedestrian route from the nearby stop on the other side of the street was, by all accounts, treacherous. Black members of the community had been lobbying for months to add a stop at the mall entrance to reduce the risk to workers arriving by bus. But their efforts had failed, and, according to the television account, there was reason to believe that powerful interests didn't want to make it too easy for Black shoppers to travel from the inner city to the suburban mall.

We use the metaphors "snapshot" and "film" to capture these competing perspectives. The "snapshot," focusing on the moment of the accident, made racism appear an absurd charge. But the backstory added by the rest of the "film" created an entirely different impression. Shifting time frames in this way works for exam writers as well as television journalists. In torts cases, there is a well-known rule/exception structure whereby one party has no duty to aid another unless the potential rescuer contributed to the victim's peril. Exam writers, then, will search for examples in which, at the moment of truth, the victim seems responsible for his own fate. A farmer might, for example, be strolling his grounds and hear a young child screaming from the bottom of a well into which the child has fallen. From a "snapshot," this appears a classic case in which the farmer is under no legal duty to attempt a rescue, whatever his moral obligations. But the exam writer may also include facts that cut the other way—e.g., the well is on the farmer's property, conspicuously marked with a "danger" sign and hidden from public view by high hedges, and the farmer has previously seen children too young to read or otherwise appreciate the danger playing close by. The "film"—bringing this broader time frame into view—suggests that the farmer may well have a duty to aid.

In our examples thus far, the "film" has revealed events occurring before "the moment of truth," but this broader perspective can bring into view subsequent events as well. The "snapshot" may, for example, reveal a donor making a charitable pledge to a private college, which is in and of itself unenforceable under American contract law. But the "film" may reveal the later payment of a significant portion of the pledge—willingly made by the would-be donor and eagerly accepted by college officials—implicitly giving rise to mutual obligations by the parties and thus an enforceable contract binding the donor to fulfill the entire pledge. The larger point is that ambiguities often arise when the snapshot tells one story and the film tells another—a situation that is frequently encountered in legal practice and that law professors may accordingly mimic as they draft your exams.

4. Differing ways to make sense of the same facts

In the patterns of factual ambiguity we've considered so far—facts on both sides of a boundary, differing perspectives, and "the snapshot vs. the film"—the parties to a legal dispute emphasize different facts as they offer competing narratives of "what went down" in the real world. In this section, we'll focus instead on the many situations in which there is little or no disagreement about "the facts" and the parties disagree instead on how we should *interpret* them.

a. "One-at-a-time" vs. "taken-together" interpretation

Imagine a Contracts exam question in which a key issue is whether an offer has been made. The alleged offeror has made the following statements at different points during a face-to-face conversation: "I'd really like to buy your watch." "If I were to buy that watch I'd probably pay around $300." And "I have $300 right here—is that tempting?" It's pretty clear that none of these three statements, taken on its own, would constitute an offer to buy the watch. On the other hand, if you read them together, perhaps an offer has been made. This kind of ambiguity obviously makes for a good exam question.

The clash between viewing individual data points in isolation and reading them together as a whole—we call this "one-at-a-time" vs. "taken-together" interpretation—gives rise to a common source of factual ambiguity. You'll find the same clash in antitrust, where a series of allegedly anti-competitive practices might each be viewed individually as just within bounds of the law but collectively over the legal line. So too sexual harassment cases might involve a series of encounters between a supervisor and an employee, where each supervisory misstep falls just within the legal limits yet the employee argues that "taken together" the interactions constitute prohibited harassment. Or to pluck an example from recent headlines, a charge of incitement to riot may seem less compelling if individual statements can be minimized or explained away, but the same allegation may be far more powerful when framed as the sum of carefully, as well as not-so-carefully, hedged provocations.

b. Lenses of generality

As we explained in the chapters on "forks in the law," exam writers will often seize upon doubts over the meaning of statutes or cases by writing questions that hinge on interpreting the law at varying levels of generality. An antitrust question about publication of a price list, for example, may be analyzed differently depending on whether the precedents are portrayed as broadly banning "anti-competitive practices," which might include publishing a price list, or as narrowly prohibiting "price fixing," in which case mere publication may be permitted.

A similar ambiguity may arise in the interpretation of facts. Many criminal statutes, for example, make it a special kind of crime ("home invasion") to break into a home. Suppose the crime victim on your exam is living in his car when the defendant breaks in and steals a computer. No one doubts that the home invasion law applies only to "homes." But is the car a "home?" One can easily imagine some judges abruptly dismissing charges with the simple conclusion that whatever else it is "a car is not a home." Yet other judges more inclined to think broadly might note that a home is where a person lives, and since the victim is living in a car, in this case a car most definitely is a home. There's no obvious right answer to this problem; it depends at what level of generality "home" is defined. That's why it would make a good exam question. And, in case this isn't already clear, it's a good exam question not because it generates "right" and "wrong" answers to whether a car is a "home" but instead because it enables the grader to reward students who see and explain the arguments for both characterizations.

Consider, to take a second example, the legal rule distinguishing between permissible "puffing" and unlawfully deceptive practices. A manufacturer can advertise a vitamin supplement as "good for you" without risk of liability, even if objective observers might view the supplement as little more than a placebo. But commercials that tout that supplement for cancer prevention better have evidence to back up the claim. Notice how "general" claims sound more like puffing, whereas "specific" claims without proof are more likely to be deemed deceptive. Your exam writer may look for a fact pattern that falls between the two poles. Consider the classic tag line in advertisements for Wonder Bread, a commercially produced staple in millions of U.S. households during the mid-twentieth century: "Helps Build Strong Bodies 12 Ways." On the one hand, the "12 ways" claim—apparently a reference to 12 biochemical processes triggered by the bland white bread—sounds pretty specific. On the other, "helps build strong bodies" may be too vague to be more than mere puffery. There is, after all, no claim that the product does the "building" itself; it only "helps," with no specification of how much. And "strong" bodies surely come in too many shapes and sizes to be susceptible to proof or disproof. In sum, then, paying careful attention to how facts can be viewed through different lenses of generality—and thus argued into different categories (home or not, puffing or deception)—is another trick for tackling the issue spotter.

c. Linguistic ambiguity

Our next example of "forks in the facts" should be the most familiar, since our chapters on "forks in the law" devoted significant attention to the multiple sources of meaning for words appearing in cases and statutes. Words play a similarly central role in the application of legal categories that rely on lay understandings and communications, and, of particular relevance here, words are the key part of almost every contract.

Any of your exams can choose to highlight the ambiguity in everyday language as a way of evoking arguments about which category best fits the facts.

Borderline cases. Some legal categories track ordinary experience in ways giving rise to interesting issues when actual experience proves other than ordinary. When we studied criminal law, courts had different rules governing searches and seizures depending on where the search was conducted. Police were afforded far greater latitude to search automobiles than homes. So our professor asked us what the rules were for searching a Winnebago, a well-known brand of motor home. This was a paradigmatic exam question because it required knowledge of the two categories and the ways in which the Winnebago straddled the boundary between them and was thus a borderline case. Similarly, property law often distinguishes between fixtures that stay with a house and chattels that the seller may take with him. The basement boiler is a fixture. The dining room table is a chattel. But what about the two-ton hot tub that sits in the pool house next to the built-in pool?

A risk in such questions is that some students may find the borderline case outside their experience. Not everyone, for example, is familiar with a Winnebago. If you draw a blank on a concept during the exam, you can try to reason your way to the concept through context, but be sure to flag in your answer that you are unfamiliar with a term, especially if it wasn't discussed in class. But in the more common case where you find yourself confused about which category something such as a Winnebago should fit into, your confusion actually means you are on completely on the right track. You have found a fork. Take it.

Words vs. actions. It's very common for there to be a difference between what people say and what they do. So why not write a question that emphasizes that difference? Let's say you have a probationary employee whose contract is very explicit that during her probationary period she may be fired at any time for any reason. The contract further states that her probationary period will end after six months, unless the employer approves her for upgrade to regular status at an earlier time. During the six-month period the boss says nothing about an upgrade. But after three months he buys her expensive new office furniture, orders her business cards, and has her name embossed on the door. In the fourth month, the boss gives her three new assignments that clearly will take until the end of the year to finish. And in the fifth month, he fires one of her colleagues and transfers all that work to her as well. When she receives an offer of employment from another firm, she declines, citing how secure she feels in her current post. If in the sixth month the boss comes to her and says she's fired because her work is no good, does she have any claim for breach of contract? The words used suggest one result, for the written contract established a six-month probationary period, and the employer never actually said it was approving her for upgrade to regular employment status. But she will surely argue that her boss's actions tell a different story.

Written vs. oral statements. To continue the theme of job security, consider the all-too-common case of an employer whose formal written policy makes clear that all employees are subject to termination "at will." Yet in an exam question the company recruiter tells the employee that "no one has been fired here in 20 years," and that "a person with your skills and experience can count on job security, something you couldn't find anywhere else in the industry." When the exam question seeks a legal analysis of the employee's discharge, it's important to note the contrast between the written and oral statements and to offer arguments about why one or the other forms the essence of the contract.

Text vs. context. Suppose your exam question tells the story of a mortgage company that takes the following actions: After the borrowers apply for a loan on a home and a thorough credit check is done, the mortgage company sends an appraiser to the home who tells the borrowers that the appraisal will be done in a couple of days. Three days later, the company emails the borrower a three-page, single-spaced PDF spelling out the details of the loan agreement. The first line of the PDF says, "Congratulations, your loan has been approved." The mortgage company's representative also calls the borrower's insurance company to make sure the home is properly insured. Then the mortgage company's attorney phones the borrower and asks when a closing date might be set. A date is chosen, and the borrower liquidates several mutual funds to have sufficient cash for the closing.

A week later, the mortgage company calls the borrower and says the deal is off. It turns out that the appraised value of the home was $50,000 less than the $500,000 expected, and a close reading of the previously emailed PDF reveals the following clause: "This agreement is conditioned on a formal valuation of the house being completed at $500,000."

The mortgage company thinks this removes any issue of its liability. Borrower says "not so fast." Your job on an exam that poses these facts would be to highlight the obvious conflict between the text of the agreement (which literally enables the mortgage company to walk away in these circumstances) and the larger context of the dealings between the parties. The context would obviously include the timing of events in which the credit check and appraisal preceded the letter, thus potentially prompting the borrower to conclude that the congratulatory message meant she'd successfully completed those steps in the lending process, an impression the subsequent insurance and closing inquiries could only serve to confirm. But there's even more to the context than that. Unless the would-be borrower is a lawyer, she is far more likely to read and react to the congratulatory opening sentence, which bore no hint of the valuation requirement, than she'd be to wade through the rest of the three-page, single-spaced email to discover and grasp the significance of what's buried in the fine print.

Multiple sources of meaning. It was our first day of law school, and it all began with Criminal Law. Over the previous week, we had moved to a new city; met countless classmates and law school staff; received class schedules and seating assignments; purchased our books from the university's bookstore; attended a multitude of orientation meetings and social gatherings; figured out where to get fresh coffee at 2:00 in the morning; and stayed up way too late struggling to understand the assigned cases. The schedule for our section announced that Criminal Law met "MTW 9:00–10:00 a.m.," so we dutifully began assembling in the designated classroom about 20 minutes before 9:00 on that fateful Monday. By 9:00 sharp, we were all in our assigned seats, casebooks and notepads open, pens and pencils at the ready. An anxious hush came over the room, and all we were missing... was the professor. By a couple minutes after the hour—and still no sign of life in the front of the room—students were consulting the schedule to double-check the day, time, and classroom information, confirming that we, at least, were where we were supposed to be. After a few more minutes, things loosened up a bit as we began to offer humorous asides about our predicament and to exchange "getting to know you" intel with seatmates. Then suddenly at 9:10, the doors flew open and the professor swooped in. Without a word of explanation or apology, we were off to the races.

Only after class did we learn one of the many secrets of American legal education, information gleaned from a passing dean we recognized from orientation: In law school, an hour is fifty minutes (don't ask), and, at our law school, classes began at ten minutes past the scheduled starting time and ended on the hour. Our next class was Civil Procedure at 11:00 a.m., and the professor was reputed to be the Darth Vader of the Socratic method, so—just to be sure—we assembled in our assigned seats well before the clock struck 11. But he kept us in suspense and burst in at 10 past the hour. Whatever else we took away from our first day of law school—and alas those scary reports about the Civ Pro prof were all too true—we learned that when it came to class meeting times, "9:00" meant 9:10; "11:00" meant 11:10; and so on.

We learned, in other words, that communities sometimes have their own languages, and that the ordinary meaning of words and expressions may accordingly give way to understandings idiosyncratic to a particular setting. Most of us had encountered this phenomenon before—like when you ordered a dozen bagels for takeout and realized when you got home that you had 13, a so-called "baker's dozen." There are likewise specialized linguistic usages in the professions (think a chef calling out "12 specials all day," confirming the total number of specials in the preparation queue); in the arts (think the painter who knows from training and experience that "painting a portrait" includes preliminary sketchwork); and in social contexts (think a teenager responding to a lengthy, heartfelt, and painstakingly drafted text message from her parents with a terse and punctuation-free "k"). And we all know longtime married couples who sometimes speak in a tongue known only to them.

What's all this got to do with law exams? A lot. When speaker and spoken-to are both established members of one of these communities, the chances of misunderstanding are obviously small. But when one of the parties is too new to a setting to be in on secret meanings—think 130 eager beavers waiting anxiously for their first law school class to start—then conflict may well arise between ordinary meanings and specialized ones. And woe unto the outsider who innocently deploys a term that has a different meaning in the locale. (One of us was traveling with spouse and six-year-old daughter in Ireland and, checking in to our hotel, asked for a "cot" so the three of us could share a room with a single bed. We should have been clued in by the desk agent's raised eyebrow and polite but skeptical query: "A *cot*?" Yes, we confidently replied, briefly wondering whether Irish families all just shared the same bed. But imagine our surprise when we returned from an afternoon of touring to find a baby crib in the room and learned that what we really wanted was a "camper bed.") And when the outsider is a layperson using terms that have common as well as legal meanings—like "offer" and "acceptance"—judges and lawyers may be genuinely confused about the speaker's intentions. One party may reply to another's proposal to sell goods by saying, "I accept your offer, but I'd like to talk to you a little more about the terms." If we read the reply through a lay understanding of terms, we may see a clear intention to continue negotiations. But if we hold the speaker to legal meanings, we may conclude that "acceptance" of an "offer" means the parties have already concluded a contract.

Ambiguities arising in situations like these are common in life, and the conflicts they generate frequently find their way into legal disputes. They are thus a prolific source of the "forks in the facts" you'll encounter on your exams.

D. Fitting Facts to Categories: Formalist vs. Purposive Reasoning

We expect by now that you have gotten the message that exam questions frequently require you to determine whether the facts fit within one legal category or another. Our illustrations have highlighted the significance of questions such as whether the facts established an "offer"; whether evidence was in "plain view" of the police; whether a tenant signed a "residential lease" rather than a commercial one; etc. In each case, the category at issue was the target of proof, and we explored the many ways in which professors can draft exam problems with facts that "straddle" the boundaries of the categories at issue, giving rise to what we describe as "forks in the facts."

But it turns out that there is more than one way to argue that particular facts do or do not fall within a particular legal category. Recall, for example, the judge who refused even to *consider* the possibility that a car could be a home for purposes of the home invasion statute. We all know the difference between a car and a home, this judge might say, and I'm not interested in legal pyrotechnics trying to convince me otherwise.

This same judge might look at our Wonder Bread commercial and con-clude that claims about "building strong bodies" *must* be "puffery" be-cause they're vague and implausible and, by gum, that's just what puffery *means*. Lawyers and law professors have a name for arguments like these—arguments that treat category placement questions as a straight-forward matter of consulting a definition and determining whether the facts at hand fall within it—and the name is "formalism." For much of the twentieth century, that style of reasoning was out of favor among legal professionals because it appeared to let judges hide behind alleged-ly neutral "definitions" without taking responsibility for the consequenc-es of their decisions. Yet that never stopped lawyers from making for-malist arguments when they helped a client or judges from relying on them in reaching decisions. Moreover, in recent years "formalism" has enjoyed a resurgence as many judges and legal academics have forth-rightly embraced "textualism" as a means of interpreting statutes and "originalism" grounded in public understanding of the text as their pre-ferred approach to constitutional law.

There is, however, an alternative approach for determining whether facts fall within the contours of a category, and that's "purposive" reason-ing. Don't let the fact we've left this approach to the end of this chapter lull you into thinking it unimportant. Indeed, this form of reasoning has been the basis for many of the most effective legal arguments we've seen in all our years of law practice and teaching. Like its formalist counterpart, purposive reasoning takes the category at issue ("offer"; "plain view"; "residential lease" etc.) as the starting point for analysis. But lawyers using this approach will look far more closely at the *purpose* served by a legal category before attempting to place the facts of a legal dispute inside or outside of it. Under this approach, placing facts within categories cannot be separated from a category's purposes, and thus your exam answers will improve if you know how to focus on purposes as well as definitions.

What might that look like? Let's work our way through an illustration. Recall once again the saga of Artiste and Patron, in which Patron makes an offer to pay Artiste $10,000 to paint a family portrait and attempts to revoke the offer after Artiste has done some sketchwork but before she's put brush to canvas on the final product. Recall further that under the Restatement of Contracts, revocation of this sort of offer is impermissible once the offeree "begins the invited performance." Artiste will no doubt argue that the sketchwork counts as the "beginning of performance"—that, in other words, the facts fall within the "beginning of performance" category. Patron, for his part, is likely to respond that the sketchwork constitutes "mere preparations"—that, in other words, the facts fall within that latter category instead.

As we've seen in this chapter, when lawyers argue over whether particular facts fall into one category or another, a multitude of ways to engage in alternative characterizations can come into play—facts on both sides of a boundary; differing standpoints; the "film" vs. the "snapshot," etc. Lawyers taking a "formalist" approach will insist upon their preferred characterizations as they pursue a simple and straightforward mission: persuade a court that the sketchwork is "really" the beginning of performance (if you're counsel for Artiste) or is "really" mere preparations (if you're counsel for Patron).

Lawyers engaged in purposive reasoning will start in the same place—i.e., with the "beginning of performance" and "mere preparations" categories. But what they do then is channel their inner difficult child and ask the question that drove parents and teachers and coaches crazy: *Why*? Why, that is, does the law draw a line between these two categories and treat cases falling on each side so differently? Why, on the facts of the Artiste/Patron problem, does the law protect Artiste once there's a "beginning of performance" yet withhold that protection if there are "mere preparations"?

As you've seen, there is often more than one answer to that question—more, in other words, than one purpose driving the rule or the decision creating the category at issue. At this point, we won't complicate our illustration by indulging a debate over the purpose behind the distinction between "mere preparations" and "beginning of performance." For ease of illustration, we will instead assume that there is only one purpose at play: "Preparations" (such as buying paintbrushes, paints, or canvas) can ordinarily be redirected to other endeavors, and thus there's "no harm, no foul" if offerors such as Patron are permitted to revoke. But "performances" (such as a family portrait, whether partial or complete) are frequently of value only to the offeror and would therefore represent a "dead loss" to the offeree if the offeror could walk away from the deal.

Armed with this purpose, the lawyers are going to make arguments about the application of law to facts that are different from those they make when they are engaged in formalist reasoning. In our example, instead of asking whether the sketchwork is "really" the beginning of performance or "really" mere preparations, the critical inquiry will be whether treating the sketchwork as the beginning of performance serves the purposes of the legal rule establishing those categories. The lawyers will therefore focus their fire on whether the sketchwork is something that can be redirected to other uses if Patron backs out, or whether it represents something of value to Patron but not Artiste. At first blush, there may seem to be an obvious answer to this question, for it is unlikely that there's much of a market for sketches of some rich guy's family, and Artiste isn't likely to have much use for the sketches of a subject who left her high and dry after a bunch of work.

At a later point, we'll rehearse some responses available to counsel for Patron, but for now we want to slow down and underline the difference between the purposive reasoning we've just illustrated and the formalist alternative. In a nutshell, with formalist reasoning, the focus is on what the categories *mean*, and with purposive reasoning the focus is on what the categories are designed to *do*. The question posed by the former focus is whether or not the sketchwork fits the meaning of the "beginning of performance"; the question posed by the latter is whether treating the sketchwork as the "beginning of performance"—and thus barring revocation by Patron—serves the purpose of the underlying legal rule.

Want to see that again? Consider the case law under the Fourth Amendment treating "homes" differently from "cars" for purposes of searches by the police, and recall the case of the Winnebago slotted right in between. Formalist reasoning will focus on whether the Winnebago is "really" a home or "really" a car. (Cards on the table: We think it's both.) Purposive reasoning, by contrast, will focus on the purposes served by the competing categories: The greater the reasonable expectation of privacy in a given setting, the stronger the argument for constitutional protection against an invasive search. On the one hand, your home is your castle, so considerations favoring the protection of privacy are strongest there; on the other, you operate your car on public streets "in front of G_d and everyone"—as a late and beloved grandmother was fond of saying—and any expectation of privacy is presumably weaker. Examined through this purposive lens, then, the facts surrounding a particular search may matter a lot. Thus, the expectation of privacy is arguably greater when the Winnebago is parked at a long-term campsite in a national forest than in the parking lot of a McDonald's during the lunchtime rush. And—whether parked or moving—we might argue for a greater expectation of privacy in the living quarters than in the driver's compartment. In sum, with purposive reasoning we're focused not on deciding what a Winnebago "really" is (home vs. car), but rather on furthering the purposes of the restriction on police searches by deciding whether and in what circumstances the occupants have a reasonable expectation of privacy.

Two questions may occur to readers following the analysis thus far. The first: "Haven't we seen this before?" And the answer is yes. The contrast between formalist and purposive reasoning in the application of law to facts looks a *lot* like the contrast between "plain meaning"- and "purpose"-focused analysis in the interpretation of statutes. Indeed, "plain meaning" interpretations of statutes and formalist reasoning about facts are consecutive stages in a classic form of legal argument: Decide what the rule means, and then decide whether the facts before us fall within that meaning. By contrast, it's "purposes all the way down" when lawyers argue about what the rule is designed to accomplish and then about how the application of the rule to the facts will best serve those ends.

Which brings us to a second question that may be puzzling some readers. Should we think about the split between formalist and purposive reasoning as just one more fork? And, if so, do these contrasting approaches to fact application—formalist vs. purposive reasoning—represent "a fork in the law" or "a fork in the facts"? The most important answer to this question is that determining the proper classification of this fork *doesn't make any difference at all to success on law exams*. No professor—not even the guys who wrote this book—will care one bit about what you *call* these arguments, so long as you learn how to deploy them effectively on an exam or in practice. Indeed, you seldom need to call them anything; you just need to *make* them.

We know from experience, however, that this answer won't satisfy readers who just can't let go until they get this sorted out, so here's an approach that may help. Because formalist and purposive reasoning are opposed ways of arguing about the application of law to facts, for exam-taking purposes we have included them in this chapter on "forks in the facts." We did so because lawyers on opposite sides of the formalist vs. purposive debate are offering different ways of looking at the facts. Moreover, there should be scant cause for confusion when a lawyer engages in formalist reasoning, for the effort to fit the facts into one category or another (e.g., mere preparations vs. beginning of performance) is plainly a "fork in the facts"; once again, it's all about differing ways of looking at the facts.

Yet the distinction between arguments about law and arguments about facts may be less clear when a lawyer deploys purposive reasoning to make her case. In effect, the lawyer will be making an argument about law and an argument about facts *at the same time*, as she asks whether it serves the purposes of the rule to read the facts this way or that. "We could argue all day over whether sketches are 'really' preparations or 'really' the beginning of performance," Artiste's lawyer might candidly concede. "But if we focus instead on the *reason* we make that distinction— protecting the reliance of vulnerable offerees who might otherwise suffer a dead loss on account of their efforts—deciding whether to permit Patron to pull the rug out isn't complicated at all. It's one thing to leave my client to her own devices in repurposing materials such as paints, brushes, and sketchpads. And it's quite another to stick her with a roomful of sketchwork she can neither use nor market." The recipe for such purposive arguments calls for equal portions of law and facts, so there's no point in attempting to affix a label that emphasizes one at the expense of the other. But we close the chapter by repeating the advice we gave a moment ago. Don't worry about what to *call* the argument; just learn how to use it to your advantage in the exam setting.

Chapter Ten

Let a Thousand Issues Bloom: "Cascading Forks"

> "From such children come other children!"
> —Yente to Golde, in *Fiddler on the Roof*

Take a deep breath! You have worked hard to reach this point in the book, and we bet you have followed its path to the point where you can spot a fork when you see one and are beginning to feel familiar, if not necessarily comfortable, with the myriad ways in which law produces ambiguities that professors test on law exams. In our experience, most law students become fairly adept at mastering the forms of ambiguity we've explored. To be sure, some get there sooner than others, so you'll want to develop study techniques that enhance your ability to "know ambiguities when you see them"—and to do so quickly in the law exam setting. We'll describe some of those techniques in the next chapter.

For now, however, we're going to step back from the mass of detail to emphasize a crucial exam-taking lesson: Don't stop with the first issue you see no matter how certain you are that it's "the answer." That's because issue-spotting exams are typically more complex than our chapter-by-chapter descriptions of all these crazy forks might suggest. Indeed, the vast majority of exam questions present more than one issue for students to identify and address.

Consider the classic exam format in Torts, in which just about every cause of action you studied in the course is buried somewhere in a long and knotty tale of woe. (It may start with an auto accident... followed by a fistfight between the angry drivers... causing the spouse of one to faint in fright and... injure his head on a nearby parked car, setting the vehicle in motion down a steep hill because its owner left it in neutral and didn't set the parking brake... where it crashes into a large pane of glass carried by two construction workers crossing the street... you get the picture.) You'll often encounter exam questions with this basic format—i.e., presenting problems that pose two or more independent issues. A less fraught Torts hypo, for example, might raise distinct defamation, invasion of privacy, and intentional infliction of emotional distress issues in connection with a series of social media posts, or a Contracts question might introduce a capacity issue at the time of formation and a warranty issue long after the deal is done. We'll have more to say about such problems later in the book, but our basic advice for coping with them is straightforward: Leave no issue behind, and keep an eye on the clock so you'll have plenty of time to hit the key points of conflict with respect to each one you see.

But in this chapter, our focus is on a different kind of multi-issue problem, one that is far more common on law exams and is in our experience more likely to trip up the unwary—that is, the exam problem in which issues give rise to further issues and those issues in turn give rise to further issues still. Such "issues within issues" are a phenomenon we think of as "cascading forks," something we've alluded to before and that we're now going to tackle head-on.

Let's pick up from the end of the previous chapter, where we introduced the use of formalist vs. purposive reasoning as a means of arguing whether the facts at hand fit within the definition of a legal term. Consider once again the Artiste/Patron dispute, in which Patron offers Artiste $10,000 to paint a family portrait and revokes the offer after Artiste completes some sketchwork but before she puts brush to canvas. Once again, Patron's best argument that "performance" has not yet begun comes straight from the formalist reasoning playbook:

> Under the law governing unilateral contracts, I am free to revoke my offer until Artiste "begins performance." The performance my offer invited was to "paint a portrait," and that performance obviously can't "begin" until there is at least some "paint" on a canvas. Artiste's sketchwork may be something to behold but—unless and until there is "paint on the canvas"—

such efforts are "mere preparations" and not the beginning of performance.

As the chapter ended, Artiste countered with a purposive argument that her sketchwork did indeed constitute the "beginning of performance" rather than "mere preparations":

> In the unilateral contract setting, we prohibit revocation by the offeror once the offeree has begun performance for a reason: to protect the offeree against the risk of nontrivial losses suffered in doing the offeror's bidding. In this case, the sketchwork is something only Patron or his family could love. Unlike expenditures on paints, brushes, or sketchpads, sketchwork can't be successfully repurposed to other projects, let alone put up for sale on the art market. So the law's purpose would best be served by treating the sketchwork as the beginning of performance, preventing Patron from leaving Artiste high and dry with a roomful of worthless sketches.

And that was the end of the chapter. *But it wasn't the end of the argument.*

Consider the responses Patron might offer to Artiste's last point. For one thing, we might expect him to stand his ground and insist on the formalist reasoning undergirding his forceful "no paint on canvas" argument. But a good lawyer—and thus a successful exam-taking student—will prepare for the prospect of losing the formalist vs. purposive reasoning argument to Artiste. So how might Patron respond if Artiste persuades the court to opt for a purposive approach? As it happens, he will have plenty to say:

- For one thing, Patron could accept Artiste's characterization of the purpose of the categories at issue (i.e., to avoid nontrivial losses to offerees who spend time and/or money on the deal) but seize on a "fork in the facts" to dispute her claim about how that purpose applies to sketchwork. Thus, Patron could point to famous sketches with high market value—from the original Gerber Baby to some of Picasso's most admired work—and thus take issue with the claim that sketchwork necessarily represents a total loss to an artist.

- For another, Patron could introduce a "competing purposes" argument, offering a different take on the purpose of the distinction between "beginning of performance" and "mere preparations." The purpose of the competing categories, Patron might contend, is to ensure that offerors are held to account once they are "benefiting from their bargain," but not a moment before. Patron bargained for a "portrait"—not for a series of sketches—and it would therefore thwart that purpose to force him to keep his side of the deal when Artiste has yet to serve up even the first brushstroke on the portrait Patron actually bargained for.

But wait, there's more! Consider the counterarguments available to Artiste with respect to each of these claims by Patron. For one thing, there's nothing in the facts to suggest that she's another Picasso or that Patron resembles the Gerber Baby, and just because *some* sketchwork has market value doesn't make it so here. For another, the terms of Patron's original offer contain a verb ("paint") as well as a noun ("portrait"), confirming that what Patron was bargaining for was an artistic *process*—with well-established protocols like preliminary sketchwork—and not merely an end product.

The punch line, then, is that Artiste's invocation of purposive reasoning gives rise to a series of further issues about the purpose of the rule and about how that purpose is best served on the facts of the problem. These "issues within issues" are typical of law exam problems and of the kinds of disputes you'll encounter in practice. We call them "cascading forks" to highlight the fact that a "choice" at one fork (e.g., purposive instead of formalist reasoning) frequently leads downstream to another fork (e.g., not that purpose, *this* purpose), with further choices producing further downstream forks (e.g., the sketchwork might or might not have market value) and so on.

So some more good news. If the Patron/Artiste hypo was a question on your law exam, you'd top the curve in almost any class with an answer that captured even half the arguments we've sketched out here. You should therefore learn to welcome rather than fear cascading forks; as you master the many ways of "getting to maybe"—and so long as you've studied the relevant course materials carefully—cascading forks will give you more than enough to work with in crafting exam answers that will impress the grader.

There is more good news still, and it's the point of this chapter. To someone new to the law, each of the individual issues we've identified in the Artiste/Patron dispute may seem like a random shot in the dark. A perfectly natural reaction is to think you'd be lucky to identify one or perhaps two of them, but to wonder how on earth you might ever be expected to come up with more. We hope you'll find our response to that concern reassuring. There is nothing random about the cascade of issues we just considered, and at this point in the book you may have seen this coming: Cascades appear in *patterns*, and learning to recognize those patterns can aid you greatly in spotting those downstream issues that might otherwise be easy to miss. We focus below on some of the most common patterns.

A. One Good Fork Deserves Another: Proliferating Forks

To quote a famous malapropism usually attributed to Yogi Berra, "When you come to a fork in the road, take it!" We're not entirely sure what the iconic Yankee catcher and manager actually meant by that, but a friendly variation on the line offers great advice for our readers: When you come to a fork on a law exam, keep going!

We will illustrate this point with a fork you are likely to encounter—on exams and in law practice—more often than any other: issues presenting a conflict between "plain meaning" and "purpose" in the interpretation of statutes and other rules. Indeed, you'll see this one so often that it will become easy to spot, and that will come in handy. But our point here is that spotting the issue is not enough, and here's a simple rule to remember: *When you encounter a "plain meaning vs. purpose" fork, push harder on both the plain meaning and the purpose.* To see why that advice might pay off, consider a question on a Legislation final that resurrects our old friend "no vehicles allowed in the park" and asks how it might apply in the context of someone arrested for weekend cycling. "Okay, I get it," a student encountering this question is likely to think right off the bat. "There's really no denying that a bicycle is a 'vehicle,' since it's used to transport people and their stuff all the time. But surely the favored form of transportation for active urban dwellers everywhere was *not* what the city council had in mind when it passed an ordinance banning vehicles from the park. OMG—bingo!—that's the issue: the 'meaning' of vehicle points one way and the 'purpose' of the ban points in another. I may survive this course after all!"

But here's where the Yogi Berra dictum comes in handy. If you cling too hard to the unmistakable conflict between meaning and purpose the bicycle example presents, the clinging can impede your ability to identify additional issues by working your way down the "cascade." For one thing, perhaps the meaning of "vehicle" is more complicated than it first appears. What if there's a provision in the ordinance assigning penalties for infractions calibrated by the weight of the offending vehicle in which the gradations are in 500-pound increments, thus suggesting that "vehicle" means cars and trucks? If that's the case, then maybe a bicycle *isn't* a "vehicle" as this ordinance defines it. For another, perhaps your first impression of the law's purpose doesn't tell the whole story either. If the city council's aim was to reduce pollution and noise, then the argument favoring a bicycle ban is weak indeed. But if the council's goal was instead to protect the mostly elderly park users from collisions with fast-moving instrumentalities, then bicycles may present as big a threat as motor vehicles. To be sure, you may have been right the first time. Depending on the particulars of the ordinance and its provenance, the arguments that bicycles are outside the meaning or inside the purpose of the ban may not be available given the facts the professor has presented and/or the legal materials you're working with. But the point is to *try*—to make sure you're not jumping to *and getting stuck on* contestable conclusions, thereby missing additional issues ripe for the picking.

Let's look at another example. Do the rocking chairs on the restaurant veranda count in the application of a "two toilets for every 40 seats" law? At first glance, there seems little doubt that a rocking chair is literally a "seat" (so rocking chairs are *within* the plain meaning of seats) or that the purpose of the regulation is to accommodate the needs of patrons sitting down for long leisurely meals (so rocking chairs are *not* within the regulation's purpose). *Voila*, another "plain meaning vs. purpose" fork. But on second thought, perhaps the "plain meaning" vs. "purpose" arguments aren't the end of the story; perhaps there are more points to be earned on the exam by pushing a bit on each "prong" in the fork. Perhaps the meaning of "seats" derives from the use of the term in the restaurant trade to denote "seats available for meal service" (so rocking chairs are

Figure One

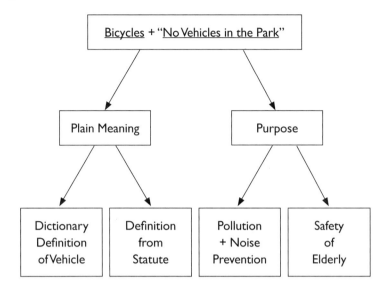

not within the meaning of seats). Similarly, if the wait for a table is long and patrons in the queue regularly use the rocking chairs for extended periods of drinking and visiting, those additional toilets may come in very handy (so rocking chairs are *within* the regulation's purpose).

To help illustrate this point about treating "plain meaning vs. purpose" issues as the beginning rather than the end of an analysis, flowcharts mapping the "issue cascades" in the bicycle case and the rocking chairs case appear respectively as Figure One above and Figure Two on the following page. If you're a visual learner—or just tired of all this dense prose—the diagrams may help you see why it's important to keep going after you identify the initial fork.

But seeing isn't always believing. From our many conversations with students over the years, we've learned that even exam-takers who see those downstream forks often shy away from writing about them in their answers. And why might that be? The first time you spot a "plain meaning vs. purpose" issue on a law exam, you'll be tempted to celebrate—and perhaps you should, since you may well have just discovered the central conflict the professor embedded in the problem. But what happens if you allow yourself to think, "Wait a minute, maybe the meaning of that term

Figure Two

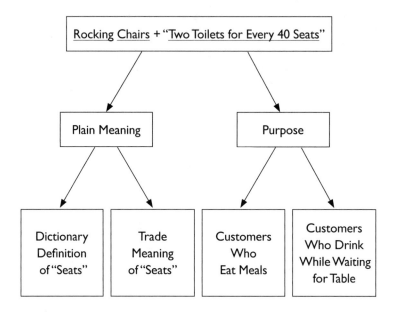

isn't so plain after all?" or "Wait a minute, maybe *that's* not the purpose of the provision"? If you come to law school assuming that exam questions have only one right answer—and once again that's the way most of us come to law school—then you may worry that questioning the components of your initial answer will lead to the conclusion that the initial answer was just plain wrong, and maybe you are missing the point altogether. But you aren't in Kansas anymore, and, in the context of law exams, although you will certainly get points for coming up with a well-crafted "plain meaning vs. purpose" analysis, you will score even more points for pressing on to argue that neither the meaning nor the purpose is so plain after all. The punch line, then, is that you should refrain from declaring "mission accomplished" when you identify a "plain meaning vs. purpose" conflict or any similarly striking issue on a law exam, for there may be additional issues lurking just "downstream" that can help you turn a good answer into an even better one.

We have two more suggestions to help you make the most of Yogi Berra's dictum. First, the advice to press on applies to *any* fork you encounter, not just to "plain meaning vs. purpose" issues. You will rightly delight in spotting a tension between the formulation of a case "holding" and the court's seemingly broader "reasoning" in the application of a key precedent to an exam problem. But as we've seen, reasoning can point in more than one direction. Recall our discussion of *Griswold v. Connecticut*—the "right to use contraceptives" case—in which some of the Court's reasons focused on protecting the marital bedroom against police intrusion and some embraced a broader and far more generalized right of privacy. (At least until the 2022 decision in *Dobbs*, post-*Griswold* cases emphasized the latter over the former, but only because lawyers were successful in persuading the courts to take the fork in one direction rather than the other.) Holdings may likewise point in differing directions, as we saw in the debate over how to read the disclosure duty imposed by *Johnson v. Davis* on sellers who know of facts "materially affecting the value of the property": Do we measure value by reference to the real estate market or by reference to the desiderata of the particular buyer? And so too when you identify a clash between "formalist" and "purposive" reasoning: As we've seen with the Artiste/Patron "sketchwork" problem, formalist reasoning can lead to more than one conclusion ("what part of 'portrait' don't you understand?" vs. "what part of hiring an artist to 'paint' a portrait don't *you* understand?"), and so can purposive reasoning ("sketchwork has no value!" vs. "tell that to Picasso!"). In each of these cases, the potential stumbling block comes from the fact that one's initial instincts about the reasoning of *Griswold* or the holding of *Johnson* or the way to understand the facts in Artiste/Patron may have prompted you to see the "reasoning vs. holding" issue or the "formalist vs. purposive reasoning" issue in the first place, and everything about "right answer culture" will understandably make you reluctant to second-guess those instincts. We promise, however, that you will be amply rewarded by your professors for actively questioning your "hot take" and embracing rather than resisting the cascading issues that further inquiry may reveal.

Our second and final point in this section is that "proliferating forks" is a metaphor for the way lawyerly argument plays out in many contexts, but it's decidedly not a one-size-fits-every-problem formula. Sometimes, for example, it will be clear that a rule has one overriding purpose. Sometimes, for another, there will be authoritative precedent attributing one meaning to a term and rejecting other interpretations. Sometimes there will be "play" on one side of a fork but not on the other—e.g., there's more than one way to read the holding of a key precedent but the reasoning was unambiguous or a later court has authoritatively declared it so. When you think you've encountered such a situation on an exam, don't offer weak or rote arguments just to achieve some false sense of symmetry ("there's more than one way to read the meaning so there must be more than one way to read the purpose!") or just to add another layer of complexity for its own sake. Sometimes one side of a fork is the right one, so don't be afraid to follow Yogi: Take it, and move on to something else.

B. Straddling a Statutory Boundary: Concurrent Forks

In many cascading forks problems, the downstream issues can be difficult to see at first, since they come to life only as you begin to grapple with the issue at the "top" of the cascade. But sometimes you'll know where to look from the start. For example, most of the statutes you study in law school—and especially those you explore in your first-year courses—address subjects that were previously governed by the common law. Indeed, for most of those subjects, the common law still governs any transaction that is "outside" the statute, and thus the "boundary" between what lies inside and what lies outside the statute is a matter of some importance. Consider the following hypothetical:

> Betty Bookbinder enters a contract with Larry Lawyer to bind Lawyer's collection of appellate briefs in 37 matching volumes. Lawyer selects cover material from among Bookbinder's extensive selection of fine leathers and stipulates, among other details, that his name should appear on each of the covers in 24-point lettering. Bookbinder finishes the work by the promised date, and Lawyer picks up the volumes, which at first blush look wonderful to him. He takes them home and realizes later that his name appears in 22-point lettering instead of 24-point. He thereupon returns the volumes to Bookbinder and refuses to pay for the work. If Bookbinder sues for breach of contract, what result?

As you'll learn in your first-year Contracts course, transactions involving a "sale of goods" are governed by the Uniform Commercial Code, and transactions involving a "service" are governed by the common law, creating what we've just referred to as a "statutory boundary." Do you see that the facts presented in our hypo are designed to straddle that boundary? On the one hand, the transaction might be characterized as a sale of goods—Bookbinder is in effect selling Lawyer a substantial quantity of fine leather and incidentally providing custom work to ensure a fit between the product and Lawyer's briefs—bringing the transaction within the U.C.C. On the other hand, the dominant component of the exchange may be viewed as a service—Bookbinder is bringing her training, skill, and experience to the task of binding a collection of briefs that already belong to Lawyer—and the transaction would therefore be governed not by the statute but by the common law. In sum, the facts can be argued on either side of the statutory "boundary," making this a classic "fork in the facts."

But the hypothetical also contains a second fork, a rule vs. counter-rule "fork in the law" that tracks the first one and renders it significant. Thus, if the transaction is a sale of goods and the U.C.C. applies, then the perfect tender rule of § 2-601 will govern. Alternatively, if the transaction is a service and the common law applies, then we'll be looking at the doctrine of substantial performance. And what difference does *that* difference make? Well, under the U.C.C.'s perfect tender rule, Lawyer has a right to reject a tender if the goods differ in any respect from the terms of the contract, and the fact that his name appeared in 22-point lettering rather than the 24-point lettering will trigger that right. But under the common law doctrine of substantial performance, Lawyer must accept the volumes and content himself with a counterclaim for any damages he's suffered as a result of the slightly smaller lettering.

We call these "concurrent forks," for the path you take at the "fork in the facts" determines the path you must choose at the "fork in the law." If we characterize the transaction as a sale of goods, then the U.C.C.'s perfect tender rule (§ 2-601) applies, and Bookbinder is out of luck. But if we characterize the transaction as a service, then Bookbinder may find refuge in the common law doctrine of substantial performance. As we did with the examples of proliferating forks, we've sketched a "decision tree" of the concurrent forks that appears below as Figure Three.

Figure Three

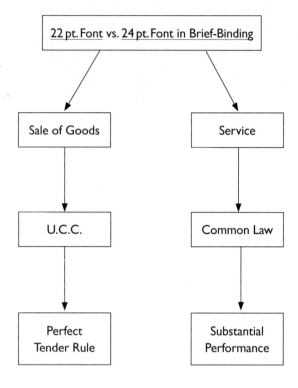

You'll encounter "concurrent forks" in most areas of legal practice and in virtually every course you take in law school. Sometimes the statutory boundary will look like the boundary between two adjacent territories. (On one side of the border, she's an "employee" protected against sexual harassment by Title VII of the Civil Rights Act; but on the other side, she's an "independent contractor" whose source of legal protection against such harassment is the common law.) Sometimes the statutory boundary will look more like the perimeter of an island. (If the country club is inside the line, then it's a "place of public accommodation" and its racially discriminatory membership policies are prohibited by the state human rights statute; but if it's outside the line, then the country club may be free to discriminate under the common law.) The point, again, is to learn to recognize the larger pattern: Watch for the "fork in the facts" that straddles a "statutory boundary," for there's almost sure to be a "fork in the law" lurking nearby.

C. Competing Domains: Bringing It All Together

Believe it or not, most law professors strive to make the study of law easier rather than harder for our students, and one way we do that is by dividing up the subject areas we teach (Contracts, Torts, Property, etc.) into discrete topics (offer and acceptance, interpretation, remedies, etc.) and each of those topics into subtopics (e.g., money damages, specific relief) and even *sub*-subtopics (e.g., the rule of *Hadley v. Baxendale*, the duty to mitigate damages; etc.). The advantage to dividing up our subjects this way is that it permits students to focus on one set of rules, cases, and/or principles at a time—an approach to learning that is far less daunting than trying to grasp the "seamless web" of the law all at once and, in any event, a lot easier to outline as you prepare for the final!

The downside, however, is that real-world legal problems seldom fit neatly into a single section of even the most sophisticated outline. Instead, they blend and bleed from one section to another, frequently crossing the most taken-for-granted boundaries of the course syllabus and the casebook's table of contents. As scary as that might seem to a beginning law student, the skilled lawyer welcomes the opportunity it provides to frame a case in a way that gives the greatest advantage to her client—and to resist her opponent's efforts to frame the case in some other way.

In an effort to assist you in developing this important skill—of learning to analyze and argue your way back and forth across the boundaries they teach you—law professors frequently design fact patterns that straddle different doctrines, or different cases, or even different bodies of law. We refer to these as "competing domains," and the "statutory boundary" situation we just finished discussing (where a hypothetical is designed to straddle the boundary between what's governed by a statute and what's governed by the common law) is an important example of what we mean.

But there is a much longer list of competing domains problems than any exam prep book could provide. And since some of them are a bit more complex than anything we've analyzed so far, we offer a few examples to give you a feel for what such competing domains may look like:

- In Contracts, you learn about the doctrine of "consideration," which requires a party asserting a valid contract to show that she gave the other party something in exchange for the other's promise, as well as the doctrine of "promissory estoppel," which permits the aggrieved party to recover based on reasonable reliance on another's promise. A classic competing domains question for that course presents a single fact pattern that straddles the two doctrines—e.g., an uncle who promises his nephew $5,000 to give up smoking, so the required forbearance could be characterized either as a mere condition on a gratuitous promise (thus falling short of consideration) or as detrimental reliance (thus justifying a claim of promissory estoppel).

- In Property, you may study one case that gives a landowner the unrestricted right to pump percolating water from his property and a second case holding a landowner liable for the subsidence of neighboring land resulting from excavation. A competing domains question would present facts that straddle the two cases—e.g., a landowner who pumps percolating water from his own land in such quantities and in such a manner as to cause subsidence on neighboring farms.

- In Employment Law, you may study the body of case law that protects public-sector employees against discharge in retaliation for exercising the right to free speech protected by the First Amendment. You may also study the common law "employment-at-will" doctrine that would permit private-sector employers to fire their employees for the same conduct. A competing domains question would present facts that straddle the two bodies of law—e.g., the discharge of a teacher at a "charter school" for statements she makes regarding a school bond issue, where the charter school might be characterized as either a public employer (so the discharge would violate the First Amendment) or a private employer (so the discharge would be lawful under the at-will rule).

So why do we think problems like these can be so complicated? Because an analysis of competing domains will often produce a mashup of "concurrent forks" as well as "proliferating forks," and—if you'll pardon a painfully mixed metaphor—that's an awful lot of balls in the air at one time for a student taking a law exam. To see just what we mean, let's return to our brief-binding hypo from the previous section. You'll recall that the hypo presented a threshold "fork in the facts," requiring an analysis of whether the transaction at issue was a sale of goods (and thus governed by the U.C.C.) or a service (and thus governed by the common law). And you'll also recall the "concurrent fork"—a rule vs. counter-rule fork in the law—lurking beneath the fork in the facts: If the U.C.C. governs, then the perfect tender rule applies and Lawyer can walk out the door because the bindings delivered (with Lawyer's name in 22-point font) differ from the bindings promised (with the name in 24-point font). But if the common law governs, then the substantial performance rule might well come to Bookbinder's rescue, barring exit by Lawyer and relegating Lawyer to a suit for any damages resulting from the two-point font difference.

But once again, that may not be the end of the argument, and once again initial impressions may give way upon closer examination. There may, for example, be an additional "fork in the facts" even after a court decides to treat binding as a service and thus apply the common law rule. Given the "vanity publishing" quality of the binding project contemplated by the parties' contract—Lawyer is proud of his handiwork and wants to see his name in lights—the font-size glitch might be characterized as a "material breach" (permitting Lawyer to walk out of the deal) rather than "substantial performance" (relegating him to an action for damages). And there may be a "fork in the facts" on the U.C.C. side as well, for Lawyer's failure even to notice the glitch when he picked up the briefs—coupled with his failure to object to it until after he had taken possession of the volumes—might constitute an acceptance of the goods, depriving Lawyer of an opportunity to reject them under the perfect tender rule. (We've once again sketched a diagram of the resulting decision tree, which appears below as Figure Four.)

In sum, the gratifying "aha" moment when you identify "concurrent forks"—two forks for the price of one!—shouldn't distract from the search for "proliferating forks" further downstream, so don't stop until you've worked your way through *all* the possibilities. But that said, it's the *fruits* of the search that will rack up points on a law exam, not a mere recitation of possibilities based on what you've read here. In other words, don't tell the professor, "Maybe Lawyer can find an argument for why the perfect tender rule shouldn't apply." If you can think of such an argument, well then, *make* it! And if you can't, move on to something else.

Figure Four

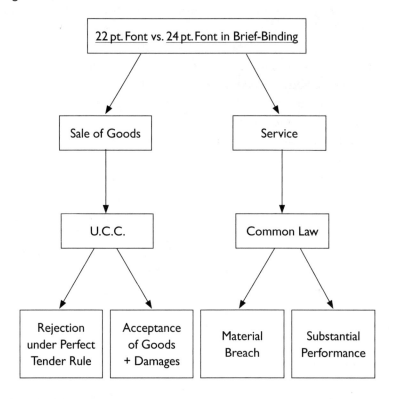

D. Creative Forks—Reading a Problem
Right Out of a Rule

We hope the many examples of cascading forks we've just explored will help you learn to recognize the patterns in which they appear and thus to anticipate downstream issues that are otherwise all too easy to miss. But before we bring this chapter to a close, we're going to focus on one more "fork"—one that offers students an opportunity to excel by taking their cues from what in our view is some of the best lawyering and judging our legal culture has to offer.

Imagine a question on your Property final that on close analysis seems to "lock you in" to a result that strikes you as profoundly wrong or unjust. Say, for example, that the question asks you to evaluate the case of a commercial tenant who 40 years earlier entered a lease agreement with a 50-year term and an option to "purchase the premises at any time during the term of this lease." Over the years, tenant spent several hundred thousand dollars renovating the building to suit its developing needs and now seeks to exercise the option to purchase. The original owner passed away some time ago and left the building to her son, who—with the lease coming to an end in just a few years—wants to keep the building for himself. Accordingly, he argues that the option is invalid under the Rule Against Perpetuities—that infamous staple of Property courses and bar exams everywhere—and the exam places the dispute in a jurisdiction that defines the rule thus: "No interest in land is good unless it must vest, if at all, not later than twenty-one years after some life in being at the creation of the interest."

At first blush, it appears that the current owner has a winning argument, since tenant is seeking to exercise the option and thus gain title to the property more than 40 years after the option was created. Yet you find yourself indignant over the prospect of tenant finding itself out on the street after all this time, and especially after undertaking all that renovation work in reliance on an option appearing in the lease agreement in unambiguous and unqualified terms.

So it's time to get to work. You reach into your bag of tricks for "getting to maybe" and take a close look at the language of the rule to see whether there's a "competing meanings" issue lurking. But alas, you don't see a plausible way to argue that the option to purchase the building is not "an interest in land," nor do you see a convincing case that the option would have "vested" not upon its exercise but at some earlier point, beating the deadline imposed by the rule. Since the meaning of the rule won't help, naturally you turn to the rule's purposes... until you recall a principle the professor stressed in class and that most courts have evidently embraced: "The Rule Against Perpetuities" is to "be remorselessly applied." So it's going to be a tough slog to convince a judge that she should soften the impact here via a purposive reading of the rule.

At this point, you're ready to conclude that the professor has drafted this problem precisely to force you to follow the law to a conclusion repugnant to anyone whose heart isn't made of stone; what choice do you have, then, but to recount the false starts and accept defeat for tenant? But in point of fact there is another possibility, and it's this: Be bold and argue that the Rule of Perpetuities just doesn't apply *at all* to an option to purchase contained in a long-term commercial lease. The point of the rule, and hence its proper scope of application—the argument would go—is "the public policy in favor of free alienability of property and against restricting its marketability over long periods of time by restraints on its alienation." And an option in a long-term commercial lease is consonant with this policy "because it stimulates improvement of the property and thus renders it more rather than less marketable." As the quotation marks confirm, we aren't making these arguments up, for they appear in a famous opinion by one of the nation's great state court judges, Ellen Peters of the Connecticut Supreme Court, when presented with the very problem under examination. And look what she did in the face of a rule that plainly applied to the facts as well as a body of precedent that precluded flexible application in the name of underlying purposes. She read the problem *outside the rule altogether*, channeling the wisdom of Obi-Wan Kenobi (had he been speaking to history rather than to Imperial Stormtroopers): "These aren't the restraints on alienation you're looking for."

Of course, this type of argument will call upon you to display a keen understanding of the reasons for the rule and why it was never meant for a situation like this. But such bold maneuvers are always worth attempting when conventional legal arguments seem to lead inexorably to an unjust result. We thus urge you to think of this as the "fork that rules them all": a choice between the ordinary application of law (on the one hand) and circumventing a rule altogether in a creative search for justice (on the other). Many of the famous cases you read in law school are venerated precisely because the judges refused to follow the path of least resistance when conventional legal arguments seemed to box them in. You could hardly do better than to follow their example when faced with a similar predicament on a law school exam.

PART III

Prepping for and Tackling the Issue Spotter

In Part II of the book, we set out to help you understand what an "issue" is and why legal problems—and thus exam questions—are chock-full of them. This Part will assist you in figuring out what to *do* with issues as you prepare for and take exams.

Chapter Eleven

Preparing for the Challenge of Issue-Spotting Exams

For the next edition of this book, perhaps we'll go all multimedia and offer a film version of this chapter. For now, let's imagine what that might look like:

> As the scene comes into focus, the big day has arrived and you're sitting in a sprawling classroom about to begin your first law exam. It's obvious you've planned carefully for this moment, for the desk before you is strewn with objets d'examen (it's a French film) including your trusty laptop (or pens, pencils, and highlighters of every hue, if you're still working with old-fashioned blue books); a full-to-the-brim water bottle; a large latte; a travel alarm clock; and—at the time of this writing, at least—several spare N95 masks together with a bottle of hand sanitizer. Superimposed over this image, a hazy phrase comes gradually into focus—"Four months earlier..."—and the camera dissolves to a gaggle of fresh-faced students crowding the entryway to the same room for their very first law school class. Silence comes over the room as students nervously take their seats and someone who looks for all the world like a famous rock star glides gracefully down the aisle toward the lectern....

Okay, this is supposed to be your fantasy, not ours. But you're reading an exam-taking book written by a pair of longtime law professors. Did you *really* think we would talk about the challenges of exam-taking without at least reminding you of things that need doing long before that day arrives? In the next two chapters—Chapter Twelve ("How to Spot Issues on an Exam") and Chapter Thirteen ("What to Do With Issues Once You Spot Them")—we'll explore a variety of techniques for making the best use of *Getting to Maybe* insights once the exam is in front of you. But attempting to deploy those techniques without first mastering the course materials would be a lot like setting out for an ocean cruise without a boat. So let's pick up from where our film clip left off and focus on the work to be done in law school *before* the final.

A. Plot Twist: Conflict and Confusion Are the Best Friends You Ever Had

We'll start with some reassuring news. The basic tools for reviewing and mastering a law school course will be familiar to anyone who has spent time in higher ed: class notes, old exams, study partners, and homemade outlines and other materials (flashcards, flowcharts, spreadsheets, etc.) to aid comprehension and recall. You did well enough in other educational settings to make your way to law school, and so you already know how to make these tools and others work for you. But as usual, there's a law school twist. In the undergraduate setting, successful exam preparation typically focuses on distillation and synthesis—bringing together lecture notes, slides, assigned readings, and other material in an effort to "get the facts right" and to identify the key points, themes, and through lines from the course. There's an important place for that kind of work in law school as well, so dust off those skills and get ready to use them again. But when it comes to preparing for issue-spotting exams, what's even more important than distillation and synthesis is the search for conflict and even confusion in the course materials. That's the stuff issues are made of, and in the pages that follow we'll offer a number of strategies for surfacing and highlighting conflict in the various stages of preparation.

We have two further introductory points. Because it's a key to success in law school, we devoted the entire first chapter to the importance of doing your own work rather than relying on commercial study aids or outlines produced by fellow students. There's no need to belabor that advice here, and for present purposes we can summarize our argument thus: The vast majority of law professors "test what they teach," and thus an exam prep strategy that puts primary emphasis on anything other than *what the professor actually taught in your class* is likely to be a poor use of your time. The lessons to be taken from a particular course and thus tested on the final vary dramatically from professor to professor—even among professors teaching the same course at the same law school—and will vary over the years with respect to a given professor. Accordingly, there is no better way to prepare for the final than by working with course-specific materials such as class notes and an outline based on the course taught this year.

Which brings us to our second preliminary point: The exams your professors have given in recent years represent their best efforts to test what they see as the most important and challenging parts of their courses. You can thus learn more about what to expect on this year's exam from prior exams than you can from any other source. So even if you are too pressed for time to follow the other preparation strategies on offer here—or even if you're otherwise confident in your own approach to study—we promise that reviewing old exams, and especially doing so with classmates, will be well worth the effort.

B. Upgrading Traditional Exam Prep Tools for Issue Anticipation and Identification

1. Class notes

When you attend a lecture as an undergraduate, you are likely to view the professor as someone with a ton of information and analysis to impart, and you expect to be graded on the basis of just how much of that information you're able to absorb, recall, and regurgitate via various assessment tools. In that setting, when class discussion digresses from the professor's prepared talking points, you may find yourself becoming impatient and perhaps even nodding off, especially if what triggers the digression is another speech-parading-as-a-question from the class know-it-all. Law professors, too, have information to transmit, and much of that information concerns the content of the rules and cases you've come to law school expecting to learn. But information transmission is not the only point—or even the principal point—of the typical law school class. Instead, class discussion is designed to focus on what lawyers *do* with rules and cases, and what lawyers do with rules and cases is *argue* about them. And when those arguments are developed and analyzed in class, the discussion will invariably bring to the surface ambiguities in the legal materials as well as competing perspectives and points of view.

Imagine, for example, a debate in Con Law over the right way to read *District of Columbia v. Heller*, a Second Amendment decision by the United States Supreme Court recognizing a "right to bear arms" in private homes free from state interference. In an extended Socratic exchange, the professor prods students to consider just how far the *Heller* right extends. Does it protect carrying a weapon *outside* the home? Carrying a *concealed* weapon in public? Brandishing a weapon during a demonstration or march? Bringing one into the U.S. Capitol? As different views are expressed and defended, it's tempting to hold your note-taking fingers in abeyance awaiting a definitive resolution by the professor. But the debate itself is often the *point* of the class. The professor might even have devised these "hypotheticals" based on her own sense of issues likely to come before the courts—as several of these questions did in *New York Pistol & Rifle Ass'n v. Bruen*, which was decided shortly before this edition of *Getting to Maybe* went to press. The more protracted and intense the competing views on offer in the classroom, the more likely it is that the professor will design an exam question presenting an opportunity to bring those views to bear in some new factual setting—e.g., a constitutional challenge to a state law prohibiting weapons in classrooms at a public university. Treat the multiplicity of views as "noise" interfering with a desire for a straightforward answer, and you may not be in a position to see more than one side come the exam. Take those views seriously, and you'll enhance your ability to "get to maybe" and excel on your answer.

To be sure, when the Socratic method is on full display, it's neither possible nor desirable to try to produce a "courtroom transcript" of the proceedings. In our experience, "transcribing" replaces "understanding" in precise ratio, and the latter is infinitely more valuable to law school study than the former. Instead of trying to take down every word, it would be wiser to *think about* what your classmates are saying and to aim to capture in your notes the basic points emerging from the seeming free-for-all. In particular, we'd urge you to identify the ambiguities in the legal materials that produced the debate in the first place. Why isn't the case under discussion open and shut? What is it about the statutory or constitutional language that makes it susceptible to multiple interpretations? Why does the professor think it worth considering alternative perspectives and points of view? In other words, the points on which the law is unclear or in flux are every bit as important to your studying as the points on which the law is clear and stable, for it's the points in contention that are likely to show up as "issues" on the final.

Class discussion may provide further hints about issues to expect on a law exam. A common teaching technique is for the professor to ask whether two of the assigned cases are consistent or inconsistent with each other. A discussion may ensue in which some students argue that the cases can be reconciled and others suggest no reconciliation is possible. It's easy to become annoyed if the professor fails to take sides. Indeed, if the professor offers no definitive view, it's tempting to conclude that the debate had no resolution and nothing worth noting was accomplished in class. But as often as not, the contrary turns out to be true. An extended classroom focus on the tension between the cases may signal that the professor views this as a pressure point for future legal development. If the professor is astute, the tensions her questions bring to the surface may eventually give rise to actual disputes you'll confront or at least read about when you're in practice. But if *you* are astute, you'll watch for the tension to show up even sooner—on your final exam.

All that said, don't let the search for conflict obscure the more straightforward roles that class notes can play in helping to anticipate exam content. For one thing, try hard to record every hypo the professor offers in class. The odds are good that a variation on one or more of them will appear on the final, and you'll be miles ahead if you've taken a second and more methodical look at them in preparation for the exam. Moreover, and at the risk of channeling Captain Obvious, if the professor identifies (say) "three key takeaways" from a particular case—while introducing it or while summarizing the ensuing discussion—you'll want to include those takeaways in your class notes as well. If the professor thinks the points are important enough to highlight in this manner, there's a good chance she'll think them important enough to test on the final. Finally, and a bit less obviously: If the professor begins class with a "do-over"—presenting a new and different take on material already covered in lecture, perhaps in response to a particularly challenging student question—the time and effort she put into the "rethinking" suggests that this is a pretty big deal to her, big enough to be ripe for testing. If you'll pardon a mixed metaphor, failing to harvest such "low-hanging fruit" in your class notes is exam prep malpractice. To put it another way, the professor is *telling* you what to expect on her final exam, if not always in so many words. So get on the clue bus and focus your preparation efforts accordingly.

2. Course outlines

Beginning law students worry a lot about closed-book exams, and many express a strong preference for an open-book format. We see how the law school equivalent of walking unarmed into a gunfight seems like a daunting prospect. But as we've confirmed in countless conversations with students who've survived an exam cycle or two, the typical exam-taker is too busy coping with the professor's questions—reading and analyzing them, and organizing and drafting answers—to leave much time for "looking things up." Simply put, if your outline is not in your head when you enter the exam room, it's not likely to be of much use in the time-pressured context of the typical law exam.

So how in the world do you get all the rules and exceptions and cases and policies and arguments and themes and the rest "in your head" as you prepare for finals? Flashcards and checklists have their place, especially when it comes to straightforward tasks like keeping track of case names (was that blasted decision on proximate cause *Peevyhouse* or *Pennoyer* or *Palsgraf*?) and remembering the fine distinctions between trespass and nuisance, replevin and trover, libel and slander, reliance and restitutionary damages, etc. But in our experience, there's no better way to "get it all in your head" than by creating an outline for the course. As exam day approaches, a course outline is likely to be *the* go-to study tool, as the time available for reviewing cases, class notes, and case briefs rapidly diminishes. Yet the principal value of an outline lies less in its utility as a last-minute study tool than in the drafting process itself, when you bring the course together and make it your own. *That's* how you master the material and "get it all in your head" for deployment on the final, whether or not you're allowed to bring the physical fruits of your labor into the exam room. In the material that follows, we offer a number of strategies for drafting an outline that can aid you in your efforts, some of them likely to overlap with techniques familiar from undergraduate and others specific to the challenges of law school exams.

a. From syllabus to course outline in fourteen (not-so-) easy weeks

Straight business: Especially during the first semester of law school, we think it's a bad idea to work in earnest on a course outline until eight or ten weeks into the semester. For one thing, it takes nearly that long for most students to begin to get the hang of basic legal reasoning skills—analyzing cases, interpreting statutes, mobilizing factual arguments, identifying issues, etc.—and the further along you are in developing those skills, the better you'll be at figuring out what belongs in an outline and what may safely be relegated to the cutting room floor. For another, an important function of outline drafting is tying the nitty-gritty details of the course to the "big picture," and the big picture frequently doesn't come into view until late in the semester. And for yet another, in the first weeks of law school most students are way too busy just trying to keep up with the daily assignments to take on the additional burden that outlining would entail.

But there *is* something you can do from the get-go to help you prepare for the eventual outlining effort: Use the course syllabus to create a template for your outline as well as an "all-in-one-place" repository for intel about what to expect on the final. Why the syllabus? Among other things, it's a definitive guide to the organization and content of the course developed by the person who, as luck would have it, will be drafting and grading your final exam—and who wouldn't want *that* person's help in preparing an outline? If the document is available in a format that permits easy cutting and pasting—e.g., Word or Excel—make a copy with the file name "Outline for [Subject]" and you're off to the races. If it's available only in hard copy or an electronic version that makes aggressive editing difficult, take the time to convert it to an edit-friendly format even if you need to do so manually.

Once you have your outline template in hand, you can use it to collect anything and everything the professor says—during class or via other communications with students—about what will or won't be on the exam (e.g., "I always test this topic" or "this is important stuff but, since we don't have time to do it in detail, I won't test it on this year's final"). You can also use the document to note updates posted on a course online platform or distributed in class—e.g., a late-breaking case involving a COVID-based claim of commercial impracticability the professor has added to the material on "excuses" listed in the Contracts syllabus. When you're ready to create a fully fleshed-out outline, the syllabus skeleton you've annotated and tweaked over the course of the semester will provide a great place to start.

b. Don't hide from conflict—<u>highlight</u> it!

Most of us come to law school expecting to learn rules by the truckload, and in this respect legal education seldom disappoints. Indeed, it's no surprise when you encounter a rule for nearly every conceivable legal problem… and even rules for problems you didn't know were problems in the first place. But what *does* come as a surprise are the many settings in which a problem generates not just one rule but two or more *conflicting* rules, substantially increasing the workload. There is, for example, the "contributory negligence" rule in tort law (which bars recovery for plaintiff's injuries when both plaintiff and defendant were at fault in bringing about an accident) vs. modern "comparative negligence" rules (which apportion damages based on the relative fault of the respective parties). Likewise, there's the rule in contract law limiting duress to situations in which perpetrator threatens victim with criminal conduct (e.g., pay me more or I'll kill your horse) vs. the modern rules under which threats of noncriminal actions may constitute duress as well (e.g., pay me more or I'll breach our contract). The availability of more than one rule for a single problem is so commonplace in American law that we devoted an entire chapter to the phenomenon—see our discussion of "rule vs. counter-rule" issues, as we referred to them back in Chapter Six.

Although most students take this unexpected source of rule proliferation in stride, some look for ways to avoid the necessity of learning all those additional rules. The most common strategy is to come up with a seemingly plausible excuse for ignoring an entire class of rules—e.g., "since the Restatement is merely 'persuasive' and not really 'law,' I'm not going to worry about it as I prepare for exams"; or "there's no reason for me to learn the nineteenth-century common law rules, since the professor isn't going to test us on a problem set in the nineteenth century"; or "I'm going to limit myself to learning the 'majority rule,' since surely that's the one the professor will be looking for on the final." But the central point of this book is that law exams test conflict—*that's where "issues" come from*—and the multiplicity of rules is an abundant source of

conflict your course outline should identify and exploit rather than ignore or conceal. Trust us that the extra work is worth your while.

But what does this mean in practice? Assume you are preparing your
Torts outline and are focused on intentional infliction of emotional distress (IIED), a cause of action available to redress the harmful psychological and physical effects of extreme and outrageous conduct—e.g.,
falsely telling parents that their child has just died. Assume further that
the professor devoted a great deal of class discussion to the problem of
whether bystander witnesses to horrific conduct (e.g., a severe beating)
can use IIED to recover against the offender, advising the class that
most courts permit such recovery but limit it to bystanders who are the
victim's "family members" (e.g., children who witness the beating of
their parents). Say the professor also spent time on the Second Restatement's formulation relaxing the "family member" requirement and extending recovery to *any* bystander who suffers physical consequences
(e.g., sleeplessness) from witnessing horrific conduct. Class discussion
may have highlighted the various arguments for and against the proposed reform—e.g., "it can be traumatic for *anyone* with a basic sense
of decency to watch the severe beating of even a complete stranger
(pro)" vs. "eliminating the 'family member' requirement would open
the door to frivolous lawsuits by greedy but essentially unfazed bystanders (con)." The upshot, as class discussion and the assigned readings revealed, is that most jurisdictions resisted this reform, and the
Third Restatement has once again reverted to the traditional "family
member" requirement.

How should you deal with all of this in your outline? It would be
tempting to ignore the reform effort altogether. After all, it didn't get
much traction in the courts, and even the Restatement has given up on
it. Why, one might think, lengthen and complicate the outline for a dog
that just didn't hunt? Yet a typical exam question designed to test the
problem of bystander IIED will pose a "hard case"—e.g., a problem in
which the traumatized bystander is the victim's fiancé. An answer that
said "no marriage license, no cause of action" would obviously get credit for recognizing and applying the traditional "family member" rule. But
an answer questioning the fairness of denying recovery to a person who
is family in substance if not yet form—and noting the benefits of the
more flexible Second Restatement approach—would get twice the points

and fare far better grade-wise. The punch line, then, is that an outline that treats conflict as signal rather than noise will stand you in better stead for a successful exam performance.

c. Include the "basics," but emphasize the "pressure points"

Don't let all our talk about highlighting conflict obscure the importance of including the "basics" in your outline. A useful outline will, for example, carefully list the elements for each cause of action you study (promissory estoppel in Contracts, adverse possession in Property, libel in Torts, etc.) and each defense as well (e.g., fraud, duress, incapacity, etc.). For Criminal Law, you'll want to do the same for each crime the course explored (homicide, burglary, embezzlement, etc.) and likewise the defenses available in that setting (entrapment, insanity, self-defense, etc.). A complete outline would also collect and organize the factors on which courts rely to reach different kinds of determinations—e.g., the multiple-factor test courts deploy to determine whether a particular activity constitutes an actionable nuisance. And of course you'll want to list all the rules you've learned (e.g., there's no duty to rescue a stranger in distress) along with the attendant exceptions (e.g., a duty to rescue may apply where a party has created the peril). Collecting and putting the "basics" together in this way not only provides an opportunity to get the details right but will also help you remember it all for ready recall on the final.

Yet there's a hidden hazard to organizing an outline in this manner. The long list of claims, defenses, rules, and exceptions can prompt one to think that the point is simply to "apply" them to the problems you encounter on an exam, "checking the boxes" as each requirement is or isn't met by the facts at hand. To be sure, there are many legal requirements that ordinarily work in this straightforward manner: a victim of a would-be homicide either is or isn't dead; a party to a would-be enforceable contract either is or isn't 18; an employer alleged to have violated a whistleblower statute either does or does not employ the statutory minimum of 15 employees. But on law exams, most professors test requirements that generate *disagreement* between the parties—that is, that generate "issues" of the sort we've been exploring throughout this book (rule vs. counter-rule, competing interpretations of a rule, competing interpretations of case law, etc.). We think of issue-generating requirements as "pressure points," and they deserve a prominent place in your course outline since that's "where the money is" on most law exams.

Let's return to the "family member" requirement for bystander IIED claims and consider just a few examples of exam questions a professor might draft to test that particular pressure point:

- Victor Victim is dragged before what appears to be a firing squad and "executed" by actors in the guise of soldiers who turn out to be firing blanks. Victor's siblings as well as his close friend Billy Bystander are firsthand witnesses to the event and have no idea that it's an elaborate hoax. The siblings can obviously bring a by-stander IIED claim, but Billy's case will generate a "rule vs. counter-rule" issue over whether to stick to the traditional "family member" requirement (in which case he's out of luck) or to follow the Second Restatement and expand liability to protect nonfamily witnesses as well (in which case his claim may proceed).

- Outrageous conduct is directed at a high school student and wit-nessed by a nanny who raised the victim from early childhood. If the governing jurisdiction is wedded to the "family member" re-quirement, can the nanny recover for bystander IIED? This sce-nario raises a "competing interpretations" issue over whether to focus on the "plain meaning" of "family member" (are you related by blood or marriage, or not?) or to interpret the term through the lens of its likely purpose (i.e., to provide a remedy only for those who—because of their relationship with the victim—are most likely to suffer trauma from witnessing a horrific event). Our nanny obviously doesn't fit within the "plain meaning" of "family member," but years of *acting* "like family" increase the likelihood that she'd *suffer* "like family" if she witnessed the vic-tim in distress. So an interpretation based on the requirement's purpose might green-light her claim.

- The "family member" requirement would likewise give rise to a host of "borderline cases" of the sort we discussed in the chapter on "forks in the facts." We saw one such case in the previous section—i.e., when the bystander is the victim's fiancé—but there are loads more where that came from. Consider, to name just a few, disputes in which the bystander has the following relationship to the victim: (1) a nonadoptive step-parent; (2) an ex-spouse;

(3) a third cousin; (4) the legal guardian; and (5) quoting the description of a modern family tie recently overheard by one of us at a family wedding, "my half-sister's real dad's second wife's parents."

Nor is "family member" the only "pressure point" presented by bystander IIED claims. Most courts require the bystander to be "present" for the trauma-inducing event, and the requirement of "presence" is thus another potential source of issue-generating disagreement between the parties. You know the drill: Is the "presence" requirement met if the outrageous event takes place on the street and the bystander views the action through a window of an apartment on the third floor of a building overlooking the street? How about a bystander who watches a recording of the event on social media? Do we interpret "presence" literally, or would the functional equivalent (e.g., via a live CCTV feed) count as well?

An outline doesn't need to go into this level of detail for exam preparation purposes. The key is to identify and highlight "pressure points" and to offer a brief example or two of issues likely to be generated thereby. Since professors mostly test what they teach, you'll have plenty of "hints" about likely candidates for this honor by the time you outline the course—from the cases you read (which may focus on a recurring dispute about the application of a particular requirement); or a series of hypotheticals conjured up by the professor ("cousins and exes, *au pairs*—oh my!"); an analysis offered in the assigned readings (e.g., tracing the history of a requirement and providing fodder for arguments about what it was designed to accomplish); or patterns evident in the professor's old exams ("she *always* asks a 'presence' question"). But including pressure points is a must if your outline is to aid in spotting them on an exam.

d. Illustrate elements, don't just list them

As suggested a moment ago, a good outline will include a comprehensive list of the elements of the causes of action, crimes, and defenses you study. But a great outline will annotate those lists with brief illustrations drawn from the assigned cases, class discussion, etc., since the critical thing in the law exam setting is not only to remember the elements but also to recognize factual settings in which they might come into play. It's all well and good if your Torts outline notes that battery requires a "harmful or offensive contact with plaintiff's body or an object closely identified with same." But your outline can bring that element to life by citing the haunting scene from *Fisher v. Carrousel Motor Hotel* in which the racist restaurateur commits battery by seizing a dinner plate from the hand of a patron of color without actually touching the latter's person. If an exam question features someone grabbing a hat from a head or a cane from an arm or an upside-down Bible from a short-fingered grasp, the facts of *Fisher* will help you remember that contact need not be with the body to satisfy battery's requirements.

e. What to do with cases

When it comes to what to do with case law in an outline, our best advice is that this depends first and foremost on what the professor does with a case in class. If she focuses almost entirely on the holding—treating the decision as no more than the source of a rule and then referring to "the [*name of case*] rule" throughout the rest of the course—she's likely to expect you to follow her lead on the final, and your outline should therefore treat the case in that way as well. If instead she emphasizes the facts—presenting the class with a series of hypos, say, that alter the facts in a variety of ways and asking whether each alteration would make a difference to the outcome—then your outline should try to capture those twists and turns, since that's how the case is likely to show up on the exam. And if class discussion is "all about the reasoning"—with a primary emphasis on the arguments and policies invoked by the court, on their wisdom and limits—then she's likely to test that reasoning on the exam, and it should therefore figure prominently in your outline. Many professors offer a mix of these approaches and other approaches still, and of course that means the outline's treatment of case law should mirror these multiple points of emphasis as well.

We have two additional suggestions that will prove useful no matter what the professor does with any particular case in class. First, your outline should include enough information about a case to trigger your recollection of the court's opinion and to enable you to recognize "similar" cases when they turn up on an exam. A substantially shortened version of the case-briefing method we discussed back in Chapter Three should do the trick, focusing on the "Three Little Questions" (who's suing whom, for what, and on what legal theory) as well as (1) the issue presented; (2) the basic facts; (3) the holding; and (4) a brief account of the reasoning. We stress that this is only a template, and—in keeping with the advice we offered above—you should adjust the format for a deeper dive into features of the case (such as the facts or the reasoning) that loomed especially large in the professor's in-class treatment.

You'll obviously be miles ahead in this effort if you briefed cases as the course progressed, and further ahead still if you took the time to supplement and correct your initial drafts based on what you learned during lecture and class discussion. You will thus have in hand a comprehensive and reliable source of information about each case, and some quick and aggressive editing can produce a streamlined version for inclusion in the outline. If you don't have your own case briefs to work with, you'll want to go back to the text of the case itself and to your class notes to gather the information you'll need to outline cases in the manner suggested above. But tempting though it may be, we do *not* recommend relying on commercially produced case briefs for this purpose. One of us just finished grading a set of first-year exams, and—not for the first time—a substantial portion of the class submitted answers making mistaken claims about a famous case that just happened to match the misinformation available from a popular commercial case-brief database. These days colleagues report similar misfires during nearly every exam cycle.

Our second and final suggestion is to keep in mind what you'll be asked to *do* with the cases you've studied on the typical law school exam. As explained at some length in Chapter Eight, the most common way professors test a student's understanding of a case is to draft a question presenting facts that are similar to the case but that include differences as well, calling on the student to muster arguments based on the similarities to "follow" the case as well as arguments based on the differences to "distinguish" it. You can enhance your ability to do this well by paying particular attention to points (2), (3), and (4) in our template—i.e., the basic facts, the holding, and the reasoning. You'll need an accurate account of the facts in order to see the similarities as well as the differences between the case you studied and the exam problem, and—again as discussed in Chapter Eight—the holding and reasoning play critical roles in constructing arguments about why and to what extent the similarities and differences matter. That chapter also contains an important discussion of the hints you can gather from lecture and class discussion about the professor's take on what "really matters" about a particular case, so we won't repeat that advice here.

f. Be sure to capture the multiple dimensions of the course

We'll wrap up the discussion of outlining where it began: with the syllabus, the best guide you have to a professor's particular approach and thus a great template for outline construction. As you'll realize once you're a few weeks into your first semester of legal studies, professors organize their teaching plans and hence their syllabi in a wide variety of ways. The "old-fashioned" approach is a focus on case law, where each section or subsection of the syllabus is more or less a list of cases. But you are also likely to encounter syllabi organized around particular clusters of rules (e.g., offer and acceptance in Contracts) or discrete subjects of governance (e.g., riparian rights in Property) or "big themes" (e.g., intention vs. consequences in Criminal Law) or different approaches to judging (e.g., originalism vs. living constitutionalism in Constitutional Law). Virtually all law professors teach with a mix of these, and a key to a useful outline is to capture each of the dimensions the professor actually emphasizes in class, treating the syllabus as merely a starting point.

A couple of quick examples should illustrate this point. Let's say your Torts professor organizes her syllabus around cases but during class discussion emphasizes the tension between "fault-based" liability (you're liable for the harms you cause only if you somehow did something wrong, such as departing from reasonable standards of precautionary behavior), and "strict" liability (you're liable for the harms you cause, even if you did nothing wrong) in connection with each of the cases covered. Your outline will obviously need to reflect this "dual focus," since your exam will almost surely pose questions testing both approaches as well. Or let's say your Contracts professor organizes the syllabus around clusters of rules but in class leans heavily on individual cases to illustrate the way the rules work—and the ways they don't. Since she's highly likely to draft an exam that is "rule and case forward," your outline should be too.

3. Old exams and study groups

The approach to outlining we've just described is not simple. But here we have not just good but very good news: You probably have ready access to a resource that has already done a great deal of the work for you. We're talking about old exams, which many professors, and indeed many law schools, routinely make available to students in some convenient format—online, in hard copy at the library, and even in bound volumes distributed to the student body. If you care about your exam performance at all—and we know you do or you wouldn't be reading this—you simply cannot pass up the opportunity to give a careful review to your professor's old exams. You'll hear this from others—and, because it's so important, you'll hear it from us again. But here we want to make the case explicitly in terms of the "forks in the law" approach to issue identification taken by this book.

Your professor may have taught the course several times before. On each exam, she will have had to invent problems that present precisely the kinds of issues we've identified in this book (e.g., rule vs. counter-rule, competing interpretations of rules, competing interpretations of case law, etc.). Working your way through these old exams can thus help you learn to hunt for issues in a sustained and systematic way. But even better, it's highly likely that some of the issues you find on old exams will show up again on yours. Most professors have particular issues they find especially interesting or at least useful for writing exam questions, and they are not shy about repeating them. So when you read over old exams, it's not merely to get generalized practice but also to familiarize yourself with your professor's exam-drafting patterns. Even the most energetic and creative professors, who like to think they are doing something new every time, in fact tend to fall back on old habits—like a poker player who can't help making a certain facial expression every time he has a good hand. Review a professor's old exams, and you'll learn to spot these "tells."

We urge you to bring along *Getting to Maybe* when you sit down with your old exams to aid you in looking for the kinds of issues we describe. But we urge you to bring along something else as well: your classmates. Once you understand that exam preparation is as much about hunting for things you don't know as memorizing things you do, you're likely to see why studying alone may not be the road to success. Finding the issues is difficult the first time through. If you do it with friends, each of you will find some issues the others don't. By the time you get to the exam, you'll have seen enough of them so that the ones actually tested will either be ones you have encountered before or sufficiently similar that you'll be likely to recognize the pattern.

Two final points. First, if your experience of study groups is anything like ours was, you'll inevitably suffer the presence of someone who routinely speaks up to unravel a consensus painstakingly reached by the rest of the group. Begrudge the outlier if you must, but heed what is said, because nonconforming views may prove quite useful in identifying potential points of contention on the final. Once again, when it comes to issue spotting, conflict rather than consensus may be the best friend you ever had.

Second, working with old exams—and doing so with study partners—is such a useful tool in exam prep that we've devoted an entire chapter to it. Thus, in Chapter Sixteen ("Putting Maybe to Work: Exam-Taking Exercises"), we offer a series of exercises designed to improve your exam-taking skills as well as an approach to group study that is ideally suited for use on old exams. Once classes are over, the reading is done, and your outlining is complete, we can't think of a more effective way to spend your time as exam day approaches.

Chapter Twelve

Spotting Issues in an Exam Problem

Enough preliminaries. It's exam day, and it's time to put your preparations to work. With the examination finally in your hands, how can you maximize the prospect of "spotting" the issues the professor has buried in the problems? What follows are the six most important lessons we've drawn from grading thousands of exams over the years: (1) despite the time pressure, spotting issues requires slow and careful reading; (2) when it comes to issue spotting, the "call of the question" is the best friend you ever had; (3) if you're not sure where to start, "brief" the dispute; (4) resist the temptation to stop with the first issue you see; (5) if the answer seems too easy, there's probably more to the story; and (6) if you finish early, "check your work." Let's explore these lessons one at a time.

1. Spotting issues requires slow and careful reading

You wouldn't be in law school if you weren't already pretty good at exam-taking, so it's natural enough to want to transplant the skills developed in high school and university to your law exams. But what worked before won't work nearly as well now, and the principal reason is a marked shift in the kind of exams you'll be taking. Simply put, if the key to success on exams in other educational settings is *what's in your head as you walk into the exam,* the key to success on a law exam *is what you can do with problems you'll encounter for the first time in the exam room.*

The typical exam question in undergrad is a prompt for you to tell the professor "everything you know" about a particular event or topic, while the typical law school exam question is a prompt for you to analyze a concrete legal dispute the way a lawyer or a judge would. Your mastery of the course materials will be indispensable, but all that work will be for naught if you don't read the problem carefully enough to identify the issues—that is, the potential points of conflict between the parties—that will jump out to experienced legal professionals. And a technique that may have worked well earlier in life—read the question until you figure out what it's "about" and then scramble to regurgitate everything you've crammed into your head on the topic—will get you a disappointing grade in the law school setting.

In recognition of this critical difference, we offer the same advice here we offered early in the book with respect to studying case law: Read the question two times before you even *think about* drafting a response. The first time through, it's fine to read quickly—to get an overview of the context, the parties and their relationship, and the nature of the dispute, and to burn up some of that nervous energy and reassure yourself this isn't mission impossible. But once you've done that we strongly suggest a... *slow... and... very... careful... read*, from the first word to the very last in order to maximize the chances of identifying every issue possible. Only then can you begin to organize and draft a successful answer.

From our own time in law school—and from decades watching students struggle with exams—we are all too familiar with the exam-day pressure upon students to devote more time to writing and less to reading. For one thing, your professor can't grade what you don't put "on paper," so—especially in the context of a time-constrained exam—you are right to be eager to start writing. For another, if you are taking the exam in a room full of eager-beaver One-Ls, it's going to seem like everyone else is already banging away on their laptops while you alone are still slogging through the question. And for yet another, you did all that studying in preparation for this exercise, so you can't wait to get down to it and begin showing the professor just how much you've learned in the course.

But if it's A's you're aiming for, you've got to resist such pressures and allow plenty of time to read through each and every exam question with a fine-toothed comb. Why is that so important? As we've demonstrated repeatedly throughout this book, law exams test and reward the ability to identify and analyze issues. But you won't be able to do that unless you *see* those issues in the first place, and—in the search for issues—*every fact counts*. So you cannot afford to skip, misread, or glide over a sentence, a phrase, or even a single word in the problem.

Consider, for example, a simple hypo in which Freda Friend attends a party at Homer Homeowner's house and is injured by a dangerous condition that Homer knew nothing about. Freda would appear to be a social guest, letting Homer off scot-free. But a closer look at the hypo reveals that the gathering wasn't just any old party. It was a *Tupperware* party, raising the distinct possibility that Freda is a business invitee—not a mere social guest—and Homer is thus liable for her injuries after all. The word "Tupperware" thus transformed a simple narrative with straightforward legal consequences into an "issue" with arguments available on both sides, and a student who misses the word "Tupperware"—or who overlooks its significance in the rush to get down to writing—won't be able to spot, let alone to analyze, this critical issue at all.

If you're thinking "But I'd never miss a word like 'Tupperware,'" we've got some sobering news: Every semester, each of us reads dozens of exams that miss the significance of critical facts conveyed by similarly conspicuous words or phrases. And while old-fashioned misreading is always a risk given the pressures of the exam setting, we've noticed a steady increase in "missed facts"—and hence missed issues—over the course of the past decade, and most professors we know report a similar pattern. This certainly isn't the result of any decline in the abilities of our students. One of the genuine pleasures of teaching in the 2020s is that we're working with some of the most talented and committed students we've ever had. We think the problem lies instead in the fact that many of today's students come to law school accustomed, as we all are these days, to doing most of their reading on smartphones, tablets, and laptops, where browsing and link-clicking—rather than careful and sustained engagement with text—are the order of the day. Habits born of years of relentless screen-skimming are difficult to break, but break them you must in order to undertake the "deep dive" required for successful issue spotting. (We offer some advice on breaking these habits back in Chapter Two ("Slow Learning").)

2. When it comes to issue spotting, the "call of the question" is the best friend you ever had

As pandemic restrictions ease, law professors everywhere look forward to the return of professional conferences, where we can renew the pleasures of catching up with old friends and meeting new ones. At such gatherings, we pose the same questions as anyone else, asking about fam-

ily, mutual friends, health and well-being, and, increasingly, the direction of the country. But the most frequently asked question in this setting
is one that reflects the central role of research and writing in academic
life: "What are you working on?" Back when we were drafting the first
edition of this book, we got a kick out of revealing that we were doing a
"how to" book on law exams, decidedly not the ordinary fare of law reviews and academic presses. But what struck us at the time was the nigh
unanimity of the reaction our revelation would prompt from fellow law
professors: "Tell them to answer the question asked!"

We always found the "do as we say, not as we do" dimension of our
colleagues' reaction somewhat amusing. Law professors are notoriously
bad at providing straight answers to student questions, though the problem stems less from contrarianism than from the impossibility of offering the simple black-and-white answers many students crave as they
struggle with law's terrain of complexity and ambiguity. In any event, our
colleagues were right, and "answer the question asked" is perhaps the
single most important exam-taking advice we can offer. (For what it's
worth, it's also important advice for entry-level legal professionals field-
ing questions from senior partners, agency supervisors, and curious
judges, all of whom will have even less patience than professors with
less-than-direct answers to their questions.)

Truth be told, exam-taking students *do* have an uncanny knack for
not answering the question asked, and the problem seems to us to resemble the famous "Far Side" cartoon contrasting "what we say to dogs"
("Okay, Ginger. I've had it. You stay out of the garbage. Understand, Ginger?") with "what they hear" ("Blah blah blah Ginger. Blah blah blah blah
blah Ginger."). We're loath to cast students in the role of Ginger, but—as
the cartoon suggests—what we're asking and what our students *think*
we're asking are often worlds apart. And, as usual, the culprit is the ill fit
between undergraduate exam-taking habits and the brave new world of
the law exam. Each grading period, we get numerous exams that read as
if the student got far enough into a question to identify the topic we're
testing—"*What a relief, this is adverse possession!*" or "*Warranties, I've got
this!*" Rather than reading through to the end and developing a careful
analysis of the problem it presents, the student then proceeds to treat the
question as inviting an "outline dump"—that is, as an occasion on which
to regurgitate everything she knows about adverse possession or warran-

ties or whatever topic the question seems to be "about." But in the nearly 50 years since we started law school, we have never, ever seen a single law exam question that actually asked, "Tell me everything you know about [insert particular legal topic]." Not once.

So if *that's* not the question, where should you look to figure out what the professor is actually asking? Nine times out of 10, the answer is about as straightforward as answers ever get in law school: It's in "the call of the question," which you'll almost invariably find at the end of the long and winding tale of mayhem and disappointment comprising the typical exam problem. Here are a few examples:

- Alvaro brings an action against Brishen for intentional infliction of emotional distress. What result under the Restatement (Second) of Torts?
- Evaluate the possible legal claims Tammi Tenant can bring in an effort to prevent Lorraine Landlord from constructing a roof over the courtyard at the apartment complex.
- After Jerimiah General uses the figures from Sloan Sub's paving bid in formulating General's own bid on the construction project—but before General hires Sub for the project—is Sub free to alter the terms of the bid? Explain your answer.

Simply put, when it comes to law exams, the "call of the question" *is* "the question asked" and thus the key to making law professors everywhere a happier lot. It is also the key to identifying the issues you'll need to analyze in constructing a successful answer. Less obvious, but equally important, is that the call of the question tells you which issues to *avoid* as you grapple with the question, saving you precious time and bandwidth. How can you get so much guidance from a simple sentence or two? Let us count the ways.

First, the call of the question may limit the search for issues to particular parties and particular disputes. Consider an exam problem with multiple players and more than one possible dispute: A betrothed and besotted couple books an upscale wedding venue for their special day, only later to learn that the venue's owner had double-booked and has revoked the reservation in favor of another couple who had booked first. As a consequence, the disappointed couple has to pay a small fortune to have the hand-painted invitations it commissioned from a pricey stationer redone to reflect the new destination. Worse still, on the very same day, their caterer abruptly and unjustifiably bails. The call of the question reads thus:

> Assume that the venue's owner is liable to the disappointed couple for breach of contract. Will the damages due the couple include the cost of the wedding invitation do-over? Explain your answer.

So what can we learn from the call of the question? For one thing, there are multiple players in the hypo: the disappointed couple, the reneging venue owner, the lucky couple whom the owner is prioritizing, the pricey stationer, and the bailing caterer. For another, there is more than one potential dispute. In addition to the couple's beef with the venue owner and troubles with the stationer, there is also the fact that the caterer has left them high and dry, so perhaps there's a contract claim there as well.

The call of the question, however, focuses only on the dispute between the couple and the venue owner, and it would therefore be a mistake even to *mention* any potential claim the couple might have against the caterer. Why do we call it a mistake? For one thing, most law exams are severely time-constrained, so every moment you spend on a dispute the professor hasn't asked you about is a moment you won't be able to devote to the dispute the professor will look to when grading. For another, the grader is not likely to react well to your frolic and will wonder whether you misunderstood the question (never a good look) or understood it perfectly well and decided to ignore it (probably worse). The lesson here, then, is that the call of the question frequently operates like a funnel, narrowing the scope of the required analysis to exclude some of the players and potential conflicts appearing in the course of the problem and directing you to focus your search for issues to a narrower field. If throwing in facts not relevant to the question asked seems like an unfriendly professorial trick, consider how likely it will be in law practice that a potential client will walk into your office with a tale of woe, and your first task will be to sort the mere slights from the harms that might create valid legal claims.

Second, the call of the question may limit your search for issues arising out of the dispute under examination. The call of the question in our wedding venue hypo asks the student to "[a]ssume that the venue's owner is liable to the disappointed couple for breach of contract." Accordingly, your answer should avoid analyzing any issues regarding whether there's a breach of contract, for that's off the table. An answer that doesn't heed this restriction will (once again) waste precious time and create the impression that you have not read carefully or that you failed to answer a straightforward question. But note that the call of the question here narrows the "search field" even further than simply taking the issue of liability out of the equation. Thus, it doesn't ask "what are the couple's damages?" Instead it asks whether a *particular* cost is recoverable as a *part* of damages: "Will the damages due the couple include the cost of the wedding invitation do-over?" If you've already taken first-year Contracts, you will recognize that this question calls for an analysis of whether and when such "consequential damages" are available to parties aggrieved by a breach, raising a series of issues such as whether the breaching party had "reason to know" of these consequences at the time of contracting. In drafting your answer, then, you'll want to resist the temptation to talk about the rules generally governing money damages or what it might have cost our disappointed couple to secure a replacement venue and to focus instead on one thing and one thing only: the cost of the invitation re-do, which will give you *plenty* to write about. The punch line is that the "funneling" function of the call of the question operates not only to restrict the parties and the disputes you should discuss but also to limit the issues you have to analyze in disputes that *are* on the table. That means less work for you—or, better yet, more time to spend on work that will actually be rewarded—and thus should be viewed as doing you a favor rather than as interfering with your freedom to write about anything and everything that pops into your head as you read the problem.

Third, the call of the question may limit your search for issues to a particular source of legal authority. Especially in first-year subjects, casebooks frequently introduce an area of law with a classic case and then proceed to trace the development of the area by offering later decisions—either as additional opinions or in the notes following the classic case—as well as the approaches to the problem embodied in the Restatement or in subject-specific statutes (e.g., the U.C.C. in Contracts) or statutory wannabees (e.g., the Model Penal Code in Criminal Law). Sometimes the point of an exam question is to have the student bring these multiple authorities to bear on a problem, identifying the difference it would make if a court follows an infamous nineteenth-century decision (on the one hand) or the modern Restatement approach (on the other). Such questions are so common on law exams that we devoted an entire chapter to them earlier in the book. (See Chapter Six ("Rule vs. Counter-Rule Issues").) But sometimes the call of the question identifies a particular legal authority and asks you to apply it, and *only* it, to the problem at hand. We saw an example of this in the call of the question that read, "Alvaro brings an action against Brishen for intentional infliction of emotional distress. What result under the Restatement (Second) of Torts?" When the call of the question narrows the inquiry in this way, you *might* get extra credit—or you *might* impress the grader—by *briefly* noting the difference it would make if some other source of law governed instead (e.g., nineteenth-century common law or the Third Restatement). But write any more than a line or two on sources of authority the professor did *not* ask about and you run the risk of prompting her to think, "Just what part of the 'the Restatement (Second) of Torts' don't you understand?" The point here, then, is that once again the wisest course is to "answer the question asked" and thus to focus unwaveringly on the issues that would arise if the legal authority the professor has specified were applied to the problem.

3. If you're not sure where to start, "brief" the dispute

The call of the question won't always direct your "search for issues" to the central dispute in an exam problem. As often as not, the prompt will broadly ask students simply to "discuss the issues" buried in a lengthy hypo without providing further guidance. When that's the case, how on earth do you go about beginning your search? We suggest deploying those Three Little Questions from the case-briefing format set out in Chapter Three: Who's suing whom? For what? And on what legal theory? Let's see how answers to each of them can guide your issue-spotting efforts.

Who's suing whom? This one is sometimes a free space on your briefing bingo card, because many "discuss the issues" questions offer a story featuring just two parties and a pretty obvious dispute between them or—when other persons are part of the narrative—a party-specific directive appearing at the end of the command (e.g., "discuss the issues that will arise in an action by Dubois against Hansberry"). Even then, answering the "who's suing whom" question carefully can be helpful in identifying issues if you cast the suit in *relational* terms, as we urged back in Chapter Three. Thus, "general contractor is suing subcontractor" offers a great deal more guidance to an issue-spotting search than "Dubois is suing Hansberry." For one thing, chances are you've studied a bunch of law governing general contractor/subcontractor disputes and, well, no law at all for Dubois/Hansberry disputes. For another, when you use proper names (or abbreviations such as "D. & H."), you run the risk of confusing the players with one another as you sort out the conflicts, and we've read many exams over the years that got into needless trouble because the student unwittingly transposed the parties in this way.

And, as you can imagine, getting clarity on exactly which disputes arise between exactly which parties is even more helpful when the events portrayed in the exam question contain a multiplayer affair—a common exam scenario in all of your courses because it is a common scenario in law as well as in life. If someone is hit by a car, it will be crucial to distinguish the potential issues arising in an action against the driver from those arising in a claim against a passenger distracting her at the time of the accident; if a bank robbery goes badly wrong, it will be crucial to distinguish the issues likely to arise in a prosecution of the shooter from those in connection with nailing the getaway driver; and if a sale of residential property blows up, it will be crucial to distinguish the issues implicated by a claim against the online mortgage lender from those in a claim against the seller's real estate agent. Keeping the parties and their differing disputes straight in settings like these will greatly aid you in zeroing in on the distinct issues presented by each respective conflict.

For what? Like "who's suing whom," this term in your "brief"—in effect, what's the party who's doing the suing trying to *get* with the lawsuit—is often a given or a "free space" that is readily apparent from the call of the question or the content of the problem itself. Our wedding venue hypo provides a good illustration of just how much guidance "for what" can provide, directing our exam-taking student's attention to the costly invitation re-do and thus to the law of consequential damages... and from there to the issues that seeking consequentials will inevitably entail. Similar guidance is evident in one of the samples we offered back

at the beginning of this section: "Evaluate the possible legal claims Tammi Tenant can bring in an effort to prevent Lorraine Landlord from constructing a roof over the courtyard at the apartment complex." Here once
again you are told exactly what the complaining party wants from a
court—*stop the roof!*—and a bit of reverse engineering can help you
identify which theories of liability/causes of action studied in Property
might get her where she wants to go. After that, it's only a small step from
identifying those potential theories of liability to pinpointing the issues
that will necessarily arise when applying each theory to the facts of the
problem at hand.

But don't despair if the "for what" *isn't* provided, for an effort to answer that question may lead you to discover more issues still. For one
thing, the facts may reveal that alternative remedies are available—e.g.,
a case in which a landowner might seek either an injunction or money
damages against invasive activity by a neighbor—in which case an analysis of the issues arising when pursuing alternative remedies may be
just what the professor is looking for. Or the facts may reveal that a
remedy the aggrieved party would strongly prefer (e.g., specific performance against the seller, since the aggrieved buyer has commitments to
sell the missing goods to a customer) is for some reason foreclosed (e.g.,
because the goods are already in the possession of an innocent
third-party purchaser)—and a recognition of the significance of that
possible dead end may be a key issue on the exam. Careful attention to
the "for what" factor, then, can also aid in your hunt for issues.

On what legal theory? Sometimes the call of the question identifies the
cause of action the professor wants you to analyze—recall once again this
example: "Alvaro brings an action against Brishen for intentional infliction of emotional distress. What result under the Restatement (Second)
of Torts?" When that's the case, you know exactly where to start in your
search for issues, for the question by its terms demands a deep dive into
the facts of the problem to see whether each of the requirements of the
IIED claim—and of possible defenses to it—is or is not satisfied. ("Did
Brishen engage in 'extreme and outrageous conduct'? Did he do so 'intentionally' or 'recklessly'?" And so on, with particularly close attention
to any recurring "pressure points," as we urged in the previous chapter.)

But more often than not, "on what legal theory" is *the* "missing piece"
in an exam problem. The call of the question—or the facts of the prob-

lem itself—may come right out and tell you just who is suing whom and just what sort of remedy the suing party wants, but leave you entirely to your own devices in determining whether there is a way to get the suing party from Point A to Point B—that is, from aggrievement to redress. Sometimes the facts suggest only one plausible cause of action, and your job is to identify the issues that claim will generate. Other times, multiple legal theories may be plausible, and the task before you is to identify the issues that will arise in connection with each. In either case, your outlining work in preparation for the exam can pay off—and pay off big—in two quite different ways. First, once you figure out the legal theory or theories in play, your outline (or your recollection of it if the exam is closed book) will be your guide to identifying the requirements of each claim—and of each possible defense—and thus to hunting for issues that will arise in determining whether the claim is viable on the facts presented. But of equal importance, your outline can aid you in figuring out *which legal theory or theories are in play in the first place*, for a thoroughgoing familiarity with the constituent elements of the various causes of action and defenses you studied may be just the hint you need to get started. *("Wait! There's a harmful contact! Could it be battery?")* The recurring "pressure points" we explored in the previous chapter may be particularly helpful in this respect. If your professor thought a particular "pressure point" was important enough to focus on—e.g., by assigning cases and/or spinning out hypotheticals illustrating it—she is more likely than not to build an exam problem around it, providing you with just the "tell" you may need to identify the missing cause of action. *("Why on earth does it matter that the passerby is the victim's "third cousin"? OMG, it's that 'family member' thing, so the professor must want us to talk about bystander IIED claims!")*

4. Resist the temptation to stop with the first issue you see

Apart from finals, perhaps the most anxiety-provoking experience for many law students is the first-year orientation party, although we may all appreciate such gatherings a bit more as the pandemic finally abates. A common strategy for introverts coping with this particular rite of passage is to cruise the room looking for a familiar face in the sea of strangers—ideally someone you knew from undergraduate or high

school, but desperate times call for desperate measures, so even someone
you just met earlier that day will do. This "start with the familiar" strategy can provide some comfort—and, as you are introduced to your
friend's friends and then to their friends, a base from which to begin
"working the room"—but it can also be self-defeating. If you spend all
evening sticking like Velcro to the one person you already know, it's going to be a mighty dull party.

You may be surprised to learn that the anxieties of law school finals
drive some students to adopt a parallel strategy on their exams. Faced
with the daunting task of analyzing a dense one-and-a-half- to two-page
single-spaced hypothetical involving (for example) a multivehicle disaster and a cast of dozens, these students panic and quickly scan the question for something, *anything* they might recognize. They focus unerr-
ingly on the first familiar issue they see ("Aha, there's a contributory
negligence vs. comparative negligence issue!") and embrace it to the
exclusion of a veritable glut of other issues lurking in the facts (e.g., issues involving negligence *per se,* inviting rescue, proximate cause, multiple causes, and damages). Sometimes the desire to cling to the familiar
is so great that it causes a majority of the class to overlook a major issue.
The question, for example, might contain a long set of complex facts
producing an obvious issue of who holds title to land under various recording statutes. Having discussed the recording issue thoroughly, however, students relax when they should press on to see whether a lurking
adverse possession claim might render the entire recording statute analysis moot. Like the party-goer who misses the chance to make new
friends, the anxious exam-taker is searching for security in an extremely
discomfiting setting. But exam-takers unwilling to venture beyond the
familiar aren't any likelier than their social counterparts to be happy with
the results of their single-minded focus.

5. If the answer seems too easy, there's probably more to the story

Assume you encounter a hypothetical on your Contracts final that
goes something like this: Seller agrees to supply widgets to buyer for
$500,000; seller breaches the contract and refuses to part with the prom-
ised widgets; buyer purchases the widgets elsewhere for $600,000 to
meet her pressing needs. What are buyer's damages? Under U.C.C.

§ 2-712, buyer is entitled to the difference between the "cost of cover" —
i.e., the cost of purchasing replacement goods—and the contract price.
Accordingly, the answer here appears to be pretty straightforward:
$600,000—$500,00 = $100,000.

But what's wrong with this picture? In a nutshell, it's this: Law exams
almost *never* test anything as easy as the ability to subtract $500,000 from
$600,000. So if you think that's the "answer," chances are you haven't yet
fully grasped the complexity of the question. We appreciate that you may
be tempted to stick with "$100,000" despite this warning; after all, simple
subtraction is something even the most math-anxious among us can
handle, while the rules governing (for example) a buyer's remedies under
the U.C.C. may seem utterly confusing by contrast. But when an answer
seems that easy and straightforward, there is almost surely an issue lurking in there somewhere that you missed the first time through. Here are
three specific ways you might go about spotting it:

(1) *Retrace your thinking step by step.* One of the most effective
strategies for spotting issues is to think the problem through
once again and undertake a careful "step-by-step" mental audit
of your initial analysis. To continue with our widget sale example, your rethinking might go something like this:

> Under § 2-712(2), Buyer is entitled to the "cost of cover" less
> the contract price. The facts state that the contract price is
> $500,000; what's the "cost of cover"? Sub-(1) of the provi-
> sion defines "cover" as a "reasonable purchase" of substitute
> goods. Buyer bought substitute widgets here for $600,000;
> is that a "reasonable purchase"? Well, we don't have many
> facts about the purchase; all we really know about it is the
> price Buyer paid, which is $600,000. Is that a "reasonable"
> figure? How would *I* know? There's nothing in the facts—
> like a market price—to compare it with. Wait a minute: I
> can compare it with the contract price, and it is a full
> $100,000 more than $500,000—that's 20% higher. That's a
> lot; maybe the issue is whether the price is just too high to
> be a "reasonable purchase."

Chances are, the ability to spot and grapple with this "reasonableness" issue is the "fork in the facts" that the professor was
attempting to test with her question, and retracing the analysis

in this step-by-step fashion is a good way of finding it if you missed it the first time.

(2) *Force yourself to argue the "other side."* Another effective strategy for "figuring out what you missed" in a question is to imagine that you are the lawyer for the party who has the most to lose from the seemingly "easy" answer. Suddenly, what seemed to be a virtue in your original answer (i.e., that it is easy to subtract $500,000 from $600,000) is outweighed by a vice (i.e., your client stands to lose $100,000!). What can you do to reduce or minimize your client's loss? Just as retracing your steps can reveal contestable assumptions, *attacking* an answer from the "other side" can achieve the same purpose. Seller's lawyer is likely to react skeptically to buyer's claim that a figure 20% in excess of the contract price was a "reasonable" cover, and that is precisely the sort of skepticism the professor is looking for—and likely to reward—on your exam.

(3) *Work out your analysis "on paper."* Don't let the way we've divided up this part of the book fool you: Spotting issues (the focus of this chapter) and dealing with them in an answer (the focus of the next chapter) are not always discrete phases of exam-taking. Indeed, our first two suggestions for ways to spot additional issues—i.e., retracing your thinking step by step and forcing yourself to argue the other side—are approaches that may yield better results if you do them "on paper" than in your head, for many of us need "to see whether it writes" in order to figure out what we think. And there's no better place to do hard thinking about an exam question than right there "on paper" where the professor can see it and reward it. To continue our example, an answer that begins with a frank admission that "$100,000 is too easy" and proceeds to discover the "reasonable purchase" issue, either by reexamining the initial assumptions or by attacking them from the other side, is the law school equivalent of the Return of the Prodigal Son (or Daughter). Since most law professors care more about the quality of your analysis than whether a particular answer is "right," you may well get more credit by showing the professor how you "found your way back" to an issue than you would for an answer that simply spots the issue and moves on.

6. If you finish early, "check your work"

One of the most common characteristics of law exams is that they ask you to do about a week's worth of analysis in four hours or less. We don't defend that tradition—indeed, we think there's a lot to be said for using the extended (eight-to-48-hour) "take-home" exam instead—but the point here is that, with the rarest of exceptions, your professor won't give you anywhere near the time that even an experienced lawyer would need to offer a thoroughgoing analysis of each question. Accordingly, if you finish an exam early because you think you've said all there is to say, *you are almost surely wrong.* Once again, you may be attempting to transplant undergraduate test-taking habits to the law school setting, and, once again, that is a serious mistake.

The point of rechecking your answers on the "memorize-and-regurgitate" college exam is to make sure that your answers are *right;* once that is accomplished, there is little to be gained by sticking around for yet another read-through. But the point of rechecking your answers on a law exam is not so much to make sure that they are "right"; once again, there is frequently no "right" answer to a law school exam question, and, even when there is, most professors are more interested in how you got there than in your accuracy at the bottom line. What you should be doing instead is carefully re-reading the questions and your answers—and, if time and exam instructions permit, even going back through your course outline—to see whether there is some issue, some argument, some angle, some complexity you missed.

One possibility, of course, is that you overlooked a particular fact altogether or skimmed over it too quickly to appreciate its significance to the parties' dispute. A colleague recommended a simple technique to help students avoid this error: Bring a highlighter to the exam and highlight each fact as you use it in your exam answer. Then, if there's extra time at the end, go back and carefully scrutinize the white space. There may be a Tupperware party hiding in there somewhere, and far better to learn of it while there is still time to adjust your answer than when a well-meaning classmate later exclaims, "Can you believe she threw in a Tupperware party? The only thing missing from that question was my grandmother."

Truth be told, we sometimes miss an issue hiding in one of our own questions, and we're absolutely delighted when student answers bring it to our attention. But in the overwhelming majority of the thousands of exams we've read over the years, students have missed one or more of the issues that we were trying to test and that would have made a difference to the final grade. Wouldn't you rather be the student who figures that out before the professor does?

Chapter Thirteen

What to Do with Issues—and What *Not* to Do—Once You Spot Them

Let's recap. Part I of the book addressed questions we've been getting from students since *Getting to Maybe* was first published in 1999—questions about how to start preparing for exams from the day law school begins. Part II explored the architecture of "issues"—the building blocks of the typical law exam question—to aid you in "spotting" them when exam day finally arrives. The last two chapters offered exam prep and exam reading advice specifically designed to help you hunt for the issues your professors are likely to test and to recognize the places you're likely to find them.

Now there's good news and bad news. The good news is that the hardest part of exam-taking is in your rearview mirror. Issue spotting is *the* critical lawyering skill—it's what lawyers in the crowd are reflexively doing while everyone else listens to a tale of woe or conflict—and, in our experience, it is the most difficult skill to teach. When we were students, law schools didn't even *try* to teach it—or, more accurately, they taught it by throwing students into the water and assuming that those who figured out how to swim on their own were "the best and the brightest." (Any resemblance to the historical persecution of witches is purely a coincidence.) Indeed, when we began teaching, it was an article of faith among our senior colleagues that a law exam was the legal equivalent of an IQ test. As one of them put it in a most revealing moment, "You've *got* to test issue spotting. How else can you tell how smart they are?"

We were skeptical then, and we aren't persuaded now, that issue spotting measures intelligence, and we're even less sure what "intelligence" means. Rather, we think issue spotting is a skill that law schools *still* don't teach very well, and—left mostly to their own devices—some students simply figure it out before others. And that's the principal reason we wrote this book. Legal issues come in patterns (rule vs. counter-rule, competing interpretations of rules, competing interpretations of case law, etc.) and, if you learn to recognize those patterns, you'll be able to "spot" issues in any subject once you've mastered the substantive material. No one should suggest any of this is easy, and there are no shortcuts—let alone any simple formulae—to get you where you need to be without considerable work. But it *can* be done, both by students who find it comes easy *and* by those who struggle at first.[*]

So that's the good news. The bad news: Though spotting issues is critical to success on law exams, it is nowhere near enough if you want to excel. So what does need to be done *after* the spotting work is complete? Here's what we've learned from watching our most successful students in action.

A. From Issue Spotting to Issue Analysis

Let's begin by imagining an exam question based on our recurring Artiste/Patron hypothetical:

> Paul Patron offers Arlene Artiste $10,000 to paint a portrait of the Patron family. Artiste explains that her other commitments make it impossible for her to promise a completed work by a particular date, and Patron responds, "I don't *want* your commitment. I just want the portrait." After Artiste spends numerous hours doing preliminary sketches—but before she has put brush to canvas and begun the actual portrait—Patron advises her that he has changed his mind and is revoking the offer. What legal rights does Artiste have against Patron?

---

[*] One of us has on multiple occasions taught academic success courses to students whose first-semester, first-year performance did not go well, and each rendition focused on issue spotting and analysis via *Getting to Maybe*. We're delighted to report that the vast majority of students in those courses, well, "got to maybe" and achieved a marked improvement in their academic performance.

Now consider two potential answers.

> *Answer #1.* Whether Patron can revoke his offer will depend on whether we apply the common law rule or the rule provided by § 45 of the Second Restatement. If we apply § 45, there will then be a second issue about whether Artiste's work so far counts as having begun performance.

> *Answer #2.* Patron can revoke if the old common law rule applies or, even if § 45 of the Restatement governs, if a court can be persuaded that Artiste has yet to begin performance. Patron's right to revoke under the common law is based on the fact that his offer seeks a performance (painting a portrait) rather than a return promise (he says he doesn't want a commitment); thus it constitutes an offer to form a unilateral contract. At common law, such offers can be revoked any time until performance is complete, and Artiste has not yet finished the painting. Section 45 of the Restatement replaces the common law rule with one more favorable to offerees in this context. It will prohibit revocation once Artiste has begun (as opposed to completed) performance. Patron will contend that since there's "no brush to canvas," performance has not yet begun. Artiste will counter that the preliminary sketchwork counts as the beginning of performance and is more than "mere preparations."

It won't surprise you that 99.99% of law professors would award a far higher grade to Answer #2 than to Answer #1. In a nutshell, Answer #1 merely *spots* the issues raised by the Artiste/Patron hypothetical, and Answer #2 *analyzes* them. But what's the difference, apart from a greater word count in the second answer?

We start by noting a crucial similarity between the two, for each recognizes that the problem presents two distinct issues, a "fork in the law" (common law vs. § 45) and a "fork in the facts" (beginning of performance vs. mere preparations). So Answer #1 has the virtue of successful issue spotting—and that's not nothing, for Answer #2 can't present an "analysis" without first identifying the issues to be analyzed. But that similarity aside, Answer #2 does two things that Answer #1 doesn't even attempt.

The first is that Answer #2 explains *why* there's a fork—why the road is split as it is—and it does so both for the "fork in the law" and the "fork in the facts." At the "fork in the law," Answer #2 identifies the facts and reasoning giving rise to the rule vs. counter-rule problem: Because Patron's offer sought a performance rather than a return promise, it may be characterized as an offer to make a unilateral contract, and the common law rule governing the revocation of such offers (revocation permitted until performance is complete) differs from the rule under the Restatement (revocation prohibited once performance has begun). In short, understanding the "fork in the law" not only helps you "identify the issue," but it also helps you to explain why there's an issue in the first place. At the "fork in the facts," Answer #2 does the same thing once again: It explains how the facts (Artiste has done sketchwork but has not begun work on the portrait itself) could lead down one road (sketchwork = the beginning of performance) as well as another (sketchwork = mere preparations).

The second distinguishing feature of Answer #2 is that it carefully explains what will happen in the dispute between Patron and Artiste if each of the issues is resolved in a particular way. If we resolve the "fork in the law" issue in favor of the common law, then Patron can revoke; if we resolve it in favor of Restatement § 45, then Patron's power to revoke depends on whether Artiste has begun performance (revocation prohibited) or undertaken mere preparations (revocation permitted). Notice how Answer #2 takes the reader carefully through each of these steps and links, from the *what* to the *why* to *what difference it makes*. It seems simple and straightforward when you read someone else's handiwork, but there's no better way to learn to do this for yourself than by practice, practice, practice—and there's no source of practice material like a professor's old exams. (We offer suggestions for how to make the best use of this resource in Chapter Sixteen ("Putting Maybe to Work—Exam-Taking Exercises").)

B. The Recipe for Argument Construction: Just Add Reasons

On law exams, analysis is good; good analysis is even better; and argument is better still. Let's take it to the next level, then, and talk about what it takes to move from "mere analysis" to "argument construction."

One way to describe the difference is to say that *an argument is an analysis that attempts to persuade.* That's an extremely useful definition for our purposes, since persuasion—of opponents, of judges, of juries—is what most lawyers do for a living and what most law exam questions are designed to test.

A concrete example may help you see vividly the difference between a mere analysis and an argument. Imagine you are a first-year associate in a Texas law firm and that Karla, the senior partner, has asked you to work on a case for one of the firm's oldest and most important clients: Arlene Artiste. (Actually, you were hoping for a quiet weekend, but you're happy with the vote of confidence the assignment seems to represent and the opportunity to impress the firm's No. 1 rainmaker.) The case, of course, is *Artiste v. Patron,* and an hour ago you gave Karla a memo that read just like Answer #2 from the previous section (i.e., the answer that analyzed the issues in the Artiste/Patron case rather than merely spotting them). You've been waiting nervously when the intercom emits a loud buzz and Karla summons you to her partner-sized office with a partner-pleasing view.

"This is fine work," she says as you walk in and sit down. "Your memo is very helpful. But you forgot something. Something big, I'm afraid. As I understand it, we have a bit of work ahead of us if we're going to win this one for Arlene. First, we'd have to persuade a court to go with the Restatement approach rather than the old common law rule. Then we'd have to argue successfully that Arlene's sketchwork was 'the beginning of performance.' Do I have it right?"

"Yes, that pretty much covers it," you respond, wondering what on earth she thinks you left out.

"So, how are we going to do that? You got cases? *Texas* cases? *Arguments*? You know, they don't let us pay the judges for ruling in our favor anymore," she teases. "We gotta convince 'em just like everybody else." She seems slightly amused by your obvious embarrassment at the lapse, and you retrieve the memo and scoot quickly from her office, heading for another long night in the firm library.

———————

But if Answer #2 doesn't tell you how to go about convincing a judge, it certainly does have the virtue of telling you exactly what it is you have to convince the judge *of.* In the same way that identifying the forks in the road offers you a blueprint for an analysis of the question, it also offers you a blueprint for your arguments as well. Your job (should you choose to accept it) is to make arguments for choosing the path of § 45 at the fork in the law, and to make arguments for choosing the path of "sketchwork = beginning of performance" at the fork in the facts, and that's not mission impossible. But you'd better get started straight away, for there's almost surely a young associate burning the midnight oil on the other side of town trying to figure out how to persuade the court to go the other way at each of those forks. Here are some suggestions that may help.

1. Keep in mind who the real judge is

The kind of persuasion that lawyers do for a living and the kind that students are supposed to do on exams are alike in more ways than just the one suggested by this story. When you think about it, a lawyer is typically attempting to persuade at least two audiences at the same time. Her primary task may be to persuade some decision-maker (the judge, the jury, etc.) to see the case her way. But for a host of reasons, she's also trying to persuade her client that she's a competent lawyer. On law exams, students are also pitching to two audiences, yet here the priorities are reversed. The question may ask them to persuade a judge or a senior partner or opposing counsel of this or that proposition, but the real point of the exercise is to persuade a second audience—i.e., the *grader*—that you are doing a good job of persuading the hypothetical decision-maker.

Surely you will want to begin that task by making arguments that your professor taught you in the course. If she assigned a series of articles that offered economic arguments on both sides of the contributory vs. comparative negligence debate and you get an exam question involving a negligent plaintiff, for heaven's sake, use the arguments she's taught you. Similarly, if you spent several classes discussing the competing virtues of various approaches to interpreting statutes (e.g., a purpose-based approach will further the legislature's aims in cases it hadn't foreseen, but a plain-meaning approach will encourage the legislature to draft more carefully in the first place), then use those arguments when you encounter a competing interpretations question on her final.

If the professor hasn't rehearsed specific arguments on a question, consider the larger "themes" she emphasized in the course. If, for example, throughout the semester your Contracts class explored the conflict between the importance of protecting reliance (on the one hand) and the importance of promoting freedom of action (on the other), then don't be afraid to draw your arguments from that resource. To continue with *Artiste v. Patron*, § 45 has the advantage over the common law approach of protecting the reliance of an offeree who is vulnerable to revocation during an extended performance; but the common law rule has the advantage of protecting the offeror's freedom of action until the moment *both* parties are bound by a contract.

2. You know more than you think you do

a. Patterns of argument for forks in the facts

An added virtue of the "forks in the road" approach we offer in this book is that many of the "issue" patterns we explore lead directly to patterns of argument. This is true in particular of the patterns we explored in Chapter Nine on "forks in the facts." Let's look at a concrete example by focusing on the second of the two issues presented in *Artiste v. Patron*—the fork you encounter if we follow the path of Restatement § 45 at the fork in the law—and watch what happens when we make the jump from mere analysis to argument:

> *Answer #3.* Under § 45, Patron may not revoke once Artiste has begun her performance. Patron will contend that since there's "no brush to canvas," performance has not yet begun. Artiste will counter that the preliminary sketchwork counts as the beginning of performance and is more than "mere preparations."

> *Answer #4.* Under § 45, the offer may not be revoked once the offeree begins performance, and it's not clear whether Artiste has met that requirement. On the one hand, Artiste can argue that she began the performance when she did the preliminary sketchwork. To an artist, such sketches are as much a part of portraiture as the brushstrokes on the final canvas, and from that standpoint she "began the invited performance" at the moment she started work on her first sketch. But Patron can counter that he asked for a family portrait—not a series of sketches—in exchange for his promise of $10,000. From the customer's standpoint (and the customer is always right!) the

"invited performance" is *the actual painting of the commis-sioned portrait*, and the preliminary sketches were "mere preparations" for that performance.

Answer #3 tells us a lot: It spots the issue (is the sketchwork the begin-ning of performance?); it tells us why it's an issue (because the sketch-work might be the beginning of performance or it might be mere prepa-rations); and it tells us what difference the issue makes to the outcome of the case (if the sketchwork is the beginning of performance, Patron can-not revoke; if it's mere preparations, Artiste is out of luck). But Answer #4 looks like Karla got hold of it and, impatient with a mere description of the parties' conflict, began to do what lawyers do and to make argu-ments for why the conflict should be resolved one way or another.

A notable feature of Answer #4 is that it draws on the differing stand-points of an artist (on the one hand) and a customer (on the other) to develop the arguments for the parties. In Chapter Nine, we identified "differing standpoints" as one of the common patterns of factual ambigu-ity that law professors use to create "forks in the facts" on their exams. As we've said before, if you learn to recognize those patterns, it will be much easier for you spot issues on exams. But the point we want to make here is that these same patterns can also help you construct legal arguments. It is a short step from recognizing an issue (depending on your standpoint, Artiste's sketchwork might or might not be the beginning of performance) to beginning to develop the arguments that lawyers would make for the respective parties (an argument based on Artiste's standpoint vs. an argu-ment based on Patron's). To put it another way, it's an "issue" precisely because there are arguments on each side of the point, so once you've spotted the issue, the arguments are right there for the asking.

Just as issues can lead you to arguments, arguments can lead you to other arguments as well. Let's continue with your saga as the associate working on *Artiste v. Patron*, and let's assume that Karla has just read the handiwork you came up with in Answer #4. "I like this," she enthuses. "'Standpoint!' Is that what they're teaching y'all in law school these days? Never knew there was a name for it, but it really does sort out the con-flict, doesn't it?" Your confidence returning, you nod your head in agree-ment and are just about to speak when she continues. "But you know, back when *I* was in law school—back before they used fancy-pants terms like 'standpoint'—they used to tell us that we ought to start by reading the contract. And if we're tryin' to figure out whether sketchwork is part of Arlene's 'performance,' perhaps it wouldn't have been such a bad idea to start by seeing whether the *contract* has anything to say on the matter."

"Well, there isn't a written contract in this case," you reply somewhat defensively.

"I know that," she snaps. "But oral agreements have terms too. What did Paul Patron *say* when he hired Arlene?"

You rifle the papers in the file, pull the memo detailing the intake interview with Artiste, and read from it: "According to Client, Patron said: 'I will pay you $10,000 to paint a portrait of my family.' There was no discussion of sketchwork at that time or at any time before Patron called Client to say that the deal was off."

"Well," Karla drawls, "if *I* were representing Paul Patron, I'd be sayin' that I didn't ask for any damn 'sketchwork,' I asked for a 'portrait,' and she ain't begun that yet. How are we going to respond to *that*?"

You return to your office, wondering whether your college roommate who went on to medical school has days like this. Karla's right about what Patron said, you muse, and what can you say in response to an argument as strong as that? Suddenly you remember that somewhere you saw an entire list of responses to arguments like that, and you reach for a book you hadn't looked at since law school. You locate the chapter titled "Forks in the Facts" and begin to thumb through the patterns of issues that had helped you so much on your law exams. You hit an entry in the "Linguistic Ambiguity" section—"literalism vs. reasonable expectations"—and a light goes on. *That's it*, you think. If Patron argues that he said "portrait," we can argue that that's just too literal. After all, if I hired you to give me a "ride" to the airport and you left home to come pick me up, my "ride" hasn't started but you would certainly contend that you had commenced performance. Similarly here, Patron is not buying a portrait from an art gallery; he's asking an artist to *paint* one for him. So if you "read between the lines" of the agreement—rather than just focusing on the words Artiste says Patron used—the likely shared understanding is that he wasn't just asking Artiste to deliver a product, but rather asking her to embark on an artistic process... a process that, in the portrait trade, routinely begins with sketchwork.

Once again regaining your confidence, you read on looking for further inspiration, and another light goes on. You hit "multiple sources of
meaning" and are reminded of the "baker's dozen." *Wow!* you think.
When you order a dozen loaves of bread from a baker, you shouldn't be
surprised if you get 13; so if you order a portrait from an artist, you
shouldn't be surprised to get sketchwork first. So even if we're stuck with
the word "portrait"—and we can't "read between the lines"—maybe
"portrait" has room in it for sketchwork.

Exhilarated by your insights, you click on your word processing program and start another memo to Karla. "Patron can be expected to argue
that he contracted for a 'portrait', not for sketchwork. But careful analysis
suggests at least two arguments in response," the memo begins.

————————————

The "forks in the road" approach thus helps your argument construction efforts in a second way. If the point of our earlier discussion was that
a fork can provide a blueprint for developing opposing arguments, the
point here is that the same blueprint can help you see a counterargument—and hence an issue that could be resolved in more than one
way—when at first you see only one side.

To be sure, when you're taking an exam you won't have a Karla looking over your shoulder saying, "But the contract *says* so." But we'll let you
in on a little professorial secret: Most exam questions are written so that
the argument on one side is pretty obvious, for that's how we separate the
merely good answers (they see the obvious argument and know exactly
where to go with it) from the excellent ones (they figure out a way to
respond to the obvious argument). And we think that the key to seeing
the counter-arguments—to knowing that you can respond to a "literal"
argument with a "reasonable expectations" or a "multiple meanings" response—is a thoroughgoing familiarity with the patterns we explored in
Part II of the book. That is why we've offered what we know seem like
nearly endless examples and illustrations drawn from different topics
covered in different courses. You need to make these patterns "your own"
by learning to recognize them when you see them in operation in a new
setting; indeed, your ultimate goal—to ensure success in law practice as
well as on law exams—should be to learn to recognize *new* patterns
when you encounter them as well.

b. Patterns of argument for competing interpretations
of statutes and cases

The "forks in the road" approach is likewise helpful in dealing with competing interpretations of statutes and competing interpretations of case law, for once again the "issue" patterns we described earlier lead to patterns of *argument*. So it is typically the case that merely by identifying the issue you have also produced a blueprint for your argument. Indeed, in one sense, developing arguments in this context may be even easier than it was with our forks in the facts, because the positions taken by lawyers in this setting are so familiar that they typically present themselves as arguments (e.g., "plain meaning," "broad holding"), and all you have to do is apply them to the particular context.

There's the rub, of course, because *applying* these arguments to a particular context will typically require a detailed knowledge of the language and purposes of the statute or of the facts and reasoning of a case or a line of cases. You can't make a plain-meaning argument if you don't know what the statute says, and you can't argue for either a "broad" or a "narrow" interpretation of a case you haven't studied carefully. No matter how good you get at these arguments, you can't deploy them effectively unless you first have a solid grasp of what it is you're arguing *about*.

3. The crucial role of policy arguments

There is a vitally important dimension to argument construction that we haven't focused on yet—"policy argument"—a dimension so important that we have devoted all of the next chapter to the topic. Law students frequently make the mistake of thinking that policy arguments should be made only in the context of questions that present themselves as "policy questions." (E.g., "You are a legislative aide to Senator Smith, and she has asked you to prepare a memorandum discussing the pros and cons of a bill that would amend the National Labor Relations Act to add the following provision....") But in fact, policy arguments have an incredibly important role to play in each of the kinds of issues we've been exploring. Indeed, in the typical rule vs. counter-rule problem discussed in Chapter Six—where, for example, the facts are set in an imaginary jurisdiction that has not yet decided whether to follow the traditional common law or the Restatement position on some issue in Torts—*policy arguments are frequently the only arguments available*, since you can't rely on a statute, or a precedent, or "the facts" to resolve the parties' conflict.

And when you confront forks in the law that involve issues of interpretation—of either a statute (Chapter Seven) or of case law (Chapter Eight)—you'll often need policy arguments in this setting as well. Take the classic standoff between "plain meaning" and "purpose" in the interpretation of a statute. Naturally the purpose side of the argument will invoke the policies the statute is designed to further, but—with or without a trace of irony—even the proponent of "plain meaning" may find it necessary to offer "policies against using policies" (e.g., "applying the rule as written will incentivize careful legislative drafting"). Indeed, as we saw in those earlier chapters, many issues of statutory and case law interpretation are really disputes over how to further this or that policy—or how to sort out competing purposes or policies—in other words, *policy* arguments.

Finally, even the application of statutes and cases to facts involves an important element of policy analysis. Recall, to take only the most dramatic example, our "creative forks" problem from Chapter Ten, where the question presented was whether the straightforward application of the arcane Rule Against Perpetuities was consistent with the policies underlying the Rule. The facts involved the validity of an option to purchase a building held by a tenant who had invested heavily in the building while doing business there for 40 years. And, because the option seemed plainly void under the rule, the tenant had nothing to go on *but* policy. So if you'd ignored that dimension of the problem, you would have had no "issue" to discuss. And recall as well the final section of Chapter Nine, where we contrasted "formalist" with "purposive" reasoning about factual applications. "Formalist" reasoning aspires to be policy-free, but purposive reasoning is nothing *but* policy argument, all the way from the language of the statute to the significance of the facts.

C. Taking the Call of the Question Seriously but Not Literally

In the previous chapter, we illustrated many ways that the "call of the question" can guide you in your issue-spotting efforts—by, for example, directing you to focus on a particular dispute or on particular parties or indeed even on a particular issue arising between them. We urged you to follow these directives "to a T" and to minimize detours to no more than a sentence or two. We stand by that advice but wish to acknowledge here two ways that the call of the question can lead you astray if you try to read too much into it.

First, on many exam questions, the call of the question consists of a broad directive to "discuss the issues that will arise in an action between A & B" with no further instructions. For the record, "A wins" is not a discussion, and the slightly better "A wins because of the dormant commerce clause" isn't either. But beyond that, the word "discuss" is pretty open-ended, and one might fairly read it as invitation to offer a few paragraphs about how the issues arising in the action relate to the broad themes from your first year in law school; or what the issues "remind you of"; or even how these issues "make you feel." To paraphrase Obi-Wan Kenobi, these aren't the "discussions" you're looking for. In law exam speak, "discuss" means "identify issues, analyze and argue about them" in the careful and detailed manner of Answers #2 and #4 above. So don't conclude from the professor's use of a seemingly vague question that a loosey-goosey answer is what will get you a good grade.

A second common professorial technique in call-of-the-question drafting is to assign the student a particular role: e.g., "You are law clerk to a justice on the state Supreme Court and have been asked to draft an opinion ruling in favor of A"; or "You are an associate in the law firm representing B, and the senior partner has asked you draft a memorandum outlining the arguments that stand the greatest chance of success." When the professor poses a question in this way, she is obviously inviting advocacy rather than neutral and detached analysis, and a successful answer will acknowledge and embrace that role. In our experience, however, an all-too-common hazard here is not that a student will fail in that effort; advocacy, after all, can be fun and is what many of us came to law school to embrace. The hazard is rather that the student will take the role too far. We have *never* read a "call of the question" that said "Be sure to ignore any arguments that cut against your position," and it's a serious mistake to lapse into one-sidedness. Whether you are drafting a judicial opinion reaching a particular result or a legal memo advocating for a particular party, competent legal work must always acknowledge and address the issues that arguments from "the other side" are likely to raise, however much you might wish that those issues would just go away. Addressing them forthrightly is thus very much a part of your charge,

despite—or really *because of*—the partisanship inherent in your assigned role.

D. Where to Focus Your Fire

In Chapter 10—our exploration of "Cascading Forks"—we explained
that you can't afford "to stop with the first issue you see" because issues
encountered on law exams frequently lead to further issues. (As the "no
vehicles allowed in the park" hypo vividly illustrated in connection with
the lowly bicycle, a "plain meaning vs. purpose" issue may well lead to
"competing meanings" issues as well as "competing purposes" issues.)
Yet when you've succeeded in identifying the many issues the professor
has buried in a problem, you may well find yourself facing a different
challenge: "How on earth can I address them all in the time permitted?"

1. Focus your fire on points in conflict

Assume you encounter an exam question involving the application of
a state whistleblower statute to a complex fact pattern. You whip through
the pertinent section of your course outline and are thrilled when
straight away you see four different points implicated by the facts. First,
there is a provision requiring would-be whistleblowers to notify the employer in writing before disclosing illegal conduct, and the facts reveal
that the employee in this case gave firm officials only a one-page photo-
copy of the statute the employer has allegedly violated. (Is that a "notice
in writing"? you wonder.) Next there is a provision stating that notification must be made to a "supervisor"—and a related provision defining
that term—and the facts reveal that the whistleblower gave the photo-
copy to the firm's general counsel, who may or may not be a supervisor
under the statute's definition. ("A fork in the facts!") Then there is a section prohibiting discharges in retaliation for whistleblowing but permitting employers to fire employees "for cause," and the facts suggest that
the employer here was motivated both by the whistleblowing and by the
employee's terrible record of tardiness. ("Didn't the professor call that a
'mixed-motive' question?") Finally, there is the jurisdictional requirement of the statute—a firm must have 10 or more employees to be
covered—and the facts state that there are 25 employees. ("*Gotcha!*")
You have an hour to draft an answer—45 minutes, now that you've read

and re-read the facts and skimmed your course outline to make sure you haven't missed anything—so where will you begin?

We've read enough exams to know that the first instinct of some will be to lead with the jurisdictional requirement. Even though most law students profess to suffer from math anxiety, it's amazing how some love to write answers carefully explaining that 25 is *much* larger than 10. To be sure, there's nothing wrong with addressing the jurisdictional requirement in these circumstances. For one thing, meeting it is crucial to the application of the statute; for another, the professor gave you a fact in the question that satisfies that requirement. But resist the temptation to expand your treatment beyond a sentence or two at the most—e.g., "The requirement of 10 employees under § 101(4) is easily met by the fact that the employer has 25." You aren't likely to "rack up extra points" by expounding on a topic about which you feel supremely confident (e.g., the difference between 25 and 10) or by detailing what you know about the history of jurisdictional requirements or the successful efforts of the small-business lobby to exempt its members from various employment statutes. And you will surely suffer from delaying your dive into topics with which you feel less comfortable (e.g., the "mixed motive" issue). To put the point in terms of "forks in the road," the professor is almost surely testing your ability to address the issues in the question about which there is genuine dispute and arguments to be made on both sides—and not your ability to tell whether 25 is bigger than 10.

2. Focus your fire on points that make a difference

Let's continue with our whistleblower example and assume that, upon carefully re-reading the facts, you realize that the whistleblower gave photocopies of the statute to both the company president and the general counsel, who happened to be in the president's office when the whistleblower dropped by. You've still got a fork in the facts: The general counsel may or may not be a supervisor under the statute's definition of that term. But before you're off on a lengthy disquisition about the facts pointing each way, force yourself to ask *what difference does it make* whether the general counsel is or isn't a statutory supervisor?

If the general counsel were the only individual to whom our whistleblower gave the alleged notice, then the general counsel's status would obviously be a vital issue. But on these facts, since the whistleblower gave a copy to the company president as well—and there's no question that's *she's* a supervisor within the meaning of the statute—the general counsel's status will make no difference to the outcome. To be safe, of course, you might devote a sentence or two to identifying the issue and even the key facts that create the ambiguity; that way, you're sure to get any "issue-spotting" points the professor is giving out. Far more important, you should briefly explain why the general counsel's status doesn't matter; chances are, that will get you more points than any discussion of whether lawyers are supervisors. But any more than a few sentences and you're twice a loser: You lose once because you've wasted time better spent on issues that *do* make a difference, and you lose again when the professor reads your answer and wonders why you gave extended treatment to an issue that wouldn't affect the outcome no matter how it was resolved.

3. Focus your fire on issues emphasized by the professor

The good news is that you've figured out that the jurisdictional requirement isn't really an issue, and that the general counsel's status doesn't really matter. The bad news is that your answer so far consists of two extremely short paragraphs making these points, and you've now got only 30 minutes left on a one-hour question that's worth 25% of the exam grade. There are two issues left—the notification issue and the mixed-motive issue—and you estimate that you could easily spend an hour writing on either of them. *What will you do?*

Whatever else you do, you should start out by writing a "road map" paragraph that briefly describes the two analyses you plan to provide. The professor can't give you credit for insights that don't appear in your answers, and by proceeding this way you offer yourself some protection against the prospect of running out of time before you reach the second issue.

But which issue should you tackle first? To resume a theme mentioned earlier, remember who your *real* judge is and that chances are she is trying, as most law professors do, to test what she taught you. So what did she teach you? If she devoted a substantial portion of the course to close and careful statutory interpretation, and if the notification question requires an involved analysis of the sort she repeatedly forced students to undertake in class, then you'd be wise to use the opportunity to "show your statutory stuff." Alternatively, if a major theme of the course was the problem of "mixed motives" in employment law, then perhaps the exam question is the perfect vehicle for bringing that theme to a close analysis of particular facts. Either way, the point is to let the professor—rather than the luck of the clock—be your guide in making your triage decisions.

4. Write till the facts run out

We close with a very important point, but one we offer more as a caution than a finely detailed prescription. On most exams, you simply won't have time to discuss every ambiguity you see. Indeed, *Getting to Maybe* has primed you for finding ambiguity everywhere you look. If you understand that "cascading forks" appear prominently in almost every exam, then you see that it's a short step to long questions that involve multiple forks. If there are three relevant statutes and two relevant cases for your problem, then even if each has only two plausible interpretations you have already 32 different combinations to discuss—trust us on the math! You are sure to tie yourself in knots if you go down every path. Accordingly, you need strategies to ensure that you aren't spending precious time on an ambiguity that the professor won't find relevant to the test.

We've just suggested several strategies for accomplishing this: Focus on disputed issues; focus on issues that matter; and focus on the points emphasized by the professor in the course. But we have one more suggestion for "keeping on track": Use the fact pattern as your guide. Although some facts are in there for "color," and some professors throw in extraneous facts "for fun," the exam question will mostly contain facts that are there for a reason. So if you find as you write that you are considering additional issues that are raised by particular facts, you are probably on the right track, and you should keep writing until these facts have been thoroughly analyzed. By contrast, if you are turning to new issues merely because they are prominent in your course outline or, worse still, if you find yourself inventing issues based on a series of "what ifs," chances are you are tying yourself in knots. Stop. Take a deep breath. And turn your energies elsewhere.

E. Getting to A+: Argument Nesting and Competing Schools of Thought

A central lesson of this book is that U.S. law is full to the brim with ambiguity—ambiguity about which rule applies and how to read it; ambiguity about how to apply a precedent in a particular case; ambiguity about how to interpret a factual scenario; etc. Judges, scholars, commentators, and others who write about law often lay claim to particular methods for tackling these ambiguities either in particular cases or across the board. Because our work stops at the exam's edge, we've avoided taking sides in these disputes or suggesting that there's a "right" way or a "wrong" way to resolve any particular ambiguity. In this we are following the lead of practicing lawyers who draw "early and often" from *all* the moves we've described—offering, for example, a broad interpretation of case X (because X will help the client) together with a narrow interpretation of case Y (because Y could hurt the client) and doing so without a trace of self-consciousness or embarrassment.

But there are limits to this methodological eclecticism, for practicing lawyers and exam-taking students alike. Lawyers first. For one thing, a lawyer may find herself before a judge who believes that there are indeed right ways and wrong ways to resolve ambiguity—a judge, for example, who thinks that all this talk about statutory purpose is hooey and that what matters is the text before you, as plain as the nose on your face. Needless to say, launching into a full-throated purpose-focused argument in that setting might not get you where you want to go. For another, if a lawyer takes positions that contradict each other during the course of arguing a case—e.g., fiercely advocating for a plain-meaning interpretation with respect to one provision in the governing statute and fiercely rejecting a plain-meaning interpretation with respect to a second—chances are pretty good the judge will notice and press the lawyer to explain the inconsistency. A good lawyer will be ready to answer that question, and a better one will anticipate and address it from the get-go.

Law students may face similar constraints when taking an exam. Some professors hold strong views on the "right way" to read a case or a statute or other legal materials. Although most of us aren't in the business of demanding servility—let alone punishing its absence with a low grade—you'd be well advised to acknowledge the professor's approach as well as its virtues rather than simply ignoring it (a really bad idea) or dismissing it without offering good reasons for doing so (possibly worse). So long as you do so, you're likely to find that even the most dogmatic professors will welcome respectful and thoughtful critiques.

Another source of constraint may come from the exam itself. Thus, if a question casts you in the role of attorney for one of the parties in a hypothetical dispute, you will do well to advance as many cogent arguments for your "client" as you can, even if these arguments seem to be in tension with one another. Indeed, we suggest forthrightly *acknowledging* the potential conflicts between the different arguments you deploy on your client's behalf. The professor is likely to admire both your understanding of the tension and your candor about it, and you may even get to the head of the class if you can come up with a persuasive argument for reconciling two seemingly inconsistent positions. (E.g., "The 'plain meaning' of the statute should be dispositive on Issue A, because people who run into trouble with respect to that issue aren't likely to have the benefit of counsel and should therefore be able to rely on the clear language of the statutory text. But Issue B is more likely to arise in the context of disputes between repeat players with built-in sources of sophisticated legal advice—like corporations and unions armed with general counsels and staff attorneys—so a purposive approach ensuring greater fidelity to legislative aims is less likely to take anyone by surprise.")

There are two further settings in which close attention to argument consistency or its opposite may pay off handsomely in an exam answer. The first, as outlined in Chapter Ten, is the context of "cascading forks," where a pattern of argument referred to by some law professors as "nesting" may emerge as the parties deploy and redeploy essentially the same argument at multiple points down the cascade. Here you may be able to earn additional credit by developing the parties' seemingly discrete arguments at each point and then stepping back to identify the larger pattern, particularly if your professor has stressed the concept of argument "nesting." A second setting in which a focus on argument consistency may secure a better grade is an area of law that is home to "competing schools of thought" over the right way to interpret the authoritative materials governing the area. Constitutional Law is the poster child for this phenomenon, but individual professors may stress "competing schools of thought" in other courses as well. In these settings, don't be surprised if the professor designs exam questions that force you not only to make legal arguments but also to identify and perhaps even critique the kinds of arguments you are making (e.g., originalist, functionalist, textualist, realist, formalist, "got no law and got no facts but my client is an upstanding member of the community, dammit," etc.).

1. Nesting: Law as a bad marriage

When spouses realize that they're having "the same fight over and over again," it's time to seek assistance from a marriage counselor. It may seem as if their conflicts are triggered by unrelated matters—who's going to do the dishes, whose parents are coming for the holidays, who gets to pick the next Netflix series for streaming—but once the argument gets rolling they quickly find themselves at the same old standoff (e.g., "why don't you tell me what you need rather than keep it to yourself until you reach a boiling point!" vs. "I tell you what I need but you never listen!"). When this pattern emerges in a marriage, it's seldom a good thing for anyone in the immediate vicinity. But when it emerges in law—where it occurs so frequently there's even a fancy name for it—it can offer exam-takers a road map for constructing arguments that will impress the grader. And if your professor stressed the "nesting" phenomenon in the course under examination, you may have an opportunity to gain even more points by spotting and explaining it when the professor has worked it into an exam.

To see what we mean, let's look at a concrete example of argument "nesting" readily built into an exam hypo. Imagine a Torts question presenting an action by the estate of Zachary against Xavier for wrongfully causing Zachary's death. The facts show that Xavier, a middle-aged Black man, was walking home along a deserted and dimly lit street when he was roughly accosted by two white teenage boys wearing ragged jeans and torn T-shirts; that Zachary—a Black man in his late 20s and wearing a business suit—came up from behind and tried to intervene to aid Xavier; and that Xavier—honestly but mistakenly thinking Zachary was one of the muggers trying to grievously injure him—gave Zachary a sharp blow to the head, killing him instantly. The exam further states that whether a defendant can plead "mistaken self-defense" is a question of first impression in the governing jurisdiction, and your Torts teacher devoted substantial class time to the pros and cons of allowing the defense and to the further question of whether the defense—if accepted—should be governed by an objective test (the mistake must be objectively "reasonable") or a subjective one (the mistake need not be objectively reasonable so long as it is made "in good faith"). As you begin drafting your answer, you realize that the question presents a "cascade of forks" coming right out of class discussion, beginning with...

> A fork in the law: Does the jurisdiction recognize "mistaken self-defense," and, if not, should it? Without it, Xavier has no defense and therefore is liable to the estate of Zachary. But if the jurisdiction accepts the defense, then we'll need to confront...

> Another fork in the law: In determining mistake, does the jurisdiction embrace a subjective test (requiring only "good faith") or an objective one (requiring reasonableness)? If the jurisdiction embraces a subjective test, then Xavier probably wins, since we're told his mistake was "honest." But if the jurisdiction embraces an objective test, then we have to confront...

> A fork in the facts: Was Xavier's conduct here objectively reasonable? If not, he loses to the estate. If so, he's liability-free.

Cards on the table: A student answer that accurately identified all three of these issues and carefully described the stakes with respect to each is going to get a pretty good grade from almost any law professor. But if your reader is like Karla, the senior partner in our Texas law firm saga—and, in this respect, most professors long for our inner Karla—she will reserve the top grades for answers that flesh out these issues with *arguments*. Cascading-forks questions, then, are another important opportunity to excel, and you can usually count on professors who want to *see* arguments on exams to *teach* arguments in the class under examination. And if you want to rack up more points still, it's an opportunity to draw on the policy arguments we explore in the next chapter.

So what arguments might be available at each of the "forks" in our mistaken self-defense problem? Turning to the first—if it doesn't do so already, should the governing jurisdiction recognize the defense of "mistaken self-defense"?—Zachary's estate is likely to stress the importance of deterring careless violence ("if you are going to kill in self-defense, you better get it right"), and Xavier's lawyer is likely to respond that we want to encourage self-help in such fraught situations ("it's not like my client could have called the police or politely asked everyone to stand still while he sorted out friend from foe").

Turning to the next "fork" in the cascade—if a defense of mistaken self-defense is recognized, should the jurisdiction apply a subjective test ("good faith") or an objective test ("reasonableness") for determining mistake?—we shouldn't be surprised if the parties dust off their respective arguments from the first fork and deploy them once again. Thus, Zachary's estate is likely to argue that we need an objective standard to deter the carelessness that a "good faith" rule might countenance. Xavier's lawyer is likely to respond that the prospect of getting second-guessed from any viewpoint except that of Xavier in the heat of the moment—and especially a viewpoint developed in the confines of a well-guarded courtroom—would discourage potentially lifesaving self-help.

And turning to the final fork—if an objective test is embraced, how does it apply here? Each side has facts in its favor, a classic exam-drafting technique we explored back in the chapter on "forks in the facts." Thus, Zachary's estate is likely to argue that a reasonable person would be careful to distinguish friend from foe before killing someone and would never have thought a 20-something Black man in a business suit was in cahoots with a slovenly pair of white teenagers. For her part, Xavier's lawyer is likely to respond that a reasonable person wouldn't risk waiting until it was too late to exercise the right of self-defense, and that in the midst of a two-on-one mugging, no reasonable person is going to take the time to check the ID of a third party who suddenly appears from behind. As the parties defend these respective positions, the debate—"look before you leap" vs. "he who hesitates is lost"—ends up replicating once more the deterring carelessness vs. encouraging self-help debate generated by the other forks.

Two takeaways here. First, an understanding of "nesting" can be of great utility in an effort to develop and deploy arguments in the exam setting. In the example just presented, the "deterring carelessness" vs. "encouraging self-help" debate generated by the problem of mistaken self-defense—a debate you are likely to have learned all about in class if the professor is testing you on it—can be reconfigured for use with respect to each of the issues in a cascade of forks, from a threshold "fork in the law" (e.g., "should we have the defense at all?") to the very last "fork in the facts" ("was the mistake here reasonable?") and everything in between. This insight can help you take an exam answer from mere issue *spotting* to the back-and-forth *lawyering* most professors are looking for.

Second, if the professor whose test you're taking taught you about argument "nesting," don't be shy about making your use of it explicit in drafting an answer. To be sure, your principal focus should be on drafting the best arguments you can in the time allotted. But an answer that does that and then "pulls the camera back" to identify the "nesting"—e.g., "the debate over deterring carelessness vs. encouraging self-help re-emerges within each issue in slightly different form, first on the larger issue of whether to allow a mistaken self-defense defense at all and then…"—is likely to be rewarded by a grader delighted to see that you not only grasped the concept taught in class but have figured out how to make it work for you in the context of a concrete dispute.

2. Competing schools of thought: Law as a child of divorce

We mentioned earlier that some professors hold strong views on the "right way" to read a case, a statute, or other legal materials, and that you'd be well advised to acknowledge that view and treat it respectfully in an exam answer. But the strong views with which you may be forced to contend may be the product of a robust methodological battle within a particular field of law rather than a dogmatic instructor. A central feature of contemporary Constitutional Law, for example, is that U.S. judges and legal academics debate not only particular issues, such as the nature of protection for gun rights, but also the larger question of how best to read the Constitution. Many who participate in this debate share a working premise that there is one "right" way to go about interpreting the U.S. Constitution. But this doesn't mean that American constitutional law has gotten *past* maybe, for there is a vigorous debate within the field about what that "right" way is, a debate we saw play out during questioning of then-Judge Ketanji Brown Jackson during her Supreme Court confirmation hearings. As we mentioned in a previous chapter, there are competing schools of thought on the topic, and the leading contenders are originalism and its proliferating spawn (contemporaneous public meaning, originalism "plus," and originalism lite); living constitutionalism; "common good" constitutionalism; and several varieties of functionalism. Your professor is likely to explore these approaches in some detail and may well identify others as well, and you'll need to master this material—in addition to a seemingly endless supply of really long opinions—even if it makes you feel like a child convinced that *life would be so much easier if your parents would just stop fighting*. In any event, the professor is likely to devise exam questions that test these theories to see what difference they make in the resolution of a particular constitutional conflict.

Here's a quick example. We'll leave the details to the professor teaching your Con Law course, but *Griswold v. Connecticut*—the case famously establishing a privacy right to purchase contraceptives and opening the door for the rights to abortion and same-sex-marriage—is often viewed as the poster child for living constitutionalism. Judges comfortable with that method of interpretation may be open to developing the existing line of cases even further, expanding the scope of reproductive freedom as well as the constitutional protection available to more transgressive forms of intimate association. By contrast, originalists—who as of this writing have laid claim to a majority on the Supreme Court—are likely to view the *Griswold* thread with regret of the sort one might associate with a night of heavy drinking and might thus be eager to bring these developments to a halt or indeed to reverse them altogether. Indeed, in the Court's recent decision in *Dobbs*, the majority cut back sharply on reproductive freedom by eliminating the constitutional right to abortion, and at least one Justice in that majority expressed a willingness to jettison *Griswold* altogether. More to the point, the commitments of the justices (or of anyone else) to the respective schools of thought are *the* principal arguments for embracing one interpretation over another, so your facility with the schools of thought will be every bit as important to success on the exam as your understanding of the case law.

Two final thoughts. First, individual professors may teach *any* course or individual topic via different schools of thought. Some of the best teaching we've seen over the years in the first-year subjects has drawn on such different approaches as legal realism, neo-formalism, law and economics, and a variety of critical theories. When the professor organizes material in this way, it's a safe bet that she'll test it that way on the final, so dismiss it as tangential at your peril. Second, whatever the topic at hand and however important schools of thought might be to the analysis, don't skip past the facts of the exam problem in the rush merely to repeat what you have learned about various schools of thought. Professors often draft problems designed to spur further critical thinking about the materials covered in the course. You might encounter a problem, for example, that calls into question the coherence of one of the schools of thought or indeed pushes it to the extreme; the targeted school may well represent an approach the professor criticized at length during class, but don't be surprised if the problem is designed to reveal the limits or shortcomings of an approach she actually seems to favor. Answers that recognize and grapple with complexities like these are going to do better than those that simply march in lockstep to positions stereotypically associated with the competing schools of thought.

F. What Not to Do with Issues: Herein of "IRAC"

You're over halfway through a book devoted entirely to law school exams, and you've probably noticed that we've yet to offer a formula or template for drafting a successful exam answer. To spare students the intense anxiety of exam week, we wish such a formula existed. But as long as the craft of lawyering involves addressing real-world problems—and it always will—it is highly unlikely that anyone will be able to tell you in advance how to structure answers to exam questions carefully designed to prepare you for the complexities of law practice. The reason is simple: It's the question itself that will dictate the appropriate organization of a response, just like the questions we all field in daily life. If your parents ask you what you plan to do after college, and you hope to head to medical school, you might lead with that conclusion and offer your reasons afterward, since most parents we know would be so thrilled by the punch line that the reasons won't matter much. But if your plan is to spend a year backpacking across Europe, you might want to head for higher ground and start your answer by stressing how hard you worked to graduate with honors as well as your eagerness in the longer term to attend graduate or professional school. But either way, you wouldn't dream of beginning your response with a robotic "The issue is what am I going to do after college; the rule is don't bite the hand that feeds you...."

(There's no need to continue; they're already asleep.) Our advice for the law exam setting is therefore quite straightforward: Take your guidance for structuring an answer from the question itself, the issues it raises, and whatever else will make your analysis as clear as possible to the reader.

We offer several examples of what this looks like in Chapter Sixteen, and—if you follow our advice to practice writing answers to our sample questions and to questions from your professor's prior exams—you are likely to get steadily better at it. Yet we completely understand that approaching a question without a definitive road map can be daunting at first and that you are likely at some point to be tempted by the lure of the so-called IRAC method, often touted by the well-meaning as a key to success on law exams. We gave the method a brief mention early in the book—in a section of the first chapter called "Some Lessons You May Need to Unlearn"—and here's what the buzz is about. IRAC—an acronym for "Issue-Rule-Application-Conclusion"—calls for the identification of an *issue* in the exam problem; and then the identification of the *rule* that governs the issue; and then the *application* of the rule to the facts of the problem; and finally a *conclusion* resolving the issue. To see this method in action, let's return to the problem of "mistaken self-defense" and use IRAC to work our way through the following exam question:

> Xavier, a middle-aged Black man, was walking home along a deserted and dimly lit street when he was roughly accosted by two white teenage boys wearing ragged jeans and torn T-shirts. Zachary—a Black man in his late 20s and wearing a business suit—came up from behind and tried to intervene to aid Xavier. Xavier—honestly but mistakenly thinking Zachary was one of the muggers trying to grievously injure him—gave Zachary a sharp blow to the head, killing the latter instantly. Zachary's estate brings an action against Xavier for wrongfully causing Zachary's death, and the governing jurisdiction (a) recognizes a "mistaken self-defense" defense and (b) applies an objective "reasonableness" test in determining whether a qualifying mistake has been made in a particular case. What result?

So here is what an IRAC-style analysis of this question would look like: The *issue*, of course, is whether Xavier can successfully claim "mistaken self-defense" against the wrongful death action brought by Zachary's estate, and the *rule* is that the mistake must be objectively "reasonable" in order for the defense to succeed. *Applying* the rule to the facts presented, Zachary's estate is likely to argue that a reasonable person would not have mistaken Zachary for a mugger, and Xavier's lawyer is likely to respond by pointing to the urgency of her client's predicament and the various impediments to identifying his would-be rescuer as friend or foe. The *conclusion* is that the reasonableness determination might go either way—a not uncommon outcome on law exams, where professors tend to test "close" cases rather than easy ones.

The IRAC analysis is thus straightforward enough, but the difficulty in reaching a firm conclusion brings us to a concern many professors critical of IRAC share: Although some advocates of the method are careful to describe the "A" term as "analysis," the far more common use of "application" suggests a syllogism with a conclusion automatically following from the premises. But on an exam question like this one—that is, a question in which there is no issue over what the rule is and no issue about how the rule should be interpreted—there must be some sort of complication when we turn to the facts, for otherwise… *there isn't any issue at all.* In other words, the "A" step in the operation will seldom come down to a simple "application" of a rule but instead will turn on an *argument* about whether the facts fall within the rule or not. As we demonstrated back in Chapter Nine, there is plenty for opposing parties to argue about even when they are focused entirely on the facts. And if there is plenty to argue about, then there's not likely to be a definitive *conclusion* to the problem, thus calling into question the "C" term as well.

Those are relatively minor quibbles, easily fixed if the "A" term is revised and the "C" term is relaxed. Of far greater concern is the fact that the four-step IRAC formula is a ticket for one train and one train only: a problem in which the rule and how to read it are perfectly clear and all that is called for is an argument about the facts. But most law professors draft questions that are *not* limited in this way and thus present issues that don't fit the IRAC rubric *at all.* If you've worked your way through Part II of this book, you've already seen those issues in action:

- *"Rule vs. counter-rule" issues, Part I.* Recall the problem in which Beau purchases land upstream from Yamila and diverts some of the flowing water to feed his sheep. The diversion diminishes the stream's flow so that it will no longer power the generator Yamila has been using for over a decade as the primary source of electricity for her family's farm. Naturally, she sues Beau and isn't crazy about his smelly sheep either. The *issue* seems clear enough—did the diminution in flow violate Yamila's rights?—but there is no "rule" addressing that question. More precisely, U.S. jurisdictions are split on the subject, and there are accordingly *two* rules that might govern. And the *analysis* and *conclusion* will differ depending on which rule applies. Thus, under the "prior appropriation" doctrine, Yamila may well have a claim against Beau for the diminution in flow since Yamila's usage of the stream predated Beau's by many years. But under the rule of "reasonable use," Beau is entitled to his fair share of the stream no matter how long Yamila has owned the adjacent lot. As long as Beau's use is reasonable—as watering sheep from a stream running through farm country would seem to be—the fact that the use deprives Yamila of the flow to which she'd grown accustomed is not conclusive. Accordingly, the IRAC formula would need to be amended to acknowledge that the issue presented in the problem is addressed by *two* rules, not one, and that each of the rules leads to a different factual analysis and a different conclusion as well. The formula for a "rule vs. counter-rule" issue, then, would be IRACRAC (Issue - (1st) Rule - Application - Conclusion - (2nd) Rule - Application - Conclusion).

- *"Rule vs. counter-rule" issues, Part II.* Sometimes professors test "rule vs. counter-rule" issues not only to see whether students can analyze the difference the choice of rule would make on a particular set of facts, but also to prompt students to debate the choice itself, mustering policy arguments—to continue our example—on each side of the prior appropriation vs. reasonable use debate. How will you know when your professor wants you to "take it to the next level" like this? If the professor is routinely using class time to explore policy debates over competing rules, chances are that's what she wants you to do on the exam. And—again to continue our example—if your professor spent class time and/or assigned readings on the arguments on each side of the prior appropriation vs. reasonable use debate, then she is surely giving you an opportunity to bring that debate to your analysis of the problem. So what does all of this have to do with IRAC? Well, for one thing, it adds another *issue* to the analysis of a rule vs. counter-rule problem. And for another, it's an I for which there is no R—that is, when there is a debate over which of two competing rules is superior, then (to paraphrase the bending spoon scene in *The Matrix*) "there is no rule" to resolve it, only arguments supporting each side. And if we add *that* debate to our already-amended formula, the result would be IARA-CRAC (Issue - Argument - (1st) Rule - Application - Conclusion - (2nd) Rule - Application - Conclusion).

- *"Competing interpretations of a rule" issues.* Recall the problem in which Horace Wholesaler receives an order from Reba Retailer for 50 high-end audio components at a total price of $20,000 and sends Retailer an acknowledgment of order by text message, promising immediate shipment of the ordered goods. Prior to shipment, Wholesaler reneges on the deal. Retailer sues, and Wholesaler asserts that the U.C.C.'s Statute of Frauds bars the claim. What result? Since the problem involves a sale of goods for a price of $500 or more, the U.C.C.'s Statute of Frauds applies, and the *issue* is whether the Statute is satisfied by the seller's text message. And at least at first blush, the *rule* seems clear, requiring a "writing signed by the party against whom enforcement [of the contract] is sought" and defining "writing" as "printing, typewriting, or any other intentional reduction to tangible form." But the effort to *apply* the rule to the facts gives rise to a second issue—how should we *interpret* the rule?—and at least two interpretations are possible. On the one hand, a text message that appears only as an electronically generated image on a smartphone screen doesn't appear to constitute the "intentional reduction to tangible form" required by the "plain meaning" of the rule. On the other hand, if the Statute of Frauds was enacted to minimize testimonial disputes over alleged oral agreements by requiring a verifiable record of the governed transactions, that purpose would seem to be equally well served by a screenshot of the text readily retrievable from a smartphone's photos feature as it is by hard copy gathering dust in a file drawer. To adjust the IRAC method to a "competing interpretations of a rule" problem, then, we would need to take account of the fact that the rule gives rise to a second issue—a conflict over its proper interpretation—and then analyze each of the competing interpretations (let's refer to them as "N" since "I" is already taken) leading in turn to two different conclusions. The amended formula would thus read (1st) Issue - Rule - Application - (2nd) Issue - (1st) iNterpretation - Conclusion - (2nd) iNterpretation - Conclusion. That's IRAINCNC for, um, short.

- *Multiplying interpretations of a rule:* Yet "plain meaning" and "purpose" aren't the only possibilities when it comes to interpreting a rule, for the language of the rule often has *more than one meaning.* Recall the problem in which an ordinance requiring restaurants to maintain "two toilets for every 40 seats" is applied to rocking chairs on a restaurant veranda. Do we give "seat" its dictionary meaning ("place or thing to sit upon") or its trade meaning ("seats available for meal service")? It is also frequently the case that a rule has *more than one purpose.* Recall the problem presented when a "no vehicles in the park" ordinance is applied to bicycles. Was the purpose to reduce noise and pollution in the park or to protect the elderly and the very young from fast-moving instrumentalities? Adjusting IRAC to fit these problems would require as many as four interpretations—competing meanings *and* competing purposes—producing different conclusions in each case: IRAINCNCNCNC.

- *Multiplying interpretations of case law:* When an exam question requires the application of precedent, sometimes the earlier case is conventionally read as producing a straightforward rule—e.g., *Hadley v. Baxendale*'s "no consequential damages for you!"—that might then be applied in a straightforward manner to the facts of a particular problem. But as discussed at length in Chapter Eight, there is almost invariably more than one way to interpret a precedent, and the possibilities abound: broad vs. narrow holdings (not to mention every holding in between); competing interpretations of the court's reasoning; competing interpretations of the language in the holding; etc. Once again, each of these interpretations may in turn lead to a different conclusion, and—in order to reflect these possibilities and permutations—we'd need to amend IRAC in ways that would threaten to crash our spellcheck program.

Not to put too fine a point on it, the effort to fit the square peg of most exam problems into the round hole of IRAC—or into any of the currently trendy copycat variants (e.g., CREAC or TRAC)—is a major source of mission failure for law students, and you don't need to try out our alphabet soup recipes in order to see why. The problem of trying to apply a rigid formula to the wide variety of issues law professors actually test is not simply a problem of proliferating capital letters, though trying to remember and differentiate multiple and complex formulae in the context of a time-pressure exam would be daunting enough. A more fundamental problem is that the four-step IRAC method *doesn't even get the order of operations right*, since in most exam questions it's "rules" that give rise to "issues" rather than vice versa. Moreover, the issue to which rules typically give rise is an issue of *interpretation*—a step that is altogether MIA in IRAC—and the issue of interpretation is almost never addressed, let alone definitively resolved, by a single rule.

In sum, as long as you don't take the "A" and the "C" terms too literally, the IRAC formula works just fine for exactly one kind of exam problem—two if you include the rare instance in which a judicial precedent can be reduced to an easy-to-apply rule—and once again that's a problem for which we know exactly what the rule is and exactly how to read it, and the only "issue" is how to apply the rule to facts. But as you've just seen, the vast majority of issues on law exams are more complex than that, and no simple multistep formula will help you to address *any* of them. Indeed, the time you would need to figure out whether IRAC would work on an exam problem would be far better spent just answering the professor's questions and leaving the futile quest for a one-size-fits-all formula behind.

So how do you go about "just answering the professor's questions" if IRAC won't do the trick? In the examples above, we were obviously mocking formulaic approaches to exam-taking, not urging you to parse the ways IRAC goes wrong to build more complicated formulas. Instead, you will find the devil in the details of the question —and the details to watch out for have been explored at length in this book. But distilled to its essence, the approach we recommend to drafting an exam answer is this: What will the parties argue about, and what will each side argue? And, if the question calls for a definitive answer, then which side has the better argument and why?

PART IV

Beyond Issue Spotting:
Somewhere Over the Rainbow

In Part III of the book, we focused on the kind of exam question you will most frequently encounter in law school, the so-called "issue spotter." In this Part, we explore two other kinds of exam questions, "policy" questions and multiple choice.

Chapter Fourteen

Policy Czars

Phillip Areeda, Harvard's late, great Antitrust and Contracts teacher, had an unmistakable style. In overcrowded yet reverentially hushed classrooms, the acknowledged master would zero in on individual students to ask, without warning, his favorite question: "Ms. Jones, if you were Czar of the Universe, how would you have decided today's case?" The question served as a powerful wake-up call for anyone still clinging to the idea that law school was principally about learning rules.

In its own way, virtually every law school exam question asks not only what the law is but what it *should* be. Thus far in the book, we have been focusing on only one kind of exam question, albeit the kind of question that appears on virtually every law exam given in U.S. law schools: the issue spotter. At first blush, Professor Areeda's Czar would seem to have little role to play in the analysis of such questions. Assume, for example, that you encounter a problem on your Property final in which a group of struggling musicians attempts to invoke the warranty of habitability against the landlord who rents them their loft space. Some facts suggest that the tenancy is a commercial one—that's what the lease says, and the loft is in a decidedly commercial district—in which case the warranty would not apply. But other facts suggest a residential lease—the musicians live as well as work in the loft, and this is known to, if not acknowledged by, the landlord—which would make the warranty claim a winner.

The problem thus presents a classic case of "concurrent forks," for the road taken at the "fork in the facts" (commercial vs. residential lease) determines the path the case will take at the "fork in the law" (the warranty of habitability applies to residential but not commercial leases). As we discussed in the previous chapter, you'll get a lot of credit with most professors for simply identifying and analyzing these issues, but you'll get more points still—as Karla stressed to her young associate—if you present persuasive *arguments* on behalf of the respective parties as well.

The point of this chapter is that behind every successful Karla is a Policy Czar: Many of the most effective arguments available to lawyers representing clients—and, more important here, to students answering exam questions—are *policy* arguments. To return to our struggling musicians, the student who identifies the commercial vs. residential lease issue; explains its significance to whether the warranty of habitability applies to the parties' lease; and carefully marshals all the facts that support the competing characterizations will surely do well on her exam. But the student who does what a first-rate lawyer would do—who offers reasons for *why* a court should choose one characterization or the other—is on her way to an "A."

Thus, the professor is likely to reward the student who points out that extending the warranty to tenants who knowingly use rental property for purposes that violate the spirit and perhaps the terms of their lease will create an incentive for tenants to ignore the obligations of private agreements they have freely and willingly entered. The professor is also likely to reward the student who argues that it will encourage subterfuge if landlords can escape legal responsibility through a commercial lease loophole even when they know they have residential tenants. And the professor is likely to save the biggest rewards of all for those students who mobilize Czar-like policy arguments such as these on both sides of a case that presents itself as a traditional issue spotter.

Every now and then, however, borrowing from Professor Areeda's playbook, law professors will cut to the chase and ask questions directly about what sort of policies the legal system should adopt. Should Congress pass a statute requiring the government to pay compensation when its actions reduce the value of an owner's property by more than 20%? Should gun manufacturers be held liable for injuries to gun victims even when "fault" lies with the criminal who misused the gun? Should Congress outlaw partisan gerrymandering? Such questions call on exam-taking skills that go beyond those we have already described.

One way to grapple with the traditional issue spotter is to understand that you must simultaneously argue issues of characterization (is the studio a residential or commercial space?) and issues of policy (what happens when we expand or contract the warranty of habitability?). Straightforward policy questions that channel Professor Areeda's Czar of the Universe allow us to isolate the policy components for purposes of exposition. But whether you are talking "big picture" or attempting to resolve a nitty-gritty dispute within a classic issue spotter, you need to be prepared for the particular challenges at stake in your brief reign as a Czar of the Universe.

A. To Know and Not to Know— That Is the Answer

The first trick to conquering policy issues is to get past two perfectly natural reactions. On the one hand, policy questions may provoke the kind of panic you might feel sitting down to dinner with your romantic partner's parents for the first time. "So kid," your prospective father-in-law chimes in, "what position do you think the United States ought to take toward the rise of China?" What you want to say, of course, is, "How the heck should I know?" But you understand that would somehow be inappropriate.

So, too, the policy aspects of law school exam questions may strike some students as somewhat unfair. We came here to have you teach us the law, the student thinks, and now you are asking us to tell you what the law should be. What was the point of all that studying if now all you want are our opinions? The answer, of course, is that professors don't want just your opinions. They are looking instead for considered analysis based on what you have learned in the course. Your initial reaction to questions like whether diversity jurisdiction should be abolished may quite honestly be "I don't know." After all, if you actually did "know," we wouldn't think of this as much of a question. But when you start to write, you will discover that although you can't provide a foolproof answer, you "know" a lot more about policy arguments than you may have thought.

A second natural reaction to policy questions is the other side of the same coin. A student who is also a landlord may believe very strongly, for example, that rent control is a bad thing. A question asking whether a particular jurisdiction should abolish its rent-control laws won't give this student pause over whether she has anything to say. To the contrary, what will strike terror in the student's heart is that the plenty she has to say won't square with her professor's not-so-hidden liberal views. The professor may have said repeatedly that answers will be judged not on which position the student takes but on how the student argues the case. But since it's unlikely the professor has taken the time to explain carefully what is meant by a well-argued case, the student's understandable feeling is that a good answer will be one that agrees with the professor's position. Yet as understandable as this feeling may be, *it's just not true*.

All the professors we know would report with pride that they've often given sterling grades to exam answers with which they strongly disagree. And all will likewise tell you of the dismally mediocre performance of students who guess at the professor's views and parrot them back devoid of all nuance or thoughtfulness. (As our own favorite professor was wont to say, "Servility will be punished.") We don't mean to deny that at the margins subtle biases may affect professorial reactions to student answers. But far and away the best grades go not to those who take "the right side," but to those who take sides "the right way." In short, you can take any side you want, as long as you temper your enthusiasm with an intelligent appreciation of the alternative point of view.

Nor is there anything metaphysical or mysterious about what makes up a good answer. As this chapter will explain, good answers to policy questions will typically (1) consider the problem from different perspectives—or what we will call different "dimensions"; (2) develop arguments within each dimension that support opposing outcomes; (3) find some aspect of the problem that's more complicated than it originally appears; and (4) above all, not despair when the analysis does not achieve either a clear resolution of the problem or even a clear identification of a simple trade-off between competing values.

We have organized this chapter to shed light on these components of good policy analysis. In "Touching All Parts of the Policy Kingdom," we describe argument "dimensions" in ways we hope will prove useful in linking policy issues to our earlier description of "forks in the road." Just as the law often presents different directions in which the lawyer's argument can take you, policy argument offers many different reasons you might want to head in one direction or another, and we'll show why that's the case. In "Heads and Tails You Win," we show how you can mix and match argument dimensions to enrich your exam answers. Finally, in "Find the Fun," we explain how no amount of memorization can prepare you for all the different policy conundrums that exams (or law practice, for that matter) will throw at you. We offer examples of some of the more familiar twists you can expect, so you won't be surprised when you encounter them, and so you can watch for countless others your professors are sure to invent.

The techniques you'll find here will enable you to extend your discussion and analysis to make persuasive arguments of the sort we described in Chapter Thirteen's discussion of "what to do with issues once you spot them." But you won't find any advice here on how to reach the "right" conclusions. Your task, after all, is to argue for one side and against its opposite, not to prove that there is an unequivocally correct solution. Indeed, if upon reflection actual resolution of the issue appears difficult to you for a whole variety of reasons, you should rejoice in the fact that you are probably getting the point. Even for Czars of the Universe, it's *Getting to Maybe* all over again.

B. Touching All Parts of the Policy Kingdom

One of our favorite definitions of a good law student is someone who will always have three or four intelligent points to make about any topic thrown her way. She may not be able to put together *more* than three or four such points, but, as we'll explain, this may not affect her performance much on law school exams.

The reason three or four points will quickly leap to mind is that there is a standard set of perspectives from which almost any policy issue can be viewed. If you go through your class notes, you are likely to discover these same perspectives appearing repeatedly throughout. We'll begin by introducing these different perspectives to emphasize the need to consider all or most of them in drafting a good policy answer. (And we'll show how this works in practice in Part V of the book, where we work our way through some sample exam questions.)

1. "Shaping" society

First and foremost, policy issues ask students to consider the future consequences to affected parties of a decision one way or another. Who will gain and who will lose if the issue is resolved a certain way? *What* will each side gain and lose? *How* will the gains and losses occur? One way to think about this approach is in terms of simple cost-benefit analysis. As we'll explain, there's more to it than such simplicity implies. But it would be perilous, if not foolhardy, to tackle a policy issue without some consideration of winners and losers.

Indeed, lawyers often differentiate between "law" and "policy" based simply on how much emphasis is placed on the consequences of the outcome. Run-of-the-mill legal issues often focus on the question of what the law has said before, via either statute or precedent, about a particular issue. By contrast, policy questions often begin with the assumption that the law is unclear and ask the decision-maker to resolve the dispute by turning to broader considerations, especially the future impact of the decision on those who will be governed by the new rule.

For the sake of convenience, we'll label arguments about a policy's impact "SHAPING" arguments, to remind you of the need to think about the shape of society after a particular rule is put into effect. So, to take one example, if your hypothetical exam question asked whether landlords should be held strictly liable for tenants' injuries, one obvious line of analysis would evaluate how landlords might be affected by such a rule and what this would do to the supply of housing in the future. In short, how would a rule of strict liability "shape" the overall housing market?

2. Administering policy

It should be immediately clear that law students may not be the people best trained to answer questions about how a particular policy will shape real-world events. Wouldn't an economist or a political scientist know better how to study the likely landlord reactions to a rule imposing strict liability?

Perhaps so. But two crucial points about exams are in order. First, law professors quite properly believe that only a very poor advocate would push for a particular legal outcome without giving serious consideration to market and other societal consequences. Economists might do better research studies, but they are less likely to find themselves in court. Accordingly, professors frequently test students' ability to consider the consequences of rule choices.

Second, the good law student will make up in breadth what she may lack in understanding of (say) regression analysis. Above all, one aspect of rule choice falls squarely within the law student's wheelhouse: How will the legal system actually *administer* the chosen rule? Like cost-benefit analysis, this question is more complicated than it might appear.

For now, let's focus on the two ways in which "ADMINISTRABILI-TY" is most likely to affect policy decisions. First, as every parent knows, the mere fact that there is a rule prohibiting something doesn't mean people won't do it anyway. Thus, the ADMINISTRABILITY inquiry is a useful reminder to would-be policymakers to pay attention to whether the announced rule will actually work in practice. If landlords are strictly liable, for example, will tenants know their rights and bring lawsuits for injuries? Will tenants sign leases that "contract away" their right to sue? And a further follow-up: Will such waivers be held valid? There's no point in adopting a rule that would, if it worked as intended, create enormous economic benefits when we suspect from the start that the rule can't be effectively applied. And this means that your discussion of how a particular policy will create winners and losers (or similar kinds of SHAPING arguments) must consider how the policy will be enforced. In your courses, you may hear this problem referred to as the relationship between the "law on the books" and the "law in action."

Second, every policy choice has an impact not only on the people being administered, but also on those doing the administering. For most law school exam questions, courts are the anticipated administrators of legal rules. So an analysis of whether State X should adopt strict liability for landlords should include a discussion of how courts might find it easier to resolve cases if the complex and fact-intensive issue of landlord fault is taken off the table. A streamlined litigation process will almost always count as a sound argument on behalf of a particular policy—not because judges and lawyers are slow or lazy, but because there are so many other cases in the queue vying for official resolution. For this reason, policy issues will often present you with an opportunity to compare the pros and cons of a "rule-like" formulation (if these three facts are present then the defendant is liable, next case please) with the pros and cons of a more flexible "standard" (we need to determine whether the landlord acted unreasonably, so we'd better call in the jury). Many of you will discuss the recurring significance of the choice between rules and standards explicitly in your first-year courses.

It's important to see, though, that bright-line rules don't always reduce judicial workload. In our example, injured tenants would presumably bring more lawsuits if it were easier to recover. Not having to prove fault would provide a strong incentive for injured tenants to take their cases to court. It might ultimately be a good thing if there were more such lawsuits. Landlords might be more careful, and tenants might receive what they deserve. But taxpayers will have to pay for more judges and court space to handle the extra load. Of course, when you're sitting in a classroom with only your exam before you, you will have no meaningful way to determine whether more judicial resources will be freed up as a result of streamlining than will be required to tackle the additional case-load. But you'll score a lot of points with your professor for raising the ADMINISTRABILITY dimension of the problem and for noticing that both landlords ("the floodgates will open") and tenants ("cases will move faster") can make use of it to help their respective cause.

3. Doing the right thing

By the time you sit down to take your first set of law exams, it's a safe bet that you'll have become a bit shy about introducing concerns of fairness or morality into your professional discussions. For one thing, you came to law school to learn new ways of thinking. You want to sound like a trained lawyer rather than an uninitiated moralist. Moreover, virtually every law student has an early experience in which a professor appears unimpressed (sometimes that's putting it mildly!) with a classmate's comments based on personal conviction. Most often, the professor is only trying to show the classmate that the issue at hand is more complicated than her deeply felt remarks suggest. Too often, however, a sharp exchange is misread by the class as a message that the law has no place for intuitions about fairness or personal views of morality. Indeed, the professorial no-nonsense attitude will sting particularly hard for students who found law school attractive precisely because of its connections to deeper ideas about politics and justice.

We have many reasons to urge you to resist suggestions that you sever notions of justice from your understanding of law. It's not good for the country for law schools to produce an army of technocrats, and it's not good for your psyche to ignore your own instincts. For our purposes, however, we will focus on only one point: Ignoring your desire to "do the right thing" (DTRT) will be disastrous for your grade point average. The trick for law school exams is not to forget about justice and morality, but to learn to present those considerations in the right way. Every policy question, indeed every law school exam question that hinges on ambiguity in the decision-making process (i.e., all of them), not only invites but also demands consideration of the underlying fairness of competing outcomes.

Consider again an exam question about imposing strict liability on landlords for injuries suffered by tenants. Your concerns about sounding unprofessional are certainly well founded. No teacher will be satisfied by answers concluding that landlords should be held strictly liable because "it's not fair for tenants to have to pay." You'll do only slightly better with the converse suggestion that "it wouldn't be fair to make landlords pay since they aren't at fault." The improvement is that you have provided a modicum of content to your notion of fairness by invoking a principle, "no liability without fault." But you still have a long way to go. After all, the whole point of strict liability is that it involves liability without fault, and courts sometimes adopt it and sometimes don't. The issue is which way to go and *why*.

Your discussion of fairness will be richer and more appealing to your grader if you work your way through the following points. Remember the discussion in Chapter Eight of the role of policy in arguments about interpreting case law? In order to determine whether established precedent should be broadened to impose on tenants the disclosure requirements already applicable to sellers—the example we analyzed at length—courts will consider the policy rationales supporting and opposing the extension. Our point in this chapter is that every exam question about policy has hidden questions of fairness that will enable you to frame multiple arguments about the desirability of opposing outcomes.

a. The unfairness of change (consistency over time)

The exam question may make you Czar of the Universe, but if you choose to adopt any policy different from current law, you need to consider the effects of transition. If applicable law now holds landlords liable only for negligence, then landlord attorneys will challenge any shift to greater liability on grounds that landlords have been relying on the old rules. Specifically, landlord lawyers may note that landlords would have insisted on paying less for buildings, charged higher rents, and taken out more insurance had they known strict liability would be in effect. Reliance will be cited as reason enough on its own to maintain the status quo. Note, by the way, that the ubiquitous nature of transition issues gives lie to the notion that policy questions are somehow softer and less rigorous than purely legal ones, for a solid grasp of the *current* law is critical to a persuasive analysis of what a particular transition will entail.

In the same vein, change will also be resisted with the argument that it's not fair to treat one group of tenants (those who couldn't recover under the old negligence rule) differently from a second group (those who would be permitted to recover if we switch to a strict liability rule). Of course, this argument is so general it would defeat any effort to change any rule. But it is used all the time by lawyers arguing against a change in the legal rules, and the fact that it has any appeal at all should remind you that some notion of "consistency" lurks behind virtually all ideas of fairness within legal argument.

b. Treat like cases alike

When the exam writer first appoints you Czar of the Universe to decide a policy question, it's tempting to focus exclusively on SHAPING arguments in an effort to predict the best possible outcome to society. But the grader will test any result you propose against results reached by other decision-makers in similar cases. If you argue for strict liability, but everyone else who has considered the issue disagrees, your contrariness alone many count as an argument against you, as the following sections suggest.

i. Consistency over space

Suppose that the vast majority of states apply a negligence rule for cases involving suits against landlords. No formal rule prevents your state from reaching a different conclusion. Indeed, many would argue that one strength of our federal system is to encourage legal experimentation by individual states. If you want your state to go it alone, however, your position will be stronger if you explain why you believe the legal system can readily cope with different rules in different places. You might say, for example, that land ownership implies a significant commitment to a particular locale, so that it would be fair to ask landlords to learn the different rules for the different states in which they hold property. Different landlord liability rules, for example, would be easier to manage than differing rules governing property that moves easily and frequently from jurisdiction to jurisdiction—e.g., regulations requiring particular safety equipment on your automobile. Alternatively, if you are arguing that your state should stay in line with others by sticking to a negligence rule, you can always stress the desirability of uniformity, but this will be particularly powerful if you can offer reasons that uniformity is especially important in this context. Perhaps it will be easier to provide landlords and tenants with information about what insurance to buy if the rules don't change as they move from place to place.

Notice how your ability to generate discussion will spring from having identified a point of comparison—the rules in other states. This technique can be replicated for virtually any policy proposal. When you recommend a solution, you can always ask yourself how this solution will fit into the broader set of legal rules that you know. Describing the fit is not only a sound analytical perspective for policymakers everywhere; it will also serve you well in writing answers to the policy questions you encounter on your exams.

ii. Consistency across social categories

When you read judicial opinions and other discussions of the strict liability issue for landlords, you'll encounter rhetoric about the dangers of transforming landlords into "insurers." At first glance, this may seem a bit mysterious. What do landlord interests hope to gain by tossing around such phraseology? If the issue at hand is whether landlords should be strictly liable, then one of the possibilities on the table is the imposition of a duty to cover the accidental losses of tenants that would indeed resemble the obligations of an insurance company, a perfectly respectable thing to be—perhaps especially to those of us who make a living in Hartford, Connecticut. How does it help the landlords' argument to resist this seemingly inoffensive comparison and decry being "an insurer?"

The law's emphasis on consistency helps unravel this mystery a bit. Landlord lawyers opposing strict liability can seek support from the way the commercial world has in the past divided certain responsibilities. They may portray a world split between value-creating business ventures, responsible for damage only when at fault, and risk-taking insurance ventures whose business is to pay for damages across the board. Landlords, according to this line of reasoning, fall into the first category and should not be treated like those ventures falling in the second.

One response to such rhetoric is to note that the legal world is not forever stuck with its pre-existing commercial categories. After all, courts and legislators are free to set the rules that best serve society, not those that robotically cater to established interests. Such casual embrace of reform, however, is itself oversimplistic. A rule that departs too drastically from existing understandings may be too unpopular to be effective. So yet another understanding of fairness you must confront is the landlord claim that to be consistent across groups the law should take seriously categories that are already in place.

Fortunately, if you are arguing for strict liability, you have a ready counter. You might note, for example, that the law already imposes strict liability on manufacturers of defective products, so existing law does not in fact maintain such a rigid distinction between business ventures and insurers. Landlords may respond that the kind of strict liability sought by tenants would go well beyond product liability and cover situations in which there's no claim that the leased premises are in any way defective. Note again, however, that what started as a seemingly open-ended discussion of the best rule ends up focusing on an analysis of similarities and differences that closely resembles what lawyers and judges do with precedents all the time.

iii. The distribution of wealth
(consistency across economic class)

Lest you think we have forgotten, let us close our discussion of fairness with the issue most likely to drive opinions about political matters. Legal thinking in the U.S. is simultaneously committed to two often conflicting views about the allocation of economic resources. Its purportedly *meritocratic* aspects accept the increasingly unequal distribution of wealth and income as a necessary, perhaps even desirable, byproduct of individuals' differing contributions to the social good based on varying combinations of native talent and personal effort. From this perspective, landlords might be portrayed as hardworking entrepreneurs struggling to make a profit while providing a vital service. The last thing they need is to have additional costs heaped upon them to pay for injuries that aren't even their fault.

Tenant interests, however, will counter by stressing the aspirational *egalitarian* component of American legal thinking. Housing could fairly be characterized as a basic need. Plus, odds are that most tenants will have fewer resources available to them than most landlords. Accordingly, tenants may offer a straightforward leveling argument that stresses how landlords are in a better position than tenants to insure against or bear the cost of unexpected losses. As beneficiaries of a legal system built to protect the rights of property owners, landlords should have no grounds to object when asked to bear a few costs.

There's plenty of room to spin out this story and link it to the SHAP- ING and ADMINISTRABILITY concerns described earlier. If additional costs are initially placed on landlords, they may ultimately be passed back to tenants through higher rents. But even so, costs will then be spread among all tenants rather than falling entirely on the injured (and hence relatively poorer) ones, since an uninsured tenant who can't cover medical costs might find herself on the street. The debate need not end there, but the point we want to make is that the clash between meritoc- racy and egalitarianism is another point of contention you can watch for in policy questions. Discussing the issue in these terms will redound to your credit, provided you are responsive to concerns that would be ex- pressed by both sides.

What won't work, however, will be global statements about fairness divorced from the context of the question. Suppose, for example, that as a true Czar of the Universe you would outlaw the landlord/tenant rela- tionship as an anachronistic throwback to the feudal period. If you spend the allotted time spinning out and defending such an outlier view, you will probably receive a very poor grade. Your mistake, however, won't be that you have taken an unpopular position. Rather, you will have com- mitted the single most common sin of all exam-takers: You will have failed to answer the question asked. Your professor wants to know about strict liability for landlords, so that's your mission—whatever your view of the underlying legal relationship.

To be sure, you might try to inform a more responsive answer with your hostility to the landlord/tenant system. You might argue, for exam- ple, that strict liability should be imposed because adding costs to land- lords will make the system more expensive and hasten its demise. Few professors will intentionally penalize you for making a pitch for deep societal transformation, and virtually none will for the direction of your views. But the task you have undertaken for yourself is enormous. A more conventional answer will assume that the landlord-tenant system as a whole will remain unchanged, with only this one issue up for grabs. And as you can see from the arguments already described, a thorough analysis of even this more modest point will keep you plenty busy in the time allotted.

If you prefer to tackle the question by using it as a springboard to re-imagine the entire system, your professor will legitimately expect a well-worked-out explanation of how housing will be provided under your new scenario (SHAPING); how the new rules will be implemented (AD-MINISTRABILITY); how transition issues will be covered (DTRT: CONSISTENCY OVER TIME); how the new rules will fit with other rules in society (DTRT: TREATING LIKE CASES ALIKE); and how the new system will address the clash between meritocratic and egalitarian views (DTRT: CONSISTENCY ACROSS ECONOMIC CLASS). We think that's a lot to tackle in the course of one exam question, and our view wouldn't change whether your direction is left (a progressive attack on private ownership) or right (a conservative attack on expansive tort recovery that deprives often middle-class landlords of justly earned income while lining the pockets of trial lawyers). If you think you can pull off a comprehensive defense of an entirely different legal system and link it to a resolution of the particular question at hand, we doubt that you'll have much to fear from a professor who disagrees with your position. Otherwise, even as a Czar of the Universe, you are better off offering a more targeted response to the question asked.

c. Building a diverse and inclusive society

We confess to some anxiety about adding this component to the analysis. As two old white guys, we ought to be doing more listening and reading than writing about race and other identity issues. But given the central importance of these issues in life and law, *not* addressing them just isn't an option, even in a how-to book on law exams. We recognize that law schools have a long way to go to create welcoming environments that support every student from every background and that issues of racial equity often reveal a particular need for improvement. At the same time, however, far more than when we were students, law schools and law faculty alike have embraced an admirable commitment to preparing students for practice in a multiethnic, multicultural society. Such preparation should and does include fostering difficult discussions of race in the classroom. Make no mistake, however, about the potential hazards in the exam context, for you may well encounter professors who react poorly when students raise issues of race that are not "front and center" in an exam question. Alternatively, you may also encounter others who will mark you down if you ignore race issues lurking just beneath the surface. Given this dilemma, you're least likely to go wrong if you take to heart a point we've made repeatedly in this book: Let the content of the exam question as well as the material you studied in the course be your guide, rather than the urge either to please or provoke your professor.

Beyond that, there's a simple proposition that can help you "do well while you are doing right" on policy questions: A seemingly neutral rule that treats everyone the same isn't neutral at all if the people affected start off in very different situations. As put most famously by Anatole France, "The law, in its majestic equality, forbids the rich as well as the poor to sleep under bridges, to beg in the streets, and to steal bread." To put the issue more concretely, consider how contemporary policy choices require consideration of long-standing historical inequities that have produced widespread inequality along racial lines. Voter identification laws appear neutral, but the evidence indicates that they will disenfranchise a disproportionate number of Black and brown voters. Exemptions from COVID restrictions for essential workers enabled many American consumers to continue buying groceries and other necessities but left workers of color on the serving end far more likely to contract, and die from, the disease.

Policymakers and judges are becoming more attuned to these disparities, and what this means for exam-writing is this: Anytime you consider arguments for or against a particular rule, you should ask yourself how that rule will land differently on different groups directly affected by the change and also what impact the proposed rule may have on those who may suffer unintended collateral damage. A question on a Property exam, for example, about a proposed zoning ordinance that limits the number of people who may live in a particular residence may seem at first blush to strike a sensible balance between family freedom and a community's desire for quiet and reduced traffic in residential neighborhoods.

But the impact of the ordinance may also fall more heavily on those whose cultural practices or religious beliefs produce larger families or on those with fewer economic resources who need more income earners in the same space to cover the rent. And as those people are frozen out of affordable housing opportunities, the character of the community might change, leading to an influx of merchants and service providers catering mostly to a wealthy clientele and ultimately to a cycle of "gentrification" inimical to cultural and racial diversity as well as social inclusion.

You should be prepared to identify and discuss such disparities. At the same time, you should avoid the rush to conclude that when you have spotted an inequity you have unlocked the key to the appropriate resolution of an issue presented in an exam question, for other considerations may come into play as well. Social Security benefits, for example, kick in at a certain age and continue until death, thus giving advantage to demographic groups with longer life expectancies (e.g., whites). Yet current law allows this approach presumably for ease of administration, but also because calibrating individual benefits to race-based actuarial predictions may strike even the most race-aware policymakers as a dangerous form of social engineering. Perhaps a more palatable approach would seek alternative reforms such as raising the benefit rates for a broad class of low-income workers and/or improving health care access (and thus the prospect of greater longevity) for everyone. Where and how to address these problems goes well beyond your duties as an exam-taker, but pointing out the underlying disparities will add to the sophistication of your answers. Even on questions as profound as racial justice you can turn recognition of conflict to your advantage without offering definitive solutions.

4. "Stay in your lane"... or what kind of Czar are you?

Another dimension that demands discussion when responding to straightforward policy questions grows out of the institutional role assigned by the exam question. You may have noticed that Professor Areeda's colorful phraseology glosses over the fact that it's judges and legislators, not Czars, who are typically asked to weigh in on legal disputes. No one tells a Czar to "stay in your lane." But American law takes the "lanes" associated with different legal institutions seriously, and you don't want to lose sight of that convention on an exam.

Return one more time to the issue of strict liability for landlords. Your professor may have phrased the question, as she may phrase virtually any policy question, in a number of ways. You might be asked whether, as a Supreme Court Justice in State X, you would be willing to embrace strict liability. Or you might be asked whether, as a legislator, you would vote for a statute imposing strict liability. Or you might be asked whether strict liability is a good idea without any explicit identification of how it might be adopted. And remember, you might even be asked that question—at least implicitly—in the context of an old-fashioned issuer spotter, in which policy arguments about the choice between strict liability and negligence would figure prominently in a high-quality analysis of a problem involving those "competing domains."

All the dimensions of policy argument we've thus far discussed (**SHAPING, ADMINISTRABILITY, DO THE RIGHT THING**) are relevant no matter how the question is formulated. But if you are directed to respond to the question as a state Supreme Court justice, you would be wise to acknowledge your role as part of a supposedly precedent-bound and less political branch of government. Here again, you can't perform well without knowing about the rules already in force. If you are considering a particular proposal, like strict liability for landlords, you may have a very different reaction to the idea if what's called for is a massive shift from a well-established negligence regime. Judges, you may argue, should leave such dramatic changes from the status quo to the legislative branch. Moreover, there's a standard line of argument that elected legislators directly answerable to the public are better positioned than judges to weigh competing social interests and thus to address what we call **SHAPING** concerns. Finally, if the question doesn't specify what your role is, you may score points for noting how you might reach a different conclusion if you were deciding as a judge or as a legislator. Not all professors agree on the limits of the judicial role, and some don't see a sharp divide between legislating and judging. But virtually all professors will expect you to **STAY IN YOUR LANE** if they have taken the time to assign a particular institutional role in the question. So don't get too carried away with the Czar of the Universe business.

5. Government noninterference and the Prime Directive: Even Czars have limits on doing the right thing

If there's a figure in contemporary pop culture who is more powerful than an ancient Czar, it would surely be *Star Trek's* Starfleet captain cruising through the universe at many times the speed of light. *Star Trek's* creators, however, captured an important part of our legal culture when in the original series they adopted the "Prime Directive" and banned the science fiction heroes from interfering with other civilizations, no matter how clearly it appears that interference would be a desirable thing to do.

In one stirring episode of *Star Trek: The Next Generation*, for example, Captain Jean-Luc Picard encounters two planets where the residents of one are deceiving the residents of the other by selling them what purports to be medicine but is actually an addictive narcotic with no curative power. Picard could radically change the culture of both planets by explaining the science to those now being exploited. But doing so would violate his sacred oath to the Prime Directive, which prohibits any interference with the ways of other cultures. So he remains silent, although the show's viewers are likely to applaud the other steps he takes to help the addicts. Placing the principle of government noninterference at the heart of the classic TV series was probably driven by the creators' reaction to the disasters of the Vietnam War, repeated decades later in Iraq. But *Star Trek* was on to something very important that will help you on exams. No matter how much power government might seem to possess, its leaders are often wise to refrain from meddling in the lives of ordinary citizens, because resistance may be swift, powerful, and unpredictable. If you need an Earthbound example of pressure on those in charge to stay their hand, consider the virulent reactions across our country when government officials imposed mask and vaccine mandates on private citizens even though the science confirmed that these public health measures could save lives.

So whatever the policy question, you should always train a skeptical eye on the claim that government action is warranted. After all, even the fiercest Czar risks cutting her tenure short if she begins issuing edicts that appear driven by whim—let's say, ordering all decorations to be green to suit her color preferences. And leaders of all stripes, including those in our more democratic culture, generally embrace the idea that each individual is a better judge of what color to paint her house (for example) than even the most omniscient government. Indeed, you might well see it as unethical to use your coercive authority to second-guess private choices in this way. So despite your role as Czar, when you are tackling a policy question, you should never lose sight of the oft-heard slogan that "America is a free country." And what this means in practice is that there are certain zones of freedom where the law, and especially the Czar, should heed the unwritten rule: "Keep Out." This is one way, for example, to think about the Supreme Court decision in *Griswold v. Connecticut* invalidating laws against birth control. And it's also a good way to approach a whole host of questions you may encounter on your exams—questions about gun control, abortion, adoption by same-sex couples, assisted suicide, vaccinations, mask-wearing, etc.

To be sure, there is a contrary directive in U.S. legal culture that runs nearly as deep as the professed commitment to "FREEDOM FIRST." It rears its head whenever voters believe government is failing to protect us from a palpable threat. Remember how those not normally fans of government action soundly criticized President Obama for underreacting to the Ebola virus? Indeed, when government does step in to help—let's say, to provide health care to the elderly—some of the direct beneficiaries are so committed to the idea of "freedom" that we see signs like the one famously brandished at a protest rally on the eve of Obamacare's enactment: "Keep Your Government Hands Off My Medicare." Yet the humorous aspect of the sign's slogan reveals the extent to which proponents of the counter-directive face an uphill battle. So strong is the professed aversion to government control that there is a tendency to forget the many critical services (from interstate highways, the courts, and the air traffic control system to Social Security and, yes, even Medicare) that are very much the product of "government interference" and to cast arguments favoring a particular intervention in "this is a free country" terms as well. Watch what can be done with vaccine mandates.

While *laissez-faire* proponents will stress the individual's "freedom of choice" ("I get to decide for myself whether I prefer the risk of COVID to the unknown dangers of the vaccine"), advocates of regulation are likely to highlight the effects of nonregulation on the freedom of third parties ("but you don't have a right to risk infecting my 90-year-old mother"). Likewise, regulation's opponents will paint a picture of a private realm of decision-making from which government should be excluded ("this is a personal matter" or "let the free market decide"), while government interventionists will stress the threats to freedom posed by the more powerful party within what we think of as the "private" sphere (a hands-off approach to the family may empower a COVID-denying angry dad to block his spouse and children from taking proper precautions; a hands-off approach to the market may enable the large corporation to steamroll its workers into taking unwarranted mid-pandemic risks). As Czar of the Universe, even you can't resolve these dilemmas. But by remembering the FREEDOM FIRST dimension of legal argumentation, you can chalk up still more points on almost any policy question.

C. Heads and Tails You Win

Our account of SHAPING, ADMINISTRABILITY, DO THE RIGHT THING, STAY IN YOUR LANE, and FREEDOM FIRST arguments is not meant to be exhaustive. Sophisticated policy argument and legal reasoning are more nuanced than anything we capture here. Our focus, however, is preparing you to write your exams. If you look at other study guides, you will find instructions on making checklists for various substantive courses. In Contracts, for example, you might analyze questions by looking for whether an offer was extended, whether it was accepted, whether a breach occurred, and what damages should be. Our list of policy perspectives can't substitute for a solid grasp of your courses any more than a simple checklist can capture all of Contracts.

But our emphasis on multiple dimensions may enable you to resolve a paradox you may have spotted within the limited guidance others provide about exams. "Argue both sides," your professors repeatedly tell you. But when you do, sometimes an exam comes back with red scrawl: "Draw conclusions. Don't be wishy-washy and indecisive." In such cases, you may wonder just who it is who can't make up his mind.

It turns out, however, that your professors aren't asking the impossible. You *can* simultaneously be decisive and argue both sides. The first step is simply to recognize the psychological bind. Your exams often demand that you carefully articulate the strongest case for at least two opposing resolutions. Should there be strict liability or not? This will push you emotionally toward seeing the merit in both outcomes and may lure you away from your initially strong feelings one way or the other. Yet your exams may also demand that you choose one outcome as better than another, and this may tempt you to repress the complexity and conflict your professor wants you to expose.

As you sit down to write, the best way to avoid the oversimplification error is to remember the kinds of arguments we have described above. Bring as many as you can to bear on the problem, and you will almost surely generate doubts about how the dispute should be resolved. Once you have generated doubts, however, you often have to bite the bullet and actually choose one route as preferable. You may be unable to refute the opposing viewpoint unequivocally, but it's enough merely to explain why you were more persuaded by one side than by the other. Pushing through doubts to a resolution is part of what judges do every day, and exams are as good a place as any to start learning to do this yourself.

I. Getting past the obvious

We're sure you've noticed how participants in hotly contested political conflict often reduce debate to one argument per side. This may be done through battling slogans (right to life vs. right to choose) or by seizing on your side's strongest point (overpolicing terrorizes the Black community vs. defunding the police helps criminals). Exam questions, however, call for more than skillfully invoking the sound bites that dominate contemporary politics. As you begin drafting an answer, you should be attempting to mobilize a multifaceted argument on each side of an issue. And if it's sound bites you long for, there's plenty of time to encapsulate the essence of your position at the end of your answer.

Let's look at a concrete example: motorcycle helmet laws. It's easy enough to anticipate the debate we'd expect on social media or cable television: "helmets save lives" versus "to hell with the nanny state." But how should we approach the topic as a question on a law exam? Using the vocabulary we've introduced in this chapter, the sound-bite version of the dispute pits the ultimate SHAPING argument (the world will be a better place if fewer people die) against a classic FREEDOM FIRST argument (keep the government out of my space). A moment's thought, however, reveals that there's much more than that to the debate. Proponents of a helmet law might appeal to some of the other dimensions we've been exploring and bolster their argument by pointing to the ways in which we already regulate highway safety through seat belt laws and mandatory air bags (DTRT: CONSISTENCY ACROSS GROUPS); by noting how insurance premiums might fall if the number of deaths and serious injuries were reduced (another SHAPING argument); by noting how police officers can more easily tell whether a cyclist is wearing a helmet than whether a cyclist is driving recklessly (ADMINISTRABILITY); or by describing the avoidable injuries to bareheaded riders as a "hidden tax" on us all in the form of increased health care costs (FREEDOM FIRST). Helmet opponents might emphasize our culture's tolerance for all sorts of dangerous activities like skydiving or snowboarding (DTRT: CONSISTENCY ACROSS GROUPS). Cyclists without helmets might actually see better and drive more carefully—with the result that there may be fewer accidents (another SHAPING argument). Helmets may be easy to detect, but there are countless motorcyclists so it might be more cost-effective to have police officers pulling over cyclists who are a danger to others than those who are merely endangering themselves (ADMINISTRABILITY).

Non-lawyers might react to this lengthy litany with impatience. "You're making a federal case out of it" is how some might put it. "The crux of the matter," they'll say, "is whether you are willing to restrict freedom to save lives, and the rest is just fluff." Perhaps. But as lawyers-to-be, your job is to begin considering multiple angles precisely when other people are rushing to the bottom line. That's why the key to excelling on a policy question is not to get stuck on any particular formulation of a problem. Think of two kids in a schoolyard yelling at each other—"Will Too!" "Will Not!" "Will Too!" "Will Not!"—and you'll have an image of how a one-dimensional answer will sound to a grader. Your multidimensional answer won't necessarily make solving the problem easier, and that's why folks anxious for results *now* may shy away from it. We promise, however, that you'll do better on policy questions—and on the policy issues lurking in traditional issue spotters—by following this approach.

2. One good argument deserves another

Breaking down policy questions into multiple dimensions helps with a second important component of a successful exam answer: responsiveness. One of the hardest things about lawyering is knowing when to meet an argument on its own terms and when to change the subject. Let's say your opponent contends that a rule you propose is too complicated to be readily administered. If, to the contrary, you think the rule is perfectly manageable, you can tackle the argument head-on. As you begin to construct your argument, however, you may conclude that an explanation of the rule's supposed simplicity is so complex that the more you say the worse you will look. In a real-life setting, as a matter of argumentative strategy you could easily decide not to address the administrability issue at all, preferring instead to focus on the fairness of your proposed rule. You just have to decide whether the judge will think you are ducking a key point (not good) or merely focusing on the strongest part of your argument (good).

In this respect, however, law school exam tactics are different. If you fail to make a particular argument, your professor won't know whether you are displaying argumentative savvy or whether you just missed a key point. Some professors will explicitly authorize or even instruct you to stick to the strongest points on each side, and—as always—you should do what they say. But our experience is that most professors will be impressed if you not only respond to a compelling argument as best you can on its own terms (meet one SHAPING argument with another) but also demonstrate how shifting the ground of the discussion may put one side or the other in its best light (e.g., by switching from SHAPING to DO THE RIGHT THING or ADMINISTRABILITY concerns).

Let's start with a simple example. Suppose your unimaginative Property professor uses the exam to revisit *Pierson v. Post*, the famous case involving the capture of a fox that has long been the first case encountered in many a traditional Property class. If you were on the New York Court of Appeals, he asks, what rules of ownership would you think should govern wild animal captures today, and why?

Of course the professor isn't likely to ask this question unless your course covered the case, so you won't be entirely surprised. But your first hurdle isn't about the case as much as it is about the professor's question, which calls for a conclusion and says nothing about "arguing both sides." That's frequently true of exam questions, and thus it's tempting in response to announce a result, present an argument to support it, and move on. You might start with something like, "I see no reason to depart from the long-standing rule of *Pierson v. Post*, because I agree with the court that requiring 'actual possession, trapping, or mortal-wounding-with-continued-pursuit' is the easiest rule to administer. Who wants uncertainty in the law of wild animals?" And if you were answering the question in a social setting, that might well end the matter.

Few professors, however, will be satisfied with such a summary conclusion. Why would you be asked to devote an hour to a question of policy if it weren't perplexing enough to raise at least some doubt about the appropriate resolution? So even without recalling the opinions in the case, you know that there must be a strong argument on the other side as well. And of course *Pierson v. Post* still appears in so many Property casebooks because the majority opinion is met by a vigorous dissent. The punch line is that policy questions, even when they don't say so explicitly, almost always require you to confront the best arguments for the opposing side.

In that iconic dissent, Justice Livingston favored a rule whereby a hunter chasing a wild animal would be awarded ownership if the hunter had a reasonable prospect of capturing the animal and remained in pursuit. Livingston wanted to discourage intruders from interfering during the hunt, for otherwise—he feared—would-be hunters wouldn't find it worthwhile to make the necessary investment in the hunting enterprise (raising and training hounds, securing and maintaining the required arms and ammo, setting the alarm for the wee hours, etc.). By now you should recognize this as a classic SHAPING argument. Livingston supports the rule he believes will generate more hunting and thus more dead foxes, and, if you don't make this point, your teacher is likely to assume you overlooked it and grade you down accordingly.

So the next step in effectively answering a policy question is to incorporate opposing arguments into your conclusion. Consider this still relatively simplistic response: "I would continue the rule of *Pierson v. Post*, because the certainty gained from a clear rule is more important than the incentive effect of a more flexible approach." Note the improvement over the wholly conclusory first try, for this answer recognizes points on both sides but comes down firmly on one of them.

Yet an obvious problem remains. Any curious reader, and surely your professor, will want to know *why* you concluded that "promoting certainty" outweighed "creating incentives for hunting" in the wild animal context. It's one thing just to say so and quite another to say so convincingly. And it's at just this point that we suspect many students begin to experience some confusion. How, sitting in the cloister of an exam room, can one meaningfully measure certainty gains against incentive losses for purposes of a valid comparison? And as long as you limit your answer to what appear to be the strongest points on each side, you risk producing arguments that seem to be talking past each other with no obvious scale upon which to weigh alternatives.

This phenomenon of arguments that cross but don't meaningfully engage is a painfully familiar part of contemporary partisan bickering. Consider, for example, the debate over campaign finance reform in which proponents stress the dangers of large contributors "buying elections," while opponents emphasize threats to "free speech." Each side has a strong point, but neither camp focuses sufficiently on how best to respond to the comparably compelling concern raised by the other side. For law school exam purposes, you can't afford to sink to partisan levels. And thus you not only need to "argue both sides" but to "argue both sides responsively."

3. When in doubt, just say no

You can further improve your *Pierson v. Post* exam answer even if the only arguments that occur to you are an ADMINISTRABILITY argument on one side (requiring capture promotes certainty) and a SHAPING argument on the other side (flexibility will spur investment). The simplest technique is just to find some way to minimize or devalue the argument that you ultimately reject. So your answer might read something like, "I would continue the rule of *Pierson v. Post* because the need for certainty remains strong while the need to encourage killing wild animals has diminished in light of demands for conservation"; or "I would continue the rule of *Pierson v. Post* because the need for certainty is powerful, while people who relish the thrill of the hunt are not likely to be deterred from the pastime by concern that their prey will be snatched at the last minute." The common theme here is that all you need to render your answer somewhat more thoughtful is a bit of brainstorming about how to explain the other side's position and then undermine it. Notice that now we have considered both sides, reached a conclusion, and, at least preliminarily, explained why we chose one argument over the other.

4. Learning to mix and match

Whole new vistas will open, however, if you keep in mind the argument dimensions we have described. Ask yourself whether the arguments that appear the strongest in favor of each side are arguments along the same dimension, or whether they appear to be talking past each other. You can then turn any difficulty created when your initial views pitted different types of arguments against each other into another opportunity to excel. All you have to do is figure out whether you can fill in what might be understood, in the *Pierson v. Post* example, as the open fields in the following chart:

	Pro-Plaintiff (hunter)	Pro-Defendant (poacher)
Administrability	?	Clear Rule Promotes Certainty
Shaping	Encourage Investment	?

You now have two questions to ask yourself. First, can you identify any arguments in favor of the dissent's pro-hunter position that directly respond to your conclusion affirming the long-standing rule of capture? Put more concretely, are there any rejoinders to the idea that *Pierson v. Post*'s capture rule provides superior ADMINISTRABILITY? Second, can you identify any arguments supporting the pro-poacher capture rule that respond to the dissent's SHAPING argument—i.e., that a more flexible approach will encourage hunting? You never know in advance whether such arguments will occur to you. But by identifying the way in which the two sides are arguing along different dimensions, you have a much better idea of just what you are responding *to*.

In case the point still seems a bit abstract, think about a family fight over where to dine one evening. Your brother touts the Chinese place around the corner because it's close. Your sister wants to go to the one across town because it's cheaper. Like the exam-taking student, you are asked to "decide the case" and give reasons. It's not easy to assess, however, whether proximity or economy should be the deciding factor.

Think how much more effective you could be if you could respond to each sibling on his or her own terms. If you choose the closer place, you might remind your economy-minded sister that the portions there are larger so that the leftovers could serve as a second dinner later in the week. Having met her concerns over cost head-on, you may now find it much easier to emphasize the importance of reducing travel time. Or, if you want to go across town, you might remind your brother of three other errands the family needs to do near the further restaurant. Since the trip needs to be made anyway, you say, why not get good food for less money? In many families, such reconciling views may occur to people only after a good deal of yelling and a decision by fiat. On law school exams, however, keeping in mind different dimensions of policy argument can provide the opportunity to address multiple considerations before you turn in your exam.

Return, then, to the *Pierson v. Post* example. The judicial opinions appear to pit an **ADMINISTRABILITY** argument on one side (certain rule) against a **SHAPING** argument on the other (protect investment to spur hunting). Your challenge, then, is to come up with an **ADMINISTRABILITY** argument supporting the flexible approach and a **SHAPING** argument favoring the court's insistence on actual capture or its equivalent. Like most things, once you have clearly identified the challenge, it's easier to accomplish. Consider this greatly improved answer: "I believe the courts should continue to adhere to the long-standing rule in *Pierson v. Post* because it provides certainty to judges and hunters and because in the end it will produce the most successful hunting as well. Critics of the rule have long argued that permitting last-minute intruders to snatch prey will discourage necessary investment. But this argument actually cuts both ways, because if we really want to ensure that the most foxes are killed, we should reward the people who actually catch the foxes, not those who spend money to chase them. 'Protecting the investor' is just a nicer name for 'discouraging competitors,' and in the end a rule that keeps foxes up for grabs until caught will promote the most aggressive hunting." Notice here that not only do you consider and respond to the other side, but you do so directly and on the other side's own terms. This is the beginning of a fully developed answer.

Similarly, if you decided to defend the dissent's position, you might write something like this: "I think the time has come to embrace a more flexible approach to the rule of capture. Not only will this give hunters greater security to invest in the necessary hunting equipment, but it will actually prove easier to administer as well. The apparent certainty of the long-standing rule is an illusion. First of all, even the famous case of *Pierson v. Post* itself carved an exception for a hunter who mortally wounded an animal and remained in pursuit. This means that when a wounded animal is taken by another, the hunter inflicting the wound might need to resort to litigation to prove, apparently via autopsy, that the animal actually would have died from the wound. But beyond that, the blatant unfairness of the rule will mean that quarrels on the hunting fields will continue. Hunters deprived in the middle of the chase won't give up merely because the intruder claims to rely on some legal rule. Feeling the prey is rightfully theirs, these hunters will be tempted to grab the animal, perhaps even violently, and then provide a court with a version of events that validates their claim. So litigation, and thus uncertainty, will continue—all at the cost of a dangerous drag on valuable hunting."

Notice here how a third dimension, the element of fairness, is deployed not for its own sake but in service of an ADMINISTRABILITY argument: Nothing will remain certain if it's not fair. This is a standard technique that presents yet another opportunity to show your stuff. And in this answer, too, you have not only considered the other side but responded on the very terms that the other side treated as dispositive. Such replies won't always be available, but they are always worth the hunt.

5. Accentuate the multiple

By now, our next recommendation may be obvious. Recognizing the multiple dimensions of policy argument provides an immediate technique for finding more in the question than what initially comes to mind. If, as in our rule of capture example, the main battle appears to center on administrability and shaping arguments, there's still plenty of room to expand the discussion to consider more of the dimensions we described earlier. Indeed, a comprehensive answer to any policy question is likely to consider many dimensions and not just the one or two that appear most immediately relevant. You need not worry if you can't think of an argument for each side that corresponds to every dimension we describe, for not all policy questions implicate all types of argument. And, we cannot stress enough, you may be able to come up with other creative arguments in addition to those we describe. Our goal is to get you rolling by helping you think like law school's version of a Czar. We have no doubt that once you do, you'll have plenty to add to the story.

Completing our rule of capture example, then, might involve the following arguments on each side. Maintaining the rule of *Pierson v. Post* might be defended on the ground that it's been the law a long time and change would be needlessly disruptive (DTRT: CONSISTENCY OVER TIME). If you are imagining yourself on a court, you might want to endorse maintaining the rule unless and until the legislature decides to change it (STAY IN YOUR LANE). You might stress the desirability of encouraging those who have snatched an animal to relish their catch without fear of a contrary claim from someone alleging to have been first to the chase (SHAPING). And you might tack on a point about keeping the government out of hunting disputes unless absolutely necessary—e.g., in case of a theft of an already captured animal (FREEDOM FIRST).

By contrast, if you want to argue for the dissent's approach, you might defend change on the ground that property law has often abandoned clear rules, like the common-enemy rule for surface waters, in favor of reasonableness standards (DTRT: CONSISTENCY ACROSS SOCIAL GROUPS). If you imagine yourself a judge, you might point out that, since judges devised the original *Pierson v. Post* rule, courts should be free to modify it. If the legislature prefers the old rule, there is nothing to stop it from restoring the *status quo ante* via statute (STAY IN YOUR LANE). You might stress the desirability of enabling hunters to feel secure when chasing an animal that no one else may come along and beat them to the kill (SHAPING). And you might note that once disputes between hunters arise, resolving them either way will necessitate government involvement, so there's no way to take a hands-off approach (FREEDOM FIRST). In the end, you might imagine the problem producing an argument chart like the one below:

	Keep Capture Rule	**Pursuer Earns Ownership**
Shaping	Encourage Competition	Reward Investor
Shaping	Promote Freedom	Protect Security
Administrability	Clarity Reduces Quarrels	(1) Old Rule Not So Clear (2) Unfair Rules Breed Disputes
Do the Right Thing	Reliance on Rule	Trend Toward Flexibility
Stay in Your Lane	Change Is for Legislature	Courts Change Common Law
Freedom First	Government Out of Hunting	Dispute-Resolution Role Inevitable

From your perspective as an exam-taker, the important components of this chart are the two alternatives identified in the top row and the argument dimensions listed in the left-hand column. It hardly matters whether you find our discussion of *Pierson v. Post* a convincing analysis of the rule of capture, or even whether you agree precisely with our characterization of the dimensions of argument. Many law teachers, for example, would characterize some of our SHAPING and DO THE RIGHT THING arguments as arguments about "rights." They might say that the party who first chased an animal could claim ownership by alleging "a right to rely." How dare someone come along and steal the fox that the defendant worked so hard to capture? In contrast, the party who actually caught the animal could assert "a right to compete." If no clear rule forbids it, then people should be able to do as they please, including grabbing an animal already being pursued.

The advantage of rights rhetoric is that it seems less political and open-ended than forthright policy analysis. The discussion about what the rule should be is recast as a battle about what the law already is, even when there's no clear guide to that determination. The emphasis on decisions taken in the past serves judges' interests in pretending not to have as much power as the Czar-image suggests. They can feign powerlessness by justifying results based on "rights" that parties supposedly have before the beginning of a dispute. We find this reliance on rights rhetoric somewhat mystifying, since you never really know which party has a "right" (e.g., to the wild animal) until after the question has been resolved. Accordingly, we tend to avoid "rights" rhetoric when talking about policy questions. But the point is to develop your ability to analyze problems in as many different ways as possible, not to mimic our style preferences. On your exam questions, you will be rewarded as much for presenting multiple arguments as for characterizing the problem exactly as your professor would.

Unless and until you develop a method of your own, one way to approach policy issues is to use a chart like ours. A straightforward policy question may make it clear what the two likely policy alternatives are. With an issue spotter, by contrast, you will be expected to identify the policy conflict on your own, in the course of mobilizing arguments on one side or the other of the many issues we explored in Part II (rule vs. counter-rule, competing interpretations of a rule, etc.). In either case, you can display the policy alternatives across the top of your chart and the various dimensions of argument along the left-hand column. After that, the task before you is to populate as many open fields as you can.

	Alternative A	Alternative B
Shaping (Policy)	?	?
Shaping (Rights)	?	?
Administrability	?	?
Do the Right Thing	?	?
Stay in Your Lane	?	?
Freedom First	?	?

And how are you supposed to know which arguments to use when filling in the open fields? Our answer is twofold. First, we have been telling you all along that *Getting to Maybe* is a tool to help you get more out of all the hard work of law school, not a substitute for it. Professors who ask policy questions and/or expect policy analyses on issue spotters will almost invariably highlight the policy dimension of various issues throughout the course. As we suggested in our chapter on exam prep, your job is to take those discussions seriously—and not to treat them as digressions, during which you cease your note-taking while waiting for the professor to resume talking about the law. (Hint: She already is.) Second, if you know that populating open fields like those in the chart is part of what you need to learn from your courses—that is, if you know you'll be called upon to address SHAPING and ADMINISTRABILITY arguments and all the rest on your final exam—you can organize your studying and outlining efforts in ways that will better prepare you for the moment of truth.

D. Find the Fun and *Snap* the Test's a Game

Now comes the fun part. We believe that most students on most exams will do pretty well with a relatively routine application of the kinds of argument we have described in this chapter. We promised at the outset, however, not only to present basic exam-taking techniques but to offer some insight into the process professors use to construct exams. You may find that insight particularly helpful when you try to tackle straightforward policy questions. On issue spotters, you'll get loads of credit simply for unearthing the policy conflicts hidden in the fact pattern, and often you'll be too busy dealing with multiple forks to take the policy analysis beyond an argument or two on each side. But on policy questions, the nature of the policy conflict is usually made clear by the question itself, and you must therefore be creative in showing how problems are not as simple as they first appear. If the grading curve is stiff, it may not be enough to do well at demonstrating the skills described in our tour of the Policy Kingdom. Moreover, the argument dimensions presented here only begin to hint at the complexity of problems and argument strategies you will encounter in practice. Indeed, it is a common professorial strategy to present what appears at first blush to be a simple policy conflict but on closer examination has layers of complexity that only the most diligent test-takers will identify and begin to unravel. Fortunately for those reading this book, professors do so in familiar and predictable ways, most of which are variations on a theme.

1. Trade-off vs. paradox

Here's the theme. Law school exam questions often require you to discuss policy questions in terms of a trade-off between competing values *and* in the less familiar terms that Deborah Stone has eloquently described as "policy paradox." Many students won't recognize this on their own because it is so seldom explained. But once you see it, you'll never look at policy questions in quite the same way again.

Let's start with a very simple example from outside the law. You are thinking about which of two houses to buy. One house is close to your workplace. The other is farther away but a little larger and more comfortable. All of us have a bottom-line-oriented friend who would be happy to sum up your decision as convenience vs. space. It's a tough choice, this friend will say, but life is full of tough choices. We have already discussed the technique of enhancing a discussion by considering other dimensions of a problem. Certainly you might expand the house selection discussion by bringing in other variables. So, if the goal is a good discussion of the choice presented—and exam questions almost always want discussions more than decisions—you might want to talk about other factors, such as which house will appreciate more in value or which will take more time to maintain. Yet we can all hear our friend's voice whispering in our ear to free our mind of minor distractions and focus on the convenience vs. space trade-off at hand.

If you want to drive your bottom-line friend nuts, however, consider the following potential wrinkles on choosing a house. Suppose the house that's farther from work is actually close to an express bus stop. If there's a special traffic-free lane for buses, the bus commuting time might be less than the driving-plus-parking time from the closer house. Consider the following statement: "The house that's farther away is, in one sense, effectively closer." At one level, this appears to be an obvious paradox. But a moment's thought reveals that, when it comes to the daily commute to work, this conclusion rings true. If we stopped here, you might say, "Great, the farther house is bigger and more convenient, so I should pick it." Alas, real-world decisions aren't likely to be so simple.

For one thing, to demonstrate the point further, the paradox may come at you from the other side as well. Suppose your family work pattern has always been that you and your spouse both enjoy heading to your downtown office on weekends for long-term work projects. It turns out, however, that the express bus does not run on weekends, and the long drive appears daunting for both of you. You can deal with this in the larger house by setting up home offices for each of you. Subtracting these two rooms, however, now actually gives you less living space in the larger house than you would have in the smaller house. Consider, then, the following statement: "The smaller house will give us more living space." At one level, this appears to be another paradox. By now, though, you get the picture.

Great fun they may be, but paradoxes like these are more likely to complicate matters than to resolve them. It might be that the bus will get you to work faster from the farther house, and so it might appear that this house is also more convenient. But there's convenience and then there's *convenience*. If you like to have your car at the office during the day to run errands, taking the bus won't work so well. If you regularly carry hardcopy documents or other bulky objects back and forth to work, the schlep to the bus stop may prove annoying. And if you more than occasionally need to work late and thus past the time the express bus stops running, then the advantages of proximity to the express route may diminish. Moreover, the rooms you plan to devote to home offices may effectively shrink the larger house, so the closer house may now seem more livable. But perhaps you can multipurpose those rooms as handy storage locales and even play areas for the kids, so there's living space and then there's *living space.*

All this means that for purposes of fully discussing which house to buy, your bottom-line friend's emphasis on a trade-off between convenience and space may greatly oversimplify the problem. In real life, such oversimplifications are often helpful to bring you to closure on a tough issue; we have all heard the phrase "don't overthink it." But if you are going to excel as a Czar of the Universe on a law exam, you don't have the luxury of ignoring the paradoxes or wishing them away.

Let's turn to a more direct application of paradox to law school policy questions. Consider how many legal and ethical problems initially draw our attention to a difficult trade-off between competing values. The debate over campaign finance reform, for example, might be seen as a contest between egalitarian ideals ("level the electoral playing field") and libertarian ideals ("candidate spending is free speech"). The debate over affirmative action is often cast—however naively—as pitting the value of diversity against the virtues of merit. Mandatory AIDS testing or mask-wearing raise issues of privacy and autonomy versus public health. It is easy to imagine writing about any one of these issues as if it were nothing but a choice between such conflicting values.

Each side could also be defended along many of the dimensions we have discussed in this chapter. So, to take the affirmative action example, proponents might stress diversity because we will be better off building a multicultural society (SHAPING); because injustices of the past warrant redress (DO THE RIGHT THING); because courts should let university officials or employers make key decisions (STAY IN YOUR LANE); and because giving a plus factor to candidates of color is easier than poring over each file for evidence of disadvantage and signs of capacity to outperform what traditional criteria might otherwise predict (ADMINISTRABILITY). Opponents might emphasize merit on the view that the best way to stop discriminating on the basis of race is to stop discriminating on the basis of race (SHAPING); that today's meritorious applicants shouldn't suffer for sins of the past (DO THE RIGHT THING); that courts are better positioned to enforce constitutional norms than universities and employers subject to market pressures (STAY IN YOUR LANE); and that affirmative action raises the impossibly difficult task of evaluating the different challenges faced by different racial and ethnic groups (**ADMINISTRABILITY**). Although this formulaic debate hardly captures the subject, it would be a good start on an exam question such as: "Affirmative action should be abolished—discuss."

Getting beyond a good start, however, will require you to look past the familiar diversity vs. merit trade-off into which the debate has been pigeonholed. To continue the affirmative action example, supporters will often make the point that a true notion of merit requires consideration of diversity. The university applicant with an unusual ethnic background may add more to classroom discussions than would just one more person with high test scores. Thus we might get the seemingly paradoxical statement that the university should admit the student with lower test scores because she is more qualified. And, of course, the mere idea that test scores measure "merit" ignores the systematic advantages some students have over others in paying for prep courses, receiving tutoring, being free from having to earn money while in school, etc. From the other side, affirmative action opponents sometimes argue that a true notion of diversity would rest on more than racial or ethnic background. In their view, more diversity can be gained by admitting a FirstGen student from a white working-class family or a conservative iconoclast who has impressed a long line of liberal teachers than from a minority applicant with a privileged social and economic background. So we might get the paradoxical statement that affirmative action hurts diversity—often put pointedly by contrasting "Cosby kids" with disadvantaged whites. The key here is that by unsettling the standard trade-off between diversity and merit, both sides have complicated and deepened the argument in ways likely to make exam-graders very happy. We urge you to keep your eyes open for such opportunities when dealing with policy issues. Of course, not every question calls for a translation of trade-off into paradox. But once you start looking, you'll be surprised how often this technique will help.

2. The pattern of paradox

No doubt some readers are wondering when we're going to make good on our promise to show you how law professors construct policy questions. Indeed, if you read through our examples of paradox in the previous section, we mostly just illustrate what a policy paradox looks like. But you need to know how to *find* it. Since paradox is everywhere, we can't provide an exhaustive guide. But this section will illustrate some of the most familiar dilemmas and paradoxes that professors use to add complexity to policy questions.

a. The short run and the long run

The initial shift from trade-off to paradox is most obvious in cases in which short-run and long-run effects of policies are likely to differ. During our years in law school, for example, rent control was a hot topic, ripe for finding its way into Property exam questions. Our guess is that by now the paradoxical aspects are a fixture in your Property course. At rent control's inception, its supporters often argued that decent housing for low-income people is more important than marginal profits for wealthy landlords (DTRT: FAIRNESS ACROSS SOCIAL CLASS). Opponents stressed the rights of landlords to do as they please with their property, noting that grocers and owners of other kinds of property don't have to lower prices to make their products affordable (DTRT: FAIRNESS ACROSS SOCIAL CATEGORIES). This approach makes it appear as though the issue is ultimately a battle between tenants (pro-rent control) and landlords (anti-rent control).

Consider the joy in the landlord camp, however, the first time someone came up with the following formulation: "Rent control is a bad thing because it's bad for tenants. Although in the short run some low-income tenants may be able to secure housing they otherwise could not afford, in the long run no one will want to invest money in a price-regulated industry. Fewer dollars will flow into housing, so fewer rental properties will be built and existing properties will not be properly maintained. The housing supply will be artificially low, and tenants will pay higher rents or become homeless more than they would without rent control." This is no mere rhetorical device; many people believe it to be true. We need not discuss the merits here. For exam purposes, what's important is how the rhetorical shift illustrates an important technique.

By changing the discussion from the short-run impact to the long-run impact, rent-control opponents can alter policymakers' understanding of the problem. What was once a perceived trade-off between tenant interests and landlord interests is re-characterized as a paradoxical choice between tenant interests now and tenant interests later. Landlords may employ this technique by sowing division within the group allegedly aided by rent control. They may say rent control helps existing tenants in the short term only at the expense of the long-term interests of younger, newer tenants seeking a foothold in the housing market. When you do it well, this kind of re-characterization will fill your grader's heart with glee. It might even help win a presidential election—e.g., "let's raise revenues by cutting taxes." So it's worth noting some of the other ways the shift can be accomplished.

b. Intent vs. effects

Suppose your Criminal Law professor asks you to evaluate legalizing drugs, such as marijuana, cocaine, or heroin. In our day (long ago!), some drug users pushed legalization pretty hard, stressing points like "the government shouldn't tell us what we can do with our bodies" (FREEDOM FIRST). This argument, however, was always a political loser among parents afraid of the effect of drug use on their kids. Only criminalization could stem the flow of dangerous drugs, the argument went, and the country should do whatever it takes to stop people from using and selling certain drugs.

Recent and increasingly successful proponents of legalization, however, shifted the ground of the debate. Rather than stressing the right of drug users to do as they please, some decriminalization advocates have conceded that public policy should be to slow down or stop drug use. They don't directly challenge the goals of current laws that impose stiff penalties for drug use. But goals, supporters of legalization say, are not enough. The key question, they ask, is what *effect* do our current laws have?

Perhaps criminal penalties don't work as intended. The black market for drugs has become extraordinarily lucrative, creating enormous incentives for pushers to get customers hooked. The high cost of drugs causes addicts to commit crimes to get money for the next fix. The drug war diverts police resources from other pursuits and fuels massive levels of incarceration. And the failure to stop drug use may breed disrespect for the law—particularly in areas where drug use is most rampant.

None of this means that we should necessarily legalize drugs. But—in the context of grappling with a law exam policy question—it illustrates the importance of stopping to consider whether the solution you propose will have the effect you intend. In the drugs example, you could do well by highlighting the trade-off between the user's freedom to experiment on his body and the society's need to combat reckless behavior and adverse health effects. But you'll do even better by noting that no clear policy alternative follows even if you decide society's interest should outweigh the individual's.

The gap between a law's intent and its effect is a pervasive source of paradox. To take another example, one of us overheard several young teenagers in a multiplex movie theater considering which of several films to see. One girl proposed *Contact*, the thought-provoking movie starring Jodie Foster about how the world might react to evidence of life on other planets. "Oh, we can't see that," replied another, "it's only rated PG." The rating system, purportedly designed to reduce the amount of sex and violence kids would see, was actually working in reverse.

Or consider the paradoxical statement that raising the drinking age may increase highway deaths. It sounds like nonsense until you hear that what happens when the age is raised is that teens drive to a nearby state with a lower limit to buy booze and then die on the road on the way home. These kinds of paradoxes are just another aspect of policy debate you can expect to find built into your exam questions. Few professors keep a list of paradoxical situations, but virtually all are happy when their policy questions have hidden twists enabling them to separate the B's from the A's. To be sure, just as legislators don't always grasp a statute's consequences, professors writing questions won't always intend the paradoxes that you identify in your answers. But we assure you that you'll be rewarded for bringing your grader up to speed.

c. Law on the books vs. law in action

The gap between "the law on the books" and "the law in action" is a close cousin of the gap between intent and effect, so we won't belabor it here. For some people, however, thinking of the gap in this way makes it easier to understand. Suppose your Tax professor poses a policy question such as: "Should the marginal rate of income taxation on the highest-earning taxpayers be increased?" This is a very difficult issue, and it's likely to draw you into discussions of fairness (meritocracy vs. egalitarianism) and incentives (will productive people work less if taxation levels are too high?). But if you get bogged down in these trade-offs too quickly, you run the risk of assuming that a higher rate of taxation "on the books" will necessarily mean more taxes will be paid "in action." Income shifting to capital gains, increased use of shelter techniques, and outright cheating, however, are all possible taxpayer reactions that your teacher will love hearing about in your response. Of course, in a theoretical discussion it would make perfect sense to say, "First let's worry about where the rates should be, and then we'll worry about how to collect the money." But successful Czars—like successful policymakers—seldom have the luxury of focusing on what *should* happen without also considering what *will* happen.

d. Categories are many-splendored things

In his 1996 acceptance speech to the Republican National Convention, presidential candidate Robert Dole tried very hard to cast his party as the party of freedom. Senate Minority Leader Tom Daschle responded for the Democrats in his speech before the Democratic convention. He claimed Democrats are the party of freedom; but, he said, where Republicans emphasize freedom *from* (presumably from government), Democrats emphasize freedom *to* (freedom to own a home, to pursue an education, etc.). Pete Buttigieg made this argument a major theme in his 2020 presidential campaign. So which party is really "the party of freedom"? Well, it all depends on what you mean by "freedom."

This kind of "category ambiguity" runs throughout virtually every policy controversy you'll find on exams—and in real-world debate as well, for that matter. Indeed, although we have placed this section under "The Pattern of Paradox," category ambiguity is actually a far larger topic in American law, and we don't pretend to offer a comprehensive treatment here. Instead, we want merely to explain how the many-splendored meaning of terms like "freedom" or "equality" can help you improve your exam answers.

As you may have figured out on your own, we have already offered some examples. The affirmative action controversy, we noted, appears to be a simple case of pitting diversity against merit until you stop and think about what is meant by "diversity" and "merit." The house shopper we described was choosing between convenience and space until we showed how "convenience" and "space" could be looked at in different ways. And these are merely the tip of the iceberg. Our public schools are filled with honors classes limited to those students who performed well in earlier grades and on standardized tests. Does this square or conflict with our commitment to equality? The familiar conflict between "equality of result" and "equality of opportunity" reminds us that the right answer is "it depends on what's meant by equality." But even this formulation contains further ambiguities that illustrate why appeals to "equality" are insufficient to solve real-world problems. If we required that honors classes be open to all comers in the name of "equality of result," would we then further insist that each student receive the same grade? If we permitted the current selection method in the name of "equality of opportunity," would we allow public schools to exclude some students altogether based on low test scores?

We can't caution you enough, then, about avoiding categorical slogans as a substitute for detailed analysis of the question at hand. Suppose Congress were to consider laws, resembling those in other countries, prohibiting election campaigning until the final 60 days before an election. Does this infringe on freedom of speech? Perhaps. But a mere recitation of "free speech" as a bar to such laws is unlikely to persuade your grader that you have thought the problem through. Or, to take another example, your Property exam has a question such as "Should landlords be prohibited from imposing requirements for the number of people in a given apartment?" Landlords may well have legitimate reasons for avoiding overcrowding—such as wear and tear on buildings or inconvenience to other tenants using shared facilities— but landlords might also use such requirements as a pretext for discriminating against families with children. Yet it certainly won't be a satisfactory answer to say "The landlords should be permitted to limit occupancy because restricting them would interfere with their property rights." After all, it all depends on what we mean by "property rights," since tenants have them too.

3. Paradox is an attitude

We could extend this chapter at great length listing still more paradoxical twists professors can write into exams. For example, suppose the question is whether an administrative agency should mandate adoption of a new safety device (e.g., automatic braking) to supplement one that's been in place for a long time (e.g., air bags). Many students may cast the problem in terms of the higher cost of the new device when compared with the safety benefits that can reasonably be expected. Imagine the grader's glee, however, when she picks up the paper that reads, "Requiring automatic braking may provide manufacturers with the necessary hands-on experience needed to invent ways to install it more cheaply, so that the sheer act of mandating automatic braking might indeed reduce its costs." (For paradoxes, after all, you can't do much better than the chicken and the egg!)

At this juncture, however, we want to make the broader point that as an exam-taker you aren't merely looking for paradox per se as much as trying to remain open to multiple perspectives on the same issue. Democrats often support minimum-wage laws because they focus on shifting money from shareholders to those at the bottom of the working class (glass half-full). Republicans often oppose minimum-wage laws on the ground that some low-paying jobs will simply disappear because of the mandated wage (glass half-empty). Good exam-takers are free to take either position as long as they carefully consider both points of view.

But if finding comfort in paradox requires an attitude, can you really learn it from reading a book like this? Some of our colleagues have told us that it's not possible to teach the kind of playfulness necessary to develop outstanding exam-taking skills. Obviously, we disagree. By now we have explained the idea as best we can. Let us close this section, then, with one more example of how turning trade-off into paradox can be fun—or at least can pave the way for Law Review performance.

Sometimes paradox arises because a trade-off between competing values just can't capture the complexity of a situation. Imagine, for example, that you are taking a seminar about the judicial confirmation process, and the exam asks you to discuss how a nominee should handle Senate testimony. Everyone can envision urging a nominee not to be too candid. The candidate might alienate an important constituency or violate the norm against comment on cases that may later come before the court. Everyone can also envision advising the nominee not to be overly diplomatic. Otherwise, the Senate may think the candidate is ducking the hard questions. A simple version of the problem is to navigate the trade-off between candor and diplomacy.

Think how happy the professor will be, however, to read an answer that describes the problem in the following way: "As my client gets ready for her Senate testimony I would urge her to be diplomatic, not as a way of hiding her true feelings, but as a way of communicating them more accurately. If her rhetoric is too sharp, the problem won't be that she'll be penalized for her views. It's that her views will be twisted out of context, and she'll be criticized for views she doesn't even hold. At the same time,

I would urge my client to be candid, not merely to demonstrate bravery and a willingness to tackle hard issues, but to generate trust. Candor, it seems to me, is the heart of diplomacy, for no one can be diplomatic unless she is trusted. Rather than a middle ground between candor and diplomacy, my client must be candid and diplomatic at different times and in different ways. This is best accomplished by practicing measured responses to the kind of questions she will receive."

The student's technique here is similar to the one we described using the affirmative action example. General categories (here, candor and diplomacy; there, diversity and merit) are critically evaluated to see if they can be meaningfully interpreted in different ways. There's still a long way to go to write a complete answer to the question. But breaking out of the conventional description of the conflict is a great way to start.

4. When in doubt, write it down

By now we imagine you've had just about enough of our efforts to show you what good policy answers will look like, and we anticipate two entirely legitimate concerns. First, you are probably thinking that it's all well and good for us to spin out multiple conflicting arguments at the leisurely pace afforded us by desktop computers and faculty offices. You have to answer policy questions under enormous time pressure and facing very high stakes. Second, we are sure you've noticed that we never quite get to the point where we actually take a stand on an issue and tell you which way you should resolve it. How, you wonder, will reading this book help you to identify a successful resolution on your own?

We have several answers. We urge you to begin by reading this chapter over carefully while working on an old policy question given by one of your professors. We are confident that the arguments we describe here will play an important role in your efforts to draft a response. We also urge you to try your hand at the sample questions in Chapter Sixteen, for the arguments will become more familiar and easier to deploy the more practice you have in using them.

Above all, however, the key ingredient we are trying to instill is confidence. When you sit down to write an answer to any question, it's human nature to long for a simple, straightforward response. As thoughts pop into your head that cause you to wonder whether there may be more to the question than your first reaction implies, there's a tendency to fear such doubts or to want to banish them. But those doubts are your friends. Include them in your answer. They may not in the end lead anywhere, and, if they don't, say that too. Remember that your professor can't know your thoughts unless they are written in your answer.

What should be clear from reading this chapter is that almost any policy proposal, no matter how attractive it appears at first blush, is susceptible to perfectly reasonable doubts. As a military general or company CEO, you might choose to hide such doubts to present a commanding image. By contrast, a true Czar of the Universe would confront these doubts head-on, confident that doing so would confirm her wisdom more than it would undermine her authority.

Likewise, as an exam-taker, your job is to explain all the angles before coming to rest upon a conclusion. Your challenge is to organize the angles into a coherent, readable answer, not to leave them out. Take heart. Those of you who work through this book have everything you need to accomplish that mission. When in doubt, just tell your grader why.

Chapter Fifteen

Multiple-Choice Exams—
A Course of a Different Color

Given our strong preference for law school examinations that require students to think through problems, spot ambiguities, and provide legal advice that clients will need, you have likely surmised that we aren't big fans of multiple-choice exams. To be sure, there are important skills the multiple-choice format can test, and more on that in a moment. But we see multiple-choice exams as a poor substitute for the traditional issue spotter because they confirm for many students the mistaken impression that the key to success is committing to memory every nook and cranny of every rule "on the books" (something lawyers seldom do), instead of reinforcing the need to interpret rules and argue about how best to apply them (which lawyers do all the time). Moreover, there's just too much "guess what the tester is thinking" built into the structure of multiple-choice questions for us to be comfortable with that format in the high-stakes setting of assigning law school grades. That's why we omitted discussion of multiple choice in our first edition.

Our experience since then, however, has convinced us that neglecting multiple choice is a conceit we can no longer afford. Multiple-choice testing is increasingly common in American law schools, and these days you are likely to face one or more multiple-choice exams in the course of your legal studies. Moreover, it isn't lost on us that most of our students will eventually be taking what will feel like The Most Difficult Multiple-Choice Test in the History of the Universe—that is, the multistate bar exam—when they graduate and head for practice.

It's tempting to blame the multiple-choice trend on a desire on the part of at least some professors to devote less time to grading exams, but many are conscientiously employing alternative means of assessment to respond to a development we've noted elsewhere in the book. Though the students we're teaching today are among the most talented and committed we've seen, they've spent most of their lives online and are thus far more accustomed to screen-skimming and link-clicking than the painstakingly careful parsing of texts required for success in law practice. Law professors have thus been looking for pedagogical and assessment tools designed to "slow their roll," for the rest of what professors try to teach will be of little use without the ability to read and absorb complex legal texts. Multiple-choice exams may help serve this purpose, at least when the questions are carefully constructed.

That said, if you've worked your way through the first fourteen chapters of this book before tackling this one, you may find yourself asking the same question we did when we first learned that some of our colleagues were giving multiple-choice exams: How on earth do you test anything useful about a shades-of-gray subject like law with questions calling for black-and-white answers? How, in other words, do you fit the square peg of the law's many "maybes" into the tiny ovals on a multiple-choice answer sheet? The short answer is that you do so by squeezing as much ambiguity as possible out of the problems you test, and an understanding of the ways in which that is accomplished may be a helpful aid in preparing for multiple-choice exams. In the materials that follow, we offer a series of examples designed to let you in on the game.

A. Bye-Bye Maybe, Maybe Goodbye

Let's start with a familiar problem, retrofitted to the multiple-choice format.

> Paul Patron offers Arlene Artiste $10,000 to paint a portrait of the Patron family. Artiste explains that her other commitments make it impossible to promise a completed work by a particular date, and Patron responds, "I don't want your commitment. I just want the portrait." After Artiste spends numerous hours doing preliminary sketches—but before she has put brush to canvas and begun the actual portrait—Patron advis-

es her that he has changed his mind and is revoking the offer. If Artiste brings suit and the jurisdiction follows the rules of offer and acceptance at common law:

A. Artiste's suit will succeed because she relied on Patron's offer.
B. Artiste's suit will succeed because she began performance.
C. Artiste's suit will fail, unless the court determines that the revocation was made in bad faith.
D. Artiste's suit will fail because she has not finished the portrait.

As we've previously seen, the Artiste/Patron problem presents a classic "rule vs. counter-rule" issue, for the outcome depends in the first instance on whether the traditional common law rule or the Second Restatement governs. Under the common law, an offer to make a unilateral contract can be revoked right up to the moment the offeree *completes* performance, and—in the problem presented here—that means Patron may revoke, since Artiste hasn't finished the portrait. Under the Restatement, revocation is prohibited as soon as the offeree *begins* the performance, and—returning again to our problem—Patron cannot revoke if the sketchwork counts as the beginning of performance. So the answer to the question of whether Artiste will prevail is (*you guessed it*) maybe, for it depends on whether the jurisdiction embraces—or can be persuaded to embrace—the common law rule or the Restatement.

But in our multiple-choice version of the problem, there is no maybe about it. And the reason is that the test-taker is told *in the question itself* that the common law rule governs, so there is only one possible result: No portrait and thus no bar to revocation. Choice D is thus the right answer, identifying the correct result (Artiste loses) and the correct reason (she hasn't completed performance).

In a moment, we're going to work our way through the other choices to see how they might lead some test-takers astray. But first we're going to let you in on a bit of authorial license and then make an important point about our choice of terminology. The license we have taken is that the right answer in most of the examples we'll discuss will be choice D. We've set it up this way for the sake of clarity, to enable us to consider and dismiss each of the other choices "in the order of appearance" as we work our way to the right one. But don't be fooled into thinking that this is what you'll encounter on real multiple-choice exams; indeed, most drafters work hard to ensure that right answers are randomly and equally distributed among all four choices. As for terminology, for each question we'll refer to the four choices as "foils" and then more specifically to the wrong choices as "distractors" or "distractor foils." (It should go without saying that we'll refer to the correct choice as "the right answer," but—as our children would predict—we'll say it anyway.) Some professors may use these terms differently than we do—e.g., referring only to wrong choices as "foils"—so it's critical to be clear about these definitions from the start.

Back, then, to Artiste/Patron, and now let's work through the foils one at a time. Foil A suggests that Artiste's reliance on the offer will save her and thus confuses the legal protection available for reliance on *promises* (typically via promissory estoppel) with the protection available for reliance on *offers* that have not yet been accepted. Foil B suggests that Artiste may secure legal protection by beginning performance and thus mistakenly applies the "beginning of performance" rule of the Restatement instead of the "complete performance" rule of the common law. And Foil C—a Hail Mary pass if ever there were one—assumes a limit on the power of revocation that doesn't exist at common law, where offerors are free to revoke before acceptance for good reasons, bad reasons, and no reasons at all.

But the more fundamental shortcoming in Foils A, B, and C is that they are not Foil D—that is, they don't apply the common law rule to the problem and don't even *try* to. In Part B of the chapter, we'll show you the specific ways in which foils like A, B, and C are designed to distract you from picking the right answer. But for now our focus is on the ways in which multiple-choice exams make a "right" answer possible at all.

Designing a question with a right answer, Step 1: How multiple-choice exams eliminate the need to choose between competing rules

a. The call of the question

So how exactly did the Artiste/Patron question eliminate the maybe—that is, dispense with the need to choose between the common law and the Restatement? The answer is simple and straightforward: By identifying the governing rule in the call of the question. As we saw back in Chapter Twelve, "the call of the question" often plays a critical role in the traditional issue spotter by narrowing the focus to particular issues and taking other issues off the table. In the multiple-choice context, the call frequently plays a similar role by choosing between competing rules you've studied and designating one of them as the applicable source of law.

It may accomplish this the way we've done it in the Artiste/Patron problem—i.e., by identifying the governing body of law, here "the rules of offer and acceptance at common law." But the call is often even more specific, as in the following examples:

- Alvaro brings an action against Brishen for intentional infliction of emotional distress; what result under the Restatement (Second) of Torts?
- Does Samantha Seller's final email constitute a firm offer under the U.C.C.?

In such cases, even if you studied another rule that might potentially govern the problem presented (e.g., the Third Restatement's approach to intentional infliction of emotional distress or the common law regulation of option contracts), the call of the question has eliminated any ambiguity about the applicable law, and the search for a "right" answer is thus greatly simplified.

b. The exam instructions

Rule clarification can be accomplished in other ways as well. For one thing, a professor may include a directive about the governing law in the general instructions for the exam—e.g., "Unless otherwise specified, you should assume that the provisions of the Restatement (Second) of Contracts govern the problems presented in the exam." Or she might issue a similar directive in class or during an exam review session—"Only the Third Restatement, folks, for emotional distress questions"—yet another reason, as we have stressed, to record every word your professor says about the final. Note that general instructions like these may apply to issue-spotting questions as well as to multiple choice, and in either case they should be followed "to a T."

There is another way a professor may—in the course of lecture and/ or the assigned readings—signal what she views as the controlling rule for the exam when there are competing contenders for the throne: i.e., by repeatedly identifying and emphasizing the "majority" rule with respect to choices that divide U.S. jurisdictions. (E.g., "While some jurisdictions have eliminated the 'family member' requirement for bystander intentional infliction of emotional distress claims, the majority continues to embrace it.") If your professor regularly resolves rule vs. counter-rule conflicts in this manner, she may also be clueing you in on what she wants to see on the final, even if she doesn't come right out and say so. To allay any doubts on the matter, we suggest asking the professor directly— after class, via email, or during an exam review session—whether you will be expected to identify and apply only "majority" rules on the exam or whether competing approaches are fair game for testing as well.

c. As the wand chooses the wizard, the facts choose the rule

One of the most vexing topics in contract law is contractual modifications: What happens if the parties agree to new terms after the contract has been agreed to but before performance is complete? If the transaction is a sale of goods—and thus governed by the U.C.C.—there is little difficulty enforcing such a modification in the absence of coercion or duress. So the parties to a contract for the sale and delivery of 1000 widgets are free at any point before performance is complete to decide to change the quantity to 500 because of supply-chain difficulties, and the change will be fully enforceable. But if the contract in question is a service or any other transaction not governed by the Code, there's a world of trouble if the contract is modified after the fact—e.g., if sailors are promised a raise in the middle of a fishing trip, they will have a heck of a time enforcing that promise when the voyage is complete. (This is the result of the ancient "pre-existing duty rule," and trust us, you don't want to hear any more about it now.)

At the risk of stating the obvious, a multiple-choice exam question testing the law of contractual modifications will "choose the rule" for you by presenting the problem in the context of a sale of goods (where modifications are typically enforceable) *or* in some other contractual setting (where the opposite is the case). This setup—where the facts choose the rule—is a common one on multiple-choice exams and can arise in any context in which there is one set of rules for some things and another set for others—e.g., public sector employees enjoy First Amendment free speech rights but private sector employees do not; landowners have one set of obligations to licensees (e.g., social guests) and another to invitees (e.g., construction contractors); etc. The bad news is that you will have to study twice the number of rules you'll actually need to answer such questions on an exam; the good news is that you'll know exactly which rule to use if you pay careful attention to the facts.

Designing a question with a right answer, Step 2: How multiple-choice exams eliminate the need to resolve conflicts over the meaning of rules and cases

The point of the previous section is that multiple-choice exams are not likely to make you guess which rule among competing possibilities governs the questions before you. But questions that "choose the rule for you" don't eliminate the prospect of ambiguity. As we saw in earlier chapters, American law is rife with disputes over the *meaning* of rules—statutory, common law, constitutional, administrative etc.—as well as the meaning of cases that interpret and apply them. Indeed, in no small part because of the deep discord associated with contemporary U.S. politics and culture, the list of issues that turn on hotly disputed questions of meaning and interpretation—from gun rights; to abortion rights; to voting rights; to the reach of the commerce clause; to the powers of administrative agencies; to the right to ignore public health regulations on the basis of religious beliefs; to the ability of employers and merchants to force employee and consumer claims to arbitration; to claims of private property trumping other kinds of rights—is growing and daunting. There is little doubt that these and similar issues will loom large in law study and classroom discussion for the foreseeable future and that law exams will test them early and often via issue spotters and policy questions. Yet while many of us have strong feelings about the "right" and the "wrong" of these matters, the questions of interpretation they present are ill-suited for testing via the multiple-choice format since they don't generate stable and objectively "right" or "wrong" answers from the law's perspective.

So if multiple-choice exams avoid testing choice-of-rule disputes as well as disputes over the interpretation of rules and cases, is there anything left to test? There is indeed. In a nutshell, most areas of law have loads of rules and cases with well-settled interpretations, and what multiple-choice exams can test is a student's understanding of the *borders and boundaries* established by those rules and cases and the *distinctions* to which the borders and boundaries give rise: the distinctions, for example, between what a statute covers and what it doesn't (e.g., a sale of goods governed by the U.C.C. vs. a service governed by the common law); or between a rule and an exception (e.g., battery is tortious but not when there's consent); or between competing legal categories (e.g., beginning of performance vs. mere preparations in the Artiste/Patron problem); or between proof of a particular element of a claim or defense and its absence (e.g., whether possession was "continuous" or not for purposes of establishing adverse possession). In our experience, such distinctions are by some distance the most commonly tested subject matter on multiple-choice exams.

But wait, a reader might object, didn't you guys devote an entire chapter to "forks in the facts"—i.e., the factual conflicts that frequently arise at the boundaries between legal categories? How does a focus on boundaries and distinctions serve the cause of "squeezing all the ambiguity" out of legal problems when—as we saw back in Chapter Nine—so many of them involve "facts on both sides of a boundary"; or disputes in which the parties come to court offering "competing perspectives"; or disputes in which a "snapshot" of the facts may look very different from the "film"; or disputes in which the facts read differently if you analyze them "one at a time" than they do if they are all "taken together"? How can you produce a "right" answer to a "which side are you on" boundary question without resolving difficult factual disputes like these? Good question! And that brings us to the third and final strategy professors commonly deploy in designing questions for multiple-choice exams.

Designing a question with a right answer, Step 3: How multiple-choice exams eliminate the need to resolve factual conflict

Let's look at another multiple-choice variation on the Artiste/Patron problem:

> Paul Patron offers Arlene Artiste $10,000 to paint a portrait of the Patron family. Artiste explains that her other commitments make it impossible for her to promise a completed work by a particular date, and Patron responds, "I don't want your com-

mitment. I just want the portrait." After Artiste spends numerous hours doing preliminary sketches—but before she has put
brush to canvas and begun the actual portrait—Patron advises
her that he has changed his mind and is revoking the offer. If
Artiste brings suit and the court follows the rules of offer and
acceptance under the Restatement (Second) of Contracts:

A. Artiste's suit will fail because she hasn't finished the portrait.
B. Artiste's suit will fail because Patron requested a portrait,
   not sketchwork.
C. Artiste's suit will succeed because she began the performance stipulated by the offer.
D. Artiste's suit will succeed if the court finds that the preliminary sketchwork constitutes the beginning of performance.

The call of the question tells us that the Restatement and not the common law governs. And, under the Restatement, an offer to make a unilateral contract (e.g., "I'll pay you $100 to climb to the top of the flag-
pole") can't be revoked once the offeree has "begun performance" (e.g.,
by actually climbing the flagpole) but remains revocable if the offeree is
engaging in "mere preparations" (e.g., by donning climbing boots before
heading for the pole). So on which side of the boundary between these
competing categories—"beginning of performance" vs. "mere preparations"—does Artiste's sketchwork fall?

As discussed at length in earlier chapters, there is no straightforward
answer to that question, for there are some pretty good arguments favoring each party. But a well-crafted multiple-choice question won't force
you to choose a side. To see just how that might be so, let's work our way
through the four foils one at a time, deploying the tried-and-true "process of elimination" to identify the "right" answer.

We can eliminate Foil A straightaway, for it assumes that Artiste must
finish the portrait to prevent revocation and thus mistakenly applies the
common law rather than the Restatement rule specified in the call of the
question. At the same time, there is something to be said for both Foil B
and Foil C. Patron would certainly contend that Foil B is right on the
money; he did indeed "reques[t] a portrait, not sketchwork," and—the
argument would continue—until Artiste starts painting the actual "portrait," she has not yet "begun performance" under the Restatement rule,

so he's still free to revoke. But Artiste will embrace Foil C, arguing that painters commonly do sketchwork as they begin a portrait—or nearly any other *objet d'art*, for that matter—and that accordingly her initial sketches of Patron's family do indeed "begin the performance" invited by Patron's offer. On this view, it is too late for Patron to revoke. Each of these foils thus offers a half-truth—a reason, to be sure, for reaching the result it favors, but a reason that pays no heed to the force of the argument on "the other side." When it comes to identifying the *right* answer, then, there's nothing to see here.

That leaves us with Foil D: "Artiste's suit will succeed if the court finds that the preliminary sketchwork constitutes the beginning of performance." There's a lot to like in this answer. First, unlike Foil A, it gets the law right and avoids the seductive lure of the common law rule. And unlike Foils B and C, it doesn't come down on one side of the factual ambiguity while ignoring the other. Instead, Foil D makes a conditional claim: *If* the court finds that the preliminary sketchwork constitutes the beginning of performance, *then* Artiste's suit will succeed. And that brings us to the critical feature of this foil: Because of its conditional nature, the statement it makes is unambiguously true. Rather than offering a contestable judgment regarding how to read the facts, the statement focuses exclusively on *the way the rule operates*—on the legal consequences of falling on one side or the other of the boundary between "beginning of performance" and "mere preparations." Foil D thus eliminates the factual ambiguity from the problem and rewards the student who understands the way the Restatement rule works (no revocation once performance has begun) and just what it would take for Artiste to succeed in her claim (persuading a court that the sketchwork was the beginning of performance). What follows, then, are some of the most common ways a professor drafting a multiple-choice exam can eliminate factual ambiguity in this way and thus create questions with right answers like this one.

a. "If" or "unless" does all the work

Note the telltale "if" in Foil D above: "Artiste's suit will succeed *if* the court finds that the preliminary sketchwork constitutes the beginning of performance" (emphasis added). Were a student to offer that sentence and nothing more on an issue spotter presenting the Artiste/Patron problem, the professor would likely red-circle the "if" and write something like this in the margin: "Please don't keep me in suspense! Should the court make that finding or not?" But in the context of a multiple-choice exam, there's no room to explain or to argue, only a demand for a single answer. Foil D delivers on that demand, dispensing with the need for any factual analysis or argument at all and (once again) casting the inquiry in conditional form—"*if* the court finds that the facts satisfy the rule, *then* the claimant wins"—leaving to some hypothetical court the task of deciding whether the "if" condition is met on the ambiguous facts. All *you* need to know is the rule itself and the distinction it creates—i.e., that the "beginning of performance" will prevent revocation whereas "mere preparations" won't—and then you can identify the foil that gets it right.

An "unless" clause can do the same work as an "if" clause. Assume the question and accompanying foils appear exactly as they do above except that Foil D reads thus (emphasis added): "Artiste's suit will succeed, *unless* the court finds that the sketchwork constitutes mere preparations for performance." Once again, the foil avoids taking sides on the disputed question of fact, sparing the student the need to resolve the ambiguity by leaving the resolution to a hypothetical court. What the foil does instead is correctly identify the issue that a court will have to resolve by stating the applicable rule and the competing categories it creates, once again eliminating any need to choose between them by evaluating the facts.

b. A passing or seemingly random word or phrase does all the work

The scariest thing most parents can imagine is something bad happening to their kid, so imagine a multiple-choice question in which—shades of *The Untouchables*—a stroller with "baby on board" begins a treacherous roll down a long and steep stairway after Betty bumps into it on the landing at the top of the stairs. The infant turns out to be fine. (We aren't monsters.) Indeed, when the stroller comes to a halt at the bottom she seems to be smiling, perhaps hoping for another ride. But in the meantime, Dutiful Dad has fainted from fright, sustaining a head injury when he hits the terrazzo floor. So it's Dad suing Betty Bumper, and the call of the question and foils read thus:

If Dad brings a tort suit against Bumper, the suit will most likely:

A. Succeed on a claim of intentional infliction of emotional distress.

B. Succeed on a claim of reckless infliction of emotional distress.

C. Succeed on both claims.

D. Fail on both claims.

On the facts given, there is little reason to doubt Dad's distress, and the problem comes right out and tells us that he's suffered physical injury as a result and that Bumper's contact with the stroller got the whole mess rolling. But in order to pick from among the foils, the test-taker needs to ascertain Bumper's *state of mind* in connection with the bump, a mystery that may seem at first to be unfathomable. One possibility, of course, is that this is a poorly drafted question—asking you, in effect, to read the professor's mind, just the way professors seem to do in a Socratic exchange during class. But another possibility is that you missed something important when you read the problem. And sure enough, a second reading reveals that Bumper "accidentally" bumped the stroller, an adverb you didn't see the first time through. (Relax: we hid it from view.) In the tort setting, that adverb does all the work, negating the possibility of recovery for either intentional or recklessness-based torts and yielding Foil D as the best answer among the available choices. Of course, you won't appreciate the significance of "accidentally" if you don't have a firm grasp of the rules governing a defendant's required state of mind in tort actions. But even if you've thoroughly mastered those rules, you may still miss the boat if you don't read the problem carefully enough to register and weigh the significance of every... single... word.

It may be helpful to note that you're more likely to encounter a multiple-choice problem like this one—meaning a problem in which a single fact turns a potentially complex dispute into a question with a right answer—when the critical fact *negates* a claim of liability rather than establishing it. The reason for this is simple: In the vast majority of cases you're likely to encounter on a multiple-choice exam, it would take multiple elements—and thus multiple facts—to establish an affirmative claim, whereas the absence of any *one* of those elements will defeat it. So be on the lookout for a seemingly passing word or a phrase that negates (for example) a required state of mind (e.g., where defendant *accidentally* bumps a stroller); or the element of causation (e.g., where Dad slips and falls *before* the stroller is bumped); or the element of reliance (e.g., where the promisee in a promissory estoppel case sold the family jewels for a mess of pottage *before* learning of the promise); or proof of damages (e.g., where the victim of a breach of contract is able to secure the promised goods from a third party *at a lower price*).

One final tip in connection with "critical facts" that might be easy to miss if you're reading too quickly. Watch out for the "late hit"—i.e., a fact that makes its first and only appearance in the call of the question, when you are tempted to think you've already finished the story and are rushing to get to the foils. (E.g., "You are the attorney representing plaintiff, and your investigation has revealed X" where X establishes that your client consented to the alleged battery; or that an allegedly defamatory statement is true; or that the consistent past practice of parties to a contract dispute undermines any claim of breach.)

c. The question stacks the deck so that only one factual resolution is possible

If a single word or phrase can *negate* a claim, it may take a whole busload of words to *establish* a claim definitively enough for a multiple-choice exam. Thus, if a liability dispute turns on whether a particular condition was "conspicuous," the element can be negated by a phrase as simple as "where none of the customers could see it"—enabling the drafter to compose a "right answer" rejecting liability on that basis. But if the drafter wants the right answer to be an affirmation of liability, then chances are she'll have to lard the problem with multiple clues—e.g., "situated in a large and colorful display" and "readily visible from the sales floor" and even "prompting comments from several customers who observed it." In poker, we call these "tells," and the job of the test-taker is to respond to the multiplicity of such hints by asking, "Why does Professor Martinez keep telling (and telling and telling) me this?" On an issue-spotting exam, mixed signals would be a feature, not a bug, for that's what the lawyers would argue about and thus what the exam-taking student would be expected to write about. But on a multiple-choice exam, the point is once again to dispense with the need for the reader to resolve ambiguous facts, and "stacking the deck" is another method by which professors may try to accomplish this to create a question with a single right answer.

B. Hiding the Ball

So if multiple-choice exams squeeze all the ambiguity out of legal problems, why aren't they a whole lot easier? We have several thoughts on that score. For one thing, legal education—and especially the first-year curriculum—is designed to train students to become skeptical readers, and one hazard of that training is that students may start to see ambiguity even when it isn't there. The shift from classroom questions that produce a multiplicity of possibilities to exam questions that seek a single right answer can be as jarring as the shift from black-and-white to color in *The Wizard of Oz*. A second difficulty is the flip side of the first. Good multiple-choice questions are extremely difficult to draft, and, judging from what we've seen over the years, not everyone is equal to the task. Students frequently find real but unintended ambiguities in the questions, reducing test-taking to guesswork since—in contrast to the issue-spotter setting—there's no place to register and explain the confusion. This hazard may be particularly acute when a well-meaning professor—intending to liven up yet another dreary account of illness, injury, and mayhem on a Torts exam—uses a popular film, book, or play as the setting for a problem, leaving readers scrambling to figure out which parts of the cultural artifact are indeed in the problem (e.g., the fact that Harry Potter is a student) and which are not (e.g., the fact that Harry Potter can talk to snakes).

Truth be told, there's not a lot you can do about ambiguous exam questions that penalize rather than reward skeptical reading—apart perhaps from keeping the risks of multiple-choice testing in mind when selecting your electives and upper-level courses. But the good news is that the most common source of difficulty in the multiple-choice setting is a feature you *can* do something about. Simply put, many professors worry that draining the ambiguity out of exam problems will make their questions too easy, so they develop techniques designed to lure students *away* from the correct answers. This reminds us of one of the first jokes we "got" when we were growing up: What has four legs and a tail, is made of cement, and howls at the moon at night? The answer, which only a six-year-old can truly appreciate: "A wolf. I just threw in the cement to make it hard." Well, in our experience professors tend to throw in an awful lot of cement when they are drafting multiple-choice questions—i.e., needless complexity and misdirection that have little meaningful relationship to legal materials or lawyering skills and are in there only to make it hard.

Following the technique we've used throughout this book, the remainder of the chapter is devoted to helping you identify the *patterns* in which such professorial distraction efforts frequently appear. Learn to recognize these patterns, and you can minimize the distractions and find your way to the "right" answers in spite of them. But there's a common thread to the patterns, and if you understand this overarching professorial strategy it can help you cope with even the "tricks" you haven't seen before: drafting a question that puts psychological pressure on the test-taker to ignore what she knows for fear that the *real* answer depends on some rule or exception or "exception to an exception" that she somehow missed despite all her diligent study.

To see what we mean, consider an SAT question asking you to identify the antonym of "overcast," where one of the options is "cloudless." This seems to you so obviously right that *it's just too easy*, so you're sure it must be wrong. You start to worry that the meaning you are ascribing to "overcast" is a slang usage in informal weather-speak (like "raining cats and dogs" or "dust devil") and that you've somehow forgotten the core dictionary meaning of the term. So you look at the other possible antonyms and see the option "underslung." You have never heard of this word—because you're not in the business of delivering medical supplies, materiel, or rations by helicopter—but now you are flailing away, trying to outsmart the question. STOP! Consider the odds that "overcast" *really* means something different from the usage you've heard a thousand times and that the correct antonym is the one word in the entire problem you've never seen before and not the word you *know* to be the opposite of the standard usage. If you've studied diligently, those odds are vanishingly small, so don't take the bait.

The broader lesson for multiple-choice law exams is a variation on the famous maxim coined by a defense secretary we seldom have occasion to quote: You go to battle with the knowledge you have, not the knowledge you fear you don't have. Don't let the questions bully you into wondering what obscure legal tidbit has somehow escaped your grasp only to find its way into Foil C on some challenging question. To be sure, there are tidbits in every subject—like the rules in Civil Procedure governing the due date for filing an answer when the 21-day period mandated by the rules would fall on a legal holiday (e.g., Thanksgiving) that is followed by a day on which the clerk's office is closed (e.g., the day after Thanksgiving in most federal offices) and then by a weekend. Testing for *that* kind of obscurity is seldom going to happen—unless, of course, the professor has stressed the operation and importance of those particular rules in class, in which case you will know all about them in any event. But here are the "tricks" professors *will* use to "hide the ball," and—with diligent preparation, careful reading, clear thinking, and just a little confidence—you can find it nearly every time.

1. When an apparent *non sequitur* shows you what the answer is, believe it

Although it's a shame that multiple-choice questions often rely on misdirection, it's an easy way to get students to take their eyes off the prize. Just watch:

> T'Challa, the new President of Nutmeg U.—the flagship public university in a small New England state—announces a change in the school's admissions policy. T'Challa declares that he has lost patience with indirect efforts to help the historically disadvantaged and plans to try a new and more direct approach. Henceforth, he announces, any applicant who can demonstrate with clear and convincing evidence that the applicant has an ancestor who was an enslaved person in the territory that now makes up the United States will automatically be given a 20-point bump in the personal profile score used by the admissions committee. In the following admissions cycle, Rex Walmsley's application to Nutmeg is rejected. Rex brings a lawsuit challenging the decision on the grounds that he was denied due process of law. Rex has no proof of having any enslaved ancestors. Instead, Rex has written a lengthy essay explaining that he deserves special consideration because of learning disabilities that make it difficult for him to compete for a spot at Nutmeg. Rex asserts that Nutmeg never read his essay nor provided him an opportunity to be heard about his unusual circumstances. The strongest argument for the claim Rex raises is:

A. Mechanical admissions policies that give mathematical preferences to some applicants over others are unconstitutional.

B. Nutmeg's policy of favoring descendants of enslaved persons is a not-so-hidden vehicle for employing racial preferences, which are unconstitutional.

C. The clear and convincing evidence standard is too high a bar, given the strength of an applicant's interest in having a fair chance to secure admission to an institution of higher learning.

D. Applicants to public universities are entitled to individualized consideration, and Nutmeg's refusal to read Rex's essay violated fundamental notions of fairness.

Let's go through the choices one at a time. By the end of your Constitutional Law course, you will have learned that the mechanical addition of points to an applicant's score based on race is unlawful under the equal protection clause. So Foil A looks like a good bet for the right answer. You'll also have learned that preferences based on race provoke intense judicial skepticism that courts refer to as "strict scrutiny." You therefore think that courts may be suspicious of preferences for the descendants of enslaved people, even though you're not entirely sure that's a race-based preference. So Foil B is at least plausible. It also seems plausible that the government can't force applicants to "bring me the broomstick of the Wicked Witch of the West" when making the case for admission to a public university, and anyway you don't completely understand the "burdens of proof" that seem to show up randomly in all your first-year subjects. Accordingly, Foil C, while confusing, is somewhat tempting too.

But here's the kicker. Whatever the validity of these points, Foils A, B, and C are simply not responsive to what the question asks. Rex, we are told, is contesting his treatment by Nutmeg "on the grounds that he was denied due process of law." He is *not* challenging Nutmeg's racial preferences; he just wants a chance to make his own case for individualized treatment. So Foil C is clearly wrong: Rex isn't trying to prove that he is descended from enslaved persons, and thus the standard of proof the university applies to such showings is irrelevant. Foils A and B are about the equal protection clause, a topic you'll have studied in depth and about which you'll be understandably eager to display your mastery. And it's entirely possible that Rex might have an equal protection claim on these facts. But the question tells us that he is pressing a due process claim instead. Accordingly, Foil D is the winner, since it's framed in classic due process terms and focused on "the opportunity to be heard."

So how can a student resist getting sucked down the rabbit hole of such tempting false foils? First and foremost, the most important advice for issue spotters is equally important in the multiple-choice setting: *answer the question asked.* The question here is about due process, so the answer will be too. Why might some students miss this obvious point? Note that the reference to the due process claim seems to be a *non sequitur*, appearing out of the blue after an extended narrative focusing the reader's attention on the country's pitched battle over affirmative action. The "wait, what?" reaction to which this sudden change of subject may give rise may prompt some exam-takers to rush right past it, but the seeming *non sequitur* is in fact a critical "tell" that the professor is burying the lead. Indeed, this is the only mention of due process anywhere in the problem, and it appears several sentences before the call of the question, another "tell" that the professor wants you to forget about it by the time you start reading the foils. And finally, even if you missed the due process reference the first time you read through the problem, you'll be saved if you remember to ask the Three Little Questions we learned in connection with case-briefing: Who's suing whom? For what? And on what theory—a.k.a. "what's the cause of action?" In this case, so long as you searched for the cause of action before choosing among the foils, you would likely have found your way back to the due process claim and out of the thicket of equal protection.

The big takeaway? Multiple-choice exams put as much of a premium on careful reading as they do on mastery of the relevant subject matter. Your job as the test-taker is to stay calm and keep your focus not on the story each question tells but on the question each story asks.

2. Definitions, friend and foe

As we explained back in our chapter on "forks in the facts," law relies heavily on categories to govern behavior. An owner has different rights to use a resource—say, a shirt or a golf club—than a non-owner. A landowner owes fewer duties to a trespasser than to an invitee. A burglar is different from an embezzler. Issue-spotting exams test a student's understanding of legal categories by telling stories in which the facts don't fit neatly into any one of them. A cashier receives money from a customer, hides it in her locker rather than putting it in the cash register, and breaks into the store at night to retrieve the funds. Is that embezzlement (because she appropriated the funds) or burglary (because she broke into the building)? Both? Neither? Presented with such a challenge on an essay exam, you would have the chance not only to show off your ability to spot the embezzlement vs. burglary "fork" but also to raise variations on the facts (e.g., is it burglary if an employee breaks into the building to retrieve his cellphone from his locker?) that might bear on the categorization. You might also address policy issues—e.g., in choosing between embezzlement and burglary, should we err on the side of the crime with the harsher penalties because the conduct at issue here is particularly blameworthy or particularly difficult to detect?

Multiple-choice exams obviously can't test or reward the creative deployment of critical lawyering skills in this manner. But what they can do is test your knowledge of how the respective legal categories are *defined*. At first, that may sound like a blessing—if you know the definitions, the answer should be easy. But beware the possibility that your professor may try to use your knowledge against you. Consider the following example:

> Tom Taylor is working the night shift at the local big-box store. The hot item on this year's holiday gift list is a toy robot named Cosmo that can, on command, motor to the kitchen and fetch you a sandwich. The Cosmo lists for $500, but Tom charges each Cosmo-seeking customer $750, explaining (falsely) that the store is running short of robots and therefore requires payment in cash. For each sale, he puts $500 into the cash register and pockets the other $250. When Tom is caught by the security guard after his activities are recorded on film, on what charge is he most likely to be convicted?
>
> A. Burglary, because he stole the funds at night.
> B. Robbery, because he threatened customers not to sell them a Cosmo unless they parted with their money.
> C. No crime, because customers got Cosmo for a price they were willing to pay and the store owner received the funds he expected to gain from each sale.

D. Embezzlement, because the store owner entrusted Tom
with the money he pocketed.

Once again, let's consider the foils one at a time, armed with the
definitions that students learn in Criminal Law. The incident took place
at night, so there's the lure for the burglary charge in Foil A. But burglary also requires breaking and entering, and here Tom was legally in
the building, so we can dismiss Foil A out of hand. Foil B characterizes
Tom's sales pitch as a "threat" to the customer, luring the reader into
considering the possibility that this is a robbery. But at this point in the
transaction, Tom is "threatening" to withhold something that belongs
to the store, not the customer, and there's no hint of any force or violence on Tom's part, so Foil B is likewise a dead end. Foil C may appeal
to dogmatic libertarians (since no one was actually killed and everyone
went home a winner) and perhaps dogmatic Marxists as well (since the
worker was relieving the owner of surplus value and then some), but it
won't fool readers who "don't leave their common sense at the door."
There's a crime here, or else retail clerks everywhere would be a *lot* richer. Yet this leaves only Foil D, which might give the reader pause since
the incident doesn't fit the classic embezzlement scenario we'd have if
Tom had charged each customer the $500 list price and put only $250
into the cash register. But slow down and think: The only reason Tom
had possession of the cash in question is that the owner authorized him
to consummate Cosmo sales on the owner's behalf, so appropriating
those funds to himself is a solid if somewhat convoluted case of embezzlement. Bingo!

Two key lessons emerge from this example. First, in preparation for
multiple-choice exams, you need to know the definitions of the legal
terms you study, and especially the distinctions between those terms,
cold. That's true for issue-spotting exams as well, but in the multiple-choice setting the definitions will often be doing all the work, so
there's no room for even the slightest error. Second, if the good news is
that your firm grasp of a definition will usually enable you to answer the
question, the bad news is that the professor may try to use that knowledge to lure you with false foils built on partial truths. The defense against
this particular Dark Art is (once again) to stay calm and read the problem and the foils with great care so you can dismiss the distractions and
zero in on the right answer.

3. Elements, friend and foe

Referring again to our chapter on "forks in the facts," we saw how professors can exploit legal doctrines with multiple elements by inventing issue spotters in which one or more of the elements is in doubt—e.g., an adverse possession problem in which it's a close call whether a squatter's possession of an island was continuous (because he would frequently head out to sea on multiday fishing trips) or open and notorious (because he slept in a cave during the day and—sporting a powerful set of night vision goggles—was out and about on the island only in the wee hours). Multiple-choice question writers mimic this style by drafting distractor foils with "near misses" on critical elements to conceal the one answer that is close enough for government work. To see what we mean, consider the following problem:

> At considerable expense, Glinda consults a leading horticulturist to learn the best ways to cultivate *Papaver somniferum*—the so-called "opium poppy"—on her suburban property without subjecting neighbors to the plant's sleep-inducing fragrances. Following the protocols offered by the horticulturist "to a T," Glinda plants poppies in a garden well removed from and downwind of her neighbor Elphaba's house. Despite the precautions, Elphaba now has trouble staying awake when she's at home and points to the poppies as the cause. If Elphaba files suit alleging private nuisance and seeking an injunction requiring removal of the poppies, she is likely to:
>
> A. Lose, because seeds from the poppies blowing onto Elphaba's property from Glinda's are too small to constitute the prohibited "invasion."
> B. Lose, because Glinda exercised the utmost care in planting the poppies.
> C. Prevail, because farming is never a lawful activity in a residential neighborhood.
> D. Prevail if Elphaba can prove causation, because the poppies are likely a nuisance.

So let's talk a little bit about private nuisance, a topic you may encounter in Torts or Property. The elements of such a claim include "[a] non-

trespassory invasion of another's interest in the private use and enjoy-
ment of land" and causation of "significant harm" by the invasion. What's
a "nontrespassory" invasion? For our purposes, the difference between a
trespass and a nuisance is that the former typically involves a physical or
tangible intrusion onto plaintiff's property and the latter does not. Thus,
for example, firing my AK-47 nonstop at all hours of the night so that my
neighbor can't sleep because of the noise is a nuisance, because there is no
physical intrusion onto the neighbor's land; errant bullets and shells, by
contrast, would constitute trespass. And what's "significant" harm? If the
nearly constant smoke from my trash fires kills most of the neighbor's
tomato crop, that would surely do the trick; the occasional interruption
of sleep when my dog howls at the moon at night likely wouldn't. A third
element—beyond the invasion and the resulting harm—is the required
state of mind. Since we're not talking about an "abnormally dangerous
activity" (e.g., dynamite blasting or harvesting various forms of the Coronavirus in petri dishes), a would-be plaintiff can succeed by proving either an intentional and unreasonable invasion (e.g., where I know full
well that my late-night gunfire is keeping you awake) or a negligent one
based on defendant's failure to exercise reasonable care in its activities.

   When you've got all that, let's consider the foils one by one. Foil A
might grab your attention because it plays on a typical reader's insecurities about his knowledge of poppies. ("Do they really have fragrances that
cause sleep, or is that just a movie thing? Are they even legal? What I *do*
know is that their tiny seeds show up on nearly every bagel—and in nearly every colonoscopy—in New York.") But don't let such fears lure you to
an obviously false foil, since the cause of action is nuisance (not trespass)
and no physical invasion is required for a nuisance claim. (And for the
record, in some jurisdictions, the physical invasion required for trespass
can be established by particulates far smaller than poppy seeds.) Foil B
may distract the reader for a different reason: It makes a factual claim that
is 100% true (i.e., Glinda "exercised the utmost care" in her planting efforts) and that sounds as if it should negate any negligence claim. But
nuisance claims don't require negligence, and Glinda's conduct can be
unreasonable for the time and place even if she undertakes it with metic-
ulous care—just as a factory can be held liable for discharging noxious
smoke even if it uses the best available technology to minimize pollution.
Foil C exploits the nagging suspicion that this isn't the time or place for

poppies by offering up a "principle" vindicating that intuition, concluding that Elphaba will win "because farming is never a lawful activity in a residential neighborhood." But it's highly doubtful that planting poppies in your garden is tantamount to "farming," and common sense tells you that many people grow fruits and vegetables in their suburban yards. Moreover, we're betting that "never" is a term you have (almost) never heard from your professor, so the claim made in Foil C is *at best* an over-statement and in any event a classic case of "brand-new" learning. Once again, if a confident statement of "the law" doesn't ring a bell, it quite likely rings hollow. That leaves us with Foil D, which sports a telltale "if," sparing the test-taker the task of figuring out whether there is a causal connection between the invasion and its consequences. As we saw in Part A of the chapter, in this manner the professor has eliminated important ambiguity from the problem and directed you to the right answer.

This question thus further illustrates the way multiple-choice questions may fool students into falling for distractor foils even when they have carefully studied the relevant legal materials. It does so in Foil A by correctly identifying a required element, but getting its content wrong; it does so in Foil B by telling the truth but not the relevant truth; and it does so in Foil C by asserting a principle that sounds remarkably "law-like" and would get you where your sense of fairness is eager to go. Your best bet for fighting off the wrong answers is by getting the elements and the corresponding requirements of proof down cold and by reading the foils with a skeptical eye, aware that the professor is likely to have planted something in each of them to distract you from the one foil that rules them all.

4. The hazards of multi-tasking

In the previous examples, there was in the end a single rule, concept, or category that governed the problem—due process in the university admissions case, embezzlement in the tale of the dishonest clerk, and private nuisance among all those poppies. And the exam-drafter's trick in each case was to lure the reader away from the right answer in the direction of misleading alternatives. Another way in which professors can complicate multiple-choice questions is by inventing scenarios in which more than one rule, concept, or category governs, multiplying the opportunities for distraction. Consider the following problem:

At the time of his death, Fred Boom owned a fee simple interest in the property at 123 Emerald Brick Road. In his will, he left the property to his daughter Judy for her life and, upon her death, to her sons Sam Crow and Tim Moon as tenants in common. Two years after Fred's death, Judy found herself in need of cash and sold her interest in the property to her best friend, Liza. A short while later, both Liza and Sam were tragically killed in an auto accident. Who owns 123 Emerald Brick Road?

A. Tim owns the property free and clear because Judy sold her interest and Liza and Sam are dead.

B. Tim owns half the property, with the other half owned by Sam's devisees or heirs.

C. Liza's devisees or heirs own the property until it reverts to Tim.

D. The property is owned partly by Tim, partly by Sam's devisees or heirs, and partly by Liza's devisees or heirs.

If you haven't had first-year Property yet—or if you have but didn't understand a word, as is the case for one of us—here's a quick primer on the two sets of rules in play in this problem. The first are the rules governing a life estate, which is what Judy inherited from Fred. Simply put, Judy owns the property until she dies and then her interest is altogether extinguished. But what happens if she sells the property during her lifetime, as she does here to Liza? Judy can sell only what she owns, and so Liza too has only a life estate. But that life estate is not measured by Liza's life. Rather, she has purchased what the law calls a "life estate *pur autre vie,*" meaning that Liza's interest terminates not upon her own demise but when *Judy* dies. So this is one set of rules you need to know to get this question right. But there's another set you'll need to know as well.

Under the terms of Fred's will, when Judy dies—and the life estate is extinguished—the property will be owned by Sam and Tim as "tenants in common." In contrast to the owner of a life estate, the ownership interests of tenants in common will survive their demise, meaning that their "heirs or devisees" (i.e., the folks who stand to inherit their stuff) will gain ownership of their interest in the property. So if one of them dies, the other tenant continues to own only his half and the deceased tenant's heirs or devisees will own the other.

Got all of that? When you do, let's work through the choices one at a time. The seemingly simple solution offered by Foil A—i.e., the land belongs to the living—may lure those who assume that the interests of Liza and Sam evaporate upon their respective deaths. But this represents a misunderstanding of the rules governing life estates as well as the rules governing tenants in common. As we've just seen, under the life estate rules Liza's interest is measured by *Judy's* lifetime, and what it means to be tenants in common is that Sam's death vests his interest in his heirs or devisees. Foil B baits a trap for those who've mastered the tenants in common rules. Its correct conclusion that Sam's interest in the property survived his death may thus tempt those in the know to stop reading and settle on Foil B, delighted they didn't fall for Foil A because they recognized that Sam didn't lose everything by dying first. But if you stop reading there, you'll get the question wrong. Foil C, avoiding any mention of measuring lives and thus trying very hard not to offer any clues about the second set of rules lurking in the question, fudges the nature of Liza's interest but is actually the first of the answers to get the life estate *pur autre vie* issue right. Since Judy is still alive, Liza's interest will indeed continue, as the foil suggests, but the problem is that the answer ignores the tenants in common rule by assuming that Sam's interest in the property didn't survive his death.

Summing up, we can dismiss Foil A (which gets both rules wrong); Foil B (which gets tenants in common right but the life estate rules wrong); and Foil C (which get life estate right but tenants in common wrong). And that leaves Foil D, the only answer that gets both rules right. Yet look how Foil D is rife with imprecision ("partly this, partly that, partly something else"), weakening its appeal to a reader insecure in his grasp of the governing rules. With all this misdirection, how can you keep your wits about you to find your way clear to the "right" answer?

Once again, slow and very careful reading is crucial. Beyond that, variations on two other lessons stressed earlier in the book are especially apt here. First, just as you shouldn't stop with the first issue you see on an issue spotter, don't stop with the first plausible answer you see in the multiple-choice setting. Thus, tempting as it might have been to seize on Foil B (because it got tenants in common right), reading Foil C might well have reminded you that Foil B was missing something (i.e., any reference to the life estate issue) and aided you in settling on Foil D (which addressed both sets of rules and got them right). The second lesson is a version of "write until the facts run out"—critical advice on an issue spotter—and the lesson here is "*think* until the facts run out." When you tackle a multiple-choice question with dense facts, you take grave risks if you slight half of them. If the professor wanted only to see if you had mastered the rules governing tenants in common, she could have written a much simpler fact pattern. But given all the material about a life estate—how Judy got one; how she sold it to Liza; and how Liza died along with Sam—a correct foil will almost surely have to address that set of rules as well. Finally, even distractor foils may contain hints about what to look for in a right answer. Thus, even without explicit mention of the life estate issue, Foil C's mention of Liza's heirs or devisees—together with its unexplained reference to the property "reverting" to Tim—might prompt you to remember that there is a second ball in the air here, beyond the tenancy in common. You can't, of course, always count on hints like this any more than a single hypo can illustrate all the tricks lurking within questions calling on you to juggle two rules rather than merely one. But what you can absolutely count on is that this pattern of burying two rules in one question is a staple of multiple-choice testing. Watch for it as you practice sample questions in preparation for exam day.

5. Getting the most out of maybe

We've devoted most of this book to the central role of ambiguity in U.S. law and to the many ways in which law exams test students' ability to "know it when they see it" and to exploit it in addressing the problems they encounter on exam questions. At a number of points, we warned of the perils of a "one right answer" mentality to a student's ability to successfully negotiate this terrain. In this chapter, we've taken an abrupt turn away from those lessons, and indeed the entirety of Part A was focused on the ways in which professors *eliminate* ambiguity when drafting questions for multiple-choice exams. Now we're going to shift our emphasis once again to show how the ability to identify ambiguity can aid you in avoiding false foils and identifying the "right" ones in the multiple-choice setting.

Suppose your Torts course has taught you that many states impose strict liability on defendants who conduct "abnormally dangerous activities" when those activities result in injuries to others. If my parachute instructor stresses the importance of pulling the rip cord at the moment she signals for me to do so, but I miss the signal because I get distracted, I am likely to recover for injuries suffered upon impact despite my inattention. Courts won't focus on whether entrusting the rip cord mechanism to skydiver trainees and/or the particular instruction protocols were "reasonable" the way they would under a negligence standard, because jumping from planes is the poster child for abnormally dangerous activity. By contrast, if you throw your back out on your first drive under the tutelage of a golf coach, to hold him accountable you'll need to convince a jury that he was guilty of negligence because golf is not abnormally dangerous for anything except maybe a nearby window.

But where exactly is the line between abnormally dangerous activities like skydiving and more earthly pursuits like golf? In your Torts class, you'll study the complex multifactor analysis courts use to draw that line and the differences between the analyses contemplated by the First, Second, and Third Restatements. If you were taking an issue-spotting exam in the course, you'd need to be at the ready to deploy those analyses to some activity your professor invented just for your exam. But in the multiple-choice setting, the one thing you can count on is that you won't be asked to make that kind of judgment call *even if the problem at hand seems to require one.* Watch.

Harry Porter receives a brand-new skateboard from his foster parents for his birthday. The manual included with the skateboard provides instructions directing first-time riders to avoid hills for the first two weeks of use so that they can get a feel for the board. Harry, however, is only nine years old and pays the manual no heed as he begins to play with his new toy. Harry is a sensible fellow, however, and so he spends over a week getting accustomed to the skateboard before attempting any major challenges. On his tenth day with the skateboard, he takes it to the top of the biggest hill in his neighborhood, and, while he is riding down, a slight wobble in the rear left wheel causes him to lose his balance, fall, and sustain serious injuries. In his suit against the skateboard manufacturer to recover for his losses, Harry will

A. Lose, because skateboarding is just not that dangerous and if anyone was negligent here it's Harry's foster parents, who should have read the manual and kept him from trying that hill.

B. Prevail, because skateboarding is an abnormally dangerous activity and thus the manufacturer will be strictly liable for Harry's injuries.

C. Lose, because Harry did not follow the directives contained in the instruction manual.

D. Prevail if the trier of fact concludes that the wobble in the wheel was the result of a defect in design or manufacture.

Let's work our way through the foils one at a time. Foils A and B suggest that everything turns on the resolution of a difficult question of fact: Is skateboarding abnormally dangerous or not? But since good arguments can be made either way, there is no way—given the limited facts presented in the problem—to determine whether Foil A or Foil B has the better of it. Faced with this dilemma, some students may begin to worry that the professor mentioned skateboarding in connection with activities most courts deem abnormally dangerous, and now they can't remember whether it was or wasn't included on that list along with dynamite blasting and skydiving. But rather than freezing with worry and indecision, students should view this unresolvable ambiguity as a clue that "these aren't the foils she's looking for" and that the question hinges on something else entirely. Let us offer, then, a corollary to one of our favorite exam-taking tips we've been giving students since we first wrote this book. On essay exams, when you find yourself in doubt, write it down, explaining the reason for doubt and why it matters to the problem at hand. On multiple-choice exams, when you find yourself in doubt, get *away* from the maybe, for chances are the right answer lies elsewhere. And in the process, the choices have been narrowed from four to two, thus doubling the odds of ending up with the right answer.

But the drafter isn't finished messing with you, for this question (like the life estate/tenants in common question in the previous section) implicates two sets of rules, not just one, and—for the careful and persistent reader—Choices C and D offer hints as to what the second set of rules might be: the rules governing product liability claims. Your Torts course is likely to identify three bases for such claims, each of them relying on proof of a "defect" in connection with an injury-causing product: defective warning, defective design, and defective manufacture. Are any of those possibilities in play here? Foil C negates a defective warning claim and is tempting because the fact it recites is true, and it's tempting to blame Harry for ignoring the warning. After all, he was surfing the hill on day 10, when the instructions manual specified a two-week practice period. But there is no suggestion in the facts that the four-day difference or Harry's inexperience played any role in the accident. Instead, the reference to a wobbly wheel points to the possibility of defective design or manufacture, and sure enough, those are the claims alluded to in Foil D. But once again the exam-taker may be feeling doubtful, for we don't have anywhere near enough facts to be sure that design or manufacturing defects are the culprit. So what on earth is there to do?

As we saw in the first part of this chapter, the telltale "if" in Foil D offers a way of getting past the maybe, dispensing with the need for factual analysis and casting the inquiry in conditional form—"*if* the court finds that the facts establish the requisite defect, *then* the claimant wins"—leaving to some hypothetical court the task of deciding whether the "if" condition is met on the ambiguous facts. All *you* need to know is the rule itself (gotta have a defect) and then you can identify the foil that gets it right.

What the question does to ensure that many test-takers will answer incorrectly, even if they know both sets of rules, is to raise the salience for the test-taker of the rule that's *not* being tested by flagging it in the first two foils. At the same time, the rule that *is* being tested is downplayed by omitting any mention of "defects" until the final phrase of the final foil. But you can avoid this trap by remembering that if you find yourself struggling with a judgment call (is skateboarding abnormally dangerous or not?) you are probably stuck on the wrong point. Let's try one more example to make sure we've got this critical lesson down pat.

There is a key distinction in First Amendment law between rules regulating the "content" of speech and rules that merely govern the "time, place and manner" of expression. This means, for example, that a local government could constitutionally enact an ordinance making it unlawful to play any music above a certain decibel level between the hours of midnight and 6:00 a.m. but could not enact an identical restriction applying only to the music of the Rolling Stones. Yet the line between what governments may and may not do isn't always clear, as the following multiple-choice question invites test-takers to consider.

> Pigblemish College, a small progressive Unitarian college in the Midwest, has been struggling to handle the security costs generated when outside speakers come to campus. During the current academic year, the college's chapter of the Free Speech Society had brought three nationally known conservative speakers to campus, and in each instance there was significant unrest, leading to nearly $50,000 in charges for the additional security required to ensure that violence did not break out. President Nimblegore, fearful that future speeches will crash the college budget, announces to the community that all campus speeches for the rest of the academic year must be canceled. It turns out, however, that only three speeches remain for the year, and all are by prominent conservatives invited to campus by the Free Speech Society. Moreover, over the course of the academic year nearly two dozen speeches had been delivered on campus by prominent liberals and progressives, without prompting any open expressions of concern from the college about security costs. Sebastian Snipe, a prominent climate change denier and one of the three canceled speakers, files suit against the college arguing that his free speech rights have been violated because the alleged concern about security costs is a pretext for shutting down conservative speech. When his case reaches court, Snipe will:
>
> A. Prevail, because President Nimblegore is clearly trying to keep students from hearing conservative voices.
> B. Prevail, because—whatever the president's motives—there is clearly a differential impact on conservative speech.
> C. Lose, because the decision to cancel "all campus speeches" is a neutral rule that applies equally to all potential speakers.
> D. Lose, because the First Amendment does not apply.

The moment you see the trick, it's a straightforward conclusion that the correct answer is Foil D. Pigblemish is a private college not governed by the First Amendment, and for that reason Snipe's lawsuit will immediately fail. But look how hard the question works to lure test-takers into getting it wrong. Only a single word appearing early in the lengthy fact pattern reveals the college's private status. And—after a narrative focused exclusively on contentious questions of campus free speech—how could the correct answer possibly bear no relationship to that issue at all? Because law students taking exams are primed to punish themselves for what they don't know, this question plays on everyone's insecurities about the uncertain line between unlawful content regulation and acceptable "time, place and manner" rules. Indeed, the other foils invite the reader to grapple with familiar issues in First Amendment law: Is a censorious motive required? Or is a differential impact enough? Or will the adoption of a facially neutral rule make all that go away? But now you are wise to this multiple-choice trick. You will almost never be asked to make a tough line-drawing call because—absent a lot more facts or a binding precedent "on all fives" with the problem—no single correct answer is possible. So instead you'll be given questions that *appear* to require line-drawing but bury the issue that actually resolves the dispute.

6. Hiding the cascade

Now that you've seen several examples of multiple-choice sleight of hand—i.e., questions that focus your attention on one place ("pick me! pick me!") while the real action is happening somewhere else ("nothing to see here")—it's relatively easy to begin to recognize variations on this theme. The examples in the previous section lured students to wrong answers by foregrounding a familiar but difficult issue and hiding the dispositive point in the shadows. The following problem—using our old friend Artiste/Patron one more time—flips that approach by hiding a difficult issue behind a straightforward one.

> Paul Patron offers Arlene Artiste $10,000 to paint a portrait of the Patron family. Artiste explains that her other commitments make it impossible for her to promise a completed work by a particular date, and Patron responds, "I don't want your commitment. I just want the portrait." After Artiste spends numerous hours doing preliminary sketches—but before she has put brush to canvas and begun the actual portrait—Patron advises her that he has changed his mind and is revoking the offer. If Artiste sues Patron for breach of contract and the ju-

risdiction follows § 45 of the Restatement (Second) of Contracts, Artiste will:

A. Lose, because Patron can revoke his offer at any time before completion of the portrait.
B. Lose, because the offer must be in writing and signed by the offeror to be binding.
C. Prevail, because the Restatement rejected the common law rule enabling the offeror to revoke at any time before performance is complete.
D. Prevail, unless the court determines that the sketchwork was mere preparations.

Everything about the way this question is constructed is designed to fool exam-takers into marking Foil C as the correct answer. The call of the question refers to only one legal rule—Restatement § 45—thus eliminating any ambiguity about whether the common law or the Restatement governs. Foil A is thus obviously—too obviously—wrong, since it employs the common law rule and not the Restatement. Foil B is likewise an obvious distractor—you need a signed writing to create a firm offer under the U.C.C., but this is a service, not a sale of goods, and the U.C.C. does not apply. Upon reading Foil C, students who have studied § 45 and have a firm grasp of the rules governing unilateral contracts will experience a "eureka" moment, since—in contrast to silly old Foil A—the statement it makes about the law governing the question is 100% accurate.

After reading Foil C, even the most conscientious student might not bother to go on to Foil D. And even those who do may not get the hint, for Foil D carefully avoids any mention of the language in § 45 establishing the trigger for protection of the offeree—i.e., "the beginning of performance." Foil D focuses instead on a term ("mere preparations") mentioned only in the reporter's notes and referring to steps taken in response to an offer but falling short of the required beginning of performance. Yet here's the rub. Foil C is absolutely right about the rule change but wrong about the outcome, since the answer—as we've seen many times before—depends in turn on whether Artiste's sketchwork constitutes the "beginning of performance" (deal!) or instead "mere preparations" (no deal!). Foil D acknowledges this ambiguity—by using the conditional "unless" clause and leaving resolution of this difficult question to some hypothetical court—and is thus the correct answer.

This is yet another example of how the ambiguity identification skills emphasized elsewhere in the book can pay off as well in the multiple-choice context. In the previous section, we saw how those skills could be used to ward off distractor foils that would force you to guess between equally plausible competing claims, signaling the need to look elsewhere for the right answer. Here your ambiguity detection antenna can help you keep your eye out for a telltale "if" or "unless" that will relieve you of the apparent need to make an impossible choice. But there is even a more important lesson to be drawn from this version of the Artiste/Patron problem. Remember our discussion of "issue cascades" back in Chapter Ten? The point there was that learning to anticipate and to recognize cascades is a critical skill in the issue-spotting context, since it can help you to avoid the temptation to "stop with the first issue you see" and instead to push on in search of additional "downstream" issues. Stopping too soon is even more likely to be a fatal exam error in the multiple-choice setting, where the exam-drafter tries to get you focused on a most familiar issue (here, the common law vs. Restatement rules governing unilateral contacts) and to lull you into forgetting that the resolution of that issue won't necessarily resolve the dispute. Here, too, you just can't stop with the first issue you see.

7. The search for the "best" answer

We can't leave this topic without stressing one final aspect of multiple-choice exams in the law school setting. Conscientious drafters of multiple-choice questions must confront the likelihood that—despite their best efforts—a strong case can sometimes be made that more than one of the available choices is arguably correct. Indeed, sometimes—and again despite the drafter's best efforts—a strong case can be made that there are problems with *all* of the options. The possibility of such difficulties—whether intended or not—is the reason it's common for instructions on multiple-choice exams to call for the "best" answer rather than the "right" one. You might wonder by what standard a particular "right" answer might be judged "better" than another or why a "wrong" answer is "better" than the rest of the lot. We sometimes do too. (Actually, one of us never *stops* wondering about that.) Yet, to echo a point we make when we're presenting exam-taking workshops to law students, from the point of view of a student seeking a high grade, the "best" answer—at least from your professor's point of view—*is* the "right" answer.

So what advice can we offer for Getting from Maybe to Best? First and foremost, focus your study on your class notes and not on commercial study aids, for clues to your professor's preferences will be found nowhere in the latter. Were there particular forms of argument (e.g., careful parsing of statutory text or a constant search for underlying purposes or policies) that she seemed to favor? Were there particular points of emphasis in the discussion of the assigned cases, where the professor signaled strong agreement or disagreement with the analysis on offer? If the exam question resembles a hypo she worked through in class, did she show her hand with respect to what she viewed as the best resolution of the problem presented? A second source of intel is the professor's multiple-choice exams from previous years, if they are available. We'll have more to say about this particular resource in the following section, but for now we'll observe that you can learn a lot about what a professor thinks is "best" by looking for patterns in the answers she liked—as well as in those she didn't—on past exams.

C. Prepping for and Taking Multiple-Choice Exams

1. The seven keys to success

So there you have it, the secrets to designing a multiple-choice question, distractor foils and all. Understanding these design features can help you anticipate the kinds of problems you're likely to encounter on an exam using the multiple-choice format. To be sure, our basic advice here is much the same as it is with respect to preparation for law school success generally. The strategies outlined in Part I of the book—doing your own work and avoiding shortcuts; unplugging and slowing down as you engage the assigned materials; and taking advantage of the case-briefing and statute-outlining methods we've recommended—will serve you as well in the multiple-choice context as they will in the issue spotter. Likewise, the exam prep advice on offer in Chapter Eleven—taking careful class notes; preparing your own outline for the course; and working with old exams and study groups—can be enormously useful in taking *any* kind of exam.

But we have seven concrete suggestions for multiple-choice success, seven ways in which we urge you to "double down" on the preparation and exam-taking techniques we recommend with a particular eye toward success in the multiple-choice context. Indeed, one of them is so important that we include it twice on our list.

First, *practice, practice, practice*. If the professor makes her multiple-choice exams from previous years available, access them and take every one you can. If she doesn't, there's no harm in asking her to do so. If the answer is no, then ask her to recommend a resource—perhaps a commercial study aid or another professor whose past exams are available—that can aid students in becoming familiar with the kinds of multiple-choice questions you are likely to encounter on her exam.

We cannot stress enough that multiple-choice exam-taking—like all exam-taking—is a skill that can be improved with effort, and no amount of reading, briefing, outlining, memorization-via-flashcards, and the rest can substitute for the actual experience of slogging your way through multiple-choice questions and struggling to identify the correct answer. Practice with a professor's old exams can also provide important intel with respect to her drafting techniques. (E.g., does the professor routinely use the call of the question to add facts to the problem or to zero in on a particular cause of action? Does the professor make frequent use of a particular doctrine—e.g., last clear chance in Torts or the obligation of good faith in Contracts—as a "Hail Mary" fourth foil that is virtually never the right answer? Does the professor often put the correct answer in Foil D, as we have done here for ease of exposition, because that gives her a chance to lure students astray with misdirection in Foils A, B, and C?) Practicing on old exams is thus not only a good way to improve your ability to address multiple-choice questions, but also a critical means of learning what to expect from a particular professor.

This brings us directly to a second important preparation technique: *Gather as much advance intelligence as you can about the professor's exam rules and protocols*. As we just said, a great way to see what you're likely to be in for is to take a closer look at the professor's old exams. But whether or not that's possible, don't hesitate to ask your professor questions such as:

- How much time and how many questions? (This will obviously help you figure out your time allocation for each question.)
- Does the professor "take off" for wrong answers? (If not, then there's no harm in guessing in a pinch.)
- Is there a particular body of law—e.g., the Second Restatement of Torts—you are supposed to work with? (Once again, an answer to this can eliminate ambiguities about which among competing rules governs the questions.)

Many professors will address these questions and others in an end-of-term memo and/or in a pre-exam review session. But if that's not happening, we urge you to ask them yourself, using whatever medium is available—during office hours or an after-class question period, via email or a classroom platform chat feature, etc.

Third, back in Chapter Eleven's discussion of course outlining, we urged you to focus in particular on what we referred to as the "pressure points" in each subject you study, the recurring points of conflict (like beginning of performance vs. mere preparations in the Artiste/Patron hypo) that professors emphasize in the course. To overstate the matter only slightly, multiple-choice exams test virtually nothing but pressure points and the distinctions to which they give rise—e.g., between what a statute covers and what it doesn't (e.g., is this a sale of goods or a service?); between a rule and its constituent exceptions (e.g., is this a battery or was there consent?); between competing categories (e.g., is the injured party a licensee or an invitee?); between proof and the absence of same with respect to particular elements of a crime, claim, or defense (e.g., did the perp have the requisite *mens rea* or not?). To prepare properly for a multiple-choice exam, then, you'll need to know these distinctions like the back of your hand.

Turning from exam prep to the exam itself, our fourth tip is that *slow reading* is even more important on multiple-choice exams than on issue spotters—and that's saying something, because we don't think there's *anything* more important on an issue spotter. As we've noted before, when it comes to legal analysis and reasoning, "every word counts." But an individual word or short phrase may count even more on a multiple-choice exam because that's one of the best "hiding places" for an ambiguity-eliminating or even a liability-establishing fact. (E.g., recall the significance of the word "accidentally" in Newborn Descending a Staircase.)

Fifth, *the call of the question* is likewise critically important on a multiple-choice exam, so read it even more slowly and carefully than the rest of the problem. As we saw earlier in the chapter, the call of the question may tell you exactly which legal rule to apply ("Has Valeria made a firm offer under the U.C.C.?") or exactly which cause of action is in play ("If Jamie brings an action against Charles for battery, the court will…"). Moreover, the call is also the place that many professors add a critical fact or two to a problem you thought you already understood—e.g., a passage providing important information about a background "trade practice" in a breach of contract case or about a widely honored professional norm in a medical malpractice case. The punch line: Every word counts *even more* when you are reading the call of the question.

Sixth, don't forget our old friends from the chapter on case-briefing, the Three Little Questions: Who's suing whom, for what, and on what theory? The answers to those questions can be an enormously helpful guide to eliminating false foils—e.g., if the question tells you that A is suing B for money damages on a claim of assault, then you can readily dismiss the foil focused on the absence of contact between the parties (it's not an element of assault); the foil that focuses on the rights of C (since she's not a party to the suit); and the foil discussing the availability of an injunction against B (since that's not what the lawsuit seeks). You will often find answers to the Three Little Questions helpfully gathered together in the call of the question, but you may find them elsewhere, for some professors hide them lest the answer be "too easy." Over the years, we've seen countless multiple-choice questions in which the identity of the cause of action (assault, breach of warranty, etc.) will *in itself* eliminate two or even more of the foils from the competition—thus virtually serving up the right answer on a plate—and in nearly every instance the wily professor hid that fact early in the problem rather than placing it in proximity to the foils.

Finally, did we mention that you should *practice, practice, practice* with multiple-choice questions? If you're not inclined to believe us on that score, perhaps it would help if we identified the original source of this advice. Each year, the Florida Bar gives an award to the bar examinee who gets the highest score out of a thousand-plus individuals sitting for the MBE portion of exam, the nationally administered multistate test covering six basic areas of law and administered in multiple-choice format. A few years back, one of us had the state's winner as a student and invited him to speak to the next graduating class about the secrets behind his extraordinary achievement. He titled his talk (you guessed it) "Practice, Practice, Practice," and he regaled the audience with humorous tales of doing practice questions while he shaved in the morning; while driving to work (via an audio file, of course); while eating meals (his long-suffering family gave him a pass); when he woke up in the middle of the night (he kept a set of practice questions on his bedstand); etc. His basic point was that *hands-on experience with the format* was every bit as important to his success as careful study of the legal subjects under examination. On the basis of hearing from hundreds of bar exam winners and losers over the years—and of a half-decade that one of us spent teaching MBE subjects for a leading bar prep company—we can't imagine more important advice.

2. Tried-and-true tips for foiling the foils

We'd be remiss if we didn't include a pair of multiple-choice tips that have been "common knowledge" forever and are still worth great emphasis here:

- It is often the case that one or more of the choices will be obviously wrong—e.g., because it misstates the applicable legal rule or invokes a doctrine that has no application in the setting presented by the question. When this is the case, eliminate the wrong answers and focus your fire on what's left. Indeed, if you're able to narrow the options down to a couple of possibilities, that can be a tremendous aid in identifying the "right" one, since you can then confine your search to particular facts or circumstances that could justify a choice between them. Moreover, even if you're reduced to utter guesswork, your odds of a bingo are considerably higher with two than with four or five possibilities.
- For most students on most multiple-choice exams, there will be some questions that you'll "get" right away and others that will seem impossible from the get-go. If you are under great time pressure—as is typically the case with law exams of every stripe—you should, if you think you can manage the disruption of skipping ahead, go through and answer all of the sure bets be-

fore heading back to tackle the more challenging problems. That way you can avoid "leaving money on the table" in the form of questions you could have answered had you reached them, and it will also free up mental and emotional bandwidth from the stress of worrying about "all those questions I haven't gotten to yet" as you struggle with the more difficult ones. But this strategy comes with a critical cautionary note: If you are working with an answer sheet, be especially careful to ensure that you're putting the right answers into the right spaces, perhaps making a conspicuous but erasable notation in the margin by each skipped question. Trust us: there may be no more devastating discovery in the history of exam-taking than to reach the 100th question on a 100-question multiple-choice exam only to realize that you're at #99 on the answer sheet.

PART V

Sample Questions & Model Answers

If we had to identify the single most important takeaway from this book, it would be that success on law exams depends not as much on "what's in your head" as you enter the exam room as it does on *what you do with the questions your professors ask* once the exam begins. In this chapter, we offer an opportunity to master that lesson by working your way through a series of sample questions and comparing your answers with ours.

Chapter Sixteen

Putting Maybe to Work—
Exam-Taking Exercises

Enough talk already. You've read through a great deal of material describing what works and what doesn't. Now we'll show you our advice in action. In this chapter, we present a series of sample exam questions and urge you to draft answers under "exam conditions" (i.e., with time limits and no outside help) and then compare your results with model answers we've provided. The questions test four basic first-year subjects: Contracts, Property, Torts, and Constitutional Law. Don't worry if you haven't taken them yet, for we introduce each question with a brief lesson on the legal materials you'll need for a trial run.

Before we get to the sample questions, we'll ask you to try your hand at an exercise we've conducted many times with our own students as well as with students at other law schools. This exercise—Part A of the chapter—is designed to help you develop a clear picture of what a superior exam answer looks like. It opens with a practice question followed by a series of answers. One of the answers is, as you might expect, a "model" response, but the rest contain common "rookie mistakes" law professors encounter while grading. In each case, we explain exactly where the answer went wrong so you don't have to learn that lesson "the hard way," via a disappointing performance on one of your exams. After reviewing this preliminary exercise, you'll be ready for "the real thing," tackling the sample exam questions in Part B on your own.

A. Preliminary Exercise:
How to Avoid Some Common Mistakes

What follows is a practice question, preceded by "a little bit of law" (the rules you'll need to draft a response), and then a series of answers. You may recognize the problem, for it is the "director's cut" of the disappearing wedding venue example we introduced in Chapter Twelve.

I. A little bit of law

Here's the American contract law you need to know to answer the exam question that follows. In a nutshell, when you're the victim of a breach of contract—e.g., when an auto dealer reneges on a promise to sell you "this year's hot car" with delivery due on a particular date—the general rule is that you are entitled to "expectation" damages: a legal term for the amount of money calculated to give you the dollar value of the promised performance. If, because of the breach, you end up paying a higher price to get the vehicle elsewhere—a likely possibility since the model is so popular—then expectation damages would include the difference between what you *expected* to pay under the terms of the original contract and what you *actually* had to pay to get what you bargained for. Your damages would also include incidental expenditures such as the search and travel costs involved in finding another supplier in a tight market.

But, to continue our example, let's say the breaching dealer had promised delivery the Thursday before Memorial Day and that you had plans to use the car for a long trip over the four-day holiday weekend. When the dealer doesn't come through, there's no time to buy another car; so you arrange for a last-minute flight to your destination, which costs you $800 in airfare plus another $200 in taxi fares to and from the airports. Does contract law entitle you to recover the $1,000 loss resulting from your unexpectedly car-less weekend? If your intuition tells you that "this is different"—that it's one thing to recover the costs of securing the promised vehicle and another thing altogether to recover the costs of a holiday re-do because you didn't have the vehicle when you needed it—the law agrees with you. Although both costs result from the breach, contract law generally says that you are entitled only to the former, the so-called "direct damages," and not the latter, which are "consequential damages." Consequential damages differ from direct damages in that they are "party specific," constituting losses to the aggrieved party that typically result from plans the latter had for particular uses of the goods, services, real estate, etc., that were to be delivered according to the contract. And the basic rule—traceable to the famous English case of *Hadley v. Baxendale*—is that aggrieved parties are *not* entitled to consequential damages.

One more thing: There has long been an important exception to this rule. Under *Hadley*, you *can* recover your consequentials if you *communicated* the prospect of the loss in question to your trading partner at the time of contracting—if, to continue our example, just before signing the purchase agreement you advised the original dealer of your plans to use the new car for a big getaway Memorial Day weekend. Modern rules—reflected in the Restatement and the U.C.C.—are even more generous to aggrieved parties, providing that the prospect of consequential losses in the event of breach need not be "communicated" to the trading partner so long as she has "reason to know" of them, again at the time of contracting. Such reasons might come from various sources, including past dealings with you, common knowledge in the trade, or from experience in business more generally. The reneging dealer here arguably had "reason to know" of the car's intended use even if you didn't specifically mention your travel plans, because the promised delivery date fell on the eve of a holiday weekend notorious for Americans of varied ages, classes, and stations hitting the road with a passion and a full tank of gas.

Once you have a handle on the foregoing principles, you're ready to take on the practice question, and we'd urge you to adopt the approach we advocated back in Chapter Thirteen: Read the question *at least* twice, once quickly to meet the players and get a sense of the dispute, and then again slowly enough to register the potential significance of every single word.

2. Practice question

Garfield and Beauregard live together in Heartache—the largest city in the State of Oz—where Garfield is a successful neurosurgeon and Beauregard is a prominent tax lawyer. After many years of focusing primarily on their professional careers, the couple finally decided to "tie the knot" and eagerly began planning a June 28 wedding. Through a little luck and a couple of key connections, they were able to reserve the Garden House in Heartache's bucolic River Park—by some distance the most expensive wedding venue in the Heartache area and likewise the most popular among those who can afford it—for their ceremony and reception.

Shortly after they'd signed the contract with Garden House, they decided they would "really go for broke" and ordered 500 hand-painted and personalized wedding invitations from Frazier & Thomas, Oz's most prestigious stationer, for a total cost of $20,000. They subsequently met with Romberg Lapin, Garden House's director of event planning, to secure the necessary information for the invitation (including the GPS coordinates, driving directions from various points, and parking instructions), explaining their desire "to get everything exactly right because we've arranged for hand-painted invitations that are costing us a small fortune."

April 1 was a terrible, horrible, no good, very bad day for the couple. First thing that morning, their wedding caterer phoned to tell them that he had decided to join the "great resignation" and close his business on May 1. And if that weren't bad enough, a short while later Romberg Lapin contacted the couple with the devastating news that Garden House had been inadvertently double-booked for June 28; that management would honor the other couple's reservation because they made it before Garfield and Beauregard; and that Garden House had no open weekend dates for the better part of a year. "Naturally we will fully refund your deposit with interest," an embarrassed Lapin explained, apologizing profusely for the mix-up.

The well-connected couple quickly made arrangements for another venue, though it cost them a pretty penny. And upon contacting Frazier & Thomas about the change in plans, they learned to their further dismay that the invitations were already finished and that they would accordingly need a replacement order—at the cost of an additional $20,000—to reflect the change of venue.

Assume that Garden House is liable to Garfield and Beauregard for breach of contract. Will the damages due the couple include the cost of the replacement order? Explain your answer.

———————

If you want to try drafting an answer to this question, give yourself 60 minutes and go for it. (That was the time allotment when this question was given on a real exam.) But you'll have plenty of opportunities in Part B of this chapter to draft exam answers, and it might instead be a good idea to see what professors are looking for—and, just as important, what they are *not* looking for—before giving it a go on your own. So don't be afraid to assume the perspective of "grading professor" and join us in taking a critical look at eight answers of the sort we've seen over the years, some of them much better than others.

3. Eight answers

Answer #1

Under the common law rule, Garden House isn't liable to the couple for the cost of the replacement order. But under the Restatement, Garden House will be liable for that cost.

This answer illustrates one of the most common "rookie mistakes" in law school exam-taking. Note that the problem is not just that it's so short; in point of fact, it is sometimes the case that the best answer in a class will be among the very shortest, albeit typically a bit longer than this one. Nor is the problem that the assessments offered by the student are incorrect; as you'll see in our subsequent answers, the student's first assertion is surely right, and there's a good case for the second one as well. The key problem is that the answer is far too "conclusory." That's a term unfamiliar to many before law school, and it signifies reaching a conclusion with little or no reasoning to support it. Lawyers are paid to <u>persuade</u>, and the audiences most lawyers address—judges, juries, legislative panels, administrative agencies, even parties on the other side of a negotiating table—are far more likely to respond favorably to compelling and cogent arguments than to bald assertions and "because I said so" pronouncements. What's missing from this first answer, then, is any reasoning that would support the conclusions offered by the answer.

Supporting your conclusions is important for a second reason: It's a hedge against the possibility that the professor might disagree with your conclusion or indeed with the assumption that the problem even has a clear-cut solution. If all you've given the professor is a conclusion she doesn't like, you are likely to get a grade you won't like. But if you've explained the reasons behind your thinking, you are likely to get at least some credit for that effort and may even impress the professor with the quality of your reasoning despite her dissatisfaction with your punch line.

*So lesson #1 from this exercise: **Avoid conclusory answers.** Now take a close look at Answer #2 to see whether it improves on Answer #1.*

Answer #2

> The general rule for contract damages is that a party suffering breach is entitled to expectation damages, the difference between what she'd get if the contract were fully performed and what she actually ended up with because of the breach. Expectation damages, in turn, are divided into two categories: direct damages, which are damages that would be suffered by any victim of the breach, and consequential damages, which are damages particular to an aggrieved party. Under the common law rule of *Hadley v. Baxendale*, victims of breach are not entitled to consequential damages unless they "communicated" the prospect of the loss to the breaching party at the time of contracting. Modern authorities apply a more permissive test, allowing recovery if the breaching party had "reason to know" of the particularized loss at the time the parties entered the contract. The damages here are clearly consequential damages. The common law then favors Garden House, while the Restatement is better for the disappointed couple.

At first blush, what we have here looks for all the world like a great exam answer—a series of confident pronouncements demonstrating a solid grasp of the legal materials and the result they'd lead to on the facts presented in the question. But don't be fooled. What we actually have is a lecture on contract law that doesn't even <u>mention</u> the dispute between Garden House and the disappointed couple until the last two sentences. This isn't reasoning. It's regurgitation accompanied by a conclusion that leaves the reader in the dark about just how the author got from the rules to the punch line. Regurgitating the law is as serious and common a mistake in first-year exams as conclusory answers. Lawyers analyze and argue—they seldom regurgitate—for the point isn't to quote or paraphrase the law but instead to use the law to analyze the facts presented in a legal dispute.

So why do good students make this mistake? For one thing, they are eager to show the professor that they "know the law" and mistakenly equate "knowing the law" with "being able to recite legal rules from memory." For another, because of their undergraduate exam-taking experience, many students equate certainty with "knowing the answer" and ambiguity with "not knowing the answer," so they'd far rather write about what they're sure of (the rules they've memorized) than about ambiguities (e.g., did Garden House really have "reason to know" of the prospect of the $20,000 loss?). But the key lesson of this book is that a deep engagement with the ambiguities presented by a question is precisely what the grader is looking for, and its absence will cost a student dearly grade-wise.

There is a danger in offering a "law lecture" that goes beyond the failure to grapple with ambiguities. It is challenging for even a seasoned lawyer to draft an accurate recitation of legal rules, let alone to do so in a time-pressured setting. Accordingly, beginning students are likely to make errors in their recitation and thus run the risk of getting graded <u>down</u> for spending precious time on something for which they wouldn't be graded <u>up</u>, even if they got it exactly right.

So lesson #2 from this exercise: **Don't regurgitate the law.** *Is Answer #3 an improvement?*

Answer #3

> Garfield and Beauregard entered a contract with Garden House for a June 28 wedding and reception. After signing, they ordered $20,000 in hand-painted wedding invitations from Frazier & Thomas (F&T). Then they met with the director of event planning at Garden House to get the information they needed (like GPS coordinates) for the invitation. On April 1, Garden House backed out of the contract because of double booking, and the couple secured a new venue. But it turned out that F&T had already completed the invitations with the Garden House info so the couple had to enter a replacement order for another $20,000. The cost of the replacement order is consequential rather than direct damages, so Garden House isn't liable to the couple for that cost under the common law rule; but Garden House would be liable under the Restatement.

This answer looks like it was written by a student who has concluded from the prior lesson—don't regurgitate the law—that they should therefore regurgitate the <u>facts</u>. To be fair, the student is on to something, because virtually all legal professionals would agree that a good legal memorandum or brief should begin with a careful recapitulation of the facts before undertaking the requisite legal analysis. But given the time constraints of the law exam setting, it is just as much a mistake to recite facts as it is to recite legal rules. Lawyers are not parrots but analysts and advocates, and thus law professors will grade students on how well they analyze and argue, not on their ability to copy or paraphrase selected portions of text.

Moreover, the same danger attending law regurgitation lurks in fact regurgitation as well: Given time pressures and exam-induced nervousness, the student is as likely as not to make unwitting errors in paraphrase or transcription, and the professor—who thought up the facts and knows them very well—will surely notice and may well penalize the errant account.

*So the lesson here is obvious: **Don't regurgitate the facts either.** But it's fair to ask, where does that leave us? If the professor isn't looking for a conclusion, or for a recitation of rules, or for a recapitulation of the facts, what on earth* is *she looking for?*

Answer #4

> Whether the couple can recover the cost of the replacement order depends on whether that cost counts as direct or consequential damages. If the cost = consequential damages, then a second question must be answered: Does the common law or the Restatement govern? If it's the common law, then there is a further inquiry: Did the couple "communicate" the prospect of this loss to Garden House at the time of contracting? If the Restatement governs instead, then we must decide whether Garden House had "reason to know" of the prospect of loss at the time of contracting.

We have, as they say, good news and bad news about this answer.
The good news is that it represents a marked improvement over the first three because the student has successfully identified the "cascade" of issues presented by the practice question, and you can't even begin to write a

successful exam answer unless you have "spotted" the issues in this way. And the issues will be familiar to anyone who has mastered the lessons of this book. The first (direct vs. consequential damages) is what we've called a "fork in the facts"; and if answer is consequential damages, then there's a "fork in the law" (common law vs. Restatement); if we follow the common law "prong," then we encounter another "fork in the facts" ("communication" or not); and if we follow the Restatement prong, then we encounter a different "fork in the facts" ("reason to know" or not). All good answers will take the identification of these issues as a starting point for the work that follows.

But the bad news is that spotting the issues is ALL this answer does. Here's a thought experiment: Imagine that the practice question is your first case as a lawyer and that you are in court, all dressed up and ready to go. The bailiff calls your case number, and you approach the lectern and solemnly intone, "May it please the court." (So far so good.) And then imagine that the entirety of your argument consists of the contents of Answer #4. (Dramatic reading suggested here.) And now imagine how the judge would surely respond: "Counsel, thank you for identifying the issues for me. But what, pray tell, am I supposed to do about them?" (It turns out Karla the senior partner isn't the only legal professional who just won't be satisfied until she hears some arguments.)

*The lesson here, then, is: **Spotting the issues is not enough.** The following answers go further and respond to the imaginary judge's query with varying degrees of success.*

Answer #5

The $20,000 price tag for the wedding invite replacement order clearly constitutes consequential damages, since it isn't a loss that parties who unexpectedly find themselves without a wedding venue would typically suffer and instead is peculiar to our wealthy, free-spending couple. Under the *Hadley* rule, the aggrieved party can't get consequentials unless the prospect of the loss was communicated to the breaching party at the time of contracting. And while the couple did let the Garden House official know that they were spending "a small fortune" on their invites—and thus needed to get accurate venue-specific information before the orgy of hand-painting commenced—the facts show that the conversation took place after the ink was already dry on the Garden House contract. So no recovery under *Hadley*. Even if the Restatement applied instead of the common law—and it doesn't, because the Restatement is merely persuasive authority—the couple is still out of luck. At the time of contracting, Garden House had no "reason to know" of a loss of anything remotely like that magnitude, since no one in their right mind would pay $20,000 for wedding invitations. The couple therefore cannot recover the cost of the re-do.

Most law professors would agree that this is a better answer than any of the previous ones because it does what lawyers do when presented with the facts of a dispute: i.e., it begins constructing arguments, offering law- and fact-based reasons for the conclusion it embraces. Argument construction is perhaps the most important skill students learn during law school, and chances are you've been building arguments all your life—indeed, that's why friends and family have been telling you "you should be a lawyer" all these years (and haven't always meant it as a compliment).

The writer here has certainly learned how to argue, but the obvious shortcoming is that he seems to see only one side of the dispute, whereas most law school exam questions are designed to test a student's ability to grapple with problems that have more than one plausible resolution. That's why we call the problems we test on exams "issues"; if there weren't another side to the story, it wouldn't be an "issue," and woe unto the client whose lawyer doesn't see the other side coming.

Once again, it's important to understand why even the best students might be tempted to argue only one side of an exam question. In the typical case, we think this springs not from a failure to see another side but from the all-too-common student mindset that exam questions call for only one answer—not two, not more, not maybe. We certainly don't blame any students for thinking this way, since the lion's share of the exams we all took during earlier stages of our education posed questions calling for a single correct answer. But learning to get comfortable with "maybe" is critical to success in law school.

A second common reason for one-sided answers is this: Law exam questions frequently ask students to "take a position"—to represent one of the parties, for example, or to predict the outcome of the dispute if it got to court. And in those cases a student might be forgiven for thinking she is supposed to offer a one-sided presentation. But a good legal advocate will invariably anticipate the arguments available to the other side and develop strategies for dealing with those arguments, so a first-rate answer should give both *sides their due even when the student is asked to pick one over the other at the end of the day.*

Thus, the next lesson of this exercise is: **Argue both sides!**

Answer #6

> The $20,000 price tag for the wedding invite replacement order clearly constitutes consequential damages, since it isn't a loss that parties who unexpectedly find themselves without a wedding venue would typically suffer and instead is peculiar to our wealthy, free-spending couple. Under the *Hadley* rule, the aggrieved party can't get consequentials unless they communicated the prospect of the loss to the breaching party at the time of contracting. And that's exactly what happened here, when the couple spoke with the venue's director of event planning and revealed they were spending "a small fortune" on their invites. Indeed, they explained carefully to Lapin that the investment they were making in the invites was why they needed to get the venue-specific information correct. The couple can therefore recover the "replacement order" consequentials in this case.

Do you see the problem? The student misread the facts in the hypo—or read them so quickly that he didn't register the fact that the conversation with Lapin took place after *the Garden House contract was signed. That is not a minor mistake. But if this is your first exposure to* Hadley *(or indeed to contract law) and you too missed the timing's significance when you read the problem, we don't think you should worry about it. Rest assured that the typical Contracts student will be thoroughly familiar with this principle by the time she finishes the course. The professor pretty clearly included the "too little, too late" conversation in the facts in order to test an understanding of the requirement that communication take place prior to or contem-*

poraneous with contract formation. And while the student here was able to recite that rule, he wasn't able to demonstrate that he knew what to do with it in the context of a concrete factual dispute.

So the key lesson here is the one we stressed back in Chapter Twelve: **Slow and careful reading is critical to success on law exams.** *In the interests of transparency, we should note that we've been presenting variations of this "question and multiple sample answers" exercise for twenty years and have only recently begun to include a sample answer that misreads the question. Simply put, misreading was less of a problem twenty or even ten years ago, when we would rarely encounter an exam answer that misread the facts in this manner. These days, though, about a quarter to a third of a typical class will get <u>at least</u> one question on the final flat-out wrong in this way, and—as we suggested earlier—we think the cause is habits developed from living life online. At the risk of sounding like a broken record—a simile that is as much of a throwback to the pre-digital age as we are—we implore you to do your law school reading and especially your exam preparation work slowly, carefully, and ideally in hard copy.*

Answer #6 goes wrong in two additional ways, and an understanding of these mistakes—each addressed at length back in Chapter Twelve—can help you reduce the dangers of misreading and improve the quality of your answers even when you've got the facts exactly right. First, recall our warning that **if the answer seems too easy, there's probably more to the story.** *The facts of the hypo here took more than a full page to state, so an answer of no more than four sentences identifying no obstacles whatsoever to a win for one side is the poster child for "too easy." In Chapter Twelve, we suggested three strategies for double-checking your initial conclusion—retrace your thinking step by step; force yourself to argue the "other side"; and work out your analysis "on paper"—any one of which might have prompted a second and more accurate reading of the facts. And recall as well our* **don't stop with the first issue you see** *admonition. Had the student here heeded that suggestion, he might have taken a closer look at the facts and remembered that Hadley isn't the only well-worn route to securing consequentials—and that the Restatement approach may offer the couple a way to prevail that does not require a misreading of the facts.*

———————

Answer #7

The couple may have had a terrible day on April 1, but their "day in court" promises to be much better. For one thing, if the "pretty penny" it cost them to land an alternative venue is greater than what they were supposed to pay Garden House, they would be entitled to that difference as part of their expectation damages. Any associated search costs—like wining and dining the proprietor of the new venue and the time spent pursuing any dead ends—would be recoverable as well. For another, the "double-booking" story sounds fishy to me. Maybe the lucky couple who bumped Garfield and Beauregard from the June 28 reservation lined the pocket of Lapin or someone else at Garden House. If so, the disappointed couple might have a "tortious interference with contract claim" against the interlopers and Lapin. And for yet another, perhaps the couple can bring a claim against the bailing caterer, if the parties had a contract (it sounds like they might have) and the disappointed couple has to pay a premium for a substitute caterer as they did for the substitute venue. As of April 1, they have less than three months to "put Humpty-Dumpty back together again." Wedding venues, caterers, photographers, etc., are likely to be in short supply for "last minute" shopping, and prices are likely to reflect that shortage.

As for the damages issue, are we sure Garden House is in breach here? Perhaps the contract has a provision permitting the venue to cancel in the event of some unexpected development, like double booking. Turning to the invite do-over, I'm running out of time, but those sound like consequential damages that weren't communicated to Garden House until *after* the parties reached whatever agreement they had, so under *Hadley* the couple won't get them. But they might have better luck under the Restatement since Garden House might have had "reason to know" … out of time… sorry!

*There are two problems here, both of them serious. You'll recall our advice back in Chapter Twelve that when it comes to issue spotting, **the call of the question may be the best friend you ever had**. The corollary to that* *point is that if you ignore it, the call of the question may be your worst enemy. In the hypo, the call of the question read thus: "Assume that Garden House is liable to Garfield and Beauregard for breach of contract. Will the damages due the couple include the cost of the replacement order?" Until the very end, the answer here addressed everything but the call of the question—including at least one would-be issue the call of the question literally took out of consideration—and that will cost this student dearly. He's likely to get no points at all for his frolics into the amount paid for the alternative venue, or the possibility of breach by the caterer, or the possibility of shenanigans between Lapin and the couple who took their place, and he's likely to lose points for questioning the breach, which the call of the question expressly stipulates. And all these misfires had an opportunity cost as well, for he ran out of time just as he reached the question the professor had actually asked.*

There is a second equally serious problem with this answer: It repeatedly fights the facts. As is often the case with exam mistakes, this one comes from a good place, for one of the principal lessons of a good legal education is the importance of healthy skepticism and critical thinking. From bicycles that turn out not to be vehicles to promises you just don't have to keep, you learn to question the obvious and the not-so-obvious alike, so professors will generally be pleased when students bring such skepticism to the reading of an exam question.

There are times when a skeptical eye can really pay off. Imagine a variation on our wedding invite problem in which we're told in passing that the bride-to-be in the couple who "bumped" Garfield and Beauregard from their June 28 reservation just happened to be the sister of the director of event planning. Were that the case, the careful reader would have a reason <u>based on the stated facts</u> to call into question the bona fides of the venue's overbooking excuse and to suspect that some sort of collusion may have come into play. To raise the prospect of a tortious interference with contract claim in that setting is a move that is likely to be rewarded by the professor—though if the call of the question directed you to focus your analysis elsewhere, you'd want to keep the insight brief and to the point, confining it to no more than a sentence or two.

But that's not the situation we have in Answer #7, where the student has conjured up the possibility of collusion between the lucky couple and Garden House management based on <u>no facts whatsoever</u> and is thus operat-

ing in the realm of wishful thinking—not much better than "Maybe every-one in this problem is 15 years old thus none of the contracts are enforceable, though whether they should all be arrested for a curfew violation is beyond the scope of this course." Similarly, when Answer #7 calls into question whether the disappointed couple and Garden House have a contract—and thus ignores the unambiguous directive to "[a]ssume that Garden House is liable to Garfield and Beauregard for breach of contract"—he isn't deploy-ing his critical thinking skills but is instead simply ignoring the problem the professor is actually testing. Come grading time, that's just not going to go well for the student.

Answer #8

Okay, the fight over the $20,000 is a fight over damages, just as the call of the question says, and clearly the disappointed couple is going to want to collect that amount and the reneging venue won't want to pay it. A full-on award of expectation damages would obviously include that amount, since it's a cost the couple would not have generated had the wedding venue kept its promise, so what's the problem? Let's start with the fact that jumps off the page: the sticker price. The $20,000 comes as a bit of a shock—I'm pretty sure I have seen online templates one can download for about $10 and that produce quite serviceable invitations—so this isn't a run-of-the-mill loss most people are likely to suffer if a wedding venue falls through. That means the $20,000 is probably "consequential damages" rather than "di-rect damages"—that is, a loss that's particular to the aggrieved party and typically the result of third-party obligations and commitments, which is exactly the case here because it is a cost arising out of the couple's dealings with the pricey stationer.

So what? Well, when it comes to consequential damages, we learned in class that there's a common law rule and a modern rule. The common law rule—traceable all the way back to *Hadley*—is that you can't get 'em, so the couple looks to be out of luck. But *Hadley* has an exception as well: You *can* get 'em if you "communicated" the prospect of the loss in question to your trading partner at the time of contracting. So does the communication exception apply here? Not quite. True, the couple did come right out and tell the director of event planning that they were paying a fortune for hand-painted invitations and needed to get details like the address and GPS location exactly right. But look at *when* that happened: The facts state that the conversation took place "shortly *after* they signed the contract"—not "at the time of contracting"—so this communication won't take the couple out of the *Hadley* rule barring consequential damages after all.

Fortunately, as Yoda famously said, "there is another"—an alternative route the analysis of this case might take. If the modern rules apply, what difference would *that* make? This isn't a sale of goods—it's a dispute about the use of a wedding venue, so it's either a service or maybe a rental agreement and the U.C.C. doesn't apply. The Restatement is thus the road to take, and the question is whether the Garden House had "reason to know" of the exorbitant costs of a wedding invitation re-do. Did it? On the one hand, maybe they'd be as surprised as I am that anyone in their right mind would pay $20,000 for wedding invites. On the other, we're told that the venue is "by some distance the most expensive wedding venue in the Heartache area" and "the most popular among those who can afford it"; indeed, it even employs its own "Director of Event Planning." It's not a stretch to think the DEP would get pretty familiar with the upscale wedding-planning practices of "the rich and famous"—that's probably his job description. And it's likely that his interaction with a couple eager to secure accurate information about location and parking for use in high-priced wedding invitations wasn't a one-off. The test, after all, isn't whether he *knew* about the price the couple was paying for the hand-painted invites, but rather whether he had *reason to know*, and these facts suggest that he might well have. So yes, I think the couple will be able to recoup the cost of the replacement order.

Moreover, I can't help but note one final aspect of the facts here that favors the couple and calls into question the fairness of the *Hadley* rule, even as it has been relaxed by modern exceptions. *Hadley* is, after all, its own exception to the general goal of contract remedies—i.e., to "make parties whole" when they are harmed by a breach. If the couple here eats the $20,000, they aren't going to be feeling very whole. The reason for the *Hadley* rule is that it isn't fair to hold breaching parties liable for losses they could not have reasonably foreseen when the parties were allocating costs and risks in the course of negotiating their contract. But in this case Garden House knew full well of the cost of the invitations when it mattered—i.e., when it breached the contract with the couple. To be sure, there is no problem in principle with Garden House cleaning up its overbooking mess with a "first in time" policy. But unless the lucky party had run up a similar tab of consequentials by the time of breach (TREAT LIKE CASES ALIKE), Garden House knowingly piled up the losses on the couple when it breached and should be made to pay (DO THE RIGHT THING). Since Garden House had "reason to know" of the consequential damages this policy argument might prove unnecessary, but it might be useful to raise to sway the court which way to turn if it was on the fence about "reason to know."

Let's get one thing clear from the start: The foregoing answer was written by two law professors, one of whom has been teaching Contracts for many years, and we drafted at our own pace in the comfort of our faculty offices. So no grader in the history of the universe would expect a law student—let alone a first-year student tackling the first set of exams—to come up with an answer quite like this one. We offer it to demonstrate just how many issues can come into play in the context of a typical exam question, and we stress that even a student who missed a couple could still get a high-end grade.

But how is a student expected to come up with any issues or arguments at all? We've got nothing but good news on that front. Most professors endeavor to test what they teach and accordingly pose exam questions that call for the deployment of arguments and analyses that were carefully canvassed in the course. In the Contracts course examined by this question, for example, there was a great deal of attention paid to the difference between direct and consequential damages and to the difference between the rule under Hadley *("communication") and the rule under the Restatement* ("reason to know") for overcoming the general proscription against consequentials, and we worked our way through a number of hypotheticals testing the "reason to know" requirement. So none of this would have come as a surprise to students taking the exam. But the reason Answer #8 went so well is that the drafters knew not only what issues to look for but also what to do with them once they found them. We have identified each of the successful strategies with bold typeface.

(a) The answer **made the call of the question its friend** by focusing exclusively on the question it asked ("Will the damages due the couple include the cost of the replacement order?") and avoiding frolics into other matters (e.g., whether there was a breach of contract in the first place or whether the couple could recover for the additional cost of securing an alternative venue).

(b) The answer **focused its fire on the points in conflict**. Thus, the answer identified and quickly put aside two issues—are the costs of the wedding invite re-do direct or consequential damages, and is the disputed transaction with Garden House a sale of goods or something else—that are not in dispute on these facts. An investment of $20,000 in hand-painted wedding invites is a poster child for a peculiar or idiosyncratic expenditure made to a third party that falls outside the realm of direct damages in a contracts case, and the couple's use of the wedding venue might be viewed as a service or perhaps even a rental of the premises, but it is not a sale and the venue isn't goods. Accordingly, the answer was right to spend no more than a sentence or two on each of these points.

(c) The drafters **did not stop with the first issue they saw**—i.e., the question of whether the couple had met the Hadley communication test via their conversation about the wedding invites with the director of event planning. Rather, it identified the "fork in the law" produced by the choice between the Hadley rule ("communication") and the Restatement ("reason to know") and proceeded to follow each prong to the next issue, a "fork in the facts" with respect to whether each of the respective tests had been satisfied in the circumstances of the case.

(d) The drafters **focused most of their fire on the issue that could make a difference**— i.e., the application of the "reason to know" *test. If* Hadley *governs, then the required communication did not take place until after the parties entered their contract, so there's just not much more to say. Indeed, at that point in the analysis, the couple's hopes would seem to be dashed at every turn: These are consequential damages so they can't get them under* Hadley, *and the* Hadley *loophole doesn't apply. So maybe "maybe" is out of reach. But a deep dive into the "fork in the facts" presented by the Restatement's "reason to know" test yields some pretty compelling arguments on each side ("$20,000? For wedding invites? Really?" vs. "Business as usual in the lives of the rich and famous and those who make a living catering to their boundless desires").*

(e) *In reaching a final conclusion, the drafters made a point to* **touch parts of the policy kingdom** *to show that courts consider the consequences of their choices.*

After reading all of this you may say to yourself, "I just never would have thought of an answer like that, and no amount of advice you can provide will change that." Relax. Once again, no professor would expect even the Most Exam-Savvy Student Ever to come up with "an answer like that," for once again it is the product of considerable professorial work and expertise. Again, a student answer could fall well short of what appears above and still set the curve in a typical law school class.

But there is an important grain of truth in the student's moment of self-doubt: Even our best former students—and we proudly count among them state and federal judges, law professors, prominent attorneys, and dedicated public servants—could never have come up with "an answer like that" without *practice.* Issue spotting and argument mobilization are *skills,* and while they may be skills that come more quickly to some than to others, they are also skills (a) that any student capable of securing admission to law school can improve with practice and (b) that even the best students need to develop and hone before they can do A-level work.

In Part B of this chapter, we'll give you an opportunity to begin that effort with several practice runs. But as we've stressed elsewhere in the book, the best possible practice for finals is to work your way through your professor's old exams. That effort will be at once easier than our exercises (since the professor's exams will test material she's been teach-

ing you all semester) and also more difficult (since we will tell you exactly which rules we are testing and real exam questions may test anything
covered in the course). But the payoff is huge, and if you review old exams diligently for each of your courses, your answers are going to look
far more like Answer #8 than might seem remotely possible now.

B. Getting Real: Sample Questions and Model Answers

Here's what you should do with each of the four sample law exam
questions that follow:

(1) Spend at least 15–20 minutes carefully studying the "a little bit
of law" section that precedes the exam hypothetical. You may
need less time if you are already familiar with the topic, but
don't worry if you think you need *more* time. Remember, this is
the "learning the law" part of the exercise, and in law school
you'll have all semester to do that in each of your courses.

(2) Devote an hour to answering the question under exam conditions. We suggest taking at least the first 15 minutes to read
and re-read the question and then using the remaining 45 minutes to draft your answer—and remember to do so without
peeking at the "model" answer! (That said, Chapters Twelve
and Thirteen have a lot of important advice about drafting
exam answers, so if you skipped them in your rush to get to
these sample questions you may want to go back and take a
look.)

(3) Take a break to clear your head. Go for a walk, a swim, a run, a
drive, take a yoga class—whatever suits your fancy.

(4) Upon your return, carefully re-read both the question and your
answer. Then it's time to work your way through our "model,"
carefully comparing it with your own. Do not be concerned if
there are aspects of the law you know from your own study that
don't appear in our models. For ease of explication, we have
tailored the model answers to the legal rules we spell out here.
And to aid you in making that comparison, we have followed
each model answer with an "Authors' comments" identifying
the particularly successful features of the answer.

We have one additional suggestion: Do these practice questions—and, even more important, work through questions from the old exams of your professors—together with two or three classmates whose work style and temperament mesh well with your own. Set up a meeting, by video chat if necessary, and identify two or three questions you're going to do as a group. You can do steps (1) to (3) individually in advance (if that's more convenient) or when you get together (if you want the "misery loves company" experience of a simulated exam setting). But in place of step (4), you may begin the group session with each of you individually reviewing the question and reading through the model answer, and then you can exchange papers and evaluate *one another's* answers.

When we've facilitated this exercise with our own students, we've followed an approach we first learned from Marc Fajer, a truly gifted law professor at the University of Miami. Thus, we've found that sharing answers works best if "graders" avoid the temptations of wide-ranging literary critique and instead confine their "corrections" to the principal errors we analyzed in Part A, inserting the brief phrases listed below in the margin by the error in question:

- did not respond to the question asked
- conclusory reasoning
- law regurgitation
- fact regurgitation
- mere issue spotting
- too one-sided
- missed an issue
- misreading/fighting the facts

To that list, you should probably add an additional entry: "wrong about the law," since beginning students in the setting of a time-limited exam will frequently make this mistake too. You will be surprised how much easier it is to identify these common errors in the answers of others than it is to see them in your own, and a session that repeats this process for one or two additional questions may lead to marked exam-taking improvement for all concerned. If your group gets along well, multiple sessions—perhaps devoting each meeting to a single substantive topic so you can focus the scope of your advance preparation—will lead to more improvement still.

1. Property

a. A little bit of law

Here's a mini-course on the "duty to disclose" in the context of a sale of residential real estate under Florida law. (If this law seems familiar, it's because we discussed it at some length back in Chapter Eight on competing interpretations of case law; and if the problem likewise seems familiar, we used a version of it as an illustration way back in our introductory chapter.)

In *Johnson v. Davis*—a leading decision by the Florida Supreme Court—a would-be homebuyer sued a seller seeking rescission of the sales contract and a return of money paid based on the seller's failure to disclose serious defects with the roof. (The parties in the case were married couples, but for ease of expression we'll refer to each side in the singular.) Under the common law doctrine of *caveat emptor* ("buyer beware"), a seller of residential real estate had no obligation to disclose such defects to a buyer; it was up to a buyer worried about defects to ferret them out. Under Florida law at the time of *Johnson*, there was an exception to *caveat emptor* for fraudulent misrepresentation, but a buyer couldn't prevail on that theory unless the seller made an affirmative misrepresentation of fact—stating, for example, that "the roof was inspected this summer and passed with flying colors" when no such inspection had taken place or when such an inspection had in fact revealed serious defects in the roof. By contrast, a seller's mere *silence* about a known defect—however significant and costly that defect might be—would not support a claim of misrepresentation.

In *Johnson*, the court took the law in a new direction and reasoned as follows:

> One should not be able to stand behind the impervious shield of caveat emptor and take advantage of another's ignorance.... The law appears to be working toward the ultimate conclusion that full disclosure of all material facts must be made whenever elementary fair conduct demands it.

Turning to the case before it, the court ruled for buyer and concluded thus: "We hold that where the seller of a home knows of facts materially affecting the value of the property which are not readily observable and are not known to the buyer, the seller is under a duty to disclose them to the buyer."

b. Sample exam question

Katie Matthews has long owned a lovely home in a suburban neighborhood outside Orlando, near Disney's Florida home. When Matthews decides to place the home on the market, it sits for a few months before the Brady family comes calling. The Bradys have two elementary school-age children and are attracted to the home because of its proximity to LaPierre Public Elementary School, about which the Bradys have heard good things. As the Bradys' broker takes them through the home, they encounter Ms. Matthews in the kitchen. The Bradys tell Matthews how much they like the home and that they hope to reach an agreement on a price soon. They also mention that they plan to send their children to LaPierre. "All three of my children attended that school," Ms. Matthews truthfully tells the Bradys.

The Bradys reach an agreement with Matthews and take title to the home in August 2019. That October, however, the Bradys' oldest daughter is attacked and stabbed by a fellow student at LaPierre. She is traumatized and left with limited use of her left arm. A thorough investigation reveals that Ms. Matthews' oldest son, Sam, was badly beaten by a fellow student at LaPierre just three years earlier. No record of the earlier assault could be found at the police station because the incident had been kept private. Similarly, no official at LaPierre was authorized to disclose information about Sam's beating or his injuries.

If the Bradys sue seeking redress, what are their chances of securing a remedy, and what arguments will Ms. Matthews be likely to raise in response?

c. Model answer

This question turns initially on how the courts interpret *Johnson v Davis*. If the case is read narrowly and confined to its facts, the holding won't extend to our very different situation. *Johnson* involved a defect (leaky roof) in the home being sold. Moving from those facts to impose a duty on Matthews to tell the Bradys about something altogether *outside* the home—i.e., the incident at LaPierre Public Elementary School—might be a stretch. The Bradys may be successful, however, in focusing attention on the court's reasoning in *Johnson*. They will highlight the court's statement that when "the seller of a home knows of facts *materially affecting the value of the property* which are not readily observable and are not known to the buyer, the seller is under a duty to disclose them to the buyer." The Bradys will argue that Matthews' silence here effectively hid what she knew about problems at the school, something the Bradys will argue would clearly affect the value. Everyone who knows real estate knows that school quality is a key in determining home prices.

Given the *Johnson* court's sweeping rejection of caveat emptor and its emphasis on the importance of ensuring honest transactions, the Bradys have a good chance of prevailing on this question of law. Matthews, however, may then raise the issue of whether a single incident involving her son is really something she should be expected to disclose. Unlike a leaking roof or a history of termite damage, it requires multiple inferential leaps to conclude that one negative event that has been kept under wraps would actually affect market value. Indeed, it may reasonably have been viewed by Matthews as an isolated incident, and the lone bully who attacked Sam has probably left the school by now. Moreover, the information about Sam is personal, and nothing in *Johnson* addresses whether its rationale should be extended into what is arguably a zone of privacy. Asking sellers to warrant all the surrounding amenities for the home and to disclose family history may be going a bit too far. In this case, Matthews has a strong chance of prevailing because courts would rightly be reluctant to turn home sellers into guarantors against any diminution in property value, however remote the cause. Indeed, doing so might well have a negative impact on the real estate market throughout the state.

Authors' comments: The first paragraph here focuses on a "fork in the law": competing interpretations of Johnson, *with one side offering a narrow reading focused on the facts of that case and the other offering a broad reading based on the court's reasoning. The second paragraph shifts to the "fork in the facts"—was the prior incident likely to "materially affect the value of the property"?—and offers two arguments to counter the "school-quality-drives-market-value" argument favoring the reneging buyers. First, it focuses closely on the facts ("pay no attention to the single incident behind the curtain") and then it embraces a "purposive" approach by arguing that the* Johnson *rule was never intended to reach private matters of family history nor indeed to require sellers to hold buyers harmless against any transaction or occurrence in the larger community that might diminish the value of the property. After considering both sides, the answer concludes with a brief policy assessment based on not treating sellers as guarantors (DTRT-CONSISTENCY ACROSS SOCIAL CATEGORIES) and on protecting the real estate market (SHAPING).*

2. Contracts
a. A little bit of law

Many laypeople—and thus many students starting law school—are under the impression that oral contracts are not legally enforceable. In point of fact, most oral contracts are every bit as enforceable as their written counterparts, but there is nevertheless a grain of truth to the conventional wisdom. *Some* contracts do indeed need to be in writing, and this is the result of an old law from England widely known as the Statute of Frauds. Its principal purpose, as you might expect, is to prevent fraud—i.e., to prevent individuals from falsely claiming the existence of a make-believe contract. The downside of the Statute of Frauds—and we bet you figured this out as well—is that an individual may use the rule to leave his trading partner in a lurch, fraudulently *denying* the existence of an agreement the parties had in fact made but not written down.

In the typical first-year Contracts course, you'll learn about which kinds of contracts are subject to the Statute of Frauds and what kind of documentation it takes to satisfy the Statute's requirements. For our purposes here, let's focus on just one of the contracts to which the Statute applies: a sale of "goods" for a price of $500 or more. ("Goods" = pretty much everything on offer at Amazon.com or at Walmart.) Section 2-201(1) of the Uniform Commercial Code governs this part of the Statute of Frauds. It provides that such a contract isn't enforceable unless three requirements are met: (1) there must be something in writing "sufficient to indicate that a contract for sale has been made between the parties" (nothing formal or elaborate is required); (2) the writing must state the quantity of the goods contracted for (100 bottles of beer; 76 trombones; two turtle doves; etc.); and finally (3) the writing must be signed by the party "against whom enforcement is sought" (typically, the party trying to back out of an agreement).

Let's watch the rule in action. Say I come to your store seeking Mason jars. You don't have any in stock, but you have several cases on order. You promise me 1,000 jars within a week at a price of $1,200, and we shake hands on it. Four days later you text me to let me know that the jars are in, and I reply that I've changed my mind. If you sue me for breach of contract, I'll be able to raise the Statute of Frauds as a successful defense: The transaction is a sale of goods (Mason jars) for a price of $500 or more ($1,200), and the Statute of Frauds therefore applies; but there is no writing and I didn't sign anything, so the Statute isn't satisfied, and I'm off scot-free.

One more thing: There is an exception to these requirements for deals "between merchants"—essentially, deals between individuals or firms who buy or sell goods in the regular course of business. The drafters of the U.C.C. worried about the consequences of the Statute of Frauds for merchants who follow the common business practice of sending a follow-up confirmatory letter or email after an oral deal is made in person or via phone. Consider the Mason jar example described a moment ago, and assume the seller sends the buyer such an email after the parties shake on the deal and the buyer leaves the store:

> 2/20/22
> Dear Beto Buyer,
> I am writing to confirm our agreement that I will sell you 1,000 Mason jars for $1,200 and deliver the goods within a week from the above date. If I have misunderstood the terms of our agreement in any way, please let me know.
> /s/ Selena Seller

So here's the rub. If *seller* tries to back out of the deal, she won't be able to raise the Statute of Frauds as a defense, for the three requirements for satisfying the Statute are easily met: There's a writing indicating a deal between seller and buyer; the writing states a quantity of 1,000; and seller signed the writing. By contrast, however, *buyer* hasn't signed anything and can therefore back out of the same deal willy-nilly. The drafters thought it was unfair to subject individuals like seller to the risk of such one-sided liability for doing what merchants do all the time—i.e., sending written confirmations of oral agreements—and therefore adopted U.C.C. § 2-201(2), an exception to the usual rules of the Statute of Frauds. That provision governs deals "between merchants" and here's what it says: If one of the parties sends a written confirmation of the contract to the other—and does so within a reasonable time after a deal is made—the confirmation satisfies the Statute of Frauds against the sender *as well as the recipient*, unless the latter gives "written notice of objection to [the confirmation's] contents... within 10 days after it is received."

What does that mean? Let's take one more look at our Mason jars hypo and assume once again that the seller sent the 2/20/22 email to the buyer shortly after the parties agreed to the sale. Even though only the seller signed the written confirmation, the confirmation satisfies the Statute of Frauds—and makes the contract fully enforceable—against the recipient buyer as well as the sending seller. So what can a recipient of a written confirmation do if she thinks the sender got it wrong? Provide "written notice of objection" to the contents of the confirmation within 10 days of receipt—e.g., "Wait, I thought we said $1,100" or "I am certain we agreed to 2,000 Mason jars" or even "I am so sorry you misunderstood, for I said I didn't want to commit to the deal until I had the opportunity to see if I could secure the Mason jars elsewhere for a better price." The recipient who protects herself with such an objection retains the benefit of the Statute of Frauds and can successfully defend against a contract enforcement suit by sender on that basis.

b. Sample exam question

At lunch on Monday, Seller and Buyer, both merchants, negotiated an oral contract for the sale of 5,000 widgets for $5,000. On Tuesday morning, Seller sent Buyer a registered and signed letter confirming the agreement and outlining the details—including the price, quantity, delivery, and payment terms—as she understood them. Buyer received the letter on Wednesday and immediately dispatched the following signed response via email: "Thank you for your letter. I spoke with my accountant after our meeting on Monday, and she pointed out serious difficulties with our deal I hadn't contemplated. I hope you'll understand, but I'm afraid I won't be able to go through with it." Attempts at settlement having failed, Seller sues Buyer for breach of contract, and Buyer raises the Statute of Frauds as a defense. How should the court rule on Buyer's defense? Explain your answer.

c. Model answer

Although Buyer has a plausible defense under the Statute of Frauds, it's one the courts should ultimately reject. Buyer's invocation of the Statute of Frauds begins with the simple observation that this is a sale of goods (widgets) for more than $500 ($5,000) and thus U.C.C. § 2-201(1) requires a signed writing by Buyer to enforce the alleged agreement against him, and "there's nothing to see here." Seller will naturally respond that the sale is "between merchants"; that § 2-201(2) therefore applies; and that its letter confirming the deal and its terms (including the quantity) will satisfy the Statute against Buyer unless the latter gave written notice of objection within 10 days of receiving the confirmation. Buyer can be expected to argue that his email satisfied the written objection requirement, but he's got an uphill battle to make that stick.

Buyer sent his email to Seller immediately upon receiving the latter's confirmation, and it certainly served to put Seller on notice that Buyer didn't want to go through with the deal. But the wording of Buyer's message doesn't do what the plain meaning of § 2-201(2) says it must do in order to preserve Buyer's Statute of Frauds defense. It's not really an "objection" to Seller's confirmation, and it doesn't take issue at all with the confirmation's "contents." Thus, the email doesn't quarrel with Seller's recapitulation of the terms agreed to over lunch, nor does it claim that what went down at lunch wasn't really a full-fledged agreement. Rather, Buyer is saying that the deal now appears *unattractive*. That's not an "objection" to the "contents" of the confirmation; it's instead an effort to repudiate an oral agreement, the existence and terms of which Buyer in no way disputes.

There's more. Buyer's frank acknowledgment that there were unanticipated difficulties with "our deal" is language literally "sufficient to indicate that a contract for sale has been made between the parties"—that, after all, is the "it" with which Buyer says he can't "go through"—and, since Buyer signed the email, the would-be objection to Seller's confirmation may well in itself constitute a signed writing satisfying the Statute of Frauds against Buyer. This would provide an independent basis—quite apart from the merchant's confirmation provision—for holding him to the contract. To be sure, Buyer can argue that his email didn't sport a quantity term, but Seller can reply that the exchange between the parties should be read as a whole and that the quantity term is supplied by its appearance in Seller's confirmation and the absence of any correction in Buyer's reply.

Buyer may attempt to escape these "plain meaning" arguments by turning to the Statute's purposes and highlighting the "cautionary" function of the Statute of Frauds. The need for a signed writing may prompt the signing party to "push pause" and take heed of the prospect of legal enforcement before committing to a deal. The writing requirement—like many legal "technicalities" in contract law—serves to slow things down to provide a cooling-off period; asking parties to put pen to paper is meant to *encourage,* not punish, second thoughts. But Seller can respond that the principal purpose of the Statute is "evidentiary"—i.e., to require documentary evidence of a deal (which we have), not to permit a party with second thoughts to "get off on a technicality" (which is what Buyer is trying to do). And whatever might be said of providing *consumers* with cooling-off periods, the paramount concern between *merchants* is evidentiary, and that concern is easily met here by the fact Buyer has at no point denied the making of the deal on the terms stated in Seller's confirmation and has even unwittingly admitted it all via his would-be objection.

In sum, then, under either a plain meaning or a purposive interpretation of the Statute of Frauds, Seller should prevail.

Authors' comments: There's no dispute that the transaction here is governed by the Statute of Frauds or that the Statute was prima facie *satisfied against Buyer via U.C.C. § 2-201(2), because we're between merchants and Seller sent Buyer a written confirmation of the oral deal. The only question is whether Buyer's email response to the confirmation enables him to retain his Statute of Frauds defense.*

Note the "fork in the law" explored in the second and third paragraphs, since the second paragraph focuses on the language of the statutory provision and the third paragraph focuses on the provision's purposes. Note as well that this fork begins a "cascade" of downstream issues about the application of each of the respective interpretations to the facts. Thus, in the second paragraph, the answer explores the "fork in the facts" created by the language of sub-(2) of the provision, with Buyer contending that the email satisfies the objection requirement—what part of "no" doesn't Seller understand?—and Seller carefully parsing the language of the provision and arguing that Buyer's email falls short of constituting the required "objection." Seller offers a second "plain meaning" argument by pointing to the language of Buyer's would-be objection and arguing that it might in itself satisfy the Statute's signed writing requirement, since it unwittingly admits that the contract exists. The brief debate at the end of the paragraph over the presence or absence of a quantity term in Buyer's objection presents yet

another "fork in the facts," nicely illustrating a clash between "taken togeth-
er" and "one at a time" approaches to reading the exchange of communica-
tions between the parties.

The third paragraph turns to the purpose of sub-(2) and raises yet an-
other "fork in the law," this one a "competing purposes" debate. We didn't
discuss those purposes in our "little bit of law" section, but most Contracts
classes in the U.S. explore the "evidentiary" and "cautionary" functions of
legal technicalities ("formalities"), so most exam-takers wouldn't need to
come up with this argument out of thin air. By the end, both sides of the
dispute have been fully considered, yet the answer returns to the facts—al-
ways a good move!—to defend a choice between them based on the argu-
ably diminished importance of the cautionary function in the context of a
transaction between commerce-savvy merchants.

3. Torts

a. A little bit of law

As a law school classmate observed "back in the day," Torts is the
course in which you learn that everything your mother warned you
about is true. The cases you'll study are teeming with evil designs, mayhem, explosions, paranoia, irresponsibility, objects falling from the sky,
and enough random accidents to make the self-quarantine a tempting
permanent lifestyle. Even the names of the doctrines you'll study—assault, battery, false imprisonment—sound like the script from a scary
movie.

One of the most controversial topics is the tort of Intentional Infliction of Emotional Distress (IIED), which pits the deep personal interest
in living a life free from bullying, revenge porn, verbal harassment, and
other forms of nonphysical abuse against the principles of free speech
and the often rough-and-tumble social practices associated with living
in a free society. Because of the latter—and reflecting the "tough love"
view that the best protection against most insulting behavior is a thick
skin—the standards of proof for securing a remedy under IIED are high:
The alleged tortfeasor's conduct must be extreme and outrageous (e.g.,
untruthfully telling someone that a close family member has died); the
resulting emotional distress must be severe (e.g., living with the horrify-
ing news overnight rather than receiving an immediate corrective); and
the wrongdoer must cause that distress intentionally (e.g., delivering the
fake news for the purpose of freaking out the listener) or recklessly (e.g.,

delivering the fake news as a joke, oblivious to the inevitable emotional fallout).

The tort may also be available to persons who weren't the target of the perp's outrageous conduct but who suffer distress as collateral damage. In such third-party "bystander" cases, the requirements of proof are more stringent still. For one thing, if you are not the target, you typically cannot recover unless you are "present" when the conduct takes place; it's not enough to hear or read about it later. Moreover, mere presence will create potential tort liability only for collateral victims who are members of the target's immediate family, e.g., when a child overhears a threat made to his parent. Absent family membership, most jurisdictions won't grant relief for a bystander claim, rejecting the effort in the Second Restatement to expand liability to nonfamily bystanders so long as they suffer bodily harm (e.g., fainting or a heart attack) as a consequence of the distress. Finally, the offender must intentionally or recklessly cause distress to the collateral victim; if he had no reasonable way of knowing, for example, that the children were nearby when he threatened the parent, there would be no liability.

b. Sample exam question

Melissa and Gary dated briefly one summer, but Melissa broke it off when she met Suzanna, the true love of her life. Melissa didn't hear from Gary again until she announced her engagement to Suzanna the following January, after which Gary began stalking her—cyber- and otherwise—and sending her a series of increasingly threatening texts and emails.

In March, Suzanna moved into Melissa's elegant Coconut Grove mansion. Late one afternoon in April—while Suzanna was still at work—Gary broke in and, brandishing a large hunting knife, angrily confronted Melissa and threatened to stab her. Elliott, a freelance film director, was in Melissa's living room at the time shooting a home furnishings commercial, and he captured the moment via a digital video recording.

The incident ended without physical injury when Melissa's private security detail intervened and expelled Gary from the premises. Eager to press charges and hoping to secure a restraining order, Melissa copied Elliott's recording onto her iMac, planning to share it with law enforcement officials the following day. Exhausted from the ordeal, she went to bed and promptly fell asleep.

A few hours later, Suzanna—who was yet to hear about Gary's visit—got home from work. Tiptoeing into the bedroom and seeing that Melissa was asleep, she gently kissed her beloved on the cheek; Melissa stirred, whispered "love you," and settled back into her deep sleep. Suzanna headed for the kitchen, where she poured herself a glass of wine before sitting down at the iMac to do one final email check before turning in. On the desktop, she noticed a WMV file captioned "Gary & Knife" and, curious, opened it and hit play. Upon viewing the video, Suzanna screamed and then began sobbing hysterically until Melissa—abruptly awakened by the disturbance—was able to calm her down hours later. Absent evidence of bodily injury caused by the obvious distress, can Suzanna prevail in a lawsuit against Gary? Why or why not?

c. Model answer

Suzanna will most likely be able to prove some of the elements of the IIED tort (extreme and outrageous conduct as well as recklessness are slam-dunks), but difficulties with her case (particularly the fact that she is not yet a member of Melissa's immediate family and was not present at the time Gary brandished the knife) may doom her claim.

Suzanna won't have much trouble showing that Gary's conduct is extreme and outrageous, because it is life-threatening and shocking beyond belief. Making threats while brandishing a knife goes well beyond any acceptable form of expressing romantic disappointment, and you'd need mighty thick skin to repel a hunting knife. But Suzanna must also demonstrate that Gary intentionally or recklessly caused her *own* distress, and, although knife-brandishing is clearly reckless, Suzanna must extend Gary's state of mind to cover not only Melissa, Elliott, and anyone else present during the incident but also those who might see the video recording. It's unlikely Gary missed the fact that Elliott had the camera on and turned his way during the incident, and certainly Gary could imagine that Melissa's loved ones would be emotionally harmed watching it—so Suzanna's case may be successful here.

But Suzanna has two more difficult challenges. First, it's unclear whether fiancées fit within the definition of immediate family members. Second, Suzanna wasn't physically present in the room when Gary brandished the knife. Overcoming these obstacles will require her to persuade a judge to expand the current contours of the rules governing IIED.

Suzanna has a relatively strong case that a fiancée should fit within the definition of family member. Gary will argue that a rule is a rule, and that once an exception is made, there will be pressure for further extensions to include next-door neighbors, close friends, and so on. But Suzanna is in a good position to suggest that fiancées are like family members in all relevant respects—close emotional bonds, serious commitment, etc.—and that including fiancées is unlikely to start us down a slippery slope because fiancées constitute a small, easily identifiable class. Suzanna will be helped here if her engagement to Melissa is provable through tangible evidence like an engagement ring, the setting of a wedding date, an announcement in the local press, or the distribution of invitations. The clearer it is that they were engaged, the easier it will be to deflect Gary's point that people might invent a potential marriage as a way of bringing lawsuits within the majority rule. (There is no point in Suzanna arguing for the relaxation of the "family member" requirement proposed by the Second Restatement, since she hasn't suffered the physical harm required by that proposal.)

Suzanna will have a harder time with the presence requirement. Certainly she can assert that watching a video recording of the event can have a striking emotional impact very much like seeing it live, as it obviously did on her. But there are two flaws here. First, because she had interacted with Melissa before viewing the recording, Suzanna already knows that Gary never made good on his threats. Second, given the proliferation of video recordings in a world of smartphones and social media, interpreting the "presence" requirement to include a viewing of a recording of an event is likely to lead to a dramatic expansion of liability for IIED. Despite the obvious pain to Suzanna, and Gary's palpable culpability, a court might well be reluctant to rule for Suzanna because of the potential for multiple lawsuits by family members who view emotionally distressing news footage, social media postings, YouTube recordings, and the like.

Authors' comments: Note that the response starts with a summary answer to the "call of the question" that draws the reader into the longer discussion and signals the most significant obstacles to recovery. A "road map" like this provides a hedge against the possibility you'll run out of time before fully addressing all the issues you see, so at least you'll get whatever points are on offer for issue spotting. It also tells the reader where you're headed, which will make the ensuing analysis easier to follow.

The second paragraph follows our advice to "focus your fire on the points in conflict" by quickly working through two elements of IIED that are no-brainers on the facts presented, the requirement of "extreme and outrageous" conduct as well as the requirement of recklessness. The third and fourth paragraphs each give more extended treatment to the "forks in the facts" that are the key issues in dispute: whether Suzanna's status as Melissa's fiancée makes her a "family member" and whether watching a video of the event after the fact will satisfy the "presence" requirement. The discussion of the family member issue offers both a fact-focused analysis (she's not a family member vs. she is the functional equivalent of one) and a policy-centered one centered on ADMINISTRABILITY (stick to the plain meaning of family to avoid the slippery slope vs. fiancées will surely feel the same degree of distress as a family member and are a discrete and easily identifiable category). The discussion of the "presence" requirement likewise presents a factual dispute (watching a video recording is "just like being there" in terms of emotional impact, but Suzanna knew that Melissa was alive and well before viewing the incident) as well as a policy argument (if video = presence, then any member of the immediate family, and perhaps their proliferating functional equivalents as well, who viewed a disturbing incident at a later point could sue).

4. Constitutional law

a. A little bit of law

One aim of the Constitution's framers was to form a government that would put an end to the trade wars that had erupted among the states during the period when the Articles of Confederation were our governing document. To that end, Article I, Section 8[3] gives Congress the power "to regulate Commerce ... among the several states." Despite this explicit grant of congressional authority, however, the Supreme Court has repeatedly held that—at least where Congress is silent—states have authority to regulate commerce in order to promote the health, safety and welfare of their citizens. Individual states have a fairly free hand here, provided they don't enact rules that conflict with federal law or discriminate against goods and services produced in other states.

The Supreme Court has invalidated two types of discriminatory state laws under what is referred to as the dormant commerce clause. First, states are generally not permitted to block other states from transacting business across state lines, and thus Georgia could not, for example, pass a statute forbidding the sale of peaches grown in Alabama. This principle was enunciated in *Philadelphia v. New Jersey*, where the Supreme Court invalidated a New Jersey law prohibiting the importation of waste from other states into New Jersey landfills. Second, absent a strong health and safety reason, states are forbidden from enacting seemingly neutral rules that have the effect of shielding state interests from out-of-state competition. For example, in *Hunt v. Washington State Apple*, the Supreme Court struck down a North Carolina law that prohibited apple sellers from stamping apple crates with any certification concerning the apples' quality apart from the grades assigned by the U.S. Department of Agriculture. Although North Carolina's rule singled out no state in particular, the Court found that superior apples grown in Washington State had previously enjoyed a competitive advantage by trumpeting the high-grade certification awarded by their home state. North Carolina failed to provide a plausible rationale for "protecting" consumers from the badge of superiority Washington's certification system provided, and thus North Carolina's labeling ban crossed the line into unconstitutional discrimination. Although courts generally do not question legislative motives when legitimate reasons for regulation exist, they are willing to reject safety rationales judged to be a pretext for boosting in-state interests. And the Supreme Court did just that in *Kassel v. Consolidated Freightways Corp.*, where it invalidated Iowa's ban on most trucks exceeding 55 feet in length, finding that the purported dangers of larger trucks (e.g., jackknifing) were merely an excuse for barring out-of-state vehicles as they traveled through the state to destinations elsewhere.

Another core principle enshrined in the Constitution is the First Amendment's command that "Congress shall make no law abridging freedom of speech," a prohibition that is also applicable to individual states under a long line of Supreme Court precedent. One question that often arises under the free speech guarantee is how far it extends to cover conduct that isn't literally "speech" but is undertaken for the purpose of protest. The Court, for example, has recognized the right of students to wear black armbands to protest the Vietnam War as well as the more controversial right to burn an American flag. Sometimes, however, the "protest" dimension of the conduct in question is insufficient to gain judicial protection for activities the government wishes to outlaw. For example, in *United States v. O'Brien,* the Supreme Court upheld a criminal conviction of a protester who burned his draft card as a sign of his opposition to the Vietnam War. The Court found that the smooth functioning of the selective service system was reason enough to require men of draft age (and only men could be drafted at the time) to have their draft card with them at all times.

b. Sample exam question

Kawanda, the recently admitted fifty-first U.S. state, has been uncommonly successful in keeping the Coronavirus at bay. Public health officials attribute the success to Kawanda's distance from the mainland together with its early imposition of a lockdown as well as a strictly enforced requirement that all persons over the age of five wear a mask at all indoor locations except for one's own home. Moreover, consistent with its long history of technological pre-eminence, Kawanda sponsored a successful program to develop and manufacture a new form of face mask, the Vibro, that has proven strikingly effective at preventing the spread of the virus. Constructed from vibronium, a rare material native to Kawanda, the masks are manufactured in the state by Panther Electronics. Panther's president, Bill Munger, is a close friend and major donor to Kawanda's Governor B. Jordan. Munger privately promises Jordan that he will provide a free Vibro for every health care worker in Kawanda in exchange for the governor's support of legislation promoting the mask. Jordan is so grateful that, as the first batch of Vibros rolls off the factory line, he uses government funds to buy a large quantity, has each one framed by a local artisan, and displays one on the lobby wall in every hospital and health care facility in the state.

Soon after this symbolic tribute, the Kawanda legislature passes and Governor Jordan signs the "Praise the Vibro Act of 2020" (PVA). This statute requires that until the end of 2023 no face mask proven less effective than the Vibro may be sold or purchased within Kawanda, and that each Vibro purchased within Kawanda will have a registration number and every owner will be required to have the registered Vibro "in their possession whenever they leave their homes." Violation of any provision of this statute is punishable by a $10,000 fine and imprisonment for one year.

Letitia is leader of the Free Kawanda movement. She observes that Kawanda has had fewer than 100 cases of COVID, and she feels strongly that the harsh measures taken by the state in response to the pandemic are an unnecessary infringement of freedom upon the state's people. She thus organizes a protest drawing over 500 people to the town square in Kawanda's capital. She arrives wearing a much cheaper mask, ironically dubbed "the Seal," that is made in Florida. Letitia purchased her Seal at a local grocery that remained open as an essential business. Studies show that the Seal is only 50% as effective as the Vibro at preventing the spread of the Coronavirus, but you can buy a Seal for $2 while the Vibro costs $300. Both masks are reusable by the owner for up to a year.

As leader of the movement, Letitia stands alone at the podium in front of the assembled crowd. She removes her Seal mask and gives a rousing speech condemning the Kawanda government, specifically touting her discovery of the "corrupt" deal between Munger and Jordan that produced the PVA, and calling for everyone in the crowd to replace their Vibro with a Seal. Then, in a dramatic gesture, she pulls her own Vibro out from her briefcase and sets it on fire, tossing it into a fireproof box so as to avoid any risk of conflagration or harm to persons in her immediate vicinity.

Letitia is immediately arrested and charged with violating the PVA by purchasing the Seal mask and by destroying the Vibro, and thus falling out of compliance with the mandatory possession requirement, at the capital rally. She hires you as her attorney and requests a memo detailing how she might challenge the act's provisions on constitutional grounds. She wants to review the best case you can make for her, to hear the best arguments Kawanda might make in response, and to get your assessment of how courts might resolve each issue.

c. Model answer

The prosecution of Letitia under the PVA raises two issues under the Constitution, first whether the prohibition on purchasing masks that are less effective than the Vibro violates the commerce clause by unlawfully discriminating against interstate commerce, and second whether Kawanda has infringed Letitia's First Amendment rights by punishing her for burning the Vibro to protest Kawanda's Coronavirus policies. Letitia's strongest defense of her purchase of the Seal is to challenge the PVA on the grounds that it violates the dormant commerce clause by favoring the local mask, the Vibro, over out-of-state competitors. But since the PVA does not on its face distinguish between in-state and out-of-state products, Letitia has work to do to persuade the courts to view the PVA through a protectionist lens. She might begin her case by pointing to the cozy relationship between Panther president Munger and the governor. The PVA, Letitia might assert, is a payback for campaign contributions and for the political boost the governor gained from the free Vibros supplied to health care workers. Moreover, Letitia will demand that Kawanda produce an extremely strong public health rationale to justify the PVA's outright ban on purchases of out-of-state products. Like the ban on 55-foot trucks in *Kassel*, Kawanda's mandate to purchase the local product can be painted as disguised protectionism unless the facts support the state's asserted motive of battling the virus.

Kawanda can be expected to push back by noting the absence of evidence to suggest the governor has done anything more than support a valid safety regulation that happened to benefit a major supporter. Indeed, Kawanda can argue that the Vibro is a highly effective mask, thus distinguishing *Hunt v. Washington State Apple*, since the regulation at issue there *disadvantaged* a superior product. At first glance, Kawanda's claim of product superiority does not appear pretextual, because the Vibro is twice as effective as the Seal, so why shouldn't Kawanda insist on everyone wearing the safer mask? But Letitia can respond that the real question is whether a single Vibro is more effective than 150 Seals, because that's how many Seals you can buy for the price of one Vibro. The $300 price tag is a lot of money for many people, and the question says nothing about Kawanda providing a Vibro for those who can't afford it. Thus, the PVA will leave the poorest citizens stranded at home without a legal mask. And, although they are reusable, masks are easily lost or damaged, making the need for cheaper masks still more imperative. Thus Letitia can argue that when it comes to the *actual* health and safety of Kawandians, the Seal is really the superior product because of its affordability, and the PVA is just a way to protect local interests against Florida competition, placing the case squarely within the reasoning of *Hunt*. Moreover, Letitia will paint the PVA as even worse than the statute invalidated in *Hunt* because the PVA imposes an outright ban on purchasing anything but the in-state product.

If the court acknowledges, as it should, that *Hunt* doesn't settle the question of how to determine what counts as a superior product, Letitia can argue for a thumb on the scale in her favor due to the suspicious nature of the dealings between Munger and Governor Jordan. Although courts would be reluctant to interfere with a legislative judgment about safety, particularly when dealing with a pandemic, the idea of "outlawing the good in pursuit of the perfect," regardless of cost or consequence, seems dubious, particularly given that those who lack $300 might be tempted to go out without a mask at all, leading to even greater risks than those posed by a less effective but far cheaper mask. None of this would have been lost on the Kawanda legislature, thus calling into question whether the PVA was a bona fide health and safety measure or merely a political payoff. And even looking past potential corruption, Letitia has a strong argument under *Kassel* that the protectionist insistence on the local product is Kawanda's paramount concern rather than safeguarding against disease. Accordingly, Letitia may succeed in striking this portion of the PVA as a commerce clause violation.

At first glance, it seems more difficult for Letitia to defend her action in burning her Vibro. She will, of course, claim that her act of symbolic protest is protected by the First Amendment and that it would therefore be unconstitutional to punish her actions despite her violating PVA's requirement that she have her Vibro with her at all times. But Kawanda will respond that Letitia's case fails because her situation is akin to *O'Brien*, where the Supreme Court upheld a criminal conviction for burning a draft card. Indeed, Kawanda may argue that there is a stronger state interest in protecting an effective and expensive mask against needless destruction in the midst of a pandemic than in protecting a draft card that can be readily replaced.

Letitia can distinguish *O'Brien* on the grounds that from a safety point of view there's nothing particularly singular about the Vibro she destroyed. She can easily borrow other masks until hers is replaced. In contrast, the Court in *O'Brien* was struck by the fact that Congress had actually *prohibited* the destruction of draft cards because the system of identifying eligible draftees depended on each person's having his card. Kawanda has enacted no such prohibition here, so any state effort to rest its case on the asserted evils of destroying a mask will prove unconvincing. Indeed, any sudden professed interest in the preservation of every mask would be difficult to square with the fact that health care facilities throughout the state are festooned with spare Vibros and *the government actually paid to put them there.* The prosecution at issue here is thus clearly aimed not at the act but at the message it conveyed, bringing it squarely within the ambit of flag-burning precedents that prohibit the state from punishing messages it doesn't like.

Kawanda is likely to respond that Letitia's crime was not burning the mask but simply not having it in her possession and so there can be no motive to squash her message. Yet because there's no evidence that Letitia went inside without her mask, Kawanda will have to justify prosecution not on a specific safety risk but on the PVA's elaborate registration and tracking system that protects masks against *any* kind of loss. Kawanda is likely to emphasize that it was the role of the draft card *in the draft registration system*—and not the intrinsic value of the scrap of paper—that prompted the *O'Brien* Court to conclude that the government's interest in protecting the integrity of that system outweighed the protester's right to disrupt it via a form of protest that might easily and effectively have been expressed in a million other ways. So too, Kawanda will argue that the registration system for masks will preserve the integrity of the state's public health interests. Letitia might respond that PVA's registration system is better suited to lining the pockets of a major Jordan supporter than to promoting the health and safety of Kawandians. Thus, the requirement of registration is more likely to promote the *purchase* of masks (by providing the government with the names of purchasers and thus a simple means of identifying holdouts) than the *wearing* of masks, which—because compliance failures are readily visible to all—can be far more effectively regulated by direct action.

In the end, Letitia may have to count on the court's discounting *O'Brien* as an artifact of its times—and as a product of the deference U.S. courts invariably accord nearly all things military—and hope that the court instead views the current dispute through the lens of the more recent flag-burning cases. But unless the court sees the Vibro registration system as unnecessary to the public health goals it was established to further, Kawanda is likely to prevail here.

Authors' comments: A significant virtue of this answer is that it addresses the commerce clause issue and the First Amendment issue in entirely separate analyses that are easy for the reader to follow and digest. The danger of a mashup is that student and professor alike might get confused—"Wait, which point are we arguing here?" In this connection, an advantage of taking an exam on a laptop is that it is easy to produce dis-

tinct analyses even when the actual drafting is more chaotic; afterthoughts and second thoughts alike can be seamlessly re-arranged and incorporated into the appropriate section of the answer. The task is obviously more challenging for those working in blue books, but rest assured that professors become fairly adept at deciphering insertions squeezed between the lines or into the margins and also at following cross-references (such as "please turn now to the commerce clause argument continued at the back of Book 2 before picking up here with the First Amendment analysis"). And one final introductory note: Since you could easily devote the full hour to either one of the two issues presented, it's a good idea to do as this answer does and use the opening to signal to the grader that you see and plan to discuss both issues, as a hedge against the possibility of running out of time while you are still discussing the first. That said, this is one place where a "pound of cure" (i.e., managing your time so you actually get to both issues) is worth significantly more than the "ounce of prevention" supplied by the opening.

Like many Constitutional Law problems, this one turns largely on "competing interpretations of case law": the commerce clause issue tests the similarities and differences between this case and Hunt v. Washington State Apple, *and the First Amendment issue asks whether the protest here more closely resembles the draft card case ("lock her up!") or the flag-burning cases ("set her free!"). Turning to the commerce clause analysis, the similarities to* Hunt *are straightforward: The PVA imposes a facially neutral ban on the sale of particular products that in its application favors an in-state product over an out-of-state competitor. (In this connection, the sudden appearance of a real state in an otherwise entirely fictional setting is a "tell" that may aid the reader in spotting the anti-import effect of the PVA.) But the differences between the facts here and those in* Hunt *exemplify how exam questions often push exam-takers in conflicting directions, something this answer handles with care. On the one hand, courts are likely to be even less sympathetic to the PVA than they were to the statute in* Hunt, *because the PVA bans all sales rather than merely imposing a rule about how out-of-state products could be certified. Yet on the other hand, the PVA stakes a stronger claim to validity because it protects an arguably superior product. Under both* Hunt *and* Kassel, *the validity of such a ban turns on whether the PVA is a bona fide health and safety regulation or a pretext for favoring in-state interests, and—even if it's not a pretext—whether the health and safety rationale is sufficiently strong to justify such an extreme measure. The answer here excels by scouring the facts for every shred of evidence that can be marshaled on either side, emphasizing on the pro-PVA side that the public health officials are tasked with battling viruses and the Vibro is in fact a significantly more effective mask than the Seal and on the anti-PVA side suspicions of a political payoff in the statute's enactment.*

The statute also seems vulnerable because the state is forcing everyone to use a very expensive local product, and here is where this answer is particularly creative. It identifies an ambiguity in the application of Hunt. The out-of-state product in this case—the Seal mask—is seemingly an <u>inferior</u> product whereas Washington State was barred from informing consumers that the apples were <u>superior</u>. But maybe the Vibro's superiority is illusory, since the Seal provides half the effectiveness for 1/150th of the cost, making the Seal the superior product for these purposes. Indeed, low-cost masks might in fact lead to greater safety because they would be more widely used, a classic SHAPING *argument.*

This answer is equally strong in its treatment of the First Amendment issue, working with the competing lines of precedent to mobilize arguments for and against the prosecution for mask-burning. The state has a strong interest in ensuring that masks—like draft cards and unlike flags—be on the person at all times. Yet unlike the government's regulation of draft cards, the government here enacted no prohibition against the destruction of masks, thus suggesting the real reason behind the prosecution is government disapproval of the message sent by the destructive act and not the act itself. But yet again as in the case of draft cards, the value of an individual mask is its connection to a registration and tracking system, though then again on the other side perhaps the registration system at issue here is regulatory overkill. The key point is that the answer neither stops with the first issue it sees nor "gives in" when one side seems to gain a clear upper hand, instead "pressing on" until it has fashioned a respectable argument out of nearly every fact presented in the question.

Exam-Taking Tips and Frequently Asked Questions

What sets *Getting to Maybe* apart from its many competitors is its frank recognition that law exams test legal reasoning and that legal reasoning cannot be reduced to any simple "check the boxes" formula. Indeed, to avoid oversimplifying or dumbing things down, we needed nearly 300 pages—pretty much all of Parts II, III, & IV of the book—to present the "basics" of legal reasoning in the ways it's typically tested on law exams. If you've worked your way through all of that—and tested your learning via the sample questions in Part V—we've got good news: You can put down this book *right now*; enjoy a well-deserved break; and bring the important lessons you've learned to the rest of your studies and/or exam prep.

But we know from experience that many readers turn to *Getting to Maybe* for help at the last minute—say a day or two before the first law school exam—and we've got good news for them too. Although end-of-term studiers should devote most of their dwindling time to course-specific materials—e.g., their class notes and course outline—we've put together this Appendix for students with only a couple of hours to spare. You'll find that it offers many valuable lessons on what to do—and, equally important, what *not* to do—in an easily accessible "test-taking tips" and "frequently asked questions" format.

The Appendix may likewise be "just what the (juris) doctor ordered" for first-year students who are feeling so pressed for time that taking on an entire book of outside reading at *any* point is simply out of the question. All of us felt that way at various stages of our first year, and many feel frazzled pretty much the whole way through. For these students as well, the tips on offer here may help and help a lot in dealing with law school exams without disrupting an already jam-packed study schedule.

Finally, the Appendix may provide a useful review for those who've read the rest of the book but did so long ago—over the summer, say, or early in the first term—and are now facing the prospect of putting that learning to use in the law exam setting. The "do's and don'ts" may help refresh your recollection of the many ways to "get to maybe" with little impact on your exam-prep timetable and whatever "me" time you've managed to salvage in spite of it all.

So here's what you'll find in the pages that follow. Appendix A—"Preparing for the Exam"—offers tips on what you can do to get ready for exams from the day classes begin until the morning of your first final. Appendix B—"Writing Exam Answers"—cuts to the chase and focuses on how to organize and write successful exam answers. Appendix C—"Mistakes to Avoid"—identifies many of the most common exam-taking misfires we've seen over the years and can help you avoid them from the get-go. And Appendix D—"Frequently Asked Questions"—addresses the questions we've most often heard from students facing the law exam ordeal for the first time. Our hope is that these materials will diminish the ordeal and enable you to excel on exams by making the most of what you've learned in your law school course-work.

Appendix A

Preparing for the Exam

The tips we offer here are designed as a supplement to good old-fashioned studying, not as a substitute for it. You can't expect to do well if you don't attend class, read the assigned material, and struggle to understand it—case closed. Often, however, students who spend what should be adequate time preparing for exams don't study as efficiently as they might. And once you've read all the cases and reviewed your class notes until you just can't look at them anymore, what should you do then? Try these tips as a way of studying smart while you are studying hard—keeping in mind of course that these are "tips" and not iron-clad rules.

Tip #1. Exam Preparation Takes All Semester

Here's the part where we tell you to prepare diligently for class, to attend class regularly, and to take good notes. We understand how tempting it is to ignore such advice; *of course* a couple of law professors are going to tell you that you need to go to every class well prepared and to write down every word we say! But consider the possibility, however remote it might seem, that the reason we want you to do these things is not to feed faculty egos, but because experience has taught us that this is your best route to success in your legal studies. Indeed, when it comes to excelling on law school exams, we think this advice is second in importance only to Tip #8 ("Read Each Question Carefully, and Answer the Question Asked"). Here's why:

Regular class attendance is crucial to exam performance

It's a common perception among nonlawyers that law is a body of "rules" that law students must memorize and be ready to regurgitate on demand in law school and, ultimately, in legal practice. But if you've been a law student for more than a week, you've no doubt begun to figure out that rule memorization and regurgitation are of very little use in class discussion and that the emphasis is far less on what the rules *are* than on how lawyers and judges *use* rules to analyze and solve problems.

For most students, this represents an abrupt departure from their undergraduate studies, where teachers frequently use class time to convey and perhaps clarify the same information contained in the reading for the course. By contrast, in law school the assigned readings are typically only the starting point for the analysis the professor pushes her students to undertake in class, and you can be sure that it is the classroom analysis that will be carefully tested on the final. As a result, class attendance is generally *the* key to preparation for the typical law exam. (If you have to miss a session, we recommend that you seek the professor's permission to have someone record it for you. A classmate's notes may do in a pinch, but—even assuming you can read the writing and decipher the abbreviations—the best they can be expected to offer is a glimpse of what you missed.)

The better your preparation, the more you'll get out of a class

Most law students quickly surmise that the cases and rules they are supposed to study in preparation for class are only the starting point for the analysis and discussion that actually take place in the classroom. But some students take this logic a step further: Since you can't learn the law's lessons simply by reading the assigned materials on your own, they figure, why bother reading those materials at all? Why not simply go to class and wait for the professor just to tell you exactly what you need to know?

The problem with this thinking is that it assumes that the point of the law school classroom experience is to teach you what the cases and materials "really mean," rather than to help you learn how to analyze, interpret, and argue about those materials and how to do so on your own. To be sure, if a particular class discussion is focused on a short and simple phrase (e.g., "a benefit previously received by the promisor" under § 86 of the Second Restatement of Contracts), you may well be able to keep up with that discussion even if you are reading the phrase for the first time right there in class. But if the focus of the discussion is any broader than that—like a complex statutory provision, or a court's opinion, or a line of cases—you're in deep trouble. Like the blindfolded person who mistook the elephant's trunk for a snake, you're unlikely to get the details right and are even less likely to grasp "the big picture."

Attendance and preparation may be even more important at the end of the semester than at the beginning

The end of the semester is invariably serious crunch time, with paper due dates, makeup classes, and professors rushing to get through their syllabi. Yet this is no time to let class attendance and preparation slip, since the material presented during the last several classes of the semester is quite likely to appear on the final. For one thing, many professors teach their courses so that concepts and issues unfold in cumulative fashion, and as a result the final two or three topics may well "bring together" various themes and problems that the professor thinks are especially important and hence worth stressing on the exam. For another, most professors draft their exams at the end of the semester—partly because we're procrastinators (just like our students!) but partly because we don't know what we'll test until we see what we've actually taught. In any event, it is only natural for us to focus our questions on the topics that are freshest in our minds, and the topics covered at the end of the course are likely to loom large in just this way.

Tip #2. Focus Your Exam Study on Your Class Notes

The reading period is nearly over, and you're spending another late night in the library. On one side of the desk is a beautifully printed, carefully organized commercial outline summarizing the main points of the topic you are studying. On the other side rests the virtually indecipherable chicken scratch that you call class notes. Although it's tempting to focus your flagging energy on the easy-to-read work of the so-called experts, don't do it. For at least two very important reasons, your class notes are your best bet.

Most professors test what they teach

Despite the widespread suspicion that your professors are out to trick you, most of us endeavor to test exactly what we've tried to teach. Thus, while a high-quality commercial study aid may offer a useful overview of a particular area of the law, nothing will provide a more accurate guide to the particular topics and issues that your professor thinks are most important—and is therefore most likely to examine—than what she actually emphasized in class. Moreover, quite apart from variation in course content, different professors focus their teaching on different lawyerly skills. Some emphasize rule application and argument; some focus on policy analysis; some embrace a theoretical perspective; some stress fact sensitivity; and most embrace some mixture of all of these and more. Whatever your own professor's approach, you can be sure that it is not captured in any study aid—unless she happens to be the author! As a result, your class notes are likely to be among your most valuable resources as you prepare for your exams.

Your class notes can help you predict questions likely to appear on the exam

Many—perhaps most—law school exam questions are simply variations on hypotheticals and problems discussed in class, so carefully working your way back through those hypos and problems is an excellent approach to preparing for the final. Indeed, some professors will signal their intention to draw explicitly from a particular class discussion by warning the students that "a problem like this will almost surely appear on the final"; obviously, it is a good idea to highlight such predictions in your class notes and to focus your study efforts accordingly.

But your notes may contain subtler hints about what will be tested as well. For example, it may be a good idea to pay special attention when the professor has gone back over particular material a second time—perhaps in response to a particularly insightful question from you or one of your classmates—and has done so in a way that suggests she has developed a new way of looking at the topic in the course of teaching it to your class. In our experience, it is more likely than not that she will focus on such "second thoughts" somewhere on the final, since she may well have experienced her own rethinking as one of the highlights of the course.

Tip #3. Prepare Your Own Outline of the Course

For virtually every law school course, there's a 1,000-plus-page casebook; a statutory and/or new-case supplement; and an extraordinary number of hornbooks and other commercial study aids. So you might wonder why we are telling you to duplicate all this professional effort by preparing your own outline for each course. Here's why:

Law exams test rule application, not memorization

Let's start with the good news. No law school exam question we have seen or heard about asks students to quote from memory an even moderately lengthy passage from a case or a statute. Thus, you need not worry about memorizing all those cases and rules and notes you have before you. What law exam questions test is not your recollection of the rules but what you can *do* with them: that is, your ability to make arguments about how to interpret and apply the rules and concepts you've studied in a variety of real-world contexts.

Thus, for example, you are highly unlikely to encounter a question that asks you to recount the definition of "goods" offered in U.C.C. § 2-105(1). Instead, you are likely to be asked to *apply* that definition to a variety of transactions. Sometimes the application will be straightforward (e.g., to the book you are reading); sometimes the application will be tricky (e.g., to the software program we used to produce it). Obviously, you will need to have a pretty good idea of "what the rules are" in order to apply them in either setting, but you can safely leave the task of memorizing vast quantities of text for regurgitation-on-demand to the interns and residents on *Grey's Anatomy*.

Don't mourn... organize!

You're right if you are thinking that we've just delivered the bad news as well: Even though you don't need to memorize all those rules, you *do* need to master them well enough to be able to explain their application to real-world fact patterns. Grasping rules and how they fit together is no easy task, and we know no better way than to prepare an outline for each course. Your outline should be designed to help you remember the rules you've studied and, even more important, to help you to understand those rules; to recognize the difficulties you're likely to encounter in interpreting and applying them; and to see where they fit in the "big picture" as your professor has presented it.

Write the outline yourself

The real point of an outline is not to have it but to *make* it. In our experience, the very process of outlining—of working your way back through the mass of course material and organizing it in a way that helps you make sense of it all—may be the most valuable part of your legal studies. In fact, we boldly predict that the more time you spend drafting and redrafting an outline, the less time you'll spend actually referring to it during the final. Of course, if you're taking a closed-book exam, you'd better not refer to your outline—or to anything else, for that matter! But even on the far more common open-book exam, you are likely to find that the outline has already done the job by helping you learn the material in the process of organizing it, thus freeing up precious exam time for reading and re-reading the questions and writing and refining your answers.

Commercial study aids are poor substitutes

Although most law professors tend to sneer at hornbooks, canned outlines, and other commercial study aids, we don't doubt that such materials can provide a useful supplement to your legal studies, provided you use them properly and recognize their limits. (See FAQ #7, "Should You Use Commercial Study Aids?") But one terribly important thing a commercial outline cannot do is provide you with the experience of organizing your *own* outline for a course; as we've said, we think the "pulling it all together" process is one of the most effective vehicles students have for learning the law. Moreover, a commercial outline is likely to fail you in a second, equally important respect: While a high-quality publication may well offer a useful general overview of a particular area of the law, your final exam is highly likely to focus on those topics and skills that your professor emphasized in class. As a result, an outline that draws on your own class notes is likely to be infinitely more useful than the one-size-fits-all version you can buy in a bookstore. Finally, commercial outlines emphasize what is clear and what is settled about the subject matter, whereas your professor is far more likely to test the unclear and the unsettled. If you organize it well, your outline can thus be a far better guide to *your* exam than a commercial product ever could be.

Outlines prepared by other students are only marginally better

In our experience, the value of outlines prepared by fellow students runs the gamut from marginally useful to downright dangerous. Most law professors update, reorganize, and even rethink the material they teach often enough to make it far too risky to rely on an outline from earlier renditions—even very recent ones—of the course. Indeed, an exam answer that draws on material the professor taught last year—but has taken the trouble to modify or transform for your class—is a surefire way to signal that you haven't taken this year's class seriously and are not up to date on the assigned material.

Outlines of the current course are obviously better, but their utility depends almost entirely on your personal role in their preparation. Thus, if your study group develops an outline through a genuine collective effort—discussing and analyzing the entire course as a group, but perhaps divvying up topics for first drafts among the individual participants—both the outline and the process of making it can be of genuine educational value. Even here, however, you are sure to find that your mastery of the material you outline yourself greatly exceeds your grasp of those parts of the course outlined by others. Once again, it is the process of outlining, and far less the product you produce, that makes a difference to exam performance.

Tip #4. Pay Special Attention to Newly Added Course Material

Many of your professors will be teaching a course they have offered a few or even many times in the past. They will see it as part of their responsibility to freshen the course at least a little each year, and the most common way they do so is by adding new material—most often cases, statutes, or articles of recent vintage. You can identify the new material by consulting the previous year's syllabus (if you can't get it from a fellow student, you might try the academic dean or the library's course reserve); by checking dates on this year's assigned readings; or by asking the professor directly what material is new, perhaps explaining that you are reviewing old exams and want to know what they did and didn't cover. But however you track it down, we encourage you to give new material prime place of study during your review, because it's highly likely to find its way onto your exam. Here's why.

Exam construction is a creative process. Your professors are looking for fact patterns that resemble key cases in some respects and differ in others. And they also strive to write questions that don't simply mimic those on past exams, so the issues you'll encounter—and the settings that present them—are fresh and inventive. You need not sympathize with your professors to recognize that this can be a challenging endeavor. With material professors are teaching for the first time, however, there's no risk that this year's exam will fall into the rut of previous patterns. The new material may thus have enormous appeal to faculty as a source of exam questions.

And that's not all. Most professors truly enjoy the process of thinking through the implications of material they are covering for the first time. Like the first bite of an ice cream cone, a new case or statute is likely to stand out as a course highlight. Writing an exam question covering such new material—and seeing what students do with it—provides an invaluable vehicle for further exploring recent legal developments. Many professors will readily seize this opportunity, and so you can seize yours by devoting extra study time to ensuring you have a handle on material recently added to the course.

Tip #5. Review the Professor's Old Exams

We believe that reviewing exams your professor has given in previous years is the most effective way to prepare for finals. Prior exams, especially recent ones, are likely to reveal the issues the professor finds significant or interesting enough to examine, and they may offer clues as to format (e.g., lengthy issue spotters vs. short-answer problems vs. policy questions) as well as content. Simply put, nothing else—not the most thorough studying, not the most popular commercial outline, not even the best book on exam-taking (this one!)—can provide you with this kind of insight into your own professor's approach.

We understand that looking at old exams can instill panic if done too early, when the questions will almost surely seem unimaginably difficult. Accordingly, you'll need to pick a time for this somewhere near the end of the course—though given the importance of the task, don't wait till the last minute either. But whenever you do it, by all means don't pass up your best opportunity to find out how your professor goes about the task of examining students!

Gather intel about your professor

As much as we pride ourselves on the universal value of the advice offered in this book, it is no substitute for learning as much as you can about the way your particular professor gives and grades exams. Many professors make this easier by holding review sessions in which they describe in advance the format (if not the content!) of the exam, and many help you out by making exams from previous years available to your class. If such exams are available, get them and go over them carefully, for you'll have no better guide to what this year's exam will be like than the questions that appeared on prior exams.

Don't wait until you are finished studying to look at an old exam

It's incredibly dispiriting to read a series of questions on topics you've never even heard of, so there's much to be said for waiting until you are well into a course before you start working your way through old exams. But we urge you not to leave this important task to the very last minute. Law school exams aren't meant to be easy, and even the best students will often feel at a loss until they actually begin working through an answer. Looking at old exams at some point early in your exam prep will give you time to incorporate the professor's particular way of thinking into your studying. Also, if an old exam raises issues that appear unfamiliar, you'll have time to determine whether the surprise is the professor's "fault" (i.e., she has changed the content of the class since last year) or your own (i.e., you missed something important in the course).

Simulate the exam experience at least once

Let's face it, taking exams is no one's idea of fun. One reason is that so much rides on your performance. But it's precisely because a lot is at stake that we recommend you practice taking an old exam. You wouldn't dream of giving a piano recital without sitting down in a quiet room and playing the piece all the way through several times before the big day. Neither should you go into an exam without putting yourself through the daunting and even intimidating experience of being alone with your questions and your blank screen! (Doing this will also give you an opportunity to practice budgeting your time among questions of varying difficulty and format; see Tip #17, "Watch Time/Credit Allocations.")

Go over old exams with your classmates as often as you can

We can't stress this enough. In our experience, many hardworking students who've been disappointed with their exam grades have turned out to be solo studiers. To be sure, working alone should play a crucial role in your legal studies. But once you feel confident about your basic understanding, group sessions reviewing old exams are perhaps the best way to test your facility with the concepts. As most law professors and more than a few lawyers have learned over the years, there is no better way to discover the holes in your own thinking than by being forced to communicate your views to others.

Moreover, studying old exams is one of those experiences that confirms the old adage two heads are better than one—and more heads, better still. Thus, no matter how good you think you are at "seeing all the angles," you're sure to unearth many more if you work your way through a question from last year's exam with a small group of classmates who have varying perspectives on life and law.

We understand "study group" sessions can become needlessly competitive if everyone insists on showing that their approach is the right one. But the way to deal with that problem is to talk about this danger in advance and agree collectively to avoid it; indeed, you can "vote with your feet" and change study groups if you find you just can't make yours work for you.

Tip #6. Consider What Questions *You* Would Ask

It's often said that there is no better way to learn a subject than to teach it. After teaching for most of our lives, we're convinced that the most learning of all occurs when we sit down to write the exam. Exam-writing forces you to look at the course as a whole; to identify the interesting issues; and to imagine where the law is headed.

This is exactly the kind of thinking that can prepare you to *take* an exam as well. Here are some helpful hints for thinking about your courses from the "top down," almost the way a CEO would think about her company. We suggest you try them after you've spent a good deal of time mastering the course material from the "bottom up"!

Pull the forest out of the trees

There is no substitute for knowing the material covered in your courses. But don't let a blizzard of detailed knowledge substitute for some quiet reflection. As the exam approaches, try to identify a small number of major issues that the professor has covered—three to six would capture the typical law school class. Have dinner with a friend unfamiliar with law and, focusing on those issues, explain the course in broad strokes—or try to before your friend falls asleep! (Do not—we repeat, *do not*—try to do this on a first date or there won't be a second one.)

Applying this technique, you might, for example, conclude Constitutional Law is about protecting individual rights from government intrusion; about dividing power between the national and state governments; and about allocating governmental power among the president, the Congress, and the courts. (Crucial as they are, it is easy to lose sight of these broader themes when you are bogged down in the details of smaller points—e.g., the rules governing the relationship between the privileges and immunities clause and the market-participant doctrine.) Then, force yourself to outline the major points the professor has tried to make about these larger issues and about how they are implicated in individual cases. (Which theme or themes are at stake, for example, in deciding whether a particular plaintiff has standing to challenge a government action?)

A related exercise is to put yourself in the position of a professor who wants to see whether her students have grasped the principal themes of the course. You might imagine a conversation with one of your classmates; what questions would you ask her if you were trying to test her this way? Even if you can't predict the professor's questions with great precision, you'll find that this kind of thinking will help immensely in your preparation for the exam.

Look for important cases pointing in opposite directions

Try to identify leading cases you have studied that take contrasting approaches to the same legal question. Based on similar facts, for example, one case might hold that a federal statute pre-empts state law while another case finds no pre-emption. Now see if you can invent a fact pattern that contains some elements of the first case and some of the second case. For example, your hypo and the first case might both address a problem requiring a uniform national standard (a factor favoring pre-emption), but your hypo and the second case might involve statutes whose wording suggests a less imperial congressional intention (a factor cutting against it).

Such hybrid fact patterns form the core of many exam questions. If you invent enough of them, you might even be able to approximate the questions on your final. But even if you don't get that lucky, you'll be developing one of the key skills you'll need for top performance, because you'll know exactly what kind of problems to look for on the exam.

Identify underlying conflicts

Every body of law is aimed at solving real-world problems. If the solutions were easy, we wouldn't need much law and there wouldn't be a whole course devoted to the subject. What makes the problems difficult is that there are often two or more important goals that are in some tension with each other.

In property law, for example, we want rules that will make owners feel safe and secure in their investments, but we don't want rules that will ban would-be competitors. In contracts, there is tension between rules that promote freedom of action and rules that protect reliance on promises.

In torts, the law must navigate between limiting liability to actors who are "at fault" and expanding it to cover any and all harms one person causes another.

Before the final, try to identify the key conflicts from your course and the situations you've studied where it's particularly difficult to reconcile those conflicts. It's a safe bet that your professor will be doing the same thing as she drafts your exam.

Look for trends and limits

Law professors frequently identify "trends" in the topics they cover, priding themselves in their forecasts of issues that are likely to arise in the future and the direction the law may take. Don't be surprised if they ask you to do the same thing on your exams.

A course such as Labor Law may make it easy to think in terms of trends. Are courts increasingly "pro-union" or "pro-management"? But every course will have some issues in which patterns and directions can be detected, even if they aren't so obvious. In Contracts, for example, the cases you've studied may reveal a recent trend toward enforcing the "plain language" of the contract, rather than understandings implicit in the transactional context. Similarly, you may have noticed—or your professor may have emphasized—that constitutional decisions are increasingly hostile to statutes that limit presidential control over hiring and firing executive officials.

A classic professorial ploy for gauging your grasp of such developments is to invent situations that "push the envelope"—i.e., that test just how far this or that trend will go before countervailing policies or concerns put on the brakes. In Torts, for example, you might detect an increasing tendency to hold market actors responsible for damages they cause even when they are not at "fault." Try to come up with situations that stretch the "no-fault" concept to the breaking point: Might gun manufacturers be held responsible when their products kill or cause injury, even if there was absolutely nothing wrong with the gun? Should an aspirin manufacturer be held liable if someone intentionally uses the aspirin to administer a fatal overdose? Questions like these frequently appear on law exams, and we can think of no better way of preparing for them than by attempting to come up with them on your own.

Consult your casebook as a source of questions

During the press of class preparation, it's sometimes difficult to take time to focus on the problems in the casebook that typically appear at the end of a chapter or a particular block of materials. These problems are designed to make you reflect upon complex topics, but you may feel pressed to move on with the assigned reading. As you begin your exam preparation, however, it's time to go back and look at these problems again, for many professors use them as inspiration for exam questions. And even if your professor doesn't build a question based on any of the problems you study, this exercise is nonetheless terrific practice for the kinds of problems you are likely to encounter on the exam.

What interests you?

Last but not least, take a few moments to consider what you find most interesting about the course. What problems would you want students to grapple with if you were writing the exam? If you'll forgive us for indulging a professional conceit, much of what you know about the subject you've learned from the professor, so it wouldn't be a coincidence if the two of you have ended up on a similar wavelength!

Looking for more detailed advice on exam preparation?
We devote all of Chapter Eleven to the subject!

Appendix B

Writing Exam Answers

Law school exams differ dramatically from those you may have encountered in other educational settings: You can't guarantee success simply by memorizing and parroting back a great deal of material, nor will elegant writing substitute for careful and critical analysis. Here, then, are some specific steps you can take to deploy the skills that got you into law school—and the hard-earned "legal knowledge" you've gained since—to master a brave new world of test-taking.

Tip #7. Carefully Read the Exam Instructions and Follow Them to the Letter

Having spent so much time in classes learning how every rule has exceptions and how some rules are made to be broken, you can be forgiven for assuming that you can safely treat your exam instructions more like guidelines. Don't do it! If you take any lesson at all from this book, it should be this. Your exam answers are written for your professors. If your professor provides page or word limits or specifies a preferred format for your answers, you should follow instructions to the letter. Here's why:

The "stuffy tuffy" may actually enjoy penalizing you

Different professors will no doubt react to violations of exam instructions in different ways. If your professor is someone we call a "stuffy tuffy"—a teacher who demands that each student come to every class meticulously prepared, who conducts relentless Socratic inquiries in a rigorous and highly formal manner, and who seems to take great delight in squeezing an extended analysis out of even the most reluctant student—chances are that he will take the same extremely demanding approach to grading your exam. Although we have always suspected that this sort of classroom style often springs from "partner envy," stuffy tuffies no doubt *believe* that their approach will best prepare you for the rigors of legal practice.

At least when it comes to demanding strict adherence to exam instructions, they have a point: Absent prior permission from the court for good cause shown, real-world judges and court clerks routinely reject pleadings and briefs that don't meet in every respect the applicable requirements governing (e.g.) page length and format, and no court anywhere has ever accepted "I didn't know about the page limit" or "I didn't have time to read the rules" or "I just forgot" as "good cause shown." The stuffy tuffy who is trying to prepare you for a career in which carelessness may harm a real-world client isn't likely to accept excuses like these either.

The "student-friendly prof" may feel bad about it, but will probably penalize you, too

Don't assume from what we've just said, however, that a professor who runs a "kinder, gentler" classroom will look more favorably on a failure to follow exam instructions. For one thing, virtually *all* law professors—from the most conservative curmudgeon to the most touchy-feely liberal; from the most traditional "black-letter" teachers to the most postmodern "theory of theory" folks—take very seriously the task of preparing their students for the rigors of law practice. More than a little of the "stuffy tuffy" lurks within all of us, and the student who fails to follow rules that are as carefully delineated as most exam instructions is highly likely to bring it out.

Our own experience leads us to make a second point: Many students seem to think that, when push comes to shove, the "student-friendly prof" won't have the heart (or the guts) to penalize a student for something as "picky" as a failure to follow exam instructions. Truth be told, they're on to something: Many professors we know—and almost all of those we like—*will* feel bad about lowering a student's grade on what seems like a technicality.

But here's the rub: For every student who just can't seem to follow instructions, there are two dozen others who take the time—*and it takes time*—to read, to grasp, and to follow them meticulously. You don't have to be in law teaching for long to conclude that letting the few get away with careless mistakes penalizes the many who strive hard for compliance. And when it comes to a choice between excusing the careless and penalizing the industrious innocent, you'll find that stuffy tuffies and student-friendly profs quickly end up in the same place.

Even if you don't "lose points," you'll make a terrible impression on the grader

A law professor faced with grading 100 or more essay exams shares something important with a law student attending a first-year orientation party with a roomful of new classmates: First impressions make a big difference. The stronger that impression, the less likely it is that further engagement will change it.

Naturally, this can cut two ways. When a professor reads an exam that begins straight off with a thoughtful and well-organized argument, she is more likely to resolve doubtful points in the student's favor later on. But when the first thing a professor notices is that an exam doesn't conform to the instructions, she is likely to get the impression that the student in question was too cavalier to read them, too careless to grasp them, or too arrogant to follow them.

While redemption is always possible—in the end, nothing beats a good answer, no matter how it is packaged—persuading the grader you've provided a thoughtful analysis of her exam *questions* may be an uphill battle if she is already persuaded that you simply ignored her exam *instructions*.

When in doubt, go find out

What should you do if you've read the exam instructions and you don't understand them—if, for example, you genuinely think that there is more than one way to read a particular directive that the professor has given? (E.g., does the word limit include the plagiarism statement you are asked to provide on the first page of the exam?) Our first and best advice is for you to take a deep breath and read the instructions once again, for the answer you seek may well be right in front of you.

Most experienced professors develop "boilerplate" instructions that they use every year. Chances are pretty good that any real ambiguity would have been resolved long ago.

But—shocking though it may seem!—even law professors make mistakes, and if after a second reading you still think the instructions are ambiguous or unclear, then for heaven's sake *ask* someone. The best place to start is with the proctor, but at many schools the professors are available during the exam precisely for the purpose of dealing with unforeseen difficulties like these. (Indeed, you may be doing both the professor and your classmates a favor by raising the point at a time when the professor is still in a position to clarify the matter for the entire class.)

If you are not able (or not permitted) to make such an inquiry, then we recommend handling the problem the way a good *lawyer* would: At the very beginning of your answer, briefly identify the ambiguity you see and explain why you've handled it the way you have. If you've spotted an unintended ambiguity, the professor may well be impressed by both your careful reading and your poise under fire. But even if you've merely imagined the problem, the professor will see that you are trying to follow the instructions, and most will appreciate that.

An ounce of prevention is worth a pound of cure

As we said a moment ago, most professors develop "boilerplate" exam instructions that vary little from year to year. As a result, the easiest way to familiarize yourself with a particular professor's "exam rules" is to study her old exams, particularly those she's given in recent years. (See Tip #5, "Review the Professor's Old Exams.") Likewise, some professors distribute exam instructions during the final class of the semester or during a review session and do so for precisely the purpose of clarifying unintended confusion and ambiguity in advance. If your professor gives you this sort of "heads-up," you should obviously take advantage of it.

Tip #8. Read Each Question Carefully, and Answer the Question Asked

When we talk to our friends and colleagues in legal academia about this book, 99 out of 100 tell us the same thing: The single most important advice for students is that they should *Answer the question!* You have probably heard the adage that the three most important considerations in a real estate deal are "location, location, location." Here, of course, the three most important things about exam-taking are "answer the question, answer the question, answer the question."

We have always resisted the urge to suggest to our more aggressive "Socratic" colleagues that students bucking this advice may simply be channeling the professor's own dogged refusal to answer any student questions in class. But given the stakes, we doubt that the typical failure to "answer the question asked" is the result of a rebellious attempt to turn the tables on the teacher. Moreover, given the obvious facility of most of our students with exams—you wouldn't be in law school if you hadn't done pretty well as an undergraduate and/or on a standardized exam like the LSAT—we also doubt that the problem lies in students' ability to answer exam questions. Instead, we think that the most common problem is that students *misunderstand* what it is that our questions are asking. Here are some brief suggestions for how to avoid falling into this trap.

Read each question carefully and *at least* twice

We've all been there: It's the final exam in your most challenging course. The proctor reviews the instructions and then signals the start of the test. You begin reading the first question, which is a complex factual scenario that goes on for a dozen paragraphs over two single-spaced pages. You're halfway through the question when you are distracted by a familiar but in this context most distressing sound: 101 sets of fingers begin clicking their keyboards. "Oh no," a little voice in your head exclaims. "They're all already busy racking up the points, and you're the only one *in the entire class* who is still reading the question! You'd better stop reading and start writing right now, or you won't stand a chance!"

While the sense of panic is a common and entirely reasonable response to the stress of the exam setting, you simply must find a way to muzzle that little voice, because the surest path to failure is to heed its advice. Simply put, you can't possibly answer the question asked unless you know what that question is, and it will take even the most gifted student two (and sometimes more) extremely careful readings to gain the necessary purchase on what the professor is asking.

Of course, you shouldn't overdo it; the point is to understand the question well enough to answer it, not to commit it to memory. And obviously you need to leave yourself adequate time to write, since grades are based on what's in your answers, not what's in your head.

But pay no heed to those around you who have rushed through the reading and are already typing away: A one-page answer that directly addresses the question asked is worth far more than a dozen pages of unresponsive blather, and in our experience the race for superior grades is won far more often by the conscientious turtle than by the careless hare.

Not every question is an issue spotter

The classic law exam question is the so-called issue spotter—i.e., the extended factual scenario that broadly invites the student to "discuss the legal issues" raised by the facts. Faced with such a question, the soundest strategy may well be to "throw in everything but the kitchen sink": i.e., to identify and, to the extent time permits, analyze each and every plausible legal issue that you can uncover. But many of the exam questions you'll encounter in law school are not nearly so open-ended. Even issue spotters frequently restrict you to an analysis of the rights and liabilities of specifically identified parties—for example, a complicated Torts question may feature a cast of more than a dozen but ask you to discuss the legal rights of only Shaniqua and Henry. Other common kinds of questions ask you to analyze a particular legal issue ("does X have a valid claim for adverse possession of Blackacre?") or to respond to a specific legal argument ("if Y claims that evidence of those prior negotiations is barred by the parol evidence rule, how should Z respond?").

Students who've embraced the "kitchen sink" strategy for open-ended issue spotters may have great difficulty shifting gears to cope with narrower and more specific questions such as these. But an answer that discusses the rights of Aaron (when the question restricts you to Shaniqua and Henry) or that analyzes the broad implications of consideration doctrine (when the question focuses on parol evidence) will persuade the grader that you didn't read the question she labored long and hard to draft, or that you didn't understand it, or that you are simply unable (or too stubborn) to answer it. When she grades such an answer, it's safe to say that she won't come up with what *you* were looking for either!

Avoid the "outline dump"

Since you were likely successful as an undergraduate, you have probably developed a facility for absorbing vast quantities of information and "giving it all back on the final." And because your undergraduate success helped you get into law school, you might reasonably expect that law exams would reward a similar form of regurgitation. Indeed, that expectation is frequently reinforced by second- and third-year students who tell the newbies that the thing to do on the final is to "show the professor you understood the course." But once again, the thing to do on the final is *to answer the question asked*. The student who ignores the question asked and responds instead by "giving it all back" will get nowhere fast.

Don't fight the question or reargue points already settled

One of the law school classroom's first lessons is to take nothing for granted, for the clever professor can take a judicial opinion that is seemingly focused exclusively on (say) whether a child can intend a battery and unearth a host of questionable assumptions made by the parties and the court (e.g., perhaps no one considered whether the victim's "horsing around" with the child just before the battery constituted "consent").

But this is yet another lesson that can get you in trouble on a law exam. Thus, if an exam question states that A has established B's liability for breach of contract and asks you to calculate the resulting damages, you would be making a serious mistake if you tried to reopen the question of liability in your answer. At best, you will waste precious time by trying to prove a point that the question has already settled. At worst, you will "fight the question" and conclude that B is *not* liable to A and thus that the professor's question regarding damages is beside the point.

To be sure, there is always the chance that you are right—that the professor has made a mistake and will reward your careful reading of the facts and perceptive conclusion. (See FAQ #4, "What If You Think the *Professor* Has Made a Mistake?") But 99 times out of 100 it is the student who has made the mistake by fighting—rather than answering—the question the professor has asked.

In a pinch, push harder, but don't B.S.

Of course, sometimes the reason that a student doesn't answer the question asked is that she doesn't *know* the answer to the question asked. Our advice here: Push harder and harder on the question, and resist the growing temptation to talk about something else. If, for example, you read a question on your Torts exam and you aren't sure what the issue is—let alone what to do with it—you should re-read the question, slowly and carefully, and then work your way back through your course outline (or your recollection of the outline if the exam is closed book) until you figure out something pertinent to say. You'll be surprised how often a question that initially seems a mystery becomes clearer as you dive in. But the very last thing you should do is draft a lecture on the history or the deep philosophical underpinnings of tort law in the hopes that *something* you say will "stick" or impress the reader. The professor will know exactly what you are up to and is likely to give you a far lower grade for your efforts than the student who at least attempts, however unsuccessfully, to grapple with the question asked. (See Tip #24, "Don't B.S.")

Tip #9. Organize and Outline Before Writing Your Answer

It takes unusual self-discipline to refrain from writing long enough to organize your thoughts. But it's well worth the effort. Law school exams, like most mental puzzles, are easier to understand if you break the problem into steps.

Suppose you are planning a trip to three foreign cities over 12 days, and your best friend asks you for a preview. You might start out by listing your plans for each day of the trip ("Well, on Sunday we'll do this . . . on Monday that . . . ," etc.). But your friend would find it much easier to follow if you started by saying something like, "My trip will last 12 days, four days each in Rome, Paris, and London." Then, as you moved into describing your itinerary for Rome, your friend would have a context to understand the trip as a whole. Better still, you'd have an easier way of remembering your plans.

Precisely the same advantages stem from outlining your exam answers. You can quickly hit the main points and place sub-issues under their correct categories. This is much easier to do before you actually begin writing. We know that you're under a great deal of time pressure to begin writing and that you won't get any credit for things you consider while outlining and then forget to include in your answer. (See Tip #12, "Explain Your Reasoning.") But virtually every professor prefers an organized essay, and outlining is the best way to provide one.

Outlining keeps you focused on the main ideas

Few aspects of law school exams are more daunting than the lengthy hypothetical with many characters, many events, and even more legal issues. It's tempting to think that unless you plunge right in, you may not have time to discuss everything. The problem, of course, is that even if you do plunge right in, you *still* may not have time to discuss everything. And you may find yourself devoting 30 minutes to the issue that happens to pop into your head first.

You simply can't afford to let the question bully you like this. Instead, take a few moments to consider the big picture. What are the three or four most important issues? Can other aspects of the question be grouped as "sub-parts" of these issues? Jot down a quick outline to this effect and then begin writing. Your outline will ensure that your answer is well organized and that you have time for the key issues.

Outlining helps you think sequentially

Another major virtue of outlining is that it will force you to consider the proper order in which to take up the issues. Every question has its own internal logic that makes it easier to take up certain issues first. For example, if the plaintiff's standing is at issue in a Con Law question, you might analyze standing at the beginning of your answer because the case cannot proceed without it. Outlining your answer won't guarantee that you will find the best sequence. But you are a great deal more likely to choose well if you pause to think before writing, rather than just diving in and discussing issues at random.

Outlining helps you avoid wrong turns

One way in which sequencing turns out to be very important is that the resolution of some issues makes other issues less pressing, sometimes even irrelevant. On the first read of a lengthy issue spotter on your Torts exam, for example, the causation issue may scream out at you for lengthy discussion. But careful outlining may lead you to conclude that negligence is the appropriate standard by which to judge the defendant's conduct and that the defendant most certainly was not negligent. If that analysis is correct, then the question whether the defendant's action caused the plaintiff's injury is immaterial. You should certainly still flag it, partly to rack up points for issue spotting and even more to hedge your bet in the event that your analysis of the negligence issue turns out to be wrong. But if you're right—and if neglecting to outline let you focus on causation, thereby missing the negligence issue—then you would have done poorly on the question, even if your discussion of causation had been first-rate.

In short, outlining can help you avoid getting sidetracked on issues that grab your attention but turn out to matter less when you've thought the answer all the way through.

Outlining helps you draft a road map

In the end, your goal is not merely to think through the answer, but to let your professor in on all that thinking as well. Your answer will accomplish that task far more efficiently if it begins with a couple of sentences explaining the major issues you will discuss and how they may fit together. Your outline, therefore, won't merely help you in your own thinking as you begin writing; it may also serve as the basis for an introductory paragraph that puts the entire question into perspective for the grader. In short, it will help you keep the forest in mind as you begin telling your professor about the trees.

Tip #10. Provide the Reader with a Brief Road Map

There's no better way to launch an exam answer than with an opening paragraph that sets forth clearly the issues you plan to discuss. This assures the reader that the main issues will be considered and signals the order in which to expect them. Some questions will be so short that no introductory road map is necessary, and in that setting drafting one may even needlessly slow you down. Never underestimate, however, the power of an introductory paragraph that confidently begins, "In this essay, I will address the following four points...."

Create a strong first impression

Suppose your professor is grading an essay answer on a Property exam. The question instructs students to discuss three theories the plaintiff can use to seek access to the defendant's land. Predictably, and regrettably, a large number of students will spend all their time on only one theory, and some won't discuss the issue of plaintiff's access at all.

Consider then how happy your grader will be when she encounters an opening paragraph that begins like this: "Plaintiff can seek access to defendant's land based on (1) the common law right of access to public places; (2) a statutory right to access on the ground that defendant has discriminated against her 'on the basis of sex'; and (3) a constitutional right to access for purposes of exercising her state-protected free speech rights." Whatever comes next, this student will already have established her ability to answer the question directly and to have identified three plausible theories.

First impressions like this are extraordinarily important. It's true you can make the same points by discussing theory (1) before you even mention theory (2) or (3). But consider the advantage of signaling the professor who is reading your analysis of the first theory that the rest of what she's looking for is on its way as well.

Put ideas in groups

An introductory road map is even more helpful when there is a long list of things that you plan to discuss. As your professor reads through your analysis of nine different issues, she may not even remember Issue #3 by the time she finishes reading Issue #8. You can help her out quite a bit simply by listing Issues 1 through 9 at the beginning of your answer. But you can do even better than that by finding some way to break the nine items into smaller subgroups.

Consider the fact that most people remember Social Security and phone numbers not by committing nine or ten individual digits to memory, but by dividing such numbers into three smaller groups. You can take advantage of this form of information processing if you can find a way to use subgroups in your road map. For example:

I will discuss (1) THE JUSTICIABILITY OF THE PLAINTIFF'S CASE—where issues of standing, mootness, and ripeness are the relevant sub-issues; (2) THE MERITS OF PLAINTIFF'S EQUAL PROTECTION CLAIM—where I'll consider in turn plaintiff's claimed loss of a fundamental right; his membership in a suspect class; and his victimization at the hands of an irrational government; and (3) PLAINTIFF'S DUE PROCESS CLAIM—where I'll analyze first the plaintiff's claim to a property interest; the possible benefits of an earlier hearing; and finally the government's claim it needs to act with dispatch.

Note that this approach goes a long way toward organizing the ensuing argument for the reader, leaving her less likely to get lost in the details. (And little tricks like using all capital letters to distinguish the major groupings from the sub-issues may also prove helpful with some professors, though others may feel like you are insulting their intelligence or needlessly yelling at them.)

Organize your own thoughts at the beginning and the end

Another advantage to an opening paragraph that provides a road map is that it encourages you to stop and think before writing. (See Tip #9, "Organize and Outline Before Writing Your Answer.") You can't write an opening description of what you plan to say unless you have thought through your answer all the way to the end. And once you are finished writing, you can go back to the initial road map and use it as a checklist to see if you have covered all the points you listed as important.

You may, however, find it enormously difficult to provide a clear road map as you begin your essay. Only after wrestling the key issues to the ground will you know for sure what the main points are. In that case, simply go back and insert the road map after you have written the rest of the answer. As it happens, this is the technique many attorneys use, adding a "summary of the argument" only after they have finished writing the body of an appellate brief. But even if you add it after the fact, drafting the road map will force you to think about the question from a big-picture perspective and help you present your answer as a well-organized whole.

Tip #11. Tackling the *Déjà Vu* Exam Question: Looking for Similarities as Well as Differences

An extremely common form of exam question offers a fact pattern that resembles the facts of one of the cases studied in the course and presents a dispute that will come out one way if courts follow the studied case and come out the other way if instead they distinguish it. We have several suggestions for writing "A" answers to such questions.

Wherein we deliver the bad news yet again

First and most obviously, you're unlikely to see the resemblance between the exam problem and the case unless you studied the case in the first place, so here's another pitch for doing the assigned readings and coming to class prepared. If you're looking for a way to avoid all that work, you're going to need a different book on law exams.

Desperately seeking similarities

If you think you may have seen a scenario like this before but are having a difficult time coming up with the right case, try isolating a particular dimension of the problem and searching your mind (or, better yet, your outline if the exam is open book) for the place you've seen it: the *transactional setting* giving rise to the problem (is this a construction subcontracting dispute?; a problem resulting from blasting or dangerous explosives?; a conflict over a defect the purchaser of residential real estate discovered only after taking title to the property?). If that doesn't do the trick, consider *the kind of legal problem* to which the facts appear to give rise (e.g., offer and acceptance? causation? title defects?); or even *the cause of action* or *legal theory* that is likely in play (e.g., promissory estoppel? *res ipsa loquitur*? adverse possession?). Narrowing the search field in this way is the best trick we know for prompting recall of a case that's just out of mental reach.

Diving for differences and a professorial secret

We'll start with the secret: No self-respecting law professor would ever give an exam question in which the facts are a 100% match with a case assigned in the course. (We already know how *that* case came out.) As a consequence, there will *always* be differences from the case somewhere in the problem: a child causes an elderly relative to fall to the ground, not by pulling out her chair but by shooting off a cap gun just behind her; the hunt is for a protected species (like a wild stallion) rather than for a fox; and so on. So if you don't see the difference(s) at first, read the problem again slowly and carefully. It's in there somewhere.

Getting to maybe for the win

Students still in the thrall of the search for "right" answers common on undergrad exams may be tempted to embrace the similarities and ignore the differences ("follow the case and rule for A!") or to highlight the differences and downplay the similarities ("nothing to see here, so rule for B!"). But the "A" answers will thoroughly canvass similarities *as well as* differences, and whatever they sacrifice in the quest for certainty they more than make up for with law school success.

Yoda's refrain: "There is another"

A common variation on questions that turn on following or distinguishing a single case is construction of fact patterns that fall "between" two cases you've studied, resembling Case A in some respects (and thus calling for a conclusion in favor of one party) yet resembling Case B in other respects (and thus suggesting the opposite outcome). The key here is (you guessed it) getting to maybe all over again. The problem will never be a perfect match with either one of the cases, and thus your analysis should be searching for similarities as well as differences with respect to each case.

Tip #12. Explain Your Reasoning

No matter how many rules you know or how insightful your analysis, you get credit for only what you actually write in your answers. It is therefore crucial to reduce to writing the thought process that leads you to your conclusions.

In mathematics, you have a chance of getting the right answer through the wrong reasoning. In chess, you might make the correct move without understanding why. But in law, an "answer" is useful only if those expected to follow the law can be made to understand *why* that result was reached. A core lawyering skill is formulating explanations to clarify the law for judges, for clients, and for the public at large. Your professor will demand that you start giving those explanations now.

Explain to show what you are thinking

Legal conclusions are often based on chains of reasoning with many "links" or steps. Even if you reach the end result that corresponds to the professor's own conclusion, your answer won't get you the grade you want unless you show just how you got there.

Consider a hypothetical statute that you are asked to analyze on your Constitutional Law exam. After some careful thinking, you conclude the statute violates the equal protection clause. So you write, "The equal protection clause has been violated," and you go on to the next question without further explanation. Reading such a response, your professor will have no way of knowing why you see an equal protection clause violation, and she is likely to grade you down even if she agrees with your conclusion. For one thing, she'll want to know what level of scrutiny you think the court should apply to the statute. If your answer is "strict" scrutiny, she'll want to know the basis for that argument. (Are we dealing with a suspect classification? Has a fundamental right been violated?) For another, she'll want to know what justification you think the government will put forth to support the statute and why you think that justification is insufficiently compelling.

This is not simply another case of professorial pickiness! If you went to court to defend an equal protection claim, the judge would ask you about all of these issues, and the bald assertion that the equal protection clause has been violated—without some further explanation—would do little to advance your client's cause. Likewise, a bald assertion on a law exam is unlikely to persuade the professor that you've mastered the course material. The more reasoning you show, the better you'll do.

Explain to improve your analysis

A major advantage of working hard to show your reasoning is that it will enhance your understanding of the problem presented. Everyone has had the experience of making up one's mind and then changing it after discovering problems while attempting to defend the original position in writing. As you force yourself to articulate each step in the reasoning process, you give yourself a chance to question each part of your conclusion.

For example, if in defending the view that the equal protection clause has been violated you force yourself to explain in writing the government's interest in the challenged statute, you might discover a more compelling interest than you initially realized. Similarly, on a Contracts exam, if you try to marshal the facts that support your initial conclusion that a material breach has occurred, this effort might help you to spot circumstances suggesting that the performance was "close enough for government work."

In short, explaining your reasoning is the best way to spot flaws in your own thinking. Best of all, as the strength of the positions you have rejected comes into view, you're likely to feel a greater need to explain why you reached your conclusion and dismissed other alternatives. Only if you carefully spell out your reasoning from beginning to end will you have earned confidence in your results.

Explain to counteract mistakes

As we've said, you will do poorly if you reach the right answer but don't explain why. Imagine, then, how your professor will react if you reach the wrong conclusion and provide no accompanying explanation. Since she can't read your mind and the only thing you put in writing was wrong, you are unlikely to get any credit at all.

By contrast, since most professors are more interested in the quality of your explanation than in the correctness of your conclusion, they're likely to award substantial credit for even a "wrong" answer that is accompanied by a cogent, if ultimately unpersuasive, argument. Indeed, since most law school exam questions present issues that could fairly be decided either way, you are likely to be safe with *whatever* conclusion you reach, whereas you are sure to be penalized if you fail to explain your reasoning. That's another reason not to fret about putting your cards on the table.

Make your assumptions explicit

Your thinking about the facts of the question is just as important as your thoughts about the law. If you argue that a federal statute pre-empts a state statute because it would not be possible to comply with both si-multaneously, be sure to explain why, as a practical matter, you think simultaneous compliance is impossible. If you conclude that a contract is voidable because one party was a minor at the time of signing, say so and explain what facts led you to this conclusion.

Making your assumptions explicit in this way may help you spot am-biguities that you missed when you first read the problem. Thus, you may have initially concluded that the plaintiff was a minor because he read comic books and rode a skateboard. Yet as soon as you write this down, you'll realize that some adults do these things. Even if you don't catch mistakes, making your assumptions explicit will ensure that your profes-sor can follow your reasoning, and that's the first step toward top-flight performance.

You have nothing to lose

Even after reading all this, many of you will still want to hold back. After all, you figure that you are more certain of your conclusions than of the reasoning that got you there. The more reasoning you write down, the greater the chance the professor will catch a mistake and discover that you don't know what you are talking about. Why not just take the best guess you can about the ultimate outcome and hope the professor will be charitable and fill in the blanks in your favor?

Because *it won't work*. You can't get away with conclusory answers because, for the vast majority of law exam questions, the professor cares far more about your reasoning than about the conclusions you draw. (See Tip #20, "Avoid Conclusory Answers.") Even a poorly reasoned answer most likely won't hurt you any more—and it may hurt you a lot less—than an answer with no reasons at all. So you might as well take a shot at pro-viding the well-reasoned answer the professor is looking for. That's what law exams are all about.

Tip #13. Draw Conclusions When They Are Called For

Many law school exam questions end with queries like, "If Juan sues Julia for breach of contract, who will prevail and why?" Such questions may cause a sinking feeling in the pit of your stomach. You believe Juan has a strong case, but you see defenses for Julia that might be successful. In truth, you're just not sure who will win.

But worry not, for you're on the right track. Odds are that the professor drafted the question precisely to generate such doubts. Do not, however, let your uncertainty cow you into silence about the outcome. If your professor has asked for a conclusion, don't leave her hanging just because the answer isn't a slam-dunk. Rather, offer your best judgment about the right result while at the same time explaining why you are ultimately unpersuaded by arguments that cut the other way. In the end, you'll have to bite the bullet and embrace one side or the other.

Use life, not school, as your model for dealing with difficult decisions

Many of you remember high school and college exams in which you were asked to solve a series of equations or to remember the precise date of a famous battle. Even if you couldn't quite calculate or remember the answer, you saw the need to venture a guess because there was no substitute for the correct response.

Law school exam questions that pull you simultaneously in opposite directions generate an understandable instinct not to reach *any* conclusions. After all, you have been trained to see what's wrong with each of the available options. Such thinking, however, remains stuck on a vision of exams where you are graded down harshly for mistakes. Think instead about Hamlet's uncertainty ("To be or not to be...") as your model of tragic error.

You wouldn't fail to make a decision affecting your future simply because there was virtue to more than one option. You may, for example, have had to decide whether to attend a private law school or a less expensive state university. Though each option had considerable virtues, either decision might have turned out to be a mistake. But attending no school at all because of the difficulty in choosing is clearly the worst decision of all.

Draw conclusions to enrich your analysis

The greatest virtue of forcing yourself to draw conclusions is that it requires you to ask yourself hard questions. Your professor may have drafted a question for which there is no ready answer. On a Property exam, for example, the language of a document may suggest that the grantor intended to place restrictions on the property, but the general rule abhorring forfeitures may suggest that the document is too ambiguous to create restrictions. You'll probably do well on the exam by spotting and explaining the contradictory interpretations.

But if the question asks for a conclusion, you must force yourself to decide whether this is a case where the grantor's intent or the rule against forfeitures should take precedence. This will force you to describe the reasons behind each rule and to take a stab at which set of reasons seems more compelling under the precise facts given. (Perhaps the forfeiture would be particularly severe, or alternatively perhaps the grantor's intent should take priority because the grant was a gift to charity.) Only by pushing toward a conclusion can you get beyond mere boilerplate recitations of the competing positions.

Say yes to one, but don't leave the other behind

The fact that a question calls for a conclusion means it's not enough to describe the strengths and weaknesses of both positions, however eloquent your descriptions. But don't be lulled into the opposite error of embracing one conclusion and ignoring the very strong points that point in a different direction. (See Tip #14, "Argue Both Sides.") A conclusion isn't well drawn unless it adequately explains why opposing positions were rejected. So as you make your case, be sure to explain not only why you chose the result you did, but also why you rejected alternatives.

Watch your emphasis on reasons vs. results

Any professor who asks you to draw a conclusion will be annoyed if you decide instead to merely recite pros and cons; indeed, some professors will find this thoroughly unacceptable. As always, you should pay careful attention to such professorial preferences and heed your own professor's stance on the need to reach decisive conclusions. (See Tip #16, "Remember Who Your 'Judge' Is.")

The same is true when it comes to emphasis. All professors will look at your reasons and your results, but what may vary is the emphasis individual graders will place on each. In general, we recommend that you never draw conclusions without reasons and that you worry more about reasons than results. But we also urge you to pay special attention to what's expected by *your* grader and adjust your emphasis accordingly.

Tip #14. Argue Both Sides

Law is a vehicle for resolving conflict through peaceful means. Accordingly, every legal problem begins with an actual or potential disagreement between people. When a client walks into your office to tell you about a dispute, you will invariably learn a little about the party "on the other side" whose views and interests are likely to differ greatly from your client's. Good legal advice will follow only if you can grasp the problem from your client's point of view *and* from her potential adversary's perspective.

Indeed, the capacity to see and argue both sides of a case is perhaps the most important reasoning skill you will develop in law school, and so you can't expect to pick it up by reading a brief "tip," however insightfully it is written! But what we can tell you is that your professors have struggled hard to invent questions that present a real challenge. They will be disappointed if you seize on some facts and arguments while ignoring others to reach a quick, one-sided conclusion. Instead, start by following these steps to ensure that your exam performance doesn't end up disappointing you as well.

Consider each person's perspective

The best way to ensure that you argue both sides is to imagine how the loser might respond to your initial foray favoring the opposing party. If your first instinct is that Juan is liable to Julia because he obviously breached their contract, ask yourself what Juan would have to say. Why *didn't* he deliver the widgets on time? Perhaps he thought they didn't really have a deal. Is there any basis for this view? Perhaps he thought Julia was supposed to call to confirm her order, or that they had additional details to work out, or that his obligation depended on some contingency that had not occurred.

The point is that in the real world there are almost always two sides to a story. On a law exam you can virtually count on that to be the case—and for good reason. To be sure, clients call on lawyers to help them with routine situations in which the rights and obligations of the parties are undeniably clear-cut. But law school would be unworthy of its status as a professional school, let alone of its place in a university, if it did not prepare you to confront the more complicated situations in which *both* parties may rightfully lay claim to some version of law and justice. Your task is to show just how each side would do so.

Seize on contradictory facts

Contradictions make many people uncomfortable. Readers of a novel in which the main character is described as generous on page 27 and stingy on page 115 might conclude the author was asleep at the wheel. We all recognize that people have contradictory characteristics, but we'd at least expect the novelist to try to reconcile them—e.g., by explaining that our hero was usually generous but stingy when it came to his own children.

On law school exams, however, you should treat apparent contradictions as cause for celebration. Suppose Demetri grants his neighbor, Wilma, what the parties term "a perpetual easement" to use Demetri's driveway for Wilma's wheelchair-accessible van. This part of the document makes it look as though Demetri intends the easement to last forever, and that it will thus be available for use by the next owner of Wilma's home who also wants access to the adjacent driveway. Suppose, however, that the same document begins with the words, "Because you, Wilma, are injured and need access to the driveway, I, Demetri, hereby grant you," etc. This part of the document makes it look as though the easement is a "ticket for one train only" and that Demetri wants the easement extinguished if Wilma moves away.

If you were drafting the document, you would do your professional best to avoid such ambiguities. But if you were drafting an exam response to the problem of whether the new owner of Wilma's home can use Demetri's driveway, you should be laughing your way to Law Review. That's because you have unearthed a fact that will help you argue Demetri's position that the easement is extinguished, and also a fact that will help you argue Wilma's position in support of the new owner that the easement "runs with the land."

Facts that send conflicting signals like these are exactly what you must identify to do well on your exam. Instead of ignoring or hiding from them because you find them confusing, you should search them out and exploit them for all they're worth. The professor labored to come up with them. She will be delighted when you highlight the contradictions and disappointed if you don't.

Use tensions in the law to your advantage

The way law pulls you in different directions takes some getting used to. Law embodies conflicting ideals such as liberty and equality. Different jurisdictions have different rules, and sometimes it's hard to tell whether, for example, state or federal law applies. Even case law is famously riddled by questions of which precedent governs.

Each of these tensions may feel like an obstacle to overcome. Who wouldn't wonder which rule really does apply, which ideal should take precedence, or even simply which prior case is controlling? But on an exam, each of these tensions is in fact an opportunity to demonstrate your mastery of the topic. If it appears to you that one important case supports a decision for the plaintiff, while another equally controlling case suggests a decision for the defendant, just *say so*, instead of throwing your hands up in despair. You are far more likely to be rewarded for identifying both points of view than you are to be graded down for your failure to reach a conclusion in which you can be 100% confident.

After all, law is a human invention designed to resolve an extraordinary range of human conflict. How could we expect it to produce simple answers in such a complex world?

Find something interesting in the question

Once upon a time you took exams that asked you straightforward questions like "name the state capital of Florida." (Tallahassee was worth 10 points—only five if the exam you took was at FSU.) But if a law professor were drafting that geography exam, she would be far more likely to complicate matters considerably by telling you that a legislative task force has decided that the state capital must be relocated and has asked you, as its chief counsel, to draft a memorandum identifying the most desirable alternative site.

An answer like "the capital of Florida should be Miami because it's the state's largest city" has the advantage of coherence, but it lacks depth. It would help if you were to add that it makes sense to have the capital be the state's largest city because today's global economy demands concentration of financial, political, and human resources. But your answer won't get interesting until you can identify a second theory that rivals the first. Maybe the capital should be Orlando, since it's more centrally located and citizens have a right to easy access to the seat of government. Only when two plausible rival theories have been identified can a productive debate occur and an interesting analysis emerge.

So, too, when professors draft law exams. For every question you read, you should ask yourself why the professor found this particular set of facts interesting. What are the competing understandings of or approaches to the case that caused the professor to ask about *this* fact pattern rather than another?

For example, if a question about landlord/tenant law involves a live-in babysitter, the odds are pretty good that the professor is interested not only in a straightforward application of the landlord/tenant rules, but also in the "big picture" question of whether those rules should apply in this unusual setting. Most professors will be looking for you to present the case for the routine application of the rules as well as the case for a special "live-in babysitter" exception, so that you can demonstrate an awareness of the choice to be made and the pros and cons of each approach. Arguing both sides, then, is a technique that can help you remember that law is about choices and that hard choices make the most interesting exam questions.

Tip #15. Stick to the Facts Presented

We know it's annoying to receive seemingly contradictory messages from your professors. "Be creative," we say. "Show some inventiveness, some imagination." And then as soon as you start strutting your stuff, we turn around and plead that you stick to the question at hand. But you really *can* satisfy both demands, as long as you keep the following points in mind.

Analogize, don't digress

Perhaps the most common form of legal analysis is the analogy. This case is *like* that case, lawyers argue, and therefore this case should be *decided* the same way that one was. Indeed, if the two cases are enough alike, the argument from analogy even gets its own fancy Latin name: *stare decisis*. As a result, the ability to identify analogous cases and situations is a vital skill, on law exams as well as in legal practice. Never forget, however, that the point of an analogy is to help you resolve the problem at hand, not to show off how much you know about some other situation.

Let's say, for example, that you get a Property exam question about parents who want to fire their live-in babysitter. The sitter claims that as a "tenant" she can't be evicted from the parents' home. She argues that her poor job performance was effectively a withholding of rent to protest the failure of her live-in quarters to comply with the warranty of habitability. In the course in question—as in many first-year Property courses—the students read *State v. Shack*, in which the New Jersey Supreme Court upheld the right of migrant workers living on their employer's property to receive visitors but declined to grant them "tenant" status. If your answer cites *Shack* for the proposition that the sitter's claim to tenancy faces an uphill climb—if migrant workers couldn't pull it off, she's even less likely to succeed—the professor will be suitably impressed. But she'll be downright annoyed if you devote three pages to the facts of *Shack*, to how the case fits in with other cases involving the rights of owners to exclude, and how it illustrates a judicial tendency to avoid constitutional issues. The professor wants to know about the *sitter's* rights—not about *State v. Shack*—and you shouldn't lose sight of that.

Be careful with the word "if"

Make up your mind which issues in the question present genuine ambiguities with plausible arguments on each side and which issues are easily resolved by existing law. For ambiguous situations, the word "if" is important, even essential. You will often find yourself writing sentences such as, "If the grantor is found to have intended that the covenant run with the land, then the new owner won't be able to violate the restriction." Here your biggest concern is to make sure you identify the facts that make the issue ambiguous and to explain what difference the competing resolutions will make to the outcome of the case.

In many cases, however, issues fairly raised by the question will be entirely clear. There may be a contract dispute between two experienced business persons who obviously fit the definition of merchant under the Uniform Commercial Code. You may be very proud of yourself for knowing the rule for nonmerchants, and therefore tempted to throw in a dangerous sentence such as, "If the parties were not merchants, then the rule would be thus and so." Or the plaintiff in an equal protection suit may be a white male. You are still feeling the thrill of learning the categories whereby equal protection suits are judged differently when brought by women or Blacks. You wonder how it could hurt to throw in sentences with beginnings such as, "If the plaintiff were Black." "If" phrases like these could hurt a lot. When the professor writes a question about merchants, she wants an analysis of merchants (and of course you should point out that you are applying the merchant rule). When the professor makes the plaintiff a white male, that's the situation he wants resolved. If you aren't careful, your professor's reaction may be something like, "If you had stuck to the facts and circumstances of the question, you might have done very well!"

Invent solutions, not scenarios

It is one thing, and generally a good thing, to invent multiple ways that a court or other decision-maker might respond to the set of facts presented in your exam question. You can do this successfully by considering various theories of liability or different remedies a court might impose. It's entirely another thing, and one you should stay away from, to invent ways that courts might respond to sets of facts that are different from those presented in the question. You might have a brilliant theory for how a court should handle the scenario in which a tenant is evicted for engaging in union organizing. But if the tenant in your question is evicted because his kid writes on the walls, that's the scenario you should discuss.

Don't write treatises about the law

The most common rookie mistake in exam-taking is ignoring the particular facts in the problem presented and offering instead a long series of general statements of law. Such answers often start off on the right foot. You read the question and correctly identify the legal issues involved. So, for example, you might observe that a dispute between neighbors over a loud radio could give rise to a nuisance suit. At this point, however, you launch into a lengthy discussion of the definition of nuisance and a description of all the nuisance cases covered in the course. This discussion wastes valuable time and takes you away from the problem presented. You may know a great deal of nuisance law, but the professor wants to hear only the parts relevant to the question at hand.

Tip #16. Remember Who Your "Judge" Is

Your law school exam is intended for an audience of one: the professor who will grade it. This is not wholly unrealistic preparation for law practice, where you will frequently find yourself trying to persuade a particular decision-maker, such as a trial judge. But for better or worse, law students have only one person to please. Don't forget these tips for doing so.

Follow your professor's advice and directives

No matter how much time we spend writing about exam excellence, this is the most important advice we can give you. Listen carefully to every word your professor says about what she wants in an exam and try to provide it. If your professor tells you that she cares most about your listing the elements of a cause of action, then forget everything you read—either here in these tips or elsewhere in this or any book—and list those elements. Your professor is in charge of your course, and it's your job to show you can play by her rules. And in case we haven't said it often enough, the clearest instruction your professor gives you on every exam is the language of the exam question itself. Pay close attention to the way the question is phrased and what the professor is looking for. Follow those instructions to the absolute best of your ability. (See Tip #8, "Read Each Question Carefully, and Answer the Question Asked.")

Think about your professor's style

It's dangerous to leap too quickly from superficial characteristics to a professor's exam preferences. Thus, your professor might arrive every day in a suit and tie or a fancy dress yet be relatively relaxed when it comes to what's expected in terms of writing style on the exam. It makes most sense to listen to what the professor actually says she wants. There is, nonetheless, something to be gained by attempting to draw some exam lessons from the way she conducts the course. If every day's class is spent on refining the holdings of cases, it's safe to assume the professor cares a lot about your ability to do so. If the professor cares in class about mastery of detail and gives a closed-book exam, then you'd better be careful throwing around details you don't quite remember. If a professor appears very interested in policy arguments, then you should find a way to work them in. And if a professor appears to value in-class creativity, then keep your imagination humming from beginning to end on exam day.

Look for course topics and themes

The increasing amount of material covered in law school courses makes it difficult for everything from your course to be tested on the exam. Nonetheless, if your Constitutional Law class spent eight weeks studying the commerce clause and you read over the exam and can't find it, read the exam again. It's unlikely your professor would have failed to test a topic on which she had chosen to spend half the course. Equally important, if your professor stresses certain themes—such as the role of the states as laboratories for government experimentation—look carefully to see if those themes have resurfaced on the exam. Law school courses vary: Some emphasize a steady diet of rules, while others hunt for an organizing principle or a set of themes. Ask yourself how your professor has approached the course, and make sure to see if you can approach the exam the same way.

Disagree freely but knowledgeably

Occasionally a professor will ask a more open-ended policy question that asks you to draw a conclusion about an issue you have studied. Suppose, for example, your Property teacher asks whether rent control should be abolished. One fear you may have is that your professor's liberal pro-tenant views may conflict with your position that rent control is counterproductive. Get over it! The overwhelming majority of professors are happy to read exams that disagree with their position. Your exam-taking concern should never be which side of an argument you are on, but only on what you can offer to support your side.

Keep the pace fast and focus on the issues in dispute

On a law exam, you get credit for analysis and argument, not for recapitulating or regurgitating law, facts, or the contents of an outline. Accordingly, an answer that begins with a two-paragraph lecture on the applicable law—or, even worse, on *in*applicable law—or with an extended regurgitation of the facts will force the professor to wade through a large block of material that won't do your grade any good even if it's accurate and can hurt you a lot if it's *in*accurate. (We address these points at greater length in Tip #18 ("Don't Regurgitate Legal Rules and Principles") and Tip #19 ("Don't Repeat the Facts").) Get to the point as fast as you can, and devote your precious writing time to the issues that produce real "maybes"—that is, the issues the parties' lawyers would argue about if this were a real case.

A sense of humor can help

Let's be clear. You want above all to stick to the point and to focus your response on answering the question asked. If you are tempted to make a joke and in doubt about whether it's in good taste, don't do it. Why risk irritating a professor who may take offense and may be unimpressed by the digression? That said, if you find easy ways to sprinkle in a little humor that's unlikely to offend the grader's sensibilities, by all means, do so. Your professors often endeavor to place a few amusing diversions in the exam questions. Perhaps the character names on the exam come from a recent hit movie or TV show. Letting us know you noticed or giving us a chuckle won't rescue a bad exam. But at the margins it certainly can't hurt if the professor is smiling as she evaluates your answer.

Tip #17. Watch Time/Credit Allocations

Most law school exams are time-pressured, some quite drastically so. Accordingly, your professor is unlikely to be impressed if you write solid answers to two of the three essay questions and handle the third one with a big, bold "OUT OF TIME." It's virtually impossible to score well if you receive no credit for an entire question, and there's no reason this should happen to you. Here are ways to avoid it.

Put your agony on paper

All of you are accustomed to doing well on exams, and most are accustomed to exams in which knowing the answer is the key. Because law exams demand analysis, not answers, there's an understandable tendency to freeze when you read a question and are genuinely not sure about the answer. Say the question on a Con Law exam asks whether the plaintiff has standing. You see a strong case that the plaintiff is "injured in fact," but you're not sure the defendant is the cause of the injury. Odds are that your uncertainty is the result of a question that the professor has deliberately drafted to invite more than one plausible conclusion. If you write down *why* you aren't sure, you are probably providing the kind of answer the professor is hoping for. But even if you're just confused—standing isn't an easy topic for any of us to master—you'll do much better writing something than nothing. The key here is that genuine uncertainty about the legal result is exactly what the professor is attempting to create. If that uncertainty makes you feel bad, writing down why is your best revenge.

Adopt a speedy style

Consider the chess concept of *tempo*, which stresses executing your plan with sufficient speed to finish before your opponent completes hers. This means, for example, that if you are trying to move your pieces into the center and trying to defend pieces your opponent has threatened, it's great to find a move that simultaneously defends and develops a piece in the center.

The law exam equivalent is to learn to write with sentences that accomplish several things at once. Thus, there's little advantage to a writing style that begins by listing various components of a legal doctrine and then proceeds to analyze them. Compare a slow-style response to a fast one for the opening of an answer responding to a hypo involving a research scientist turned down for a government grant who alleges her application was denied for political reasons.

> *Slow*: The Supreme Court in *Allen v. Wright* identified three factors to determine whether a plaintiff has standing: (1) has the plaintiff suffered injury in fact? (2) is the defendant's injury caused by the defendant's conduct? and (3) if the plaintiff prevails, can the court provide a remedy that will adequately redress plaintiff's grievance? Under the first factor we see that the plaintiff has suffered an injury because she sought grant funds and received none. Under the second factor, plaintiff has greater difficulty because she may not be able to show that she would have received the grant were it not for the illegitimate political reasons. The third factor is also problematic, because even if

the court were to find the grant denial improper, no grant funds may remain to award to the disappointed applicant.

Fast: There's no question about the plaintiff's injury (she failed to get the grant), so the real problems with establishing standing are proving causation (there's no guarantee plaintiff would have received the grant even if the process had been free of taint) and demonstrating redressability (there may be no grant funds left to award to the disappointed applicant).

The fast answer has *tempo* because it combines a demonstration of knowledge with an analysis of the problem rather than attempting to perform these tasks separately.

Force yourself to move on

There's not much more to say than that. If you have 10 more points to make about Question 2 and only 30 minutes left, do you think those 10 points will help you more than spending the same 30 minutes on Question 3, which you haven't even begun? If you've been writing about Question 2 for an hour, odds are you have already covered the main points. If you haven't, spend five more minutes on a quick outline of these points, and move on.

Outline when you must

If you are running out of time, you may need to resort to outlining to finish an answer. Make no mistake about the limits of the outline format in the law exam setting: Your answer will be graded on the basis of the quality of the analysis and the cogency of the arguments, and an outline is a poor vehicle for anything more than issue spotting and argument-bites. But the professor can't grade what you don't include in your answer, so an outline in service of a last-minute scramble for points is infinitely superior to blank space. To outline, merely identify the issues you'd discuss in full if you had the time. One neat trick is to list the factors that might push you to one conclusion or the other. For example:

If time allowed, I'd address the issue of whether the plaintiff has standing:

For Standing	Against Standing
For Standing	**Against Standing**
injury clear	causation doubtful
clear legal question for court	hard to see court redress
plaintiff clearly not a bystander	

An outline like this may earn you some much-needed issue-spotting points. But beware: Some professors refuse to read answers that aren't written in prose, and virtually all vastly prefer analysis and arguments to bullet points. So while this strategy can sometimes save the day, you should employ it only in a pinch.

Looking for more detailed advice on writing exam answers?
We devote all of Chapter Thirteen to the subject!

Appendix C

Mistakes to Avoid

Like all endeavors, law school exams offer endless opportunities for mistakes, from the simplest failure to read the question to the subtlest misunderstanding of complex legal doctrine. Certain errors, however, repeatedly appear, in large part because professors are asking you to do things on law school exams that differ markedly from what you did in college and even from what you've done in your legal research and writing courses. Here are some mistakes we have seen frequently in the course of grading thousands of exams.

Tip #18. Don't Regurgitate Legal Rules and Principles

We noted in Tip #1, "Exam Preparation Takes All Semester," and you have no doubt already discerned, that merely memorizing and restating rules won't get you very far in class discussion. It won't get you very far in the exam setting either, for on the one hand "the rules" *are not enough* and on the other "the rules" *are way too much* when it comes to writing law exams. Here's how you can learn to avoid both pitfalls.

Rules are not enough, Part I: You get credit for *applying* the law, not for regurgitating it

Unless you decide to specialize in handling the legal problems of first-year law students, chances are you'll never have a client walk into your office and ask, "What are the seven elements of adverse possession?"

Instead, most clients will offer up "facts"—events that have already taken place or things that they think (or worry) might happen—and ask you to explain the legal implications and consequences.

Imagine, for example, that a client tells you that he and his brother have been mooring their sailboat at a seemingly abandoned dock near their beach house for the past eight summers, and that they want to know the risks of spending a substantial sum to fix up the dock. It may be useful to briefly explain the concept of adverse possession and to describe the elements, but if you stopped there, you wouldn't have helped the client with his problem. What will help him is an analysis that *applies* each of the elements to the particular facts and circumstances he has presented. (They moor at the dock only in the summer; would that constitute "continuous use"? Does merely tying the boat to the dock establish "actual possession"?)

So, too, with a law exam presenting this client's problem as a question. While a brief explanation of adverse possession and a listing of the elements may be a good starting point, what separates the superior answer from the barely passing answer is the ability to apply those legal concepts to the facts and, in particular, to identify the difficulties or ambiguities that might arise in the course of that application.

Rules are not enough, Part II: An ounce of analysis is worth a pound of law

If you weren't successful as an undergraduate, you wouldn't be in law school today. Yet frequently undergraduate success is the result of committing to memory the contents of lectures and readings and parroting those contents back on quizzes and finals. It would therefore be no surprise if you found yourself tempted to deploy the same technique in law school by using the law exam to demonstrate to the professor that you have "learned a lot of law."

The difficulty with this kind of thinking is that although it is indeed necessary to "learn a lot of law" in order to succeed in law school, it is nowhere near sufficient. The typical law exam tests your ability to *use* legal rules and principles to analyze and argue about particular facts and problems. To be sure, you can't use rules you don't know, but merely showing that you "have them in your head"—for example, to continue our illustration, by briefly reciting the elements of adverse possession—is only a start. To excel, you have to show that you know how to apply the rules, and, to do that, you've got to use them to analyze the facts and problems presented in the question.

Rules are too much, Part I: Lengthy quotations of legal rules waste precious time

The typical law school exam is comprised of a set of questions that could easily take you a week or more to answer fully, but—for better or for worse—you have only three or four hours within which to complete your work. As a result, time is at a premium, and you need to use every available minute analyzing the facts presented in light of the legal rules and principles you've learned in your coursework. To be sure, brief quotations of pertinent rules (e.g., the "clear and present danger" test in Constitutional Law or a "definite and seasonable expression of acceptance" under U.C.C. § 2-207 in Contracts) may demonstrate to the grader that you know precisely what is in dispute in a particular problem. But the ability to quote verbatim lengthy excerpts from cases, from statutes, from the federal rules, or from the Restatement would be useful only to a monk copying sacred scripture before the invention of the printing press. For a law student faced with the task of writing an exam, it is of no use at all.

Rules are too much, Part II: A lengthy paraphrase may be even worse than a lengthy quotation

Some students seem to think they will get credit for merely regurgitating legal rules if they put them "in their own words" instead of quoting them verbatim. But this is a lose-lose proposition.

At best, reformulations are merely a waste of time that would be far better spent *applying* the legal rules to the facts presented in the question. (A clever law student could, for example, come up with more than 5,000 ways in which to rearrange the seven elements of adverse possession, but he won't get any credit for such efforts from the professor.)

At worst—and, given the high-pressure setting of a law exam and the formidable challenges of legal drafting, this is an extremely common scenario—the would-be paraphraser will restate the rule incorrectly. If she gets the rule wrong in a way that makes a difference in the analysis of the problem, the mistake may have a devastating effect on her entire answer. But even if she gets the rule wrong in a way that doesn't really matter, her sloppiness is likely to make a poor impression on the grader. Depending on the professor, this may result in points off as well—all for doing something for which she wouldn't get any credit even if she'd done it properly!

Tip #19. Don't Repeat the Facts

In your first-year legal writing course, you may have learned that the best way to begin a legal memorandum is by restating the facts of the problem you've been asked to research. Although this may be a useful format for memo writing, it's a bad way to organize an answer for most law exams. Here's why:

You get credit for *analyzing* the facts, not for copying them into your answers

Clients want their lawyers to help them make legal sense of facts that the clients know all too well. So as law students you can expect to be rewarded for your ability to "make legal sense" out of the facts you're given—i.e., to analyze them in light of the legal principles you have learned in your courses. By contrast, the ability to parrot back facts is useful mostly to a parrot.

Thus, for example, if a hypothetical on a first-year Property exam explicitly states that "Sally holds a vested remainder," the student who begins his answer with "Sally holds a vested remainder" or even "The legal interest that Sally holds is a vested remainder" is going nowhere fast. At the same time, his classmate who starts straight away by discussing the significance of the fact—i.e., by explaining what difference it might make to the legal analysis of the problem—is already miles ahead (e.g., "*Because* Sally holds a vested remainder, she faces no problems under the Rule Against Perpetuities…").

Repeating the facts wastes precious time

We make the same point here that we made about regurgitating legal rules: On law exams, because time is at a premium, you need to use every available minute *answering* the questions. Time spent merely *repeating* them is a complete waste.

Repeating the facts conveys uncertainty and adds nothing of value to an answer

Deep down most students already know that fact regurgitation won't get them the grades they desire. So why, it is fair to ask, do so many students nevertheless fall into parrot mode when they come face to face with their laptop screen? Here's one answer we hear from students, particularly those who are unhappy with their exam performance: "After reading the question, I was so confused and stressed out that the only thing I was sure of was the facts. So I figured I couldn't go wrong by repeating them and getting at least *that much* right."

But here's the rub: This strategy is far more likely to highlight rather than conceal your confusion, for a student who begins an answer by repeating the facts is sending the message loud and clear that he isn't sure how to respond to the question. At best, it will make a poor first impression. But the downside risk is greater still. After all, the grader *invented* those facts; indeed, she probably spent a lot of time working out the details. So she will quickly recognize her own work as well as the fact you've added nothing of consequence to it, and she is not likely to reward you for wasting either your time or hers.

Attempts to paraphrase are likely to get you in trouble

Once again, you can't solve the regurgitation problem—whether you are regurgitating law or facts—by paraphrasing rather than quoting. At best, you will succeed only in wasting the time spent rephrasing rather than analyzing the facts presented. At worst, you will get the facts wrong in some small but significant way that can undermine your entire answer. Consider, for example, a Contracts hypothetical in which some facts suggest that Omar has made an "offer" and other facts suggest that he has only invited one; a paraphrase of the hypothetical that even inadvertently emphasizes one view and ignores the other is a deadly error, since the professor is undoubtedly testing to see whether the student can argue the facts *both* ways. In sum, you gain nothing—and stand to lose a lot—by attempting to paraphrase the facts.

The facts are already written down

If you pull into a tollbooth and ask directions to the George Washington Bridge, the attendant might well repeat your question back to you: "So, you want to get to the bridge?" Your kids in the back seat might crack wise ("Duh, how did he ever guess?"), but the toll collector is no doubt making a legitimate attempt to ensure he heard the question right before trying to answer it. Unlike the toll collector, however, a law student who wants to make sure she has the facts right can—and indeed she *should*—simply go back and read them again; she gains nothing by repeating them into her answers.

Tip #20. Avoid Conclusory Answers

Imagine you and your best friend have just finished reading a great novel like Dostoyevsky's *Crime and Punishment*. You're excited to talk about it and you call your friend on the phone. "Did you like the book?" you ask. "Yes," he says. "Do you think there was any merit to Raskolnikov's original thinking about justifications for murder?" you inquire. "No," he replies. "What do you think ultimately led to Raskolnikov's downfall?" you press on. "Guilt," he mutters. Not much of a conversation, is it?

Your professors can't write like Dostoyevsky. But we do our best to pose problems we find interesting and that we hope will challenge you to think. So, if after a long fact pattern we put a question to you like, "Does Jill's suit have merit?" it is highly unlikely that "yes" (or "no" for that matter) will prove a satisfactory answer. We are at least as interested in why you have drawn a particular conclusion as in the conclusion itself.

Nor is this a mere aesthetic preference. Your professional life will depend on persuading people to act and judges to rule as you wish. It's unlikely that clipped conclusions will push them in the desired direction. You might be able to get by with one-word answers when you are telling a client that "yes" she may go forward with her plans. But if your answer is "no," you had better have a detailed explanation for why and a further consideration of other possible alternatives and why those will or won't work. Explaining why is the watchword of a successful practice, and that goes double for exam performance.

Be wary of conclusory terms

It is seldom a good idea to begin a point in your essay with phrases like "it is obvious that" or "clearly." If you are correct, and the point you are making is obvious, then the chances are good that this isn't the issue the professor is hoping to see you discuss. So if it is "obvious that Zhang will sue Samantha for breach of contract," then it's likely the important issues are what defenses Samantha has and whether Zhang will ultimately prevail. Alternatively, and still worse, the point you are making may not be obvious at all. You are not likely to get the grade you'd like with an answer that says "it's obvious the rule against perpetuities doesn't apply" when there's a strong argument that it does.

Don't say what, say why

Law school exams often present ambiguous circumstances. A contract or deed can be interpreted in different ways. A statute can be read to have different meanings. A defendant can be seen as having acted negligently or not. It's important to choose which interpretation of events is more compelling. But it's not enough. In many cases, for example, when there are only two plausible readings, you could pick the right one 50% of the time just by guessing. So the professor is unlikely to be impressed with a mere conclusion. If, for example, you see no evidence of a defendant's discriminatory intent, it's a good first step to say the defendant isn't liable because the intent element is missing. But if you don't go on to explain why you see intent as an element of the applicable antidiscrimination statute—based on the plain meaning of the language, the legislative history, the case law interpreting similar statutes, or some other factor—then your answer is stopping short. Every conclusion you draw should have a why attached to it.

Always anticipate rejoinders

Even after you have spelled out all the reasons you believe a legal issue should be resolved in a particular way, you are still only halfway home. You should next ask yourself what arguments a hypothetical opponent might raise that would push the decision-maker in the opposite direction. After you have written down how you would respond to the strongest arguments that cut against your position, you will then have truly tackled the question the way it was written. Anyone can reach a conclusion if the arguments the other way aren't adequately presented. But to write a persuasive answer you need to rebut the best that the other side has to offer. (See Tip #14, "Argue Both Sides.")

Don't stop because you think you've nailed the issue

Exam questions often provide you with eureka moments of recognition. You see what the question is driving at, and you can't wait to tell your professor what the issue is and how it should be resolved. Given time pressure it's very tempting then to move quickly to the next issue or question. But such happy moments can lull you into a false sense of security. If the issue is screaming out at you, so will it be apparent to your equally studious classmates. Odds are good that there are complications to the argument, so take a deep breath and reflect before moving on.

Tip #21. Avoid Disquisitions on Topics Outside the Course

Although you may sometimes have your doubts, your professors generally aren't out to fool you and mostly strive to test exactly what they teach. Accordingly, you can rest assured that the vast majority of them would never ask you to address an exam question on a topic not covered in the course. Professors put a great deal of effort into explaining the issues they address, and they want to find out how much you have learned. So if you are convinced that the real issue on one of your Property exam questions is whether the defendant violated the antitrust laws, go back to the drawing board and search for the property law issue that you are undoubtedly missing. The antitrust issue is likely a mirage, and, even if it's actually there, it is surely not the issue your Property professor is testing.

This doesn't mean you should never make quick mention of a legal issue you believe is relevant even though you never discussed it in class. Most professors greatly value creative thinking and are delighted if you raise facts about the real world that you know from personal experience. But if you find yourself going on and on about something from a topic never covered in your course, or from some other field, or worst of all from a commercial outline, *stop!* The grade you save may be your own.

Know your topics well, and use your syllabus as a guide

Many students would readily agree that it's foolish to spend time writing about issues not covered in the course. It's one thing, however, to avoid talking about antitrust issues on a Property exam, and quite another to remember every issue covered in a Property course so that you know whether it's fair game for testing. There's always the fear that, even though you don't remember covering something, it was in fact a focus of considerable scrutiny the one day you missed or during that hazy week when you had the flu.

Our first reaction to this is that if you are taking school seriously you probably remember a lot more than you think. If you really don't remember covering something, you probably didn't cover it. Often the professor will provide a syllabus with headings that make the course issues easier to remember. And if the exam is open book, there's probably no better document to have on hand. But here, we say again, there are no substitutes for knowing the material. Topics discussed in class should be your first study priority. Topics in the readings should be next. These two will keep you plenty busy and in any event will surely exhaust the list of topics typically tested on the exam.

You can't afford to waste time

It's the rare exam question that doesn't contain several difficult issues built on the main topics of study. A Constitutional Law question focused on state action may also involve an issue on the merits and even a standing question as well. But imagine that you wrote your moot court brief on the immunity of public officials to lawsuits, though the topic was never covered in your course, and imagine further that you see an immunity issue lurking in the facts if the defendant is found to be a state actor. If you insist on showing off to the professor how much you know about immunity, you risk running out of time to talk about the merits and may even miss the standing issue altogether. *So don't do it!* If the professor spent time teaching you about standing, that's probably what she wants to hear about. Remember, your task on the exam is to convince her that you have mastered the material covered in the course. You'll have plenty of time for a disquisition on the immunity issue when you meet up with your classmates for a post-exam drink, though frankly we wouldn't overdo it there either.

Venturing beyond the course risks needless mistakes

Going outside the course material not only wastes time, it increases the odds that you'll make mistakes. You aren't likely to get much credit for discussing material the professor isn't testing. But the professor is certain to be displeased if you bring up other issues and then get them wrong. Moreover, mistakes during extramural frolics are highly likely for at least two reasons. First, no matter how well you know some other body of law, you aren't likely to know it as well as you know the material that you've devoured while getting ready for the exam. Second, most areas of law offer considerable room for interpretation. You are familiar with your professor's take on the material that you covered in the course. But you will be hard-pressed to predict her understanding of other topics. Material you picked up as gospel somewhere else—whether that be in another course or from a commercial outline—may strike your professor as poppycock. Quoting it back to her isn't likely to improve your performance.

Be brief and you will be saved

Sometimes you just can't resist discussing other topics. Sometimes you'll even be right. You'll have spotted an issue from another body of law that actually is as relevant to the problem as anything your professor intended to test. Though such occasions will be rare, they are not out of the question, and you don't want knee-jerk tips-following to inhibit you. So if, upon reflection, or at least as much reflection as you have time for during an exam, you are convinced that an issue outside the course is crucial, flag it. Explain *briefly* why and how you think it's relevant and *move on!* If you're right, you'll may well be rewarded with credit for creativity. If you're wrong, you'll risk little time, and the professor is unlikely to penalize provided your principal focus remains on the issues she is actually trying to test.

Tip #22. Don't Leave Your Common Sense at the Door

This is a good rule for most of life, but exam pressure makes it hard to follow, especially when you are eager to show off your newly acquired legal learning. Here are some simple points that will help you sound not only like a student who has begun to master the law's lessons but also like someone whom your professor can imagine someday handling a client's affairs.

Rules are made to be broken

You worked hard all semester learning rules so complicated they made your head swim. You know now that landlords are bound by a warranty of habitability and that if an apartment doesn't comply with the housing code the tenant has grounds to withhold rent. You also know that providing hot water is an essential part of almost every housing code. Rote rule application might lead you to conclude that a tenant in an exam question could stay rent-free for months in a luxury apartment merely because there's no hot water in the Jacuzzi. But you know in the real world this would never happen. It shouldn't happen on your exams either.

Don't ignore your experience

It's easy to get confused about legal terminology. You may recall that the Supreme Court has found a "fundamental right to travel" without remembering precisely what that means. It might also occur to you that any state rule that restricts your freedom, let's say to hunt as you wish, could be described as interfering with your travel rights. "I can hunt in my home state without any special training in gun safety, so why can't I do that in the state next door?" But however savvy it sounds to your legal mind to challenge state hunting restrictions as unconstitutional infringements on travel, you know in your bones, even if you've never picked up a gun, that states routinely regulate things like hunting, and out-of-state hunters are unlikely to be exempt from the rules applicable to locals.

Be very careful, then, about reaching exam conclusions that contradict the way you know the world to be organized. In short, if your recollection of the commerce clause cases convinces you that it's unconstitutional for a state to operate a public university, you probably should rethink your understanding of the cases before telling your professor at the University of State X to relinquish his or her paycheck.

Pay attention to consequences

You have carefully mastered the requirements of "due process of law." Your exam question posits a scenario in which a student must maintain a B average to receive a tax credit for college tuition. In that scenario, a lot is obviously at stake in every student grade, and a review of the professor's grades could surely find errors, so you wonder whether every student at a public university has a right to a formal hearing to contest any grade below a B. *Time to slow down.* However logical this might sound, if you want to push this point, you need to take careful account of the implications of such a dramatic shift in ordinary practice. How many grades below B do you think are awarded in the nation's public universities in one year, and what would it cost to provide hearings in all cases? On what basis would the hearing examiner decide whether the original grade was fair? Would such hearings bog universities down in endless procedure and interfere with the professor's control over her classroom? If you are prepared to offer answers to such questions, then you might score points with your interpretation of "due process." But whatever you do, be particularly careful about tossing out conclusions of law without some grasp of how your ideas will play out in the real world.

Distinguish the *is* from the *ought*

Suppose you have a creative theory that would—if forthrightly accepted by the courts—invalidate a practice that your experience tells you goes on all the time. You may remember, for example, that the Supreme Court has found unconstitutional state action in the judicial enforcement of racially restrictive covenants. Your exam question is about a neighbor who holds Ku Klux Klan rallies in his backyard and calls the police to evict any Blacks who seek to attend. If you want to argue that *in principle* there's no difference between the cops' involvement here and the courts' involvement in the covenants case, more power to you. Your professor will reward you for creativity, especially if you are sensitive to available counter-arguments. But if instead you summarily conclude that the cops can't help the neighbor, you will have confused what you think the law should be with what it is, and that won't help your exam grade.

Tip #23. Avoid Writing Philosophy Lectures

Law school classes spend a great deal of energy on time-honored questions of law that transcend individual subjects. When should rules be strictly enforced and when should an exception be made? When should the needs of the community eclipse the rights of the individual, and vice versa? Do citizens owe allegiance to immoral laws? Like most students, you may have developed strong views on such questions. Save those views for an occasion on which the professor asks for your opinion. In the meantime, use your understanding of deeper issues to focus on the question at hand. Seeing how the exam problem is only part of a much larger issue should help you write a better answer to the question. But it doesn't invite or authorize a lengthy philosophical essay about the issue itself.

Always keep the question in mind

You have studied so hard and learned so much that the temptation is almost irresistible to let the professor in on your newfound erudition. Don't give in! The professor wants your analysis of the question at hand, not your thoughts on big-picture questions or related legal issues. Let's say your Constitutional Law exam has a hypothetical statute that bans cloning and you are asked to discuss a constitutional challenge to the statute. You see right away that Supreme Court cases protecting birth control and same-sex marriage but refusing to protect abortion, bigamy, or a right to die provide the relevant precedents for your analysis. *Good!* Now go back and tell us how these cases will help you analyze the cloning statute. But don't spend your time writing about the ways that privacy has been a contested concept since the time of John Stuart Mill or about the history of "fundamental rights" analysis.

Analogize with a purpose

Figuring out how your exam problem resembles other problems you've studied is crucial to successful exam performance. But it's not enough to point out that your case is "like" *Singh v. Jones*. You have to show how *Singh v. Jones* will or won't help resolve your case.

Dinner table discussion provides a useful model here. Let's say teenage Jenny sits down and explains a recent problem at work involving a co-worker. Everyone can tell the difference between responses from two types of family elders. Aunt Sarah, the family sage, might reply as follows. "I faced a problem like that once. Here's how I handled it. Based on my experience, here's what you might try to cope with your situation." Note how Aunt Sarah "cited a precedent" but then immediately brought the topic back to Jenny's problem. That's what you want to do on an exam.

Now consider Uncle Fred's response to Jenny. "Gee, dear, that reminds me of a story. Back when I was your age…." Fifteen minutes go by, and Fred is still telling his tale. You recognize Uncle Fred as the family blowhard, and that's how you'll sound if your answer starts off, "This case reminds me of *Singh v. Jones*," and you then spend the rest of your time going on at length about that case.

Stay at the question's level of generality

Here's a good opportunity to remind you once again of the single most important rule of exam-taking: "Read Each Question Carefully, and Answer the Question Asked." (See Tip #8.) This time we want to urge you to read the question with an eye toward the level of generality that the professor is seeking.

Thus, if the professor asks whether Felipe can sue Sam when Sam draws water from a well lying under tracts of land owned by each, don't write a treatise on the difference between traditional rules of capture and the doctrine of correlative rights. Focus instead on whether Felipe will prevail and under what circumstances. If, however, the professor asks for a comparison of the pros and cons of handling conflicts over water via traditional rules of capture, then by all means write at length about the wisdom of competing approaches. Don't switch instead to a more general discussion of whether we should have a private property system or to a less general discussion of whether in one particular case the traditional capture rule would be preferable. Ask yourself for each question whether the professor wants analysis of a particular fact pattern, a competing rule choice in a narrow area, or a general thematic discussion. Respond accordingly.

Tip #24. Don't B.S.

You open up your Torts exam and carefully read through the first long hypothetical. Terror fills your heart as you realize you just don't get what the question is driving at. You understand that issues of negligence are involved, but you are afraid you won't be able to figure out how. The thought occurs to you that it would be a shame for you to do poorly on a negligence question. After all, you spent hours studying negligence, and you could write a sterling essay on the general characteristics of negligence and how it fits into tort law as a whole. You figure the professor won't penalize you too much if you demonstrate sound command of the general principles, even if you only tangentially refer to how they fit back to the question. Offering this kind of fluff-filled response may even have worked for you in college. So you are thinking of attempting it again.

Don't even try. We law professors pride ourselves on our ability to spot exam-dodging evasions, and it will be a matter of professional self-respect that we come down hard on you. There's a pretty simple reason.

If your experience as law students is anything like ours was, you've probably already figured out that law professors aren't hired on the basis of (a) drop-dead good looks; (b) a sense of humor; (c) compassion for students or other living things; (d) an ability to bring boring material to life; (e) an ability to bring complex material to crystal clarity; (f) an ability to cope with the world going on outside of the "ivory tower"; or (g) an ability to grade exams expeditiously. To be sure, many law professors (present company excluded, of course) possess one or more of these traits, and, if you're as fortunate as we were, you'll even have some who possess almost all of them. But there is only one talent that is common to virtually every professor currently teaching in an American law school; moreover, once you understand the nature of this common talent, everything else about legal education—from the way we grade through the selection criteria for Law Review—begins to make an odd sort of sense.

Here's the secret: *What professors are good at is taking law exams.* Most of us have taken tests successfully throughout our lives. We went to law schools that happen to produce law professors; we did well enough on our law school exams to persuade others who did well on *their* law school exams to hire us for positions as judicial clerks, government attorneys, or associates in blue-chip firms; we even did well enough on our law school exams that our law school professors (who had also done well on *their* law school exams) were willing to recommend us for jobs in the legal academy; and we were ultimately hired by other law professors who in turn hold their own jobs because they too did well on *their* law exams.

If you think about it for a little while (and we try not to), test-taking skills are a pretty paltry talent in the grand scheme of things. This may be one reason for the old adage that A students become law professors, B students become judges, and C students become rich. But the one thing you can count on is that a group of people selected for their ability to take tests will be able to spot it when you are bluffing in your efforts to take yours. So go back and read that Torts hypothetical again. Take a stab at what you think the question is really about. Our bet is that you have a better idea than you think. But we're sure you won't get anywhere trying to bull your way through.

Looking for more detailed advice on avoiding rookie mistakes? Chapter Sixteen is full to the brim with examples of the most common exam-writing mistakes and the ways to avoid them!

Frequently Asked Questions

We generally offer review sessions before our exams, during which we entertain student questions about the course and the exam. We also sometimes hold feedback sessions during which we answer questions about an exam we've just graded. Here are some of the questions we hear most often from our students.

FAQ #1. Do You Need to Cite Cases by Name?

Precedent is a central feature of U.S. law, and accordingly, "doing things with precedent"—following it, extending it, limiting it, distinguishing it—is a skill frequently tested on law school exams. When an exam question presents a scenario resembling one or more of the cases you've studied, it will be a whole lot easier to "do things" with a case if you remember its name. But it is entirely possible to perform superbly even if you can't call the name to mind, and—just as important—merely citing a case by name is no substitute for applying it to the problem at hand. Here's what we mean:

Forgetting case names is no cause for alarm

Law school exams are not memorization exercises. Many are open book, but even closed-book exams seek primarily analysis, not information. So if you get a question about a state constitutional amendment requiring U.S. senators to be younger than 70 years old, you'll score well if you say the Supreme Court's invalidation of state-imposed term limits appears to extend to all state-imposed qualifications, including a maximum age. If your analysis is sound, the professor is unlikely to care whether you mentioned the name of the case on which your analysis relies.

Citing cases is not nearly enough

In contrast, you won't score well at all on a question about a state's effort to retire senators at age 70 by noting that the closest case to your facts is *U.S. Term Limits v. Thornton* if you then go on to dismiss that case as irrelevant because it involved length of service rather than age requirements. You got the case name right and accurately identified the way in which your exam problem factually differs from the real case. But the glib distinction between the cases is too pat and misunderstands the Supreme Court's argument about the dangers of state-imposed qualifications for federal office. You would have done much better to remember the argument and forget the case name.

Case names are fabulous shorthand

Assume for a moment you are writing a history essay about the U.S. Senate in the second half of the twentieth century and you want to describe the sudden increase in the number of female senators following the 1992 election. You could attribute the change partly to the fallout from the Clarence Thomas/Anita Hill hearings. Let's say, however, that your mind goes blank for a moment and you just can't remember either Clarence Thomas's or Anita Hill's name. You could convey roughly the same point to your reader if you wrote something like, "Female voters were stirred up following a contested hearing before the Senate Judiciary Committee in which a former female subordinate of a Supreme Court nominee accused the nominee of sexual harassment." If this were an exam, your grader would be unlikely to penalize you for forgetting the names Thomas and Hill.

But consider the downsides of forgetting. First, it takes a lot longer to describe the event than merely to reference it by name. This is particularly true of law cases, which are often two words long. Second, if you have to describe the event you will inevitably omit details or even make an error in description. By contrast, a mere reference to the Thomas/Hill hearings draws the reader into a shared community in which you both rely on your stock recollections of the event and suggests that you remember the whole event as it happened. For much the same reason, case names can prove wonderfully helpful, even though very few professors actually look through answers to see whether the names of the relevant cases are there or not.

FAQ #2. Does the IRAC Method Help?

If we had to answer this question with a flat "yes" or "no," we'd pick "no" without a moment's hesitation. As we said early in the book, in our combined three-quarters of a century of law teaching—and in the thousands of exam answers we've read over all those years—neither of us can recall a single occasion in which a first-rate exam answer was organized around the so-called IRAC method ("issue-rule-application-conclusion"). In the paragraphs that follow, we'll explain the two principal reasons we strongly advise students to avoid IRAC (or any other simple formula for that matter) unless the professor grading your exams has explicitly given that method the green light.

Not all questions are the same

Many students conclude that if you try hard enough, you can squeeze *any* question—no matter what size or shape—into the neat little four-corner hole provided by IRAC. As we know firsthand, since we've done it twice, you can write an entire book about the salient features of law-exam-taking that such a rigid approach ignores. But the bottom line is that different kinds of questions call for different kinds of answers.

As the first letter of the acronym suggests, IRAC is designed for use with the traditional issue spotter question—the extended factual scenario full to the brim with legal issues of varying degrees of obviousness. But there are at least four kinds of issues that issue spotters test, and the IRAC method is utterly useless for three of them. It works okay when there is only one rule governing the issue at hand and only one way to read it and all that's left is figuring out how that rule applies to the facts. Even here, the "application" term makes it sound like you are presenting a syllogism—where a conclusion follows logically from the rule and the facts—and you'll get many more points from the vast majority of professors if you offer *analysis* and *argument* rather than mere *application*. For another, "conclusion" suggests that there is only one way the facts can be analyzed, but in the vast majority of exam problems you'll encounter there is more than one plausible outcome. Yet if you substitute "analysis/argument" for "application" and you don't take the "conclusion" term too literally, IRAC may help you get started down the right road… on this kind of question and only this kind of question.

By contrast, the formula is of little use if there is more than one rule that might govern the dispute (e.g., is a riparian rights case arising in the State of X governed by the rule of prior appropriation or the reasonable use doctrine?); or if there is more than one way to interpret the rule (is the Statute of Frauds—which requires a document "in writing" for some contracts—satisfied by a text message?); or if the facts resemble a case you studied and the case can be read in more than one way (does the right to bear arms in public places recently recognized in *Bruen* apply to AK-47s?). No "rule" resolves questions like these, and you can waste a lot of time looking for one or trying to "apply" the law to the facts when what the question calls for is not "application" but instead *interpretation*. The formula is similarly useless when the professor dispenses with the issue-spotting format—as professors often do—and asks a straightforward policy question ("Should the State of X make landlords strictly liable for tenant injuries?") or gives you a conclusion and asks you to fashion arguments based on current law to get there ("What are the best arguments available to a party seeking to challenge the constitutionality of a state law prohibiting affirmative action?").

By our count, then, there's a one-in-six chance that IRAC can get you where you want to go, calling to mind a famous game of chance the name of which we dare not speak. Are you feeling lucky?

IRAC is too slow

We have stressed all along that law exams put you under tremendous time pressure. Consider, then, how poorly suited IRAC is to cope with this challenge. Although we've devoted our whole book to teaching you how to deal with exam questions where there is no one "right" answer, you can't ever forget that law exams still ask *questions*. You want to answer them as best you can, even if there is more than one way to do so.

Consider how slow IRAC is as a means for answering a question. You pull into a gas station and ask how to get to City Hall. Suppose the person behind the counter says, "I see your issue is that you want to get to City Hall. The rule is that you want to take the most direct route. To apply that rule, take a left at the light, go three blocks and turn right, and you'll come to it in about a mile. So what I want you to do is take a left at the light, go three blocks and turn right." You've got your answer, but you'll probably have to restrain yourself from yelling at the person to get to the point. That's how an IRAC answer may seem to your grader.

Ah, you say, but the City Hall example is unfair, because there was a clear answer and so the question didn't resemble a law exam. Okay, then, imagine that there are two ways to get to City Hall, the scenic route and the quick route. A speedy response might go like this: "Take a left at the light, go three blocks and turn right, and you'll come to it in about a mile. Or, if you want a more scenic trip, don't turn left until your second light, and go the same three blocks and turn right. This takes a bit longer, but you'll go by some nice Christmas lights." Let's say, however, that your town guide is suffering from IRAC disease. So he says to you, "There are two issues here. The first issue is where you want to go, but that one's easy since you are headed to City Hall. The second issue is whether you want the quick route or the scenic route. Now I suppose there are reasons why you might want either. [He then launches into a life philosophy discussion contrasting how the early bird gets the worm with why it's good to stop to smell the roses.] So, if you want the quick route turn left at the first light, go three blocks and turn right and proceed for a mile. If you want the scenic route, turn at your second light, go three blocks and turn right. [He then restates everything he just said to form a conclusion.]" You'll get your answer both ways, but your quickest route in the second scenario would have been to ask someone else for directions.

FAQ #3. What If You Realize You've Made a Mistake in Your Answer?

You are halfway through a question on your Criminal Procedure exam when you realize you have been evaluating the constitutionality of a search that a husband made of his wife's suitcase. Suddenly you remember that the pertinent provisions of the Constitution govern the behavior of public but not private actors. What should you do when you have traveled so far down the wrong path?

Don't panic

Your first instinct may be anger with yourself for pursuing a line of analysis that turned out to be a nonstarter. So you'll have a strong desire to delete, strikethrough, or rip up everything you have done and start over. But in our view, you should resist the temptation to overreact. Indeed, the first thing to do is to go back and carefully read the question again, for you may discover that your first instinct was right and that the wrong turn wasn't so wrong after all. (In the situation here, perhaps you'd been unconsciously swayed by the husband's having spoken with the police before the search and, at their urging, broken into the suitcase.)

But even if the re-read confirms your worst fears, you shouldn't despair. Mistakes like these often occur because the professor drafted the fact pattern with ambiguities deliberately designed to lure you into error. So the professor is not going to penalize you for heading down the wrong path... so long as you correct your mistake before submitting your exam. It's harder to do that, of course, if you are handwriting answers, but with the miracle of word processing you can minimize your mistake. You might insert a statement such as, "If this had been a police search it would have violated the Fourth Amendment, but since the husband searched his wife's suitcase no constitutional violation is present." Indeed, if you are lucky, the question may have been designed to lead you astray for the very purpose of provoking discussion on why the Constitution applies only to official violations of privacy, thereby leaving those whose privacy has been violated by private actors vulnerable to criminal prosecution. If that's the case, you'll suffer little and perhaps even gain from a preliminary section indicating why the search would have been illegal had it been conducted by the police.

Go back and signal your mistake before it happens

Should you conclude that you've just "gone down the rabbit hole" for several pages, don't wait until the end of the passage to signal the mistake ("Sorry—the last six pages should be ignored") and force the professor to make that needless journey with you. The waste of your own time is bad enough for your grade; wasting the professor's time may be even worse. Far better, then, to go back to the spot in your answer where you initially went wrong and signal your error. In the problem at hand, you might insert something like, "In the analysis that follows I treat a search by a husband as if it were a police search for purposes of the Fourth Amendment. I understand that this confuses a basic point about the application of the Constitution to private vs. public actors." This may be the best you can do, but all the better if you can point to facts in the problem that led you astray. You might, for example, say that the husband's quick trip to the police station suggests that he and the police had cooperated in advance on planning the search and that the husband was thus acting as a police agent. This will raise further difficult issues about what a private actor can do when cooperating with the authorities, but at least it will make what was a tangent now seem relevant to the facts in the problem. The important point is that an advance signal of your error is your best protection against being graded down severely.

Move quickly and confidently down a new path

Whatever else it will cost you, a lengthy digression or a mistaken evaluation will take time away from the analysis the professor expects. So if you conclude that you've made a mistake, go back and signal it and *then move on!* Ask yourself what issues you might have missed because you were busy focusing on something that now seems mistaken. Also, try as hard as you can to resist being flustered by your mistake. Everyone makes errors when confronting complex fact patterns for the first time. When you start down your new path, continue to use the same confident tone you had before. You want to learn from your mistakes but not be intimidated by them.

FAQ #4. What If You Think the *Professor* Has Made a Mistake?

You are reading through a long problem on your Property exam that appears to raise issues about the nature of the state action doctrine and its application to judicial enforcement of restrictive covenants. At the end of the question the professor asks, "How does the Rule in *Shelley's Case* apply to these facts?"

You are convinced that the professor has erred. The Rule in *Shelley's Case* is a mostly dead letter doctrine about interpreting grant language in property deeds. You are convinced your professor meant to ask, "How does the rule in *Shelley v. Kraemer* apply to these facts?" (*That* Shelley is the leading United States Supreme Court case on the topic of racially restrictive covenants.) Or, you might spot a professorial mistake in an unintended ambiguity rather than in a simple error. Suppose your exam question asks you about three constitutional law theories and asks you to pick a case that illustrates the strengths and weaknesses of each theory. Are you supposed to choose one case and discuss all three theories or pick one case to illustrate each theory? What should you do in such cases when things just aren't clear?

Ask about apparent errors

The first thing to do in an exam situation in which you think there's an error or an ambiguity is to ask about it. If the professor is present at the exam, ask her. If you are right and the error is a significant one, the professor may have an opportunity to correct it for you and the whole class before it's too late. If you are wrong, the professor may simply tell you there is no error. This will remove any uncertainty you may have had. Or you may get the silent treatment from either the proctor or the professor. In that case, you are no worse off than you were before. There's certainly no harm in asking, and the quest for an ounce of prevention is well worth any potential embarrassment.

Flag apparent errors where you cannot resolve uncertainty

If you can't get to the professor, or if the professor won't answer your question, and you still believe there's an error, then explain in your answer why you think the professor made a mistake and how you believe the question is supposed to read. This lets the professor in on your thinking as she begins to evaluate your answer. The worst thing you can do, of course, is simply to assume the professor made an error and—without making that assumption clear—proceed to answer the question you think the professor meant to ask. If your assumption is mistaken and the question is correct as written, you will almost surely lose points for misreading the question.

If you have time, answer the question both ways

If your uncertainty remains unresolved, you must deal with it in your answer. If the final line of the question reads "discuss Carl's causes of action" and you believe the professor meant to ask about Carla's causes of action, then tell the professor about both. First indicate you know what the question says and answer that one first. Then explain how you think the question was supposed to read and answer that one too.

Rethink your assumptions

Before spending a great deal of time responding to anything other than what appears on the exam, make sure you haven't missed something. Most professors spend a great deal of time proofreading exams, often consulting colleagues for a double-check. Minor, easy-to-miss typographical errors that nonetheless change the meaning of the question sometimes slip through. It's unlikely, however, that you will find major errors. If it seems to you that a professor has really goofed, like asking about the wrong case, stop and think again. If the question is one of a series of short essays, maybe the apparent mistake is intentional. When the professor asks how does Case A apply, maybe what she wants to hear is "it doesn't and here's why."

If, however, you have an hour to analyze the significance of what you are convinced is an irrelevant case—or more generally if you are positive that the question as written isn't what you are supposed to answer—then flag the error and do your best to cope with it.

FAQ #5. What If You Don't Know What a Word Means?

Your professors will try hard not to use unfamiliar terms without defining them. But occasionally they won't realize that something that seems entirely familiar to them may turn out not to be familiar to you. Our favorite example is a Criminal Law exam involving a warrantless search of a Winnebago—a large vehicle on wheels that you can live in for extended periods but also drive around on camping trips. The Supreme Court has granted the police greater latitude to search automobiles than to search private homes. The exam drafter thought that a Winnebago posed the perfect intermediate case that would force his students to consider the reasons for the automobile vs. home distinction. Unfortunately, many of his students didn't know what a Winnebago was, and this made it almost impossible to grade the question in a manner that was fair both to the students who *did* know (and were thus able to provide the analysis the professor was looking for) and to those who *didn't* (and thus went off on all sorts of tangents).

When there's a professorial misfire like this one, your unfamiliarity with the word in question isn't likely to hurt you. At the other extreme, if it's a word that was discussed at length in class or in the assigned materials, then ignorance is likely to cost those who don't recognize it. But for cases falling in the middle—i.e., you just don't know the meaning of the word though most of your classmates do—an ounce a prevention is the way to go since there's virtually no chance of a remedy after you've turned in your exam. So here's what to do to avoid this predicament.

Bring a dictionary to all open-book exams

The whole point of open-book exams is to allow you to simulate more closely the real world in which attorneys can look things up. Although you are most likely to want to look up cases and statutes, you never know when you might want to check on a definition. This goes double if English is not your first language. If you have taken steps to cope with your language difficulty and still come up blank, a brief statement that the word in question does not appear in your dictionary is likely to persuade your professor that his choice of words—rather than your vocabulary—is the problem. But since in most cases you won't be permitted to search online, you'll be out of luck if you show up without a dictionary.

If the professor is present, ask for a definition

Many professors check in on their students during exams precisely to ensure there are no unanticipated problems. If you ask, the professor may be more than happy to tell you the meaning of a word. She may decide that the word is harder than she expected and announce the definition to the whole class. Either way, you'll find out what you needed. If the professor won't tell you, at least you'll have tried your best. But if you keep mum, the professor is extremely unlikely to give you a break when you email her the next day and explain your problem.

If the professor is absent, ask the proctor for help

At some schools, professors don't attend exams, and monitoring is done by proctors. Proctors are much less likely to tell you the meaning of a word, because this might interfere with the professor's goals. A proctor might, however, be willing to call the professor during the exam to seek permission. This is certainly worth a shot and is a whole lot better than sitting there in ignorance.

If all else fails, highlight in your exam that you don't know a word

If the professor is not there and the proctor refuses to answer your query or help you out—or, as at some schools, there is no proctor or the exam is given remotely—you should at least flag for the professor that you were confused about the meaning of a word. This may not help you much, but the point of law exams is not generally to test vocabulary. If you explain your confusion in your answer, there's a decent chance the professor will give you a break.

FAQ #6. Does the Professor Want "Black-Letter" Answers?

We often hear students complaining that Professor X spent all his class time on big-picture questions of social policy and then focused his exam on mundane questions of law. Such complaints miss a basic point. Every law school professor, no matter how abstract or theoretical, will insist that you learn basic legal rules. If you don't, no amount of policy argument, fancy theorizing, or other exam-taking wizardry will save you from a poor performance.

This doesn't mean, however, that your professors are seeking merely "black-letter" law. While knowing the black letter is necessary to exam excellence, it is not sufficient. Your job is to convince the professor that you know how to *use* the rules, not merely that you have memorized them. So your challenge is to demonstrate that you have mastered the black letter and that you can apply it to the exam problems. Here's how to do both at the same time.

Use black-letter law to spot issues

You don't need to have attended law school to recognize certain basic legal issues. A pedestrian struck by a car traveling 90 miles an hour through city streets is likely to have a cause of action against the driver. But the more law you know, the more you will be able to spot subtle problems. Suppose instead that the driver is on an interstate highway traveling at 60 mph when a child runs into the road chasing a Frisbee. The driver swerves, avoiding the child, but a passenger in the car is so frightened he has a heart attack and dies. Can the passenger's family successfully sue the driver? This sounds like a typical Torts exam question.

Every bit of black-letter law you know can help you spot legal issues. If you know there's a legal doctrine called negligence per se that renders people liable for damage they cause while violating safety statutes, then you'll want to know what the speed limit was on the highway where the accident occurred and whether it took place in a jurisdiction where negligence per se applies. If you know that the negligence per se doctrine is sometimes found inapplicable because the injured party is not someone whom the safety statute was intended to protect, then you will see an issue of whether speed limits are really meant to protect passengers from heart attacks. (Passengers seem a likely protected group, but perhaps heart attacks fall outside the scope of intended protection.) If you understand that a tort suit requires proof of causation, then you might see an issue of whether the driver—rather than the child—was the proximate cause of the harm. Finally, if your course covered so-called "guest statutes" that at various times and places have immunized drivers against most suits by passengers, then you'll want to know whether any "guest statute" is available here. The point is you can't spot any legal issues if you don't know black-letter law. So in one sense your professor wants, even demands, a black-letter answer.

Go beyond black-letter responses

The whole point of law school exams, however, is to place you in situations in which black-letter law doesn't lead to easy solutions. Suppose you encounter a hypothetical deed in which a rich landowner grants his large estate, Chic Acres, "to my cousin William, but if William should ever attempt to transfer Chic Acres to a member of the Proud Boys, then Chic Acres is to go to my niece Chelsea in fee simple." The first rule that occurs to you is the one prohibiting "restraints on alienation," which would preserve William's right to sell to whomever he wants despite what the deed says. But then you remember that another rule *permits* restraints on alienation as long as they merely bar sale to some discrete group of persons, such as a will provision intended to keep the property out of the hands of a disfavored branch of the family. If *that* rule applies, then a court may well uphold the restriction at hand. You recall further your professor explaining that the rule disfavoring restraints typically applies in cases involving "general" or broadly applicable restrictions whereas the rule upholding them comes into play mostly in cases involving a "limited" restriction that won't unduly restrict the new property owner's ability to find a suitable buyer. Now you are ahead of the game because you have identified black-letter rules on both sides of the dispute as well as a "sorting hat" rule to help identify which rule will apply to which cases.

But you are not finished! You must proceed to analyze the question of whether a court would be more likely to view the restriction at hand—i.e., a ban on sales to Proud Boys members—as a "general" (and thus invalid) restraint or instead as a "limited" (and thus permissible) restraint. You might discuss the size of the disfavored group (e.g., "the population of Proud Boys in the county where Chic Acres is located is much larger than the typical branch of a family tree") or you might note "the undesirability of asking courts to expand the exception for families in ways that allow restrictions on property rights to turn on political affiliation." But it's less important which factors you stress than that you recognize that the court has a choice to make. If all you do is prove to the professor that you know the black-letter rules, you won't do well because you won't explain how a choice between them might be made. In this important sense, black letter is not enough.

FAQ #7. Should You Use Commercial Study Aids?

Let's face it: If we told you that the answer to this question is "no," you wouldn't believe us, for hornbooks, outlines, canned briefs, and the like are as much a part of American law school life as the Socratic method, yearly tuition increases, and the TGIF. Indeed, if we thought there were no place in legal education for commercial study aids, we wouldn't have written this book! But the key word here is "place." A high-quality commercial product can do some things for you, but other things you'll have to do for yourself—other things, in other words, that even the best commercial outline simply cannot replace.

The good news: A high-quality commercial study aid can help you spot the trees in the forest

The typical law school course tends to treat "black-letter" rules as merely a starting point for analysis. When you study the perfect tender rule in Contracts, for example, your professor may seem to spend about 30 seconds on U.C.C. § 2-601 (buyer may reject goods "if the goods or the tender of delivery fail in any respect to conform to the contract") and devote the next two classes to increasingly complex variations and exceptions (e.g., what if the buyer has invariably accepted similarly nonconforming deliveries in the past? what if the buyer signs for the delivery after the seller notifies him of the nonconformity?). Meanwhile, the individual without any experience in business transactions (i.e., the typical law student) may still be trying to figure out the rule itself. Although the professor is unlikely to test "the rule itself"—and is in fact far more likely to examine the variations and exceptions explored in class—a high-quality commercial study aid may nevertheless help students get the comfort and grounding they need before they can join the professor "at the next level."

So, you ask, how can I determine which of the many commercial study aids on the market is a high-quality product? The classics—Prosser on Torts; Farnsworth on Contracts; Chirelstein on Tax; Glannon on Civil Procedure; Chemerinsky on Constitutional Law; Singer on Property—are classics for a reason, and you can seldom go wrong with judicious reliance on any of them. Beyond that, the best source for a recommendation is your professor, who may well have a favorite and who may in any event be willing to help you steer clear of the shoddier products on the market.

The bad news: The most useful outlines are made, not purchased

One terribly important thing a commercial outline cannot do is provide you with the experience of organizing your *own* outline, and, in the end, there is no better way to grasp either the fine details or the "big picture" of a course. Indeed, the very process of outlining—of working your way back through the mass of material before you and of organizing it in a way that helps you make sense of it all—may be the most valuable part of your legal studies. (See Tip #3, "Prepare Your Own Outline of the Course.")

More bad news: The most useful outlines are tailored to your professor's course

While a commercial study aid may offer a useful overview of a subject, nothing will provide a more accurate guide to the particular topics and issues that your professor thinks are most important than what she actually emphasizes in class. Moreover, quite apart from the variety of course content, different professors focus their teaching efforts on different lawyerly skills. As a result, an outline that draws heavily on what *your* professor actually did in class is likely to be your most valuable resource as you prepare for your exams.

Still more bad news: Commercial study aids may emphasize the wrong skills

Earlier in the book, we quoted a law school classmate who aptly described the experience of reading a case for the first time as akin to "stirring cement with your eyelashes." It is no surprise, then, that many students turn to commercial study aids to help them shortcut this difficult task.

Canned briefs, for example, purport to find legal rules for you, by offering you a pre-digested case analysis for each of the cases covered in the casebook. That they frequently do this shoddily is a defect that we won't belabor here, but the principal problem is that *you* should be undertaking the case analysis yourself; what kind of lawyer would you be if you couldn't give legal advice based upon the current case law until that case law made its way into a hornbook?

Moreover, whether you learn a supposed rule by analyzing a case on your own, by reading a canned brief, or by finding it in a hornbook or commercial outline, simply knowing that rule just won't get you very far. The crucial skill—for success on law exams as well as in law practice—is rule application, and that too is a skill you can develop only with great practice; no commercial product can do it for you.

Perhaps the worst news yet: Commercial study aids may waste valuable time

It's tough enough to find the time to read the cases for all of your courses; to brief and think about them; to attend all your classes well prepared and to take good class notes; and—as exams near—to begin to outline your courses. If occasional or even relatively frequent reference to a high-quality commercial outline helps you clarify your understanding of this or that particular point as you go along, then by all means avail yourself of that assistance. But if you treat your commercial study aid as simply *another* massive text to read, digest, and attempt to integrate with the required materials—or, worse, if you attempt to do this with more than one of the commercial products available for the course in question—you'll find that the added value you get in exchange for all that time and effort will be practically nil. And if your experience of law school is anything like ours was, you don't have that kind of time to waste.

About the Authors

Richard Michael Fischl is Constance Baker Motley Professor of Law at the University of Connecticut. After graduating *cum laude* from Harvard Law School in 1978, he spent four years with the Division of Enforcement Litigation at the National Labor Relations Board and a year with the Litigation Unit of the California Agricultural Labor Relations Board. During his time with the NLRB, he was principal author of the agency's successful Supreme Court briefs in *NLRB v. Hendricks County REMC* and *NLRB v. Transportation Management Inc.* In 1983, he joined the faculty at the University of Miami, where he taught until his appointment at Connecticut in 2006. The year of his departure, he was the recipient of Miami's Golden Apple award for outstanding teaching and service, and he is a three-time finalist for UConn's Perry Zirkel '76 Distinguished Teaching Award.

Prof. Fischl teaches Contracts; Labor Law I & II; and a seminar on the history of American legal thought. He has devoted much of his career to working with students seeking to improve their performance on law exams; indeed, his contributions to *Getting to Maybe* are in large measure a product of that experience. He developed and offered the first for-credit academic success course at Miami; he has taught multiple academic success courses at UConn; and over the years he has offered exam-taking workshops for first-year students at numerous law schools, including Harvard and the University of Minnesota.

Prof. Fischl's research interests focus on union organizing and collective bargaining, the individual contract of employment, and legal theory.

He has offered American work law courses as a visiting professor at Yale and Cardozo Law Schools; has taught comparative labor law at University College London and Eberhard-Karls-Universität in Tübingen, Germany; and has lectured widely on labor law topics. His scholarship has appeared in the *Berkeley Journal of Employment & Labor Law*; *Columbia Law Review*; *Law & Social Inquiry*; *New York University Review of Law & Social Change*; and *Yale Law Journal Online*.

Jeremy R. Paul served as dean of Northeastern University School of Law from 2012 until June 2018, when he returned full time to the faculty. He teaches Constitutional Law and Property, and for several years he co-directed the University's Media Advocacy master's program, which he helped found. He has served for ten years as co-editor of the Association of American Law Schools' *Journal of Legal Education* and is the editor of the SSRN Journal of Legal Education.

A 1978 graduate of Princeton University, he received his law degree from Harvard in 1981. Before coming to Northeastern, Professor Paul served for 23 years on the faculty of the University of Connecticut School of Law, where he was dean and the Thomas F. Gallivan, Jr. Professor of Real Property Law from 2007 until 2012.

Professor Paul's scholarly work has been published in the *Texas Law Review*, *Michigan Law Review*, *University of Southern California Law Review* and *Washington Monthly*. In addition to co-authoring *Getting to Maybe*, he is author of a widely used introduction to legal reasoning, "A Bedtime Story," published in the *Virginia Law Review* and recently translated into Portuguese. He is a frequent contributor to the legal and popular press, with articles appearing in the *New York Law Journal*, the *ABA Journal*, *The National Law Journal*, *The Hartford Courant* and other outlets.

In addition to his long-term career in teaching, Professor Paul served as a law clerk to Judge Irving R. Kaufman of the US Court of Appeals for the Second Circuit; as Professor-in-Residence at the Appellate Staff of the Civil Division of the US Department of Justice; and as assistant to the president of Travelers Group. He has also taught at the University of Miami and at Boston College Law School.

Professor Paul is a fellow of the American Bar Foundation and the Connecticut Bar Foundation, and a member of the Executive Committee of the AALS Section on Empirical Study of Legal Education and the Legal Profession.

Hypos and Cases and Bears, Oh My: Not Quite an Index

On the following pages, you'll find a series of lists that may be helpful if you're attempting to find—or to re-locate—specific ideas or discussions appearing in the book. Here's a guide to the lists:

Where You'll Find the Forks

The "forks in the road" approach to issue-spotting, explained, 71–77
Forks in the law
    The concept explained, 73–75 (with illustration), 79
    Types
        Rule vs. counter-rule forks, 80–84
            Recurring patterns
                Traditional rule vs. modern rule, 80–81
                Different rules for different jurisdictions, 81–83
                Common law vs. statute, 83–84
            How professors test rule vs. counter-rule forks, 84–87
                Generally, 84–85

Where you'll find our core exam-prep
& exam-taking advice

Where you'll find other key concepts

Where you'll find our hands-on exercises

Where you'll find our hypotheticals
(in order of first appearance)

Where you'll find the cases we discuss
(we've omitted those making merely a brief cameo)